LAW AND AGING
Essentials of Elder Law

Second Edition

Ronald J. Schwartz

PEARSON

Prentice Hall

Upper Saddle River, New Jersey 07458

Library of Congress Cataloging-in-Publication Data

Schwartz, Ronald J.
  Law and aging : essentials of elder law / by Ronald J. Schwartz.-- 2nd ed.
    p. cm.
  ISBN 0-13-117322-7
  1. Aged--Legal status, laws, etc.--United States. 2. Aged--Medical care--Law and legislation--United States. 3. Estate planning--United States. I. Title.

  KF390.A4S39 2004
  346.7301'3--dc22

                              2004000065

Director of Production & Manufacturing: Bruce Johnson
Executive Editor: Elizabeth Sugg
Managing Editor—Editorial: Judy Casillo
Editorial Assistant: Cyrenne Bolt de Freitas
Consulting Editor: Athena Group, Inc.
Marketing Manager: Leigh Ann Sims
Managing Editor—Production: Mary Carnis
Manufacturing Buyer: Ilene Sanford
Production Liaison: Denise Brown
Production Editor: Robin Reed/Carlisle Publishers Services
Composition: Carlisle Communications, Ltd.
Design Director: Cheryl Asherman
Senior Design Coordinator: Christopher Weigand
Cover Design: Kevin Kall
Cover Printer: Phoenix Color
Printer/Binder: Courier Westford

This book was set in 10.5/12 Times by Carlisle Communications, LTD. and was printed and bound by Courier Westford. The cover was printed by Phoenix Color.

THE INFORMATION PROVIDED IN THIS TEXT AND CD-ROM ARE NOT INTENDED AS LEGAL ADVICE FOR SPECIFIC SITUATIONS, BUT ARE MEANT SOLELY FOR EDUCATIONAL AND INFORMATIONAL PURPOSES. READERS SHOULD RETAIN AND SEEK THE ADVICE OF THEIR OWN LEGAL COUNSEL IN HANDLING SPECIFIC LEGAL MATTERS.

10 9 8 7 6 5 4 3
ISBN 0-13-117322-7

CONTENTS

WHAT'S ON THE CD-ROM?

The enclosed CD-ROM includes reference materials that can be invaluable to the practice of elder law. It includes questionnaires, sample documents, statistics on aging, and a wide variety of resources to help the elderly.

QUESTIONNAIRES

The CD-ROM includes a number of questionnaires that the elder law professional should be prepared to use with a client, based on the services the client is seeking. The answers to these questions will guide the representation of the elderly client. The disk includes the following sample questionnaires:

- Elder Law Initial Confidential Questionnaire
- Confidential Will-Planning Questionnaire
- Guardianship Intake Questionnaire
- Checklist for Clients and Their Families When Altering Their Living Arrangements

DOCUMENTS

There are also a number of sample documents that the elder lawyer can use in daily practice. It is important to note that these documents are not to be used verbatim. Each client's individual needs and preferences will dictate the appropriate language to be used in personally prepared documents. Furthermore, some states have statutory forms, which should be used to make sure the document will be recognized by that state. Always consult with an attorney before executing any legal documents. The following sample forms are on the disk:

- General Durable Power of Attorney (The Powers Themselves)
- Health Care Proxy (with organ and tissue donation provisions)
- Living Will
- Predesignation of Guardian
- Revocable Living Trust
- Supplemental Needs Trust

RESOURCES

Elder law professionals are often called upon to intervene in situations affecting the client's financial welfare, physical health, and psychological well-being. A complete list of community resources is an invaluable tool for the elder lawyer. This collection of resources, when combined with local community resources, can provide the elder lawyer with the tools necessary to service a client's myriad needs. Always check for updated resources as the practice of elder law is constantly changing. The following resources are included:

- IRS Service Center Offices
- State Offices on Aging
- Where to Report Elder Abuse
- Where to Write for Vital Records
- Identity Theft—state statutes, credit reporting agencies, and sample affidavits.
- A Profile of Older Americans—providing statistical data on the elderly.
- Elder Law Resources—a comprehensive list of resources published by the federal government.
- A Sample Patient's Bill of Rights—from a nursing home residency agreement.

CD-ROM CONTENTS

ACKNOWLEDGMENTS

Elder law is a special and wonderful area. It is most rewarding and most gratifying to be able to make a real contribution to the quality of the daily lives of the elderly. To be effective in this field, the practitioner must have compassion for the elderly as well as a keen understanding of the many societal and physiological factors that directly impact upon the aging process.

I received a firsthand education from my father, Hermann, a Hungarian veteran of the trenches of World War I, who at age 66 retired from his various post-war occupations to become what may be the first elder law paralegal in this country (and perhaps even in the world)! I worked closely with my father. As the years passed, I developed an understanding of the problems that confront and often bewilder the elderly and began to respect and appreciate the aging process. My mother's death during that period added yet another dimension to my understanding of other problems commonly faced by surviving spouses and their children.

During those years, my general practice of law, which had always focused upon estate and probate work, began to change. My clients were living longer as a result of modern medical technology; a need to counsel the elderly in their very special age-related, medical-legal problems became apparent. Armed with the firsthand education I had gained from handling my father's affairs, I began to assist other children and their elderly parents through the aging process.

Accordingly, I wish to thank my father, who worked tirelessly with me until the age of 94. He died at the age of 97. He was a true inspiration to me and was really responsible for developing my interest and abilities in elder law.

Of course, I also wish to express my gratitude for the able assistance provided by my legal, paralegal, and clerical staff, without whom this book could not have been completed. I would especially like to thank my two associates, Dory Salem, Esq. and Christopher Marlborough, Esq. for their technical assistance.

In addition, I would like to express my appreciation to my reviewers, Labron K. Shuman, Delaware County Community College; Michael Pener, Johnson County Community College; Laura Barnard, Lakeland Community College; and Susan Patterson, Attorney, for their insightful comments.

Lastly, I thank my elderly clients and their families for allowing me to be of assistance to them, helping me to understand the daily problems of aging in America, and for teaching me so much.

Ronald J. Schwartz, Esq.

PREFACE

Since the publication of the first edition of this book in 1998, the legal landscape has changed dramatically. The events of September 11, 2001, in New York City, where I practice elder law, have forever changed the legal concerns of all citizens of this country, young and old. My clients have been more focused than ever on planning for future disposition of their assets. They are concerned about making new wills, setting up trusts for their families, and establishing powers of attorney, health care proxies, living wills, and other estate planning devices. There seems to be a sense of urgency that I have never seen in my 40 years of practice in the field.

Congress has passed several new laws in the areas of taxation, patients' rights, and entitlement programs that affect every American. The chapter on financial planning required a complete revision to reflect the Economic Growth and Tax Relief Act of 2001 implemented by President George W. Bush. The new law poses serious planning problems because of the sunset provisions encompassed therein.

The full effects of the Health Insurance Portability and Accountability Act of 1996 (HIPAA), passed shortly before the publication of the first edition, are just now being recognized in relation to medical privacy issues. In addition, the threat to prosecute elder law attorneys under the HIPAA for providing advice to their clients, has receded as former U.S. Attorney General Janet Reno and a federal court have both declared those provisions to be unconstitutional.

The tragic case of Terri Schiavo, a Florida woman in a persistive vegetative state, has caught the public's attention, highlighting the importance of having a living will and choosing the proper person to carry out your wishes.

The legal concept of patient self-determination has changed with the conviction of Dr. Jack Kevorkian in Michigan, the passage of physician-assisted suicide legislation in Oregon, the reaction of U.S. Attorney General John Ashcroft, and the ensuing court challenge to Mr. Ashcroft's directive.

With the advent of the information age, identity theft has become a major problem in the United States, so the chapter on elder abuse has been expanded to include this phenomenon.

In addition to responses to current trends, the book has been expanded to include two new chapters. Chapter 2, Diseases of Aging, provides information on the prevalence, treatment, and prevention of diseases that disproportionately affect older persons. Chapter 8, Love and Marriage among the Elderly, recognizes that many elderly are widowed, divorced, or in a second marriage, and their estates require special consideration when there are children from a prior marriage. In addition, that chapter considers the financial effects of catastrophic illness on the well spouse.

Case law relevant to the materials has been added to give the reader a more sophisticated understanding of some of the legal issues addressed by elder lawyers, with an emphasis on constitutional law. The cases have been edited for brevity.

Finally, more sample documents, a statistical profile on the elderly, and a list of helpful resources are included on the CD-ROM.

The field of elder law continues to grow and adapt to changing demographics in this country. It is the fastest growing area of law and has attracted many professionals to the specialty. More courses are being taught at the paralegal level, as well as in law schools, throughout the country. Many law schools have established elder law clinics to provide pro bono services to seniors in the community, while giving law students the opportunity to learn firsthand the kinds of legal problems that face the elderly. I am a special adjunct professor at Brooklyn Law School and St. John's University in New York City, and I have seen the growing interest among students in the field. I believe that the zealous representation of the elderly is a noble pursuit, and I hope that my students and readers will feel the same.

CHAPTER 1

Introduction

PREVIEW

In America today, the elderly represent an ever-growing percentage of the population. Statistical information suggests that by the year 2030 one in every five Americans will be over the age of 65 and that the baby boomer generation born between 1946 and 1964 will account for approximately 76 million Americans. Thanks to this graying of the population, the specialty of elder law has rapidly developed in the last 15 years, providing elderly individuals and their families with the assistance to solve the many problems relating to aging and life course planning. This chapter provides an introduction to the medical, social, financial, and legal issues associated with aging and to the role the elder law professional should take in life course planning. It also has a discussion on how to succeed as an elder law professional.

THE AGING OF AMERICA

The population of the United States is graying. Americans are living longer, and their lives are healthier and more productive. As a result, the number of elderly citizens is rapidly increasing. Statistical information helps us realize exactly how America's population is changing.

CURRENT LONGEVITY STATISTICS

- Approximately 42 million Americans are over age 60
- Approximately 35 million are over age 65
- Approximately 13 million are over age 75
- Approximately 3 million are over age 85
- Fastest growing age group, 1980–1990: 85 to 90 years
- Fastest growing age group, 1990–2000: 90 to 95 years
- Median age group, age 36

Longevity has been extended as a result of dramatic advances in science and technology. America is becoming a society of longevity. There are currently over one million Americans over the age of 100. According to the U.S. Census Bureau, 76 million Americans were born between 1946 and 1964. This aging generation, dubbed *baby boomers,* will have a significant impact upon the resources of American society. Currently, the baby boomers represent almost 30 percent of the U.S. population. During the next 12 to 30 years, the boomers will enter the over-65 age group. By 2011, the first baby boomers will be ready for retirement. Every day 5,574 people celebrate their 65th birthday. By the year 2030, one in five Americans will be over 65. They will need the assistance of skilled professionals to solve the many problems related to aging and life course planning. Americans are being granted the wonderful opportunity to live longer, healthier, and more active lives, and with that comes new responsibilities.

Today, elder law firms are very active in assisting the elderly and their families in life course planning. The specialty of elder law has rapidly developed in the last 15 years. It is the fastest-growing area of the law. Professionals that practice in this field will be in ever increasing demand for years to come.

ACTUARIAL PREDICTIONS

- In the year 2010, 39 million Americans will be over age 65.
- In the year 2030, 70 million Americans will be over age 65.
- In the year 2050, 10 percent of the United States population will be over 85.

Life Expectancy Today

- A 65-year-old healthy male has a life expectancy of 81 years.
- A child born today has an average life expectancy of 76.9 years.

MEDICAL, SOCIAL, FINANCIAL, AND LEGAL ISSUES ASSOCIATED WITH AGING

Medical

As people live longer, the likelihood of their immune systems breaking down increases. (This occurrence is professionally known as *decompensation*.) The elderly are more likely than younger population to be afflicted with the following illnesses and conditions:

- Acute confusional state
- Alzheimer's disease
- Amyotrophic lateral sclerosis (ALS)
- Arthritis
- Behavioral disorders
- Cancer of the prostate, colon, breasts, and uterus
- Cataracts
- Cerebral vascular accident
- Coronary artery disease
- Diabetes
- Glaucoma
- Hearing impairments
- Hypertension
- Osteoporosis

- Parkinson's disease
- Persistent vegetative state
- Pneumonia
- Pressure sores
- Macular degeneration
- Multisystem failures
- Nephritis
- Organic brain syndrome (OBS)
- Senile dementia
- Stroke
- Transient ischemic attack (TIA)

Some of those illnesses and conditions are catastrophic, precipitating radical adjustments. Others are progressive in nature and require more subtle changes in lifestyle. Consider, for instance, Alzheimer's disease. The graph illustrated below vividly reveals that the number of new Alzheimer's cases will increase dramatically. As demographic changes evolve and the population ages, the incidence of this dreaded disease is expected to increase to epidemic proportions. Remind clients to have dessert first, while they can remember to!

ALZHEIMER'S TOLL AS COUNTRY AGES

Health researchers estimate that the number of Americans with Alzheimer's disease, currently about 4 million, will grow to 10 million to 14 million by 2050 as the population ages.

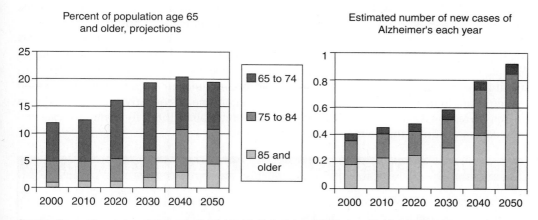

Sources: Census Bureau (population projections): Liesi E. Herbert, Laura A. Beckett, Paul A. Scherr and Denis A. Evans, "Annual Incidence of Alzheimer Disease in the United States Projected to the Years 2000 Through 2050," in *Alzheimer Disease and Associated Disorders,* Vol. 15, No. 4, 2001.

Social

The Well Elderly

Elderly people who are basically in good health may continue to live independently, by themselves or with their spouses. Their business involvement may be curtailed, voluntarily or involuntarily, due to company retirement policies. Reaching age 65 may result in mandatory retirement, and the world of the retiree may undergo subtle and radical changes. Medical insurance issues resulting from retirement must be resolved. Retirees find themselves confronted with more leisure time. For some, this is a special time to pursue old hobbies, new interests, and recreational activities. For others without varied interests and involvement, these long unstructured hours can precipitate boredom, depression, and associated medical consequences. The empty nest syndrome and waning health may require a change in existing housing. Some people relocate to warmer climates, which may be more conducive to better health and outdoor activity. The gradual, or sometimes radical, change of lifestyle due to ill health or death of a spouse requires emotional adjustment as people progress through their seventies and eighties. The elderly may experience feelings of isolation as they are separated from their families who are in other geographical areas. Grandparents forego the pleasures of watching their grandchildren and great-grandchildren grow up.

Even in the normal course of aging, health and personal needs change. Situations will arise that cause the elderly to become increasingly dependent upon their families. Some have done advanced planning as part of life course planning. Others have not, and they need the assistance of legal counsel and health care professionals to adjust their lives to fit their changing needs. The elder law attorney and her or his staff, consisting of paralegals, social workers, geriatric care managers, and nurses, are uniquely equipped to solve these problems.

The Ill Elderly

The elderly face involuntary changes of lifestyle as a direct result of the illnesses of aging. Many of these disorders require hospitalization. Unfortunately, these elderly patients are being discharged from hospitals too soon. This occurs because hospitals must follow Medicare regulations that assign specific lengths of stay to particular illnesses. This Medicare regulatory procedure is known as **diagnostic related grouping.** Whereas in the past patients could remain in the hospital until they were well enough to return to the community, patients today are being discharged "sicker and quicker" because hospitals can no longer afford to treat patients for an extended period of time. Frequently, patients must then be transferred to less costly skilled nursing and rehabilitation facilities for continued care and treatment, sometimes for the remainder of their lives.

Diagnostic Related Grouping
Medicare regulations that assign specific lengths of hospital stays to particular illnesses.

ALTERNATE LIFESTYLES FOR THE WELL AND ILL ELDERLY

- Placement into a life care community
- Placement into an independent living facility
- Placement into an assisted-living facility
- Obtaining home care assistance in the community
- Placement into a long-term care facility
- Hospice care

Financial

Financing the future is a major concern of aging Americans. Traditionally, most people retired at 65, and many died a few years later. Now, as a benefit of advanced medical technology, lives are being extended. However, no adequate financial provisions have been made by society, business, and government to compensate adequately for this phenomenon.

Financial planning to protect assets for people while they are healthy is a must if their elderly years are to be as comfortable as possible!

1. The wealthy are concerned about estate planning to avoid or minimize estate taxes on their assets.
2. The middle class may transfer their assets or purchase long-term care insurance (or they may be in a position to do both). They may also require estate tax planning to reduce the burden of potential estate taxes.
3. The poorer class requires information on how to access state and federal programs designed to help the elderly in medical care, drug prescriptions, housing, food, and other critical necessities of life.

Financing catastrophic illness causes great anxiety to the elderly and their families, regardless of economic status. Nursing home costs are staggering, an average of $40,000 per year in this country, and can go as high as $120,000 or more per year in the greater New York area. How can the average person meet these costs? What are the options and choices?

1. *Private Pay:* The individual pays nursing home costs from personal assets. When the assets are exhausted, that person can apply for public assistance. Timely financial and legal planning can avoid or minimize the use of personal assets.
2. *Long-Term Care Insurance:* Private insurance purchased by the policyholder covers costs of skilled nursing facilities, room, and board and also provides coverage for assisted-living facilities, home care, and respite care.
   - The current average annual premium for a long-term care insurance policy with a standard risk is $1,000 at 60, $1,500 at age 65, and $2,000 at age 70.
   - 3.5 million long-term care policies have been issued to date.
   - One hundred and thirty-five insurance companies offer long-term care insurance.
   - Over 1,000 U.S. employers provide long-term care insurance for their employees, and some even provide coverage for their employees' parents.
   - The average age of an individual who purchases long-term care insurance is 67.
   - Women are more likely to need skilled nursing care—33 percent of males and 50 percent of females will spend some time in a skilled nursing facility.
3. *Medicare:* It is a federal entitlement program providing coverage of a portion of medical costs. Long-term care coverage is also provided under this program, but is limited as follows:
   a. Coverage available for rehabilitation only—custodial care does not qualify.
   b. As of 2004, coverage pays first 20 days in full—21st through 100th day (less a patient-paid deductible of $109.50 per day) is also included. The deductible increases annually.
   c. 72-hour hospital stay required prior to entry into nursing facility.
   d. Limited hospice care, usually up to 210 days.
4. *Medicaid:* It is a federal entitlement program administered by the individual states. It provides funds to pay for nursing home care and home care for indigent individuals and families.

Legal Issues

A major portion of this book is devoted to documents that every elderly American should possess. The documents listed below are routinely prepared by the elder law professional. All clients, regardless of age or wellness, should be encouraged to execute these documents. The aging process may result in a person's physical or mental incompetency and/or incapacity, preventing the ability to make personal and financial decisions and ultimately requiring the appointment of a guardian or conservator. There may be an inability to make medical decisions.

The following advanced directive documents are a necessity if judicial intervention is to be avoided, and the family or appointee named in these legal instruments will be permitted to act on behalf of elderly persons according to their wishes:

- Health care proxy (medical power of attorney)
- Durable power of attorney
- Predesignation of appointment of guardian

This precautionary life course planning achieves the goal of helping the elderly to retain their dignity, self-respect, and independence.

Note: A living will should also be executed. This legal document is a statement by a person *indicating* that he or she does not wish to be kept alive artificially. This document does not appoint someone to make decisions.

THE ROLE OF THE ELDER LAW PROFESSIONAL

The major ethical issue that confronts every elder law professional is "Who is the client?" Is it the incapacitated elderly client, the spouse, their children? Most often it is the elderly person who is the client, regardless of who makes the initial contact. The elder law professional's relationship with the client is very important. The first contact that the client has with the law firm occurs during a telephone conversation or at the initial interview in the office, at the hospital bedside, at the nursing home, or sometimes even at the client's home. The client's first impression of the elder law practice is based upon this very significant contact. Therefore, it is of the utmost importance to know how to respond appropriately to the new client. A keen understanding of the aging process and its impact upon the clients and their families will facilitate this. It is easier to work with clients who have an ongoing relationship with the firm because the foundation of trust has already been established.

It is also important to consider the circumstances prompting the client to consult with the elder law attorney. For example, the initial interview is often precipitated by a crisis, in which case the elder law professional must be sensitive to the needs of the client and to the distress and despair of the family. The demeanor of the law professional is critical in these situations. One must be mature, patient, knowledgeable and kind, responsive, and caring, yet firm. A warm smile and sometimes a pat on the back goes a long way to reassure clients and give them confidence in you as you work with them throughout their ordeals.

Clients must be reassured of the genuine interest that the firm has in assisting them and their families. It sometimes maybe necessary to protect the client against overreaching family members who may be involved in financial and/or physical abuse of the client. Only a person willing to serve these special needs should consider employment in this unique, emotionally demanding, and rewarding field of the law.

HOW TO SUCCEED AS AN ELDER LAW PROFESSIONAL

- Maintain honesty and dependability.
- Take responsibility for every task undertaken.
- Learn to analyze details.
- Listen to what the client does not say.
- Be persistent and work hard; complete projects quickly and efficiently.
- Never give up; there is a solution to all problems.
- Never stop learning; the field of elder law is constantly growing and changing.
- Remember that a positive approach is the key to success.
- Learn to communicate effectively with the clients, their families, and other elder law team players.
- Return all calls from the clients within 24 hours of their receipt.
- Be innovative; if you think something in the office can be done more efficiently, do not be afraid to discuss this with the elder law team.
- Be organized, and stay that way.

The elder law team consists of lawyers, paralegals, nurses, geriatric care managers, and social workers. They assist the client in the medical, social, emotional, financial, and legal aspects associated with aging. Whereas the nurse may be called upon to make medical evaluations and recommendations and the social worker and geriatric care manager may assess and make new living arrangements for the clients, the paralegal is the coordinating link of the elder law team, working in all phases of the process.

REFERENCE

See the CD-ROM for A Profile of Older Americans: 2002, issued by the Federal Administration on Aging. It is an excellent study of the aging population and confirms the ever-increasing need for elder law legal services.

REVIEW QUESTIONS AND EXERCISES

1. What social, financial, and legal issues does America face due to the graying of the population?
2. What medical, social, financial, and legal issues does the elderly individual face in his/her day-to-day affairs?
3. Describe the needs of the well elderly versus the ill elderly, and indicate how the elder law professional should deal with these groups.
4. Explain the steps that an elder law professional should recommend to a client in connection with planning for continued financial solvency. What steps should be taken for healthy individuals? What steps should be taken for clients who are suffering from a catastrophic illness?
5. Explain the importance of drafting advanced directives for all clients, not just elderly clients.

CHAPTER 2

Diseases of Aging

PREVIEW

It is medical certainty that as we age, we become more susceptible to illness and disease. It is important for the elder law legal professional to understand the etiology of age-related diseases and the toll they take upon the elderly client. Many elder law clients suffer from the afflictions discussed in this chapter. A basic knowledge of the diseases of aging will result in a more effective and productive initial interview of the elder law client. Disability, disease, delivery of health care services, and financial planning among the elderly are of great concern not only to the field of elder law, but to society in general.

The most common illnesses of the elderly (and those discussed in this chapter) are Alzheimer's disease, dementia, Parkinson's disease, cerebrovascular disease (strokes), pneumonia, diabetes, hip fractures, and arthritis. Many of these diseases are chronic, lead to the disability of the elderly patient, and eventually may cause death. The prevalence of these conditions increases with age. The most common disabling diseases are arthritis, hip fracture, and Alzheimer's disease.

ALZHEIMER'S DISEASE

Defining Alzheimer's Disease

The disease was first discovered by the German physician Dr. Alois Alzheimer in 1906 in a middle-aged patient who developed memory problems. The disease progressed to severe dementia and death at age 51. **Alzheimer's disease (AD)** is very complex, affecting the brain, and is one of the most devastating diseases of aging. It is a metabolic disorder with neurological implications. This affliction is a public health issue of enormous proportions and is considered by epidemiologists to be a silent epidemic. The most commonly reported form of **dementia** is Alzheimer's-related dementia. There are no known causes or cures for this illness, which mainly affects the population over 70. However, there are many cases of middle age victims. It is the fourth leading cause of death in America, after heart disease, cancer, and stroke. Former President Ronald Regan and actor Charlton Heston are among the four million Americans suffering from the disease. Actress Rita Hayworth and columnist Dear Abby died of it.

Alzheimer's Disease
This is the most common cause of dementia after age 50. It is a progressive neuropsychiatric disease caused by metabolic change in the brain cells and neuron degeneration. The disease is characterized by the loss of cognitive functions as well as behavioral disturbances. Approximately four million people in the U.S. suffer from it. Its cost to society is about $90 billion per year, including all services rendered to the stricken individuals. It is the fourth leading cause of death of people 65 years or older. It appears to occur twice as frequently in females as in males.

Dementia
Refers to a large number of brain diseases in which there is slow progressive deterioration of cognitive ability and personality traits and severe behavior changes. Results in memory loss, disorientation as to time and place, intellectual decline, and finally, impaired judgment.

Warning Signs

- Memory loss
- Difficulty in performing familiar tasks
- Problems with language
- Disorientation to time and place
- Poor or decreased judgment
- Problems with abstract thinking
- Misplacing things
- Changes in mood or behavior
- Changes in personality
- Loss of initiative

Progression

The duration of Alzheimer's disease varies widely among its sufferers. It can last anywhere from three to 20 years. The average is about eight years from onset to death. The areas of the brain that control memory and thought processes are the first to be infected, and as the disease advances, the remaining brain cells begin to die. Eventually, if there are no other diseases affecting the patient, the complete loss of brain function will cause death.

Biology of Alzheimer's Disease

There are two types of brain lesions associated with the disease:

1. Amyloid plaques, which are abnormal, insoluble clumps of protein fragments that are deposited outside of brain cells
2. Neurofibrillary tangles, which are clumps of altered proteins that are found with the brain cells

Scientists believe that a form of abnormal metabolic processes causes the formation of the plaques. Research is ongoing to find medications that will destroy these clumps of protein.

Age and Genetics

Current studies indicate that the greatest known risk for contracting the disease is aging. Ten percent of people over 65, and 50 percent over 85, suffer from Alzheimer's disease. Family history also plays a significant role. The chances of illness are increased if a parent or a sibling has the disease. Risk is 20 percent familial (genetic) and 80 percent sporadic. Recently released research reveals that high cholesterol and high blood pressure may also be risk factors. The disease is twice as common in women as in men, perhaps because women live longer.

Stages of the Disease

There are three clinically recognized stages of the disease. The patient undergoes a slow but steady decline from one stage to another, with the final stage ending in death.

Early Stage

The most common early signs of Alzheimer's disease are recent memory loss, the inability to learn and remember recently learned information, language problems, mood swings, and personality changes. For example, although it is normal to forget appointments and telephone numbers, patients in this stage of the disease will forget these things more frequently and not have the ability to remember them at a later date. There are increased signs of irritability, hostility, and agitation as a response to the effects of the memory loss. The patient may get lost on the way to a familiar neighborhood store. The language problems are exemplified by the inability to remember simple words or by substituting unusual words, making his/her speech or handwriting difficult to understand. A person afflicted with the disease may not be able to find the word for a toothbrush and will ask for "that thing for my mouth."

Intermediate Stage

During the intermediate stage of Alzheimer's disease, the patients require assistance with the activities of daily living, such as bathing, dressing, eating, and toileting. There is a complete loss of the ability to learn and recall new information. Memory of remote events is present, in a diminished form. Wandering and agitation become more prevalent. There is more evidence of poor and decreased judgment. They may dress without regard to weather conditions, wearing a heavy sweater on a hot day and going out in a cold winter day wearing nothing but a short sleeved blouse. People with Alzheimer's disease often misplace things in unusual places. A bracelet can be found in the refrigerator, a wallet in the freezer. They are prime targets for telemarketers and home repair contractors and are often the victims of financial abuse. (See Chapter 15, Elder Abuse.) In this stage, the patients become disoriented as to time and place. Unable to find their way to the bathroom or bedroom, they often appear confused and are subject to a significant risk of falling or accidents.

Terminal Stage

In the terminal stage of the disease, the patients are unable to walk, completely **incontinent,** and unable to perform any of the activities of daily living. Confinement to a skilled nursing facility is usually necessary. There is an increased risk of the following:

- Malnutrition because they no longer can swallow or eat
- Pneumonia, especially from aspiration
- Extensive bedsores

In this severe stage, the patient is unable to speak and eventually lapses into a **coma,** with death occurring from some form of infection.

Incontinence
The inability to control bodily elimination functions.

Coma
The medical state of a deep stupor, being completely unaware of one's surroundings, and unable to hear or respond.

Diagnostic Testing

The diagnosis is usually based upon history, physical examination, laboratory tests, and the exclusion of other causes of dementia. The diagnostic process includes the following:

- Comprehensive medical history, including family health
- Mental status evaluation
- Testing of memory, reasoning, vision-motor coordination, and language skills
- Physical examination
- Testing of sensation, balance, and nervous system
- Brain scan to detect a stroke as a possible cause of dementia
- Laboratory tests of blood of urine
- Psychiatric evaluation

Medications Used in Treatment

The five drugs approved by the Food and Drug Administration for the treatment of the Alzheimer's disease are:

COGNEX®	Approved in 1993
ARICEPT®	Approved in 1996
EXELON®	Approved in 2000
REMINYL®	Approved in 2001
NAMENDA®	Approved in 2003

These drugs cannot alter the progression of the disease, but they often minimize or stabilize the symptoms. The necessity of nursing home placement is often delayed by the use of these drugs. The first four medications belong to a class of drugs known as cholinesterase inhibitors. They are designed to prevent the breakdown of acetycholine, a chemical messenger in the brain that is critical for memory and other thought processes. Reminyla® appears to be most effective in treating early to middle stages of the disease. It does not affect the patient's sleep cycle as the other drugs do and allows the patient to lead a more normal life.

Namenda® is the newest medication and is the first of a new class of NMDA Antagonists. It is not a wonder drug. It improves memory and thinking for a small number of patients. However, it significantly slows down the pace of deterioration of patients suffering from the disease. While the other cholesterol inhibitors currently available are most effective in early stages of the disease, Namenda works effectively in advanced stages.

Recently released medical studies indicate that a class of drugs called **Statins,** used to lower cholesterol, can be also effective in dissolving the plaque formation commonly found in the brain tissue of Alzheimer's patients. People with a high levels of cholesterol are apparently more likely to contract the disease than those with lower levels.

Alzheimer's Statistics
- Approximately four million Americans have Alzheimer's disease.
- By the middle of this century (2050), 14 million Americans will have AD unless a cure or means of prevention is discovered.

- One in 10 people over 65 and nearly half of those over 85 have AD. A small percentage of people in their 30s and 40s get the disease.
- A person with AD will live an average of eight years from the onset of the disease, but some patients live for 20 years or more.
- U.S. society spends at least $100 billion a year on AD. Most private health insurance does not cover the long-term care most patients need. Medicare has just begun limited coverage.
- Alzheimer's is costing American business $61 billion a year. Of this, $36.5 billion is the cost to business of caregiving (lost productivity from absenteeism of employees who care for family members with Alzheimer's); the rest is the businesses' share of the costs of health and long-term care.
- More than seven of 10 people with Alzheimer's disease live at home. Family and friends provide almost 75 percent of the home care. The remainder is paid care, costing an average of $50,000 per year. Most families are required to pay almost all of that out of pocket unless the patient is on Medicaid.
- Half of all nursing home residents suffer from AD or a related disorder. The average cost for nursing home care is $50,000 per year, but can exceed $100,000 in some areas of the country.
- The average lifetime cost per patient is almost $200,000.

The Future

Today, the only reliable method of diagnosing Alzheimer's disease is by an autopsy of the patient's brain. The only diagnostic method that has been developed by medical science is the exclusion of the other causes of dementia, such as stroke or depression. Therefore, cognitive testing at early stages of symptomatic onset is very important.

There is little that can be done currently to arrest the progression of Alzheimer's disease. Early diagnosis of the disease appears to be critical to effective treatment. New neuropsychological testing is being developed to detect traces of the disease before it becomes apparent to the patient and family. Genetic research is ongoing to see how variations in a gene can indicate an increased risk of contracting the disease. Genetic linking may be used to establish a predisposition to the disease. A genetic component is likely because Alzheimer's runs in families. A shared environmental factor is also under study. Many countries are involved in the Human Genome Project focusing on genetic causes for the disease. The Weitzman Institute in Israel is one of the leaders of research in this field.

A recent study in *The New England Journal of Medicine* (June 19, 2003) revealed that leisure activities such as reading, playing board games, playing musical instruments, and dancing were associated with a reduced rate of Alzheimer's-related dementia in the elderly.

PARKINSON'S DISEASE

Parkinsonism is a chronic neurological condition named after Dr. James Parkinson, a London physician who was the first to describe the syndrome in 1817. **Parkinson's disease** is a slow, progressive disease that affects a small area of cells in the midbrain known as the **substantia nigra.** Gradual degeneration of these cells causes a reduction in a vital chemical known as **dopamine.** This decrease in the production of dopamine causes the symptoms of the illness.

Parkinson's Disease
A degenerative process that occur in the basal gaglia. A chronic nerve disease, it generally appears in midlife or later and progresses slowly in severity. It results in rigid posture and expressionless face. There is a slow, regular tremor of the hands. The gait is slow and shuffling, and turning is done in one piece. Muscles are rigid and weak, and movements tend to be limited in range and force.

Parkinson's disease is a prominent cause of disability in people over age 50. There are about one million cases in America, with 50,000 new cases diagnosed each year. The incidence increases with age, peaking at about 75 years. The estimated overall life-time risk is 2.5 percent. Although mostly afflicting the elderly, Parkinson's can also strike younger people. Actor Michael J. Fox was diagnosed with Parkinson's at age 30. Other celebrities with the disease include former Attorney General Janet Reno and boxer Mohammed Ali.

This disease is always progressive, but at variable rates. It can progress rapidly, and the patient can be completely disabled within five years from onset, More often, however, the course of the disease is slower and more protracted, allowing the patients to remain functional for many years.

Causes

- Decrease in production of dopamine
- Viral encephalitis
- Side effect of certain drugs
- Cerebral atherosclerosis
- Brain tumors
- Head trauma
- Carbon monoxide poisoning

Symptoms and Signs

Resting Tremor
A tremor of a limb that increases when the limb is at rest.

Bradykinesia
A slowness of an voluntary movement and speech.

- The most common initial symptom of Parkinson's is tremor, usually in one hand or sometimes in both, involving the fingers in a pill-rolling motion. Tremors often occur at rest. A **resting tremor** is a tremor of a limb that increases when the limb is at rest. The tremors disappear during sleep.
- Muscular rigidity is a condition of hardness, stiffness, or inflexibility of a limb.
- **Bradykinesia** is a slowness of all voluntary movement and speech. Patients attempting to walk suddenly find that their feet are frozen to the ground.
- Gait becomes shuffled, with short steps, and the patient's arms fail to swing.
- The face can become masklike, with a lack of expression and diminished eye blinking.
- Speech becomes slow and monotonous.
- Dysphagia, difficulty in swallowing occurs, and the patient tends to drool.
- Activities of daily living are affected, *e.g.,* the patient has difficulty tying shoelaces.
- Mood abnormalities, including depression or anxiety, dementia, and intellectual impairment, appear.

Treatment

No curative therapy is available for Parkinson's disease. Levodopa combined with Carbidopa is the single most effective drug therapy available for treatment. This drug combination changes into dopamine when it interacts with the brain. Recent medical trials have shown that an operation involving deep brain stimulation will significantly reduce tremors. The procedure involves inserting electrodes into the brain, which in turn produce electrical charges counteracting the tremors. The latest experimental treatment makes use of gene therapy.

STEM CELL RESEARCH: MIRACLE OR MURDER?

"It is not too unrealistic to say that this research has the potential to revolutionize the practice of medicine and improve the quality and length of life." These are the words of Harold Vargas, former director of the National Institutes of Health, describing the future benefits of embryonic stem cells. Stem cell research may soon treat or cure a number of diseases that strike the elderly disproportionately, including Alzheimer's disease, Parkinson's disease, diabetes, and ALS (Lou Gehrig's disease). Biologists report that successful treatment for Parkinson's disease may be only a few years away.

Embryonic stem cell research involves using the healthy undifferentiated cells of a human embryo to replace the damaged cells of a person with a neurological disorder. The stem cells then develop into the specialized cells they are replacing. Embryonic stem cells are derived from unused embryos donated from fertility clinics, which would otherwise discard them.

Critics of federally funded stem cell research argue that the use of embryonic cells is tantamount to government-sponsored abortion, because embryos must be destroyed in order to obtain the cells. On the other side of the debate is the scientific community, which has been outspoken in favor of stem cell research and its potential for cure. Joining the scientists are a number of celebrities who have been personally affected by some of the diseases that could be eradicated by stem cell treatment including Mary Tyler Moore (who has juvenile diabetes), Michael J. Fox (who has Parkinson's disease), Christopher Reeve (who has a severe spinal cord injury), and former First Lady Nancy Reagan (whose husband Ronald suffers from Alzheimer's disease).

In August 2001, President Bush limited federal funding of stem cell research to a small supply of pre-existing stem cells from an even more limited number of sources. Identical cells could then be cloned from those original cells, providing a supply of cells for future research, but no new embryos would be destroyed. This compromise did not satisfy advocates on either side of the debate but has allowed for stem cell research to evolve from its "embryonic stage," with the hope of curing some of the elderly's most debilitating diseases.

STROKE

Stroke is a cardiovascular disease. It affects the blood vessels that supply blood to the brain. A stroke occurs when a blood vessel bearing oxygen and nutrients to the brain bursts or is clogged by a blood clot or other particles (cholesterol or plaque). The brain does not get the required blood and oxygen as a result of this rupture or blockage. Deprived of oxygen, nerve cells in the affected area begin to die within minutes of the onset of the stroke. The devastating effects are permanent. Dead brain cells can never be replaced.

There are two main categories of strokes:

- Brain hemorrhage
- Brain ischemia

Stroke
A sudden loss of brain function caused by a blockage or rupture of a blood vessel to the brain.

Brain Hemorrhage

In this instance there is bleeding within the brain or skull tissue. This category is then further subdivided into:

1. *Subarachnoid hemorrhage*—bleeding into the spaces and spinal fluid around the brain. This occurs when a blood vessel on the surface of the brain ruptures and bleeds in to the space between the brain and the skull, but no bleeding occurs in the brain itself.
2. *Intracerebral hemorrhage*—bleeding directly into the brain when a defective artery in the brain bursts, flooding the surrounding brain tissue with blood flowing from the compromised blood vessel. This is commonly known as a cerebral hemorrhage.

Hemorrhage from an artery in the brain is often caused by trauma to the head or a burst aneurysm. Aneurysms are blood-filled pouches ballooning out of a weak section of an artery wall. Hypertension or elevated blood pressure can cause an aneurysm. If the ballooning artery bursts, the artery walls are compromised, and blood leaks into the surrounding tissue. A burst aneurysm can be fatal.

When any type of hemorrhage occurs, there is a loss of blood supply. Brain cells deprived of blood and nutrients quickly die. The amount of bleeding that occurs determines the extent of the cerebral hemorrhage. When a blood vessel in the brain bursts, pressure from the blood compresses part of the brain. If the victim survives, the pressure gradually diminishes, and the brain may then regain some of its function.

Brain Ischemia

Here there is an injury to brain tissue caused by an inadequate supply of blood and nutrients.

1. *Cerebral thrombosis*—is the most common form of brain ischemia, occurring when a blood clot (thrombus) forms and blocks the blood flow in an artery supplying blood to a part of the brain. Blood clots are usually caused by fatty build-ups called atherosclerosis. They most often occur at night or the first thing in the morning. TIAs (transient ischemic attacks) or mini-strokes are warning signs of impending strokes.
2. *Cerebral embolism*—occurs when a clot (embolus) formed in another part of the body, often the heart, enters the blood stream and is carried along until it lodges in an artery leading to or in the brain. The flow of blood is then blocked.

Prevention

Good health habits go a long way in preventing strokes:

- Control hypertension
- Treat cardiac disorders
- Treat coronary artery disorders
- Treat congestive heart failure
- Treat all heart arrhythmias
- Lower cholesterol levels

- Stop smoking
- Do not abuse drugs or alcohol
- Exercise regularly
- Maintain normal weight
- Avoid overeating
- Avoid exhaustion

Recovering from a Stroke

Recovery hinges upon two important factors: (a) the extent of the injury, and (b) the personal and socioeconomic circumstances of the stroke victim. A person who had a good quality of life before the stroke has a good chance of recovery, provided the injury is not too severe. Asset structure of the patient plays a significant role in recovery. A stroke survivor who can afford to hire caregivers, therapists, and buy or rent rehabilitation equipment has a better chance at recovery and returning to an active and useful life. Depression is a common complication. Therefore, a good mental attitude is important.

FALLS AND HIP FRACTURES AMONG OLDER ADULTS

Seriousness of This Problem

- In the United States, one out of every three adults 65 years old or older falls each year.
- Falls are the leading cause of injury deaths among people 65 years and older.
- In 2001, more than 11,600 people over 65 and older died from fall-related injuries.
- Of all fall deaths, more than 60 percent involve people who are 75 years or older.
- Fall-related death rates are higher among men than women and differ by race. White men have the highest death rate, followed by white women, black men, and black women.
- Older adults are hospitalized for fall-related injuries five times more often than they are for injuries from other causes.
- Of those who fall, 20–30 percent suffer moderate to severe injuries that reduce mobility and independence and increase the risk of premature death.

Other Health Outcomes Linked to Falls

- Among older adults, falls are the most common cause of injuries and hospital admissions for trauma.
- Falls account for 87 percent of all fractures for people 65 years and older. They are also the second leading cause of spinal cord and brain injury among older adults.
- Each year in the United States, one person in 20 receives emergency treatment because of a fall. Advanced age greatly increases the chances of hospital admission following a fall.
- Among older adults, fractures are the most serious health outcomes. The most common are fractures of the pelvis, hip, femur, vertebrae, humerus, hand, forearm, leg, and ankle.

Where People Fall

- For adults 65 years or older, 60 percent of fatal falls happen at home, 30 percent occur in public places, and 10 percent occur in health care institutions.
- Of all fractures from falls, hip fractures cause the greatest number of deaths and lead to the most severe health problems.
- Women sustain 75 percent of all hip fractures.
- People who are 85 years or older are 10–15 times more likely to experience hip fractures than are people between the ages of 60 and 65.
- Most patients with hip fractures are hospitalized for about two weeks.
- Half of all older adults hospitalized for hip fractures cannot return home or live independently after their injuries.
- In 1991, Medicare costs for hip fractures were estimated to be $42.9 billion.
- Because the U.S. population is aging, the problem of hip fractures will probably increase substantially over the next four decades. By the year 2040, the number of hip fractures is expected to exceed 500,000.

Factors That Increase the Risk of Falling in Older Adults

- Factors that contribute to falls include problems with gait and balance, neurological and musculosketetal disabilities, psychoactive medication use, dementia, and visual impairment.
- Environmental hazards such as slippery surfaces, uneven floors, poor lighting, loose rugs, unstable furniture, and objects on floors may also play a role.

Reducing the Risk of Falling

- Maintain a regular exercise program. Exercise improves strength, balance, and coordination.
- Take steps to make living areas safer. Remove tripping hazards, and use nonslip mats in the bathtub and on the shower floor. Install grab bars next to the toilet and in the tub or shower, and have handrails placed on both sides of all stairs.
- Ask physician to periodically review all medications in order to reduce side effects and interactions.
- Have an ophthalmologist check vision each year. Poor vision increases the risk of falling.

Costs of Fall Among Older Adults

The cost of fall-related injuries is usually expressed in terms of direct costs. Direct costs include out-of-pocket expenses and charges paid by insurance companies for the treatment of fall-related injuries. These include costs and fees associated with hospital and nursing home care, physician and other professional services, rehabilitation, community-based services, use of medical equipment, prescription drugs, local rehabilitation, home modifications, and insurance administration. Direct costs do not account for the long-term consequences of these injuries, such as disability, decreased productivity, or diminished quality of life.

Fall-Related Injuries
- In 1994, the average direct cost for a fall injury was $1,400 for a person over the age of 65.
- The total direct cost of all fall injuries for people age 65 and older in 1994 was $20.2 billion.
- By 2020, the cost of fall injuries is expected to reach $32.4 billion.

Fall-Related Fractures
- The most common fall-related injuries are osteporotic fractures. These are fracture of the hip, spine, or forearm.
- In the United States in 1986, the direct medical cost for osteoporotic fractures was $5 billion. By 1989, these costs exceeded $6 billion.
- Over the next 10 years, total direct medical costs for osteoporotic fractures are expected to double.

DIABETES

There are 17 million people, or 6.2 percent of the population in the United States, who have **diabetes.** While an estimated 11.1 million have been diagnosed, 5.9 million people are unfortunately not aware that they have the disease. Each day approximately 2,200 people are diagnosed. About 800,000 people aged 20 years or older will be diagnosed this year. Diabetes is the fifth deadliest disease in the United States. In 1999, it contributed to almost 210,000 deaths. It is a chronic disease that has no cure.

A Silent Killer

Many people first become aware they have diabetes only when they develop one of its life-threatening complications:

- *Heart disease:* Heart disease is the leading cause of diabetes-related deaths. Adults with diabetes have heart disease death rates two to four times higher than the normal population.
- *High blood pressure:* About 73 percent of adults with diabetes have blood pressure greater than or equal to 130/80 millimeters of mercury (mm Hg) or use prescription medications for hypertension (normal blood pressure is 120/80).
- *Blindness:* Diabetes is the leading cause of new cases of blindness among adults 20–74 years old. Diabetic retinopathy causes from 12,000 to 24,000 new cases of blindness each year.
- *Kidney Disease:* Diabetes is the leading cause of treated end-stage renal disease. In 1999, a total of 38,160 people with diabetes began treatment for end-stage renal disease. In 1999, a total of 114,478 people with diabetes underwent dialysis or kidney transplantation.

Diabetes
A disease in which the pancreas does not produce or properly use insulin, a hormone that is needed to convert sugar, starches, and other food into energy needed for life.

- *Nervous system disease:* About 60–70 percent of people with diabetes have mild to severe forms of nervous system damage. Such damage includes impaired sensation or pain in the feet or hands, slowed digestion of food in the stomach, carpal tunnel syndrome, and other neurological problems. Severe forms of diabetic neurological disease are a major contributing cause of lower extremity amputations.
- *Amputations:* More than 60 percent of nontraumatic lower limb amputations in the United States occur among people with diabetes. From 1997 to 1999, about 82,000 nontraumatic lower limb amputations were performed each year among people with diabetes.
- *Dental disease:* Periodontal or gum diseases are more common among people with diabetes. Among young adults, those with diabetes are often at twice the risk of those without. Almost one third of people with diabetes have severe periodontal disease with loss of attachment of the gums to the teeth measuring 5 millimeters or more.
- *Other complications:* Uncontrolled diabetes often leads to biochemical imbalances that can cause acute life-threatening events, such as diabetic ketoacidosis and hyperosmolar (nonketotic) coma. People with diabetes are most susceptible to many other illnesses and, once they acquire these illnesses, often have a worse prognosis than people without diabetes. For example, they are more likely to die with pneumonia or influenza than people who do not have diabetes.

Cost of Diabetes

Diabetes is one of the most costly health problems in America. Health care and other costs directly related to diabetes treatment, as well as the costs of lost productivity, run $98 billion annually.

Medical Definition

Diabetes is a disease in which the pancreas does not produce or properly use insulin, a hormone needed to convert sugar, starches, and other foods into energy. The cause of diabetes is yet to be found. Both genetics and environmental factors such as obesity and lack of exercise appear to be significant factors. There are two major types of diabetes:

- *Type 1:* An autoimmune disease in which the body does not produce any insulin, most often occurring in children and young adults. People with Type 1 diabetes account for 5–10 percent of the reported diabetic cases.
- *Type 2:* A metabolic disorder resulting from the body's inability to make enough or properly metabolize insulin. This is the most common form of diabetes. Type 2 diabetes accounts for 90–95 percent of all reported cases. It is now nearing epidemic proportions due to an increased number of older Americans and a greater prevalence of obesity and sedentary lifestyles.

Gestational diabetes develops in 2–5 percent of all pregnancies, but disappears when the pregnancy is over. Women who have had gestational diabetes are at increased risk for developing Type 2 diabetes later in life. Diabetes can also result from specific genetic factors, surgery, drugs, malnutrition, infections, trauma to the pancreas, and other illnesses. People who undergo open-heart bypass surgery and remain on a heart–lung machine for an extended period of time develop pancreatitis and the resulting diabetes.

Those at Greater Risk for Diabetes

Type 1

- Siblings of people with Type 1 diabetes
- Children of parents with Type 1 diabetes

Type 2

- People over age 45
- People with a family history of diabetes
- People who are overweight
- People who do not exercise regularly
- People with low HDL cholesterol or high triglycerides
- Certain racial and ethnic groups
  - *African Americans:* African Americans are 1.7 times as likely to have Type 2 diabetes as the general population. An estimated 2.3 million African Americans, 10.8 percent, have diabetes.
  - *Latinos:* Latinos are almost twice as likely to have Type 2 diabetes. For example, diabetes affects 1.2 million, or 10.6 percent, of the Mexican American population.
  - *Native Americans:* The overall prevalence of Type 2 diabetes in Native Americans is 12.2 percent versus 5.2 percent for the general population. In some tribes, 50 percent of the population has diabetes.
- Women who had gestational diabetes or who have had a baby weighing nine pounds or more at birth.

Warning Signs

Often people with Type 2 diabetes have no symptoms.

Type 1:
- Frequent urination
- Unusual thirst
- Extreme hunger
- Unusual weight loss
- Extreme fatigue
- Irritability

Type 2:
- Any of the Type 1 symptoms
- Frequent infections

- Blurred vision
- Cuts/bruises that are slow to heal
- Tingling/numbness in the hands or feet
- Recurring skin, gum, or bladder infections

PNEUMONIA

Pneumonia
A major infection or inflammation of the lungs in which the air sacs in the lungs fill with pus and other liquid, causing oxygen to have trouble reaching the blood.

Pneumonia is the most common fatal infection. Until 1936, pneumonia was the leading cause of death in America. With the discovery of antibiotics, pneumonia was reduced to the sixth leading cause of death by disease and the fourth leading cause of death in the elderly (1997).

Physicians often refer to it as *a special enemy of old age.* Hospitalized elderly have a substantially greater chance of contracting pneumonia than younger patients do. At any given time, it is estimated that 2.1 percent of nursing home residents have some form of pneumonia.

Pneumonia is a major infection or inflammation of the lungs. The air sacs in the lungs fill with pus and other liquid. When this occurs, oxygen cannot reach the blood supply. If there is too little oxygen in the blood, body cells cannot work properly. Because of this and the rapidly spreading of infection throughout the body, pneumonia can and often does cause death.

Pneumonia affects the lungs in two ways. Lobar pneumonia affects a section (lobe) of a lung. Bronchial pneumonia (or bronchopneumonia) affects patches throughout both lungs.

Causes

Pneumonia is not a single disease. It can have more than 30 different causes, of which five are especially important:

- Bacteria
- Viruses
- Mycoplasmas
- Other infectious agents, such as fungi, including pneumocystis
- Various chemicals

Bacterial Pneumonia

Bacterial pneumonia attacks all ages of the population, from infants to the elderly. Alcoholics, the debilitated, post-operative patients, people with respiratory diseases and viral infections, and people who have weakened immune systems are at greater risk.

Pneumonia bacteria are present in some healthy throats. When body defenses are weakened by illness, old age, malnutrition, general debility, or impaired immunity, the bacteria multiply and cause serious damage. When a person's resistance is lowered, bacteria work their way into the lungs and inflame the air sacs.

The tissue of part of a lobe of the lung, an entire lobe, or even most of the lung's five lobes becomes completely filled with liquid. The infection quickly spreads through the bloodstream, and the whole body is invaded.

Streptococcus pneumoniae is the most common cause of bacterial pneumonia. A vaccine is available for this form of pneumonia.

The onset of bacterial pneumonia can vary from gradual to sudden. In the most severe cases, the patient may experience shaking chills, chattering teeth, severe chest pain, and a cough that produces rust-colored or greenish mucus.

Temperature may rise as high as 105° F. The patient sweats profusely, and breathing and pulse rate increase rapidly. Lips and nailbeds may have a bluish color due to lack of oxygen in the blood. A patient's mental state may be confused or delirious.

Viral Pneumonia

Fifty percent of all pneumonias are believed to be caused by viruses. More and more viruses are being identified as the cause of respiratory infection, and though most attack the upper respiratory tract, some produce pneumonia, especially in children. Most of these pneumonias are not serious and last only a short time.

Infection with the influenza virus may be severe and occasionally fatal. The virus invades the lungs and multiplies, but there are almost no physical signs of lung tissue becoming filled with fluid. It finds many of its victims among those who have pre-existing heart or lung disease or are pregnant.

The initial symptoms of viral pneumonia are the same as influenza symptoms: fever, a dry cough, headache, muscle pain, and weakness. Within 12 to 36 hours, there is increasing breathlessness; the cough becomes worse and produces a small amount of mucus. There is a high fever, and there may be blueness of the lips.

In extreme cases, the patient has a desperate need for air and extreme breathlessness. Viral pneumonias may be complicated by an invasion of bacteria, with all the typical symptoms of bacterial pneumonia.

Mycoplasma Pneumonia

Because of its somewhat different symptoms and physical signs and because the course of the illness differed from classical pneumococcal pneumonia, mycoplasma pneumonia was once believed to be caused by one or more undiscovered viruses and was called *primary atypical pneumonia.*

Identified during World War II, mycoplasmas are the smallest free-living agents of disease in humankind. Mycoplasmas are not classified as bacteria or viruses but have characteristics of both. They generally cause a mild and widespread pneumonia. They affect all age groups, occurring most frequently in older children and young adults. The death rate is low, even in untreated cases.

The most prominent symptom of mycoplasma pneumonia is a cough that tends to come in violent attacks but produces only sparse, whitish mucus. Chills and fever are early symptoms, and some patients experience nausea or vomiting. Patients may experience profound weakness that lasts for a long time.

Other Strains of Pneumonia

Pneumocystis carinii pneumonia (PCP) is caused by an organism believed to be a fungus. PCP is the first sign of illness in many persons with AIDS.

It can be successfully treated in many cases. It may recur a few months later, but treatment can help to prevent or delay its recurrence.

Other less common pneumonias may be quite serious and are occurring more often. Various special pneumonias are caused by the inhalation of food, liquid, gas, dust, or fungi. Foreign bodies or a bronchial obstruction such as tumor may promote the occurrence of pneumonia, although they are not causes of pneumonia.

Rickettsia (also considered an organism somewhere between viruses and bacteria) causes *Rocky Mountain spotted fever, Q fever, typhus,* and *psittacosis,* diseases that may have mild or severe effects on the lungs. *Tuberculosis pneumonia* is a very serious lung infection and extremely dangerous unless treated early.

Treatment

If a person develops pneumonia, chances of a fast recovery are greatest under certain conditions—if the person is young, if the pneumonia is caught early, if defenses against disease are working well, if the infection has not spread, or if the person is not suffering from other illnesses.

In the young and healthy, early treatment with antibiotics can cure bacterial pneumonia and speed recovery from mycoplasma pneumonia and a certain percentage of rickettsia cases. There is not yet a general treatment for viral pneumonia, although antiviral drugs are used for certain kinds. Most people can be treated at home.

The drugs used to fight pneumonia are determined by the germ causing the pneumonia and the judgment of the treating physician. After a patient's temperature returns to normal, medication must be continued according to the physician's instructions; otherwise the pneumonia may recur. Relapses are known to be far more serious than the first attack.

Besides antibiotics, patients, when needed, are given supportive treatment: proper diet and oxygen to increase in blood levels. In some patients, medication may be necessary to ease chest pain and to provide relief from violent cough.

The vigorous young person may lead a normal life within a week of recovery from pneumonia. For the elderly, however, weeks may elapse before they regain their accustomed strength, vigor, and feeling of well-being. A person recovering from mycoplasma pneumonia may experience weakness for an extended period of time.

Prevention

Because pneumonia is a common complication of influenza (flu), getting a flu shot every fall is good pneumonia prevention. A vaccine is also available to help fight pneumococcal pneumonia, one type of bacterial pneumonia. The elderly, who are usually at high risk of getting the disease and its life-threatening complications, should be vaccinated.

There is an increased incidence of pneumonia as a result of the aging process. Many elderly patients contract the disease and die. The greatest risk of contracting pneumococal pneumonia occurs in the segments of the population that:

- Have chronic illnesses such as lung disease, heart disease, kidney disorders, sickle cell anemia, or diabetes

- Are recovering from severe illness
- Are age 65 or older

ARTHRITIS

Osteoarthritis (OA), or degenerative joint disease, is one of the oldest and most common types of arthritis. It is characterized by the breakdown of the joint's cartilage, which is the part that cushions the ends of bones. Cartilage breakdown causes bones to rub against each other, causing pain and loss movement.

Most commonly affecting middle-aged and older people, OA can range from very mild to very severe. It affects hands and weight-bearing joints such as knees, hips, feet, and the back and is a leading cause of physical disability in people over age 65.

Osteoarthritis (OA or Arthritis)
The breakdown of bone cartilage in the joints, which causes bones to rub against each other, causing pain and loss movement.

Causes

There are many factors that can cause OA. Although age is a risk factor, research has shown that OA is not an inevitable part of aging. Obesity may lead to osteoarthritis of the knees. In addition, people with joint injuries due to sports, work-related activity, or accidents may be at increased risk of developing OA.

Genetics have a role in the development of OA, particularly in the hands. Some people may be born with defective cartilage or with slight defects in the way that joints fit together. As the person ages, these defects may cause early cartilage breakdown in joints. In the process of cartilage breakdown, there may be some inflammation, with enzymes released and more cartilage damage.

Diagnosis

Physicians make a diagnosis of OA based on a physical exam and history of symptoms. X-rays are used to confirm the diagnosis. Most people over 60 reflect the disease on X-rays, and about one-third have actual symptoms.

Treatment Options

Treatment of osteoarthritis focuses on decreasing pain and improving joint movement and may include the following:

- Exercises keep joints flexible and improve muscle strength.
- Many different medications are used to control pain, including corticosteroids and Non-Steroid Anti-Inflammatory Drugs (NSAIDs). Glucocorticoids are injected into joints that are inflamed and not responsive to NSAIDs. For mild pain without inflammation, acetaminophen (Tylenol®) and aspirin are often helpful.
- Heat/cold therapy gives temporary pain relief.
- Joint protection prevents strain or stress on painful joints.

- Surgery relieves chronic pain in damaged joints.
- Weight control prevents extra stress on weight-bearing joints.

Those at Risk

- Osteoarthritis affects an estimated 20.7 million Americans, mostly after age 45.
- Women are more commonly affected than men.

Other Information

- OA is responsible for more than seven million physician visits per year.
- Eighty percent of people with OA report some form of limitation in movement or activities.
- Knee OA can be as disabling as any cardiovascular disease except stroke.
- As many as 50 percent of the people who have OA do not know what type of arthritis they have and cannot make informed decisions about their care because treatment options vary among the more that 100 forms of arthritis.
- Musculoskeletal conditions such as OA cost the U.S. economy nearly $65 billion per year in direct expenses and lost wages and production.

PERSISTIVE VEGETATIVE STATE

Persistive vegetative state is defined as the loss of cortical function in the brain while retaining brain stem function. Medical experts say patients in a persistive vegetative state show no evidence of language comprehension or expression or voluntary responses to sight, sound, touch, or smell. Because their brain stem functions, they can often breathe normally. No form of medical treatment available today can cure or ameliorate this condition. Patients are devoid of thought, emotion, and sensation; they are permanently unconscious.

Persistive vegetative state is caused by a lack of oxygen to the brain tissue. The cerebral hemisphere can only be deprived of oxygen for four to six minutes before permanent damage is caused; brain stem cells can live for 15 to 20 minutes without oxygen.

At present, 35,000 people in this country are in a persistive vegetative state. While relatively rare compared to Alzheimer's disease or diabetes, the effects are so dramatic that the condition warrants notice. And its cost is enormous, up to $500,000 per year to maintain one patient.

Prognosis is extremely poor. Of the 100,000 people who fell into a persistive vegetative state between 1970 and 1990, only three patients were able to make even a partial recovery. The longest anyone has ever been in a persistive vegetative state and made any recovery is 22 months. While patients have no cortical function, they do exhibit involuntary reflexes, grimacing, and rhythmic blinking, which family members sometimes misinterpret as communication. Unfortunately, this can create a false sense of hope for families.

Medical and legal experts strongly advise that everyone draft a living will stating whether they want to be kept alive through lifesaving procedures should they enter a persistive vegetative state. See also Chapter Four, Advance Directives, and Chapter Eleven, Patients'

Rights in Health Care Decision Making, for more information on persistive vegetative states and the benefits of a living will.

SUICIDE IN THE UNITED STATES

The Problem

- Suicide took the lives of 29,199 Americans in 1999.
- More people die from suicide than from homicide. In 1999, there were 1.7 times as many suicides as homicides.
- Overall, suicide is the 11th leading cause of death for all Americans and the third leading cause of death for young people aged 15–24.
- Males are four times more likely to die from suicide than are females. However, females are more likely to attempt suicide than are males.
- In 1999, white males accounted for 72 percent of all suicides. Together, white males and white females accounted for more than 90 percent of all suicides. However, during the period 1979–1992, suicide rates for Native Americans (a category that includes American Indians and Alaska Natives) were about 1.5 times the national rates. There were a disproportionate number of suicides among young male Native Americans during this period, as males 15–24 accounted for 64 percent of all suicides by Native Americans.
- Suicide rates are generally higher than the national average in the Western states and lower in the Eastern and Midwestern states.
- Nearly three out of every five suicides in 1999 (57 percent) were committed with a firearm.

Suicide among the Elderly

- Suicide rates increase with age and are highest among Americans aged 65 years and older. The 10-year period, 1980–1989, was the first decade since the 1940s that the suicide rate for older residents rose instead of declined.
- In 1999, men accounted for 84 percent of suicides among persons aged 65 years and older.
- From 1980–1998, the largest relative increases in suicide rates occurred among those 80–84 years of age. The rate for men in this age group increased 17 percent (from 43.5 per 100,000 to 52).
- Firearms are the most common method of suicide by both males and females 65 years and older, accounting for 78.5 percent of male and 35.0 percent of female suicides in that age group.
- Suicide rates among the elderly are highest for those who are divorced or widowed. In 1992, the rate for divorced or widowed men in this age group was seven times that for married men, 1.4 times that for never-married men, and over 17 times that for married women. The rate for divorced or widowed women was 1.8 times that for married women and 1.4 times that for never-married women.
- Risk factors for suicide among older people differ from those of the young. Older people have a higher prevalence of depression, a high incidence of social isolation, and a greater use of highly lethal drugs and alcohol. They also make fewer attempts per

completed suicide, have a higher male-to-female ratio than other groups, have often visited a health care provider before their suicide, and have more physical illnesses.

REFERENCES

The *Merck Manual of Geriatrics,* 2nd Ed. (1995)
Alzheimer's Association–www.Alz.org
American Heart Association–www.Americanheart.org
American Diabetes Association–www.Diabetes.org
National Parkinson's Foundation–www.Parkinson.org.
National Centers for Disease Control–www.cdc.gov.
Arthritis Foundation–www.Arthritis.org.
National Institutes of Health, (stem cells)–www.Nih.org

REVIEW QUESTIONS AND EXERCISES

1. What are some of the most common diseases to affect the elderly? Discuss any interaction you may have had with people with these diseases. How were the families and friends of the ill individual affected?

2. What is Alzheimer's disease, and what are the warning signs? What are the different stages of the disease? What steps should the elder law professional take to ensure that all clients' needs are protected?

3. What is Parkinson's disease, and what are warning signs?

4. What is a stroke? Describe what happens to a stroke victim. How can a stroke affect the capacity of a client to create legally binding documents?

5. What is diabetes? What is the difference between Type 1 diabetes and Type 2 diabetes? Which of these is more common in the elderly? What are the warning signs of diabetes?

6. What is pneumonia? What are the different kinds of pneumonia, and how do they differ in effect? What are the causes of pneumonia? How can pneumonia be prevented and treated?

7. What is osteoarthritis, and what are the causes of arthritis? How can arthritis be treated?

8. What are the risk factors for suicide among the elderly? What minimizes the risk of suicide among the elderly population? Discuss suicide among the elderly.

CHAPTER 3

Initial Interview

PREVIEW

The elder law professional's relationship with a client is very important. The initial interview can have a significant impact on how the elder law professional–client relationship develops. In building a good rapport with the elderly client, it is important to remember that clients and their families often require more personal attention and hand-holding than other clients. This chapter provides an understanding of the basic tools needed for the initial interview. There is a discussion of the documents that the client should bring to the initial interview, the questions that should be asked of the new client, the role and demeanor that the elder law professional should take, and how the elder law office should be designed.

The first contact that any client has with the elder law team is vital. The elder law professional must often assess the situation to determine whether immediate crisis intervention is necessary or whether the client can wait for a scheduled office visit.

ASSESSING NEED

Situations Requiring Immediate Crisis Intervention

1. *Death of a client:* Client's family needs assistance in making funeral arrangements, locating the decedent's will, and reviewing procedures concerning death.
2. *Discharge from a hospital:* Where should the patient go next?
3. *Sudden catastrophic illness:* How are the affairs of the ill individual to be handled?
4. *Elder abuse issues*

Nonemergency Situations

1. General issues concerning estate planning, finances, transfer of assets, tax considerations, Medicaid eligibility planning, drawing of wills, setting up trusts, and other advance directive documents
2. Management of progressive disorders
3. Medicaid applications
4. Nursing home placement
5. Assisted-living arrangements

6. Elder abuse issues
7. Nonfamily disputes

In nonemergency matters, the elder law professional should schedule initial interviews with the clients, advising them to bring certain documents to the interview. This should be followed up with a letter of instruction about the necessary documents and confirming the appointment. A frequent response will be, "I don't have these documents. I can't find them. What should I do?" Clients should be encouraged to come to the office even though they do not have all of the documents and information requested. Calls from the client should be returned promptly. It is important to remember that the elderly client and immediate family require more personal attention and guidance than other clients.

PREPARATION FOR THE INITIAL CLIENT MEETING

The client should be instructed to bring the following documents and other important papers and materials to the initial interview:

- Last will and testament
- Codicils to wills
- Power of attorney
- Health care proxy
- Living will
- Advance directive for the appointment of a guardian
- Do not resuscitate (DNR) orders

If the client has the documents listed above, they should be reviewed to see if they are current and effective; if not, new documents should be drawn up. Documents that have "stale" dates may present a problem when they are presented for enforcement.

Personal Papers
1. Birth certificates
2. Death certificates of family members
3. Driver's license
4. Medicaid card
5. Social Security card and award letter (Is the Social Security benefit being electronically deposited to bank account?)
6. Passport or citizenship papers
7. Certificates of marriage
8. Prenuptial, postnuptial agreements
9. Divorce decrees—annulment and separation agreements, alimony and property settlement agreements
10. Adoption papers
11. War separation awards, *e.g.,* Holocaust victims
12. Veteran's Administration benefit awards
13. Change of name court decrees
14. SSI or disability benefit awards

Proof of Ownership of Property

1. Deeds to primary residence, vacation properties, business and industrial properties; mortgage loan agreements and reverse mortgage agreements in connection with these properties; statement of current mortgage balance
2. Cooperative apartments—shareholder's certificates and proprietary leases
3. Leases on rental apartments
4. Time-share agreements
5. Closing statements for real property or businesses sold within the most recent 12 months
6. Family partnerships or limited liability companies

Financial Papers

1. Bank passbooks
2. Bank statements and cancelled checks
3. Income tax and gift tax returns for the most recent 36 months. Have gift tax returns been filed for all transfers? If any tax audits, provide tax authority's decision. Are there any pending audits? If during this current taxable year there were any sales of capital assets that would be subject to potential capital gains tax, provide transaction details or stock losses, provide all details.
4. Itemized list of any unusual medical expenses
5. Estate tax returns of spouse or parent who has died within the most recent 36 months
6. Trust agreements—living trusts, revocable trusts, irrevocable trusts, supplemental needs trusts, charitable trusts, life insurance trusts, and testamentary trusts in which the client is either the grantor or the beneficiary
7. Brokerage accounts—current statements of assets
8. List of individually held stocks, dividend reinvestment plans, bonds (including U.S. savings bonds, which should be checked to determine actual cash value and if they are still accruing interest), mutual funds, foreign investments, etc., specifying the number of shares, date acquired, market value at date of death, current market value, and registration of ownership
9. List of pension plans, *e.g.,* IRAs, Keoghs, 401(k)s, etc.
10. Annuity contracts—Who are the beneficiaries? What is the cash surrender value?
11. All current and prior wills and codicils
12. List of all pending inheritances
13. Basic inventory of all assets and how they are held
14. List of all automatic bill payments

Insurance Policies

1. Homeowner's insurance policy
2. Personal articles floater
3. Umbrella policy
4. Automobile/boat insurance policy
5. Life insurance policies—VA policies; personal and business policies upon client's life and upon the life of client's spouse. Who are the beneficiaries? Is there any cash surrender value? Should these policies be cashed in? Are there any outstanding loans against the policy?
6. Health insurance policies

7. Long-term care insurance policies
8. Accident and disability policies
9. Has third-party notification been arranged in case of nonpayment of a premium?

Other

1. List of all debts, including credit card obligations and promissory notes
2. Documents pertaining to any litigation in which the client is involved and judgments or liens that have remained outstanding for the most recent 20 years against the client
3. Pending guardianship or conservatorship proceedings
4. Garnishments of salary
5. Bankruptcy proceedings
6. Child support obligations
7. Location of safety deposit boxes and ownership
8. Cemetery plots, prearranged funeral contracts, and burial accounts
9. Third-party notification in case of nonpayment of clients financial obligations
10. List of any assets that may be missing or unclaimed

INITIAL CLIENT MEETING

The initial meeting may take place at the lawyer's office, a medical institutional setting where the client is currently confined, or at the residence of the client, at which time the elder law professional will ask the client to complete a questionnaire. The client may need assistance in completing the questionnaire. See the CD-ROM for the Elder Law Initial Confidential Questionnaire.

There are special circumstances of which the elder law professional must be cognizant when the initial interview takes place at a hospital or nursing home. Generally, the visit should be scheduled for normal visiting hours. It is usually not necessary to notify the facility of the meeting. Some facilities may require the presence of a social worker during an interview. The family should be consulted as to the best time to visit. When is the patient most alert? Is patient receiving pain medication? When does the patient receive physical therapy? Is the patient suffering from any cognitive impairment? Institutional patients should not be visited early in the morning because at that time they are being cleaned, fed, and medicated. Patients suffering from **sundown syndrome** may not be alert in the late afternoon or evening.

The issue of privacy is also present when a meeting occurs in an institution. A patient may not have a private room and may feel uncomfortable discussing personal matters in the presence of another patient in the room. If the patient is ambulatory, the elder law professional should request institutional personnel for assistance in moving the patient to an area where the interview can proceed in privacy.

Sundown Syndrome
Many elderly clients tend to be more alert during the day than in the late afternoon or evening.

Initial Interview

The elder law professional's task during any initial interview, whether in a residence, an institutional setting, or a law office, is to extract familial and financial information to determine the client's financial, social, legal, medical, and mental status and provide assistance to the client or family members that have sought help. This may not be easy, because clients are often unable to focus on the key issues and may want to tell their life stories. The elder law professional must guide them, gently but firmly, by insightful questions.

It is vital, too, that the client be informed at the onset of the interview that everything discussed is confidential, in accordance with the privileged communications laws, which apply to the attorney, the paralegal, and the entire elder care law team. (Discussions with governmental authorities are not confidential.)

The initial interview with the elderly client begins with obtaining the following information:

1. Client's name
2. Address
3. Social Security number
4. Date and place of birth
5. Citizenship
6. Occupation
7. Marital status: divorced, widowed, second marriage
8. Children: first marriage, second marriage, stepchildren; ages of children
9. Are any of the family members incapacitated, incompetent, disabled, receiving Medicaid, Social Security insurance, or disability benefits?

Some information can be obtained directly, but more subtle information must be obtained artfully. First and foremost, the legal professional must develop a sense of who is the client. Is it the person who contacts the elder law firm? An adult child or a spouse? A friend? Or is your client really the elderly person himself or herself?

In most situations, the client is the elderly person who needs assistance, not the contact person. The primary obligation of the law firm would ultimately be to protect the elderly person, even if doing so adversely affects other family members. This is a critical ethical issue that often presents major problems.

In addition, it is essential to determine:

- What are the family relationships? Are the relationships good between the parents and children? Any "black sheep" in the family? Are there any animosities? Any sibling rivalry? Is the client willing to discuss any problems that may exist between parents and children? Is there any overreaching or undue influence by family, caregivers, friends, or neighbors? Are there any problems between spouses? Is there any evidence of domestic, spousal, or self-abuse?
- Are the clients involved in family businesses?
- Does the client or family member exhibit any type of personality disorder? The most common disorder exhibited by elderly clients is paranoia. Is he or she distrustful and suspicious? Is the client schizophrenic? Is behavior bizarre? Is he or she is fearful and frightened? Does he or she appear to be highly emotional, nervous, or histrionic? Does he or she exhibit a dependent personality that prevents functioning? Are you comfortable working with this client and the client's family?
- Is the patient competent? Is a psychiatric evaluation required? Will a guardianship or conservatorship proceeding be necessary? What is the family's care plan? If the client (patient) is in a nursing home, does the family want to keep the patient there, or do they want to bring the patient home? If the person is in the hospital, does the family want to bring the patient home, or is continued hospitalization required? If they bring the patient

home, can they take care of the patient at home? Will the discharge from the nursing home to the community be a "safe discharge"? Should an assisted-living facility be considered? Are the family members being reasonable and rational in their expectations?

- What is the client's domicile? Does the client have multiple residences, *e.g.,* New York and Florida? Does the client own a home, condominium, cooperative apartment, time-shares? If so, are these premises mortgaged, and what is the current balance? Is there a reverse mortgage against the premises, or is the property free and clear? Is there a co-owner with that client? Is there a life estate on the real property? Does a homestead exemption exist? Are the real estate taxes subject to a veterans or senior citizens exemption? Review title to all assets.

- Does the client have Social Security and/or SSI disability benefits? If so, how much? Suggest electronic deposits of all pension benefits.

- Does the client receive any pensions, IRA distributions, annuity distributions, 401(k) benefits, union benefits, or Holocaust reparations? How much and from where?

- Does the client receive Medicare benefits? If so, does the client have both Part A and Part B?

- Is the client a veteran eligible for any benefits?

- Does the client have a Medicare supplemental insurance policy?

- Does the client currently receive Medicaid benefits? If yes, home care or institutional care? For how long? Has Medicaid filed any liens against the beneficiaries' real property? Has Medicaid instituted any recovery actions?

- Has interest been posted to bank passbooks within the most recent six months? If interest has not been posted regularly, the funds may have been turned over to the state comptroller's office as abandoned property. This turnover often occurs with elderly persons. If funds appear to be missing, contact should be made with the state abandoned property office to see if any funds were deposited there for the benefit of the client. Most states have individual web sites that provide information as to abandoned property.

- Does the client have long-term care insurance, and what is the coverage?

- What is the client's financial situation? All federal, state, and local income and gift tax returns filed in the most recent three years will need to be reviewed. These will reveal an excellent picture of his or her asset structure and lifestyle. It is necessary to determine the value of the client's net estate. *Gross estate minus liabilities = net estate.* The gross estate is determined by adding up all of the client's existing assets and potential assets, *e.g.,* proceeds of a personal injury suit, inheritance from a spouse or living parent, repayment of a loan. From these assets are deducted any debts or potential liabilities resulting from lawsuits or other business transactions. This brings us to the *net estate* for estate planning purposes.

The review of assets will assist in determining if an application for Medicaid assistance is recommended and when it should be filed. Because of the **36-month lookback rule,** we must determine whether there have been any transfers of assets within that window of time. See Chapter 10 for a more detailed discussion of the law. A determination will have to be made regarding Medicaid planning and the need to **spend down** in order to qualify for Medicaid. Should the client transfer assets at this time as a method of reduction of the net estate, or should spending down be considered? Transfer of assets enables the elderly to:

- Become Medicaid eligible
- Reduce their estates so as to minimize or avoid inheritance tax, both federal and state
- Avoid probate costs, fees

36-Month Lookback Rule

Under the 36-month Lookback Rule (applicable to outright transfers) and 60-month Lookback Rule (applicable to certain transfers in trust), eligibility for Medicaid may be denied if the person going into the nursing home transferred assets for less than fair market value within 36 or 60 months before his or her application for Medicaid benefits. The period of ineligibility begins with the month in which the resources were transferred and lasts for a number of months equal to the total value of the transferred property divided by the average cost of nursing home care to a private patient in that state.

Spend Down

The process by which an elderly person divests him- or herself of assets in order to qualify for Medicaid.

- Possibly avoid the necessity of a guardianship or conservatorship
- Remove the burden of management of their personal and financial affairs, thereby giving them peace of mind and more independence

The initial interview will provide a basic picture of the client's financial, social, and medical status. Having gathered this information, the elder law attorney is now ready to begin the planning process.

THE MULTIFACETED ROLE OF THE ELDER LAW PROFESSIONAL

Dealing with an elderly client can be very tricky. Therefore, a keen understanding of the aging process and its impact upon the clients and their families is necessary. It is important for the elder law professional to realize that all tasks, however simple or complex, require the same understanding of the nature and psychology of the elderly.

Be aware that an elderly person may have hearing and vision impairment. If you sense that your client is hard of hearing, give him or her the opportunity to read your lips or speak louder. Have a hearing amplifier available to assist clients that exhibit hearing loss. If you sense that your client has vision problems, write bigger. Be aware that the elderly fatigue easily. Do not have an extended interview.

Clients get tired. On the other hand, beware of the client who wants to spend the afternoon talking to you.

Exhibit a combination of patience, sensitivity, and persistence during the interview in order to elicit as much pertinent information about the client as possible. A good rapport with the client will go a long way to instill confidence in the client that the elder law firm will properly manage his or her affairs.

THE ELDER LAW OFFICE

The elder law office should create a comfortable setting for elderly clients and their families. The ambiance should be soft and homelike to create a low-key atmosphere in which the elderly and their families can explore their problems. Wheelchair access is essential.

The office should be safe. There should be no slippery floors or area rugs. There should be handrails on all staircases. Outdoor steps, driveways, and sidewalks should be kept free of ice and snow in winter. The inside temperature of the office should remain a comfortable 70 degrees. Overly cool temperatures in the waiting room during summer heat should be avoided. Straight-backed chairs are recommended for the waiting room. Low, comfortable sofas are not appropriate because clients may find it difficult to get up once they are seated.

The office should be equipped with an augmentative hearing device to aid hard-of-hearing clients. This consists of an amplifying device with headphones. Many clients are diabetic; it is considerate to offer them a glass of juice or other snack if they so desire. Poor vision is common in the elderly. Every desk should be equipped with a magnifying device to assist the client in reading documents.

Last but not least, the elder law office should be equipped with an easily accessible bathroom. It will be greatly appreciated. The staff also should know how to respond in the event that a client becomes ill while in the office. Staff meetings should be held to discuss responses to medical emergencies occurring in the office or in a client's home during a consultation. Medical emergency telephone numbers should be readily available. Caring and consideration are essential elements in the practice of elder law.

REVIEW QUESTIONS AND EXERCISES

1. Discuss what situations may be considered emergency situations requiring immediate crisis intervention versus situations that are nonemergency situations. In what ways should the elder law professional's initial interaction differ between nonemergency and emergency situations? In what ways should the initial interaction be similar?

2. What information/documents are important to obtain from an elderly client in the initial interview? What should the elder law professional do if the client does not have these documents and/or information readily available?

3. Identify your client. Discuss how the needs of the elderly client may differ from the needs of the person who contacted the elder law office. Discuss how to deal with any potential conflicts of interest and how to determine who is the client.

4. In addition to the basic information gathered in the initial interview, what should the elder law professional be cognizant of?

5. What skills are especially necessary for the elder law professional?

6. Discuss how the elder law office should be designed and how this may differ from a typical law office.

CHAPTER 4
Advance Directives

PREVIEW

Advanced directives are legally binding documents created by healthy individuals that provide detailed instructions on how the client wishes his or her medical and legal affairs to be handled in case of incapacity. This chapter provides an understanding of the contents of these advanced directives, when and how they should be used, and how to assist in their preparation and execution. The advanced directives discussed in this chapter include the durable power of attorney, the health care proxy, the living will, the directive for anatomical gifting, and the appointment of a guardian.

INTRODUCTION

The first step in almost every elder law matter, even in a crisis situation, is to have legal documents prepared so that the family, friends, or significant other can responsibly and efficiently handle the legal and medical affairs of the person who is elderly or ill. These documents are called **advance directives** and are known individually as:

- Durable power of attorney
- Health care proxy (medical power of attorney)
- Living will
- Directive for anatomical gifting
- Appointment of a guardian
- Last will and testament (discussed in Chapter 5)

> **Advance Directives**
> Legal instruments executed by an individual directing others on how to responsibly and efficiently handle his or her legal and medical affairs.

They are called advance directives because the elderly, while competent and physically able, can direct in advance what should be done under certain circumstances while the patient is alive and when he or she dies. The legal professional must have a thorough understanding of the contents of these documents, when they should be used, and how to assist in their preparation and execution. These documents play an essential role in disability and life care planning as the aging process takes place in all our lives.

POWERS OF ATTORNEY

A **power of attorney** is one of the most powerful instruments recognized by our legal system. Before legal professionals can appreciate the significance of a power of attorney, they must understand the basic concept of this legal instrument and how it is used in the law.

> **Power of Attorney**
> A legal instrument executed by a competent adult authorizing another individual to act in a fiduciary capacity on his or her behalf.

37

Statutory Authority

All powers of attorney derive their authority from statutory legislation, and all states have enacted some form of power of attorney legislation. Most states follow the Uniform Power of Attorney codification, while other states have adopted their own format. STATED BELOW ARE GENERAL PRINCIPLES.

Definition: Power of attorney—A power of attorney is a legal written instrument executed by a competent adult authorizing another individual to act in a fiduciary capacity on his or her behalf. Its origin is in the law of principal and agent. The **principal** appoints an **agent** (also known as the **fiduciary**) to act for the principal under certain circumstances and to carry out specific duties set forth in the power of attorney. The agent who is the recipient of the power(s) becomes the **attorney-in-fact** for the principal. The act of the agent is considered the lawful act of the principal, provided the agent acts in full legal conformity of the power(s) vested in the agent. In sum, by executing this document, the principal confers upon the duly appointed agent certain power(s) specified in the body of the document. *The principal must be competent at the time of execution* and understand the nature and consequences of this vesting of power in another person(s) or agent(s).

The instrument defines the powers given to the agent, *e.g.,* general through limited.

The Principal

The Principal
The person from whom the power of attorney originates.

The principal is the person from whom the document originates. He or she must be an adult and must have mental capacity. There is no requirement of citizenship.

The Agent

The Agent
The beneficiary of the power of attorney transferred by the principal.

The agent is the person to whom the principal transfers her or his powers. Agents must have the implicit trust of the principal, since their function is to act on behalf of the principal, and their acts are deemed those of the principal. If they do not adhere to these strict fiduciary rules, they may be found guilty of malfeasance of office and could be subject to criminal and civil convictions. Self-dealing is strictly forbidden, unless it is specifically permitted in the instrument.

Who may act as an agent?
1. An adult who is a competent individual. (There is no citizenship requirement.)
2. A corporation authorized to act as a fiduciary, *e.g.,* a bank or a trust company.

PRACTICE TIP

The elder law attorney would not be a good choice for an agent because of potential conflicts of interest that often arise in fiduciary relationships.

The elder law professional should be aware of the most commonly asked questions by clients:

1. I have a spouse and four children. Who should act as the agent?
2. I am in a second marriage with two children from a prior marriage. Who should act as the agent?
3. I am a widow/widower/divorced with four children. Who should act as the agent?
4. I am single with no children. Who should act as the agent?
5. Should the agents act separately or jointly?
6. What if the proposed agents live in another state?
7. What if the proposed agents are elderly?
8. Do I have to ask the proposed agents if they will accept the responsibility before naming them in the document?
9. Do the agents get a copy or an original of the document, and if they do, when do they receive it?
10. Where should I keep the document once it is executed?
11. Do I have to tell my children or my spouse that a durable power of attorney has been executed?

Other Considerations

1. The principal should always appoint at least one substitute agent to avoid the possibility of a vacancy in office that would result in the power of attorney becoming ineffective.

SCENARIO

The principal appoints one agent. The principal becomes incompetent, then the agent dies, leaving a vacancy in office. The principal, now incompetent, can no longer appoint a substitute agent. At this point, the document is worthless.

2. The principal may appoint multiple agents. They can be appointed to act as follows:
   a. Jointly or the survivor—The agents A & B (or as many as designated) must act together in concert in order for any act to be legal. "A" or "B" cannot act alone to legally bind the principal. If A dies or is unable to act, B can act alone or vice versa.
   b. Severally—A or B can act separately on behalf of the principal without the necessity of a unanimous decision to bind the principal.

   A is not a substitute for B, and B is not a substitute for A.

3. Substitute appointments—In the event that the primary agent or agents cease to function, then the substitute agent or agents can function.
4. The principal should also consider the ability of the agents to act together, especially if they are the children of the principal. Is there a possibility of friction between the children? Do they live in different parts of the country? Will it be practical for them to act together? If one child is named and not the other, will this create resentment among the siblings? Will the emotions of the parties likely interfere with the proper execution of the agent's fiduciary duties?
5. There are four basic types of powers of attorney:
   • General power of attorney
   • Durable power of attorney

- Springing durable power of attorney
- Limited power of attorney

General Power of Attorney

General Power of Attorney

A legal instrument executed by a competent adult authorizing another individual agent to act in a fiduciary capacity on his or her behalf. The power automatically ceases upon the incapacity of the principal.

The **general power of attorney** is the standard power of attorney that is used in basic business transactions. It is often used in the transfer of real property where principals, knowing they may be out of town, grant an agent the authority to sign contracts of sale, closing documents, deeds, and mortgage agreements in their stead. In real estate transactions, the power may be limited to a particular transaction so stated in the document, or it may be a continuing power to handle multiple transactions over an extended period of time. The general power is also used in financial transactions such as banking and transfers of stocks, bonds, and other securities. The general power of attorney can be used for any type of transaction as specified within the power. It can contain all of the powers found in the other types of powers of attorney, but it has one significant difference: *it ceases upon the incapacity of the principal*, resulting in the agent's loss of all authority. This power of attorney can be revoked at any time. This type of power is ineffective in financial planning for the elderly because the basic purpose of the power of attorney is to permit the agent to function and carry out duties when the principal has reached the state of incapacity.

It should be noted that the general power of attorney is similar to the durable power of attorney and the springing power of attorney in that they all cease upon the death of the principal.

Durable Power of Attorney

Durable Power of Attorney

A legal instrument executed by a competent adult authorizing another individual agent to act in a fiduciary capacity on his or her behalf.

The **durable power of attorney** is considered the most powerful instrument in our legal system because of the powers granted in the document. It is the cornerstone of advance planning and, as such, is an invaluable document, provided there are adequate safeguards in place to avoid the ever-present possibility of fraud and abuse. It permits the transfer of authority from a competent principal to a trustworthy agent. The execution of an advance directive durable power of attorney by the elderly principal while still competent can avoid the excessive cost and unpleasantness of judicial intervention in the form of a conservatorship or guardianship proceeding.

The court has the authority to revoke any power of attorney that was obtained by fraud or abuse. This often occurs in guardianship or conservatorship hearings.

Durable power of attorney legislation has been enacted in every state. A durable power of attorney can contain all of the same powers as the general power of attorney but it also contains the following special language: "*This power shall survive the incapacity of the principal*," or stated in another way: "*This instrument will not be affected by the subsequent disability or incompetence of the principal*." This special language will prevent the durable power of attorney from becoming ineffective *upon the subsequent incapacity of the principal*. All powers granted in the durable power of attorney will remain in effect until the death of the principal, when all powers cease, or until such time as the principal revokes the powers, which he or she *can* do while still competent. (See the CD-ROM for power of attorney and revocation forms.) Some states do not permit revocation. This is an irrevocable power of attorney. Review local statutes.

Springing Durable Power of Attorney

The **springing durable power of attorney** is a standard durable power of attorney, but with one unique feature: it springs into effect only upon the happening of a certain event and becomes effective only if and when this special *condition precedent* occurs. The usual condition precedent is the incapacity or incompetency of the principal. The springing power differs from the general power and durable power of attorney in that *no power is transferred when the document is executed*. (The principal may be uncomfortable with a general power or a durable power of attorney because power is transferred immediately upon execution.) With a springing durable power of attorney, it is the principal's intent to have the agent act only if the principal becomes incompetent or incapacitated.

In order to activate the springing durable power of attorney, the agent must establish the incompetency or incapacity of the principal. Obtaining the necessary medical proof often delays the agent from acting in situations where time is of the essence. Questions can also arise concerning the definition of incompetency or incapacity. Further complicating this situation is the fact that physicians are often reluctant to declare a person incompetent or incapacitated for fear of malpractice and the fact that the incapacity of the principal can also be contested. The springing durable power of attorney, although superficially appealing, is not commonly recommended by the elder law attorney because of the inherent problems described above.

As you can see, each of the powers of attorney have distinct advantages and disadvantages. In practice, the durable power of attorney is the document of choice because:

1. It enables the principal to give the document containing the powers to the agent if the principal wants the agent to act immediately.
2. It enables the principal to retain the document in his or her possession if the principal does not want the agent to act immediately.

The principal can keep the document or instruct an attorney to hold the document until such time as the principal wants the agent to act, *e.g.,* in the event of illness or incapacity. This procedure avoids the necessity of having the patient declared incompetent or incapacitated by a physician.

A springing durable power of attorney ceases to be operative when the principal regains capacity. However, in cases where there is prolonged illness, the appointment of a guardian or a conservator by the judiciary system does not automatically terminate any form of power of attorney. It may, however, depending upon the circumstances, create the suspension of the power for a certain period of time.

The Execution of Powers of Attorney

Factors to Consider

1. The principal must have the legal capacity to execute the power of attorney. If there is any question as to whether the principal understands what he is signing, it is strongly recommended that a physician's affidavit be obtained confirming the principal's capacity. If the principal can sign only with an "X" or his signature will differ significantly from that already on file with a third party, it is also critically important to obtain a physician's affidavit to confirm the capacity of the principal. The document must not only be notarized, but there should be two independent witnesses to this type

Springing Durable Power of Attorney
A legal instrument executed by a competent adult authorizing another individual agent to act in a fiduciary capacity on his or her behalf that takes effect upon the happening of a condition precedent, usually incompetence or incapacity of the principal. Medical proof will have to be obtained before a durable power of attorney can "spring" into effect.

of signature. If a physician's affidavit is not available, the affidavit of the attorney who was present when the power of attorney was executed may be accepted by the third-party financial institution.

2. All forms of powers of attorney must be in writing.

3. The document should be notarized, even if not required by the law of the jurisdiction.

4. Some jurisdictions additionally require that the document be witnessed by at least two independent witnesses.

5. All pages of the document should be initialed by the principal at the foot of the page. Any hand-written alterations to the document must also be initialed. Some states require that the principal initial each individual power that is granted to the attorney-in-fact.

6. Powers of attorney should be executed in multiple originals. The more extensive the principal's assets are, the more originals will be required. You will find that when the agent acts pursuant to powers granted on behalf of the principal, the agent will often have to surrender the original document to a bank, stock transfer agent, or title company for recording, etc., and may never get it back. Photocopies of the original document will not be acceptable. If the power of attorney must be recorded, it will be returned to the agent, but it may take months for the original to be returned.

7. The legal professional should retain one original of the fully executed instrument in his or her office. This should be kept in a vault along with the client's will and other important documents. It is not unusual for a lawyer to receive a panic call from an attorney-in-fact stating that the original instrument was mislaid. Invariably, in these cases, the principal is already incompetent.

8. The general power of attorney and the durable power of attorney are effective immediately upon execution. The springing durable power of attorney springs into effect in the future when the condition precedent set forth in the document is met.

9. In some jurisdictions, the end of the statutory general power of attorney form, directly after the notary acknowledgments, is an affidavit that is a significant part of the document. When the agent is ready to use this document to conduct the principal's business, the agent must sign this affidavit before a notary public for the purpose of inducing a third party to act. The agent must represent the following therein:

    a. That the principal is still alive and is known to the affiant and is the person who signed the power of attorney.

    b. That the document annexed to this affidavit is a true copy of said power of attorney.

    c. That the agent was appointed on the specified date.

    d. That the agent has no actual knowledge or notice of revocation or termination of the power of attorney by death or otherwise.

    e. That the power of attorney is therefore still in full force and effect.

10. Some states require statutorily defined proof that the party giving the power of attorney has the legal capacity to do so.

PRACTICE TIP

When executing and drafting powers of attorney, it is very important to comply with the local statutes currently in force and to review cases in local jurisdiction.

Use of Forms

The publication of legal forms is a major industry serving the legal profession. The legal professional will find that there are preprinted forms at relatively inexpensive prices in every jurisdiction in this country. These forms provide the bare essentials that are found in statutes. It should be noted that practically all statutes permit the attorney-drafter to expand these powers to incorporate the specific needs of the client. For this reason, it is recommended that the use of these forms be avoided. Attorneys can use the statutory language and expand upon it to suit the needs of the client.

Powers of Attorney for Banks and Other Financial Institutions

Some banks and stock brokerage and other financial institutions require the use of their own in-house powers of attorney.

The elder law attorney should determine if in-house forms are necessary and review their scope. These forms should also be reviewed beforehand to make sure that they are in the best interest of the client. The lawyer may recommend that certain provisions be excluded and that others be included. In many situations, the preprinted in-house forms used by banks and other financial institutions do not include important provisions concerning durability, e.g., they lack the following language: "*This document shall be durable and shall survive the incompetency of the principal.*,"

PRACTICE TIP

A power of attorney may be rejected because the execution date is "stale." The financial institution or title insurance company may require the document to have been executed within the previous 6 to 12 months. In some instances, the third party may also insist on a physician's affidavit to the effect that at the time of execution the principal was mentally competent to execute a power of attorney. To avoid this problem, it is good practice to advise the client to keep the power of attorney current by updating it periodically.

PRACTICE TIP

The legal professional should determine the banks, brokerage houses, etc., in which the client has accounts, obtain the in-house forms, and have them executed simultaneously along with the other powers of attorney that have been prepared by the elder law office.

Powers of Attorney for Health Care Providers

The Health Insurance Portability and Accountability Act of 1996 (HIPAA) requires that health care providers maintain the privacy of patient information or face civil and criminal penalties. As a result, health care providers have become much more cautious when it comes to releasing information. The power of attorney should be drafted to allow the attorney-in-fact to acquire the principal's medical records and other confidential information with specific reference to the HIPAA provisions.

Powers of Attorney for Federal and State Agencies

1. **Internal Revenue Service**

   The Internal Revenue Service sometimes does not recognize a durable power of attorney executed pursuant to state law, even though the principal specifically delegates to the agent the power to represent the principal in connection with all tax matters. In view of this, the client should be advised to execute the *Internal Revenue Service Power of Attorney Form 2848—Power of Attorney and Declaration of Representative.* This permits the agent to sign the principal's name on all federal tax returns and to represent the principal in any tax audits or appeals. It is crucial when completing Part I, Item 5 of Form 2848 to add the following power: The power to *"sign any and all tax returns and to receive, endorse, and cash refund checks."* Unlike other power of attorney forms, this form does not have to be notarized or witnessed. It is also a good practice to have the client execute *Form 2821-Tax Information Authorization,* which permits the agent to obtain copies of the principal's prior tax returns.

   Recent changes in IRS procedures now permit the spouse of a physically incapacitated person to sign a joint income tax return on behalf of the ill spouse, provided that a dated statement is attached to the return stating the reasons therefore. The incapacitated spouse is required to give oral consent.

   Copies of both forms can be found on the CD-ROM, can be obtained from the Internal Revenue Service in quantities free of charge, or can be downloaded from the IRS web site (www.irs.gov). (However, the IRS accepts copies of these forms.)

2. **State or Local Taxing Authorities**

   It is also recommended that the client execute state and local taxing authority powers of attorney because many states and local jurisdictions do not recognize the standard durable power of attorney, especially in the area of income tax and estate tax. These forms can be obtained from the state or local taxing authorities directly or downloaded from their web sites.

3. **Medicaid Power of Attorney**

   Many jurisdictions have their own procedures for filing Medicaid applications, which often necessitate the filing of a power of attorney.

Reliance by a Third Party upon the Acts of the Agent

Often a third party who is required to rely upon the act of an agent is reluctant to do so because of fear that the principal may come back at a later time and disavow the act of the agent. To avoid this potential problem, the following language should be included to protect the third party:

I, for myself and for my heirs, executors, legal representatives and assigns, hereby agree to indemnify and hold harmless any such third party from and against any and all claims that may arise against such third party by reason of such third party having relied on the provisions of this instrument.

The above clause is found in the New York State statutory power of attorney. Many states have incorporated similar clauses in their enabling legislation. A clause may be drafted to protect the agent from the principal's inappropriate acts.

Revocation

A power of attorney may be revoked at any time by a principal so long as the principal retains capacity. The revocation should always be in writing. Oral revocation is ineffective because it lacks proof. The written notice of revocation must be signed by the principal, notarized, and/or witnessed. It should be served upon the agent, and upon any third parties who are relying upon the agent's authority and who are known as such by the principal. Service should be made personally or by certified mail, return receipt requested.

It is essential that every third party be served with this notification of revocation or termination. Until the third party receives actual notice, he or she may legally rely upon the agent's authority to bind the principal. If the client wants to enhance the ability to revoke, it is common practice in Texas, for example, to provide that a power of attorney may be revoked only by filing the revocation in the real property records of the county where the power is to be exercised. Of course, this makes the power of attorney more difficult to use. This procedure is stated as follows in the typical, statutory, durable power of attorney:

> *To induce any third party to act hereunder, I hereby agree that any third party receiving a duly executed copy or facsimile of this instrument may act hereunder and that such revocation or termination hereof shall be ineffective as to such third party unless and until actual notice of knowledge of such revocation or termination shall have been received by such third party.*

Check local statutory requirements for revocation of a power of attorney. Some states may not permit revocation. The document may be irrevocable. (See the CD-ROM for the revocation of power of attorney form.)

Death of a Principal

All powers of attorney automatically cease upon the death of a principal. Then the duly appointed executor, personal representative, or administrator of the principal's estate takes over.

Recognition of Powers of Attorney by Other States

In general, one state will not recognize a power of attorney executed in another state. Therefore, it is incumbent upon the client to execute a statutory power of attorney for the state in which he or she wishes to delegate powers to an agent to conduct business. It is the legal professional's duty to obtain these statutory forms. Often a client is *domiciled* in one state and has *residences* in several states. **Domicile** refers to the place intended to be your permanent home, from which you file tax returns and vote, etc. A domicile is distinguished from a **residence** because one could have simultaneous residences in many states, but only one domicile. It is necessary, therefore, for such clients to have powers of attorney drawn for the

Domicile
A place where an individual has a fixed permanent home to which he or she always has the intention of returning when absent. An individual may have only one domicile. Domicile is significant because it controls the jurisdiction of taxing authorities, voting rights, etc. Domicile is determined under state law. Therefore each state may declare a person domiciliary for tax purposes.

Residence
Place where an individual may live. One may have several residences in different localities.

state of domicile and for each state of residence, each state of business, or each state where they own investment real property.

Fraudulent Use of Powers of Attorney

The fraudulent use of powers of attorney by designated fiduciaries has increased. It is not uncommon to hear horror stories in which elderly people have been robbed of their life savings by trusted family, friends, and home health care workers who have converted the assets of the principal to themselves. Studies are being conducted throughout the country to determine whether it is time to enact legislation strictly regulating the use of powers of attorney to prevent their fraudulent use, in this case, financial abuse of the elderly. With that in mind, New York State has recently modified its durable power of attorney statute. It now requires the principal to initial each separate power to make the said power effective. Only the powers that are specifically authorized by the principal are delegated to the agent. (See Chapter 15, "Financial Abuse of the Elderly.")

DURABLE MEDICAL POWERS OF ATTORNEY

American medical technology has made far-reaching advances in the ability of health care providers to keep patients alive for indefinite periods of time. The use of **Miracle of Life** support systems can extend the process of dying for no other purpose than to keep the patient alive, regardless of the quality of life. Statistics indicate that typically at least 50 percent of one's entire lifetime medical expenses are spent during the last six months of life. And to no avail . . . the individual dies anyway. So, some ill men and women have pushed for measures like physician-assisted suicide.

Prolonging or Ending Life

Dr. Jack Kevorkian, sometimes referred to as Dr. Death, is a self-described zealot in the area of physician-assisted suicide. Dr. Kevorkian created many headlines in 1998 when the television news show *60 Minutes* broadcast Dr. Kevorkian assisting Thomas Youk in ending his life. Following this interview, which showed Dr. Kevorkian personally injecting Mr. Youk with a lethal injection (as opposed to most physician-assisted suicides where the patient administers the drugs his/herself), Dr. Kevorkian was tried and convicted of second-degree murder and sentenced to a prison term of 10 to 25 years. (For more information, see *People of the State of Michigan v. Kevorkian,* 639 N.W.2d 291 (Mich. App. 2001), which can be found in Chapter 11.)

Still, in recent years, the issue of assisted suicide by the terminally ill or chronically ill has focused debate on the question of whether and how life should be prolonged and who should make these decisions.

In the past, when a person became ill, the family or close friends stepped in to direct medical treatment without a problem. Today, however, due to the high rate of divorce, remarriage, malpractice fears, longevity, elder abuse, and Dr. Jack Kevorkian's concepts of physician-assisted suicide, this is not possible. The fact that a spouse or parent-child relationship exists or that an individual wishes to terminate one's own life is not sufficient.

Further complicating the issues are the life-sustaining miracle machines and modern technology to which we referred above. To ensure that a person's own wishes in the form of medical directives can be implemented in the event of temporary or long-term incapacity, a person must designate beforehand, in writing, a trusted representative to carry forth these wishes. The designated agent should be capable and willing to handle the financial and medical affairs of the person in the person's best interest.

The **health care proxy** is a legal instrument that enables medical treatment to be conducted according to one's predetermined directives. It avoids involving family members and friends in costly court proceedings in order to implement the patient's oral wishes that were known previously to trusted family and friends.

Surrogate Health Care Decision Making

Historical Background

The law presumes that a person is competent. This legal presumption of competency gives the individual the legal right to consent to or to refuse medical treatment. Case law in every state is quite clear; a competent adult has the right to determine his or her own health care, as provided by federal and state constitutional rights to privacy. Any competent person can refuse medical care, surgery, nutrition, and hydration, even if this course of action will eventually cause death.

Common law also protects the individual from "unauthorized touching," a tortious act known as assault and battery as well as trespass. The landmark case in this area is *Scholendorf v. Society of New York Hospital*[1] decided by Justice Cardozo in 1914. The New York Court of Appeals ruled that the plaintiff, Mrs. Scholendorf, had been subjected to unauthorized surgery, or tortious assault, and thus awarded her damages.

Health Care Proxy
An advance directive legal instrument wherein an individual appoints another to make medical and health care decisions for him or her in the event the individual is unable to do that. It operates on the principal and agent rule.

SCHOLENDORF V. SOCIETY OF NEW YORK HOSPITAL
105 N.E. 92 (N.Y. 1914)

Cardozo, J.

In the year 1771, by royal charter of George III, the Society of the New York Hospital was organized for the care and healing of the sick. During the century and more which has since passed, it has devoted itself to that high task. It has no capital stock; it does not distribute profits; and its physicians and surgeons, both the visiting and the resident staff, serve it without pay. Those who seek it in search of health are charged nothing if they are needy, either for board or for treatment. The well-to-do are required by its by-laws to pay $7 a week for board, an amount insufficient to cover the per capita cost of maintenance. Whatever income is thus received is added to the income derived from the hospital's foundation, and helps to make it possible for the work to go on. The purpose is not profit, but charity, and the incidental revenue does not change the defendant's standing as a charitable institution. *People ex rel. Society of N. Y. Hospital v. Purdy*, 28 N.E. 249.

To this hospital the plaintiff came in January, 1908. She was suffering from some disorder of the stomach. She asked the superintendent or one of his assistants what the charge would be, and was told that it would be $7 a week. She became an inmate of the hospital, and after some weeks of treatment, the house physician, Dr. Bartlett, discovered a lump, which proved to be a fibroid tumor. He consulted the visiting physician, Dr. Stimson, who advised an operation. The plaintiff's testimony is that the character of the lump could not, so the physicians informed her, be determined without an ether examination. She consented to such an examination, but notified Dr. Bartlett, as she says, that there must be no operation. She was taken at night from the medical to the surgical ward and prepared for an operation by a nurse. On the following day ether was administered, and, while she was unconscious, a tumor was removed. Her testimony is that this was done without her consent or knowledge. She is contradicted both by Dr. Stimson and by Dr. Bartlett, as well as by many of the attendant nurses. For the purpose of this appeal, however, since a verdict was directed in favor of the defendant, her narrative, even if improbable, must be taken as true. Following the operation, and, according to the testimony of her witnesses, because of it, gangrene developed in her left arm, some of her fingers had to be amputated, and her sufferings were intense. She now seeks to charge the hospital with liability for the wrong.

In the case at hand, the wrong complained of is not merely negligence. It is trespass. Every human being of adult years and sound mind has a right to determine what shall be done with his own body; and a surgeon who performs an operation without his patient's consent commits an assault, for which he is liable in damages. *Pratt v. Davis*, 79 N.E. 562; *Mohr v. Williams*, 104 N.W. 12. This is true, except in cases of emergency where the patient is unconscious, and where it is necessary to operate before consent can be obtained. The fact that the wrong complained of here is trespass, rather than negligence, distinguishes this case from most of the cases that have preceded it. In such circumstances the hospital's exemption from liability can hardly rest upon implied waiver. Relatively to this transaction, the plaintiff was a stranger. She had never consented to become a patient for any purpose other than an examination under ether. She had never waived the right to recover damages for any wrong resulting from this operation, for she had forbidden the operation.

❋ ❋ ❋

The focal issue in surrogate health care decision making is the patient's liberty rights versus the state's interest in keeping patients alive under any and all conditions, regardless of their quality of life. The Due Process Clause of the Fourteenth Amendment of the United States Constitution guarantees the patient's rights. There has been continuing case law in this area:

1. The *Quinlan* case in New Jersey[2]
2. The precedent-setting *Cruzan* case[3]
3. The *O'Connor* case in New York[4] (The full text of this case is found in Chapter 11.)

Karen Ann Quinlan was the first significant case wherein a court (N.J. Supreme Court, 1976) authorized the termination of life support systems. Karen Ann Quinlan was a young girl who at age 22 ingested drugs and alcohol, causing aspiration and blockage of her airway passage.

This resulted in her going into a comatose state that eventually left her in a persistent vegetative state. She was put on life support systems, including a respirator, feeding tube, and catheter to keep her alive. *(She did not have any advance directives.)*

IN RE QUINLAN

355 A.2d 647 (N.J. 1976)

The opinion of the Court was delivered by Hughes, C. J.

THE LITIGATION

The central figure in this tragic case is Karen Ann Quinlan, a New Jersey resident. At the age of 22, she lies in a debilitated and allegedly moribund state at Saint Clare's Hospital in Denville, New Jersey. The litigation has to do, in final analysis, with her life—its continuance or cessation—and the responsibilities, rights and duties, with regard to any fateful decision concerning it, of her family, her guardian, her doctors, the hospital, the State through its law enforcement authorities, and finally the courts of justice.

Due to extensive physical damage fully described in the able opinion of the trial judge, Judge Muir, supporting that judgment, Karen allegedly was incompetent. Joseph Quinlan sought the adjudication of that incompetency. He wished to be appointed guardian of the person and property of his daughter. It was proposed by him that such letters of guardianship, if granted, should contain an express power to him as guardian to authorize the discontinuance of all extraordinary medical procedures now allegedly sustaining Karen's vital processes and hence her life, since these measures, he asserted, present no hope of her eventual recovery. A guardian ad litem was appointed by Judge Muir to represent the interest of the alleged incompetent.

The matter is of transcendent importance, involving questions related to the definition and existence of death, the prolongation of life through artificial means developed by medical technology undreamed of in past generations of the practice of the healing arts; the impact of such durationally indeterminate and artificial life prolongation on the rights of the incompetent, her family and society in general; the bearing of constitutional right and the scope of judicial responsibility, as to the appropriate response of an equity court of justice to the extraordinary prayer for relief of the plaintiff. Involved as well is the right of the plaintiff, Joseph Quinlan, to guardianship of the person of his daughter.

✳ ✳ ✳

THE FACTUAL BASE

On the night of April 15, 1975, for reasons still unclear, Karen Quinlan ceased breathing for at least two 15 minute periods. She received some ineffectual mouth-to-mouth resuscitation from friends. She was taken by ambulance to Newton Memorial Hospital. There she had a temperature of 100 degrees, her pupils were unreactive, and she was unresponsive even to deep pain.

✳ ✳ ✳

The experts believe that Karen cannot now survive without the assistance of the respirator; that exactly how long she would live without it is unknown; that the strong likelihood is that death would follow soon after its removal, and that removal would also risk further brain damage and would curtail the assistance the respirator presently provides in warding off infection.

It seemed to be the consensus not only of the treating physicians but also of the several qualified experts who testified in the case, that removal from the respirator would not conform to medical practices, standards, and traditions.

The further medical consensus was that Karen in addition to being comatose is in a chronic and persistent 'vegetative' state, having no awareness of anything or anyone around her and existing at a primitive reflex level. Although she does have some brain stem function (ineffective for respiration) and has other reactions one normally associates with being alive, such as moving, reacting to light, sound and noxious stimuli, blinking her eyes, and the like, the quality of her feeling impulses is unknown. She grimaces, makes stereotyped cries and sounds and has chewing motions. Her blood pressure is normal.

✳ ✳ ✳

Here a loving parent, qua parent and raising the rights of his incompetent and profoundly damaged daughter, probably irreversibly doomed to no more than a biologically vegetative remnant of life, is before the court. He seeks authorization to abandon specialized technological procedures which can only maintain for a time a body having no potential for resumption or continuance of other than a 'vegetative' existence.

We have no doubt, in these unhappy circumstances, that if Karen were herself miraculously lucid for an interval (not altering the existing prognosis of the condition to which she would soon return) and perceptive of her irreversible condition, she could effectively decide upon discontinuance of the life-support apparatus, even if it meant the prospect of natural death. To this extent we may distinguish Heston, supra, which concerned a severely injured young woman (Delores Heston), whose life depended on surgery and blood transfusion; and who was in such extreme shock that she was unable to express an informed choice (although the Court apparently considered the case as if the patient's own religious decision to resist transfusion were at stake), but most importantly a patient apparently salvable to long life and vibrant health;—a situation not at all like the present case.

We have no hesitancy in deciding, in the instant diametrically opposite case, that no external compelling interest of the State could compel Karen to endure the unendurable, only to vegetate a few measurable months with no realistic possibility of returning to any semblance of cognitive or sapient life. We perceive no thread of logic distinguishing between such a choice on Karen's part and a similar choice which, under the evidence in this case, could be made by a competent patient terminally ill, riddled by cancer and suffering great pain; such a patient would not be resuscitated or put on a respirator in the example described by Dr. Korein, and a fortiori would not be kept against his will on a respirator.

Our affirmation of Karen's independent right of choice, however, would ordinarily be based upon her competency to assert it. The sad truth, however, is that she is grossly incompetent and we cannot discern her supposed choice based on the testimony of her previous conversations with friends, where such testimony is without sufficient probative weight. 348 A.2d 801. Nevertheless we have concluded that Karen's right of privacy may be asserted on her behalf by her guardian under the peculiar circumstances here present.

If a putative decision by Karen to permit this non-cognitive, vegetative existence to terminate by natural forces is regarded as a valuable incident of her right of privacy, as we believe it to be, then it should not be discarded solely on the basis that her condition prevents her conscious exercise of the choice. The only practical way to prevent destruction of the right is to permit the guardian and family of Karen to render their best judgment, subject to the qualifications hereinafter stated, as to whether she would exercise it in these circumstances. If their conclusion is in the affirmative this decision should be accepted by a society the overwhelming majority of whose members would, we think, in similar circumstances, exercise such a choice in the same way for themselves or for those closest to them. It is for this reason that we determine that Karen's right of privacy may be asserted in her behalf, in this respect, by her guardian and family under the particular circumstances presented by this record.

Regarding Mr. Quinlan's right of privacy, we agree with Judge Muir's conclusion that there is no parental constitutional right that would entitle him to a grant of relief In propria persona. Id. at 801. Insofar as a parental right of privacy has been recognized, it has been in the context of determining the rearing of infants and, as Judge Muir put it, involved 'continuing life styles.' See *Wisconsin v. Yoder*, 406 U.S. 205, (1972); *Pierce v. Society of Sisters*, 268 U.S. 510 (1925); *Meyer v. Nebraska*, 262 U.S. 390 (1923). Karen Quinlan is a 22 year old adult. Her right of privacy in respect of the matter before the Court is to be vindicated by Mr. Quinlan as guardian, as hereinabove determined.

✱ ✱ ✱

DECLARATORY RELIEF

We thus arrive at the formulation of the declaratory relief which we have concluded is appropriate to this case. Some time has passed since Karen's physical and mental condition was described to the Court. At that time her continuing deterioration was plainly projected. Since the record has not been expanded we assume that she is now even more fragile and nearer to death than she was then. Since her present treating physicians may give reconsideration to her present posture in the light of this opinion, and since we are transferring to the plaintiff as guardian the choice of the attending physician and therefore other physicians may be in charge of the case who may take a different view from that of the present attending physicians, we herewith declare the following affirmative relief on behalf of the plaintiff. Upon the concurrence of the guardian and family of Karen, should the responsible attending physicians conclude that there is no reasonable possibility of Karen's ever emerging from her present comatose condition to a cognitive, sapient state and that the life-support apparatus now being administered to Karen should be discontinued, they shall consult with the hospital Ethics Committee or like body of the institution in which Karen is then hospitalized. If that consultative body agrees that there is no reasonable possibility of Karen's ever emerging from her present comatose condition to a cognitive, sapient state, the present life-support system may be withdrawn and said action shall be without any civil or criminal liability therefor on the part of any participant, whether guardian, physician, hospital or others. We herewith specifically so hold.

Modified and remanded.

The *Quinlan* case highlights two critical points:

1. The constitutional right of privacy includes a right to refuse medical treatment.
2. That right is personal, and a relative does not have authority to make that decision without a guardianship relationship or a health care proxy and only when it is clear that he is carrying out the wishes of the incapacitated person.

In the *Cruzan* case, the Supreme Court decided that a person's liberty interest under the due process clause of the Fourteenth Amendment includes the right of a person to refuse all medical treatments, even though it might lead to the death of that person.

CRUZAN V. DIRECTOR, MISSOURI DEPT. OF HEALTH
497 U.S. 261 (1990)

Chief Justice REHNQUIST delivered the opinion of the Court.

Petitioner Nancy Beth Cruzan was rendered incompetent as a result of severe injuries sustained during an automobile accident. Copetitioners Lester and Joyce Cruzan, Nancy's parents and coguardians, sought a court order directing the withdrawal of their daughter's artificial feeding and hydration equipment after it became apparent that she had virtually no chance of recovering her cognitive faculties. The Supreme Court of Missouri held that because there was no clear and convincing evidence of Nancy's desire to have life-sustaining treatment withdrawn under such circumstances, her parents lacked authority to effectuate such a request. We granted certiorari, 492 U.S. 917 (1989), and now affirm.

On the night of January 11, 1983, Nancy Cruzan lost control of her car as she traveled down Elm Road in Jasper County, Missouri. The vehicle overturned, and Cruzan was discovered lying face down in a ditch without detectable respiratory or cardiac function. Paramedics were able to restore her breathing and heartbeat at the accident site, and she was transported to a hospital in an unconscious state. An attending neurosurgeon diagnosed her as having sustained probable cerebral contusions compounded by significant anoxia (lack of oxygen). The Missouri trial court in this case found that permanent brain damage generally results after 6 minutes in an anoxic state; it was estimated that Cruzan was deprived of oxygen from 12 to 14 minutes. She remained in a coma for approximately three weeks and then progressed to an unconscious state in which she was able to orally ingest some nutrition. In order to ease feeding and further the recovery, surgeons implanted a gastrostomy feeding and hydration tube in Cruzan with the consent of her then husband. Subsequent rehabilitative efforts proved unavailing. She now lies in a Missouri state hospital in what is commonly referred to as a persistent vegetative state: generally, a condition in which a person exhibits motor reflexes but evinces no indications of significant cognitive function. The State of Missouri is bearing the cost of her care.

". . . (1) [H]er respiration and circulation are not artificially maintained and are within the normal limits of a thirty-year-old female; (2) she is oblivious to her environment except for reflexive responses to sound and perhaps painful stimuli; (3) she suffered anoxia of the brain resulting in a massive enlargement of the ventricles filling with cerebrospinal fluid in the area where the brain has degenerated and [her] cerebral cortical atrophy is irreversible, permanent, progressive and ongoing; (4) her highest cognitive brain function is exhibited by her grimacing perhaps in recognition of ordinarily painful stimuli, indicating the experience of pain and apparent response to sound; (5) she is a spastic quadriplegic; (6) her four extremities are contracted with irreversible muscular and tendon damage to all extremities; (7) she has no cognitive or reflexive ability to swallow food or water to maintain her daily essential needs and . . . she will never recover her ability to swallow sufficient [sic] to satisfy her needs. In sum, Nancy is diagnosed as in a persistent vegetative state. She is not dead. She is not terminally ill. Medical experts testified that she could live another thirty years." *Cruzan v. Harmon*, 760 S.W.2d 408, 411 (Mo.1988) (en banc) (quotations omitted; footnote omitted).

In observing that Cruzan was not dead, the court referred to the following Missouri statute:

"For all legal purposes, the occurrence of human death shall be determined in accordance with the usual and customary standards of medical practice, provided that death shall not be determined to have occurred unless the following minimal conditions have been met:

"(1) When respiration and circulation are not artificially maintained, there is an irreversible cessation of spontaneous respiration and circulation; or

"(2) When respiration and circulation are artificially maintained, and there is total and irreversible cessation of all brain function, including the brain stem and that such determination is made by a licensed physician." Mo.Rev.Stat. § 194.005 (1986).

Since Cruzan's respiration and circulation were not being artificially maintained, she obviously fit within the first proviso of the statute.

After it had become apparent that Nancy Cruzan had virtually no chance of regaining her mental faculties, her parents asked hospital employees to terminate the artificial nutrition and hydration procedures. All agree that such a removal would cause her death. The employees refused to honor the request without court approval. The parents then sought and received authorization from the state trial court for termination. The court found that a person in Nancy's condition had a fundamental right under the State and Federal Constitutions to refuse or direct the withdrawal of "death prolonging procedures." App. to Pet. for Cert. A99. The court also found that Nancy's "expressed thoughts at age twenty-five in somewhat serious conversation with a housemate friend that if sick or injured she would not wish to continue her life unless she could live at least halfway normally suggests that given her present condition she would not wish to continue on with her nutrition and hydration." *Id.*, at A97-A98.

At common law, even the touching of one person by another without consent and without legal justification was a battery. See W. Keeton, D. Dobbs, R. Keeton, & D. Owen, *Prosser and Keeton on Law of Torts* § 9, pp. 39–42 (5th ed. 1984). Before the turn of the century, this Court observed that "[n]o right is held more sacred, or is more carefully guarded, by the common law, than the right of every individual to the possession and control of his own person, free from all restraint or interference of others, unless by clear and unquestionable authority of law." *Union Pacific R. Co. v. Botsford*, 141 U.S. 250, 251 (1891). This notion of bodily integrity has been embodied in the requirement that informed consent is generally required for medical treatment. Justice Cardozo, while on the Court of Appeals of New York, aptly described this doctrine: "Every human being of adult years and sound mind has a right to determine what shall be done with his own body; and a surgeon who performs an operation without his patient's consent commits an assault, for which he is liable in damages." *Schloendorff v. Society of New York Hospital*, 105 N.E. 92, 93 (1914). The informed consent doctrine has become firmly entrenched in American tort law. See *Keeton, Dobbs, Keeton, & Owen*, supra, § 32, pp. 189–192; F. Rozovsky, *Consent to Treatment, A Practical Guide* 1–98 (2d ed. 1990).

The logical corollary of the doctrine of informed consent is that the patient generally possesses the right not to consent, that is, to refuse treatment. Until about 15 years ago and the seminal decision in *In re Quinlan*, 355 A.2d 647, cert. denied sub nom. *Garger v. New Jersey*,

persistant Vegetative State.

429 U.S. 922 (1976), the number of right-to-refuse-treatment decisions was relatively few. Most of the earlier cases involved patients who refused medical treatment forbidden by their religious beliefs, thus implicating First Amendment rights as well as common-law rights of self-determination. More recently, however, with the advance of medical technology capable of sustaining life well past the point where natural forces would have brought certain death in earlier times, cases involving the right to refuse life-sustaining treatment have burgeoned. See 760 S.W.2d, at 412, n. 4 (collecting 54 reported decisions from 1976 through 1988).

In *In re Storar*, 420 N.E.2d 64, cert. denied, 454 U.S. 858 (1981), the New York Court of Appeals declined to base a right to refuse treatment on a constitutional privacy right. Instead, it found such a right "adequately supported" by the informed consent doctrine. *Id.*, at 70. In *In re Eichner* (decided with *In re Storar*, supra), an 83-year-old man who had suffered brain damage from anoxia entered a vegetative state and was thus incompetent to consent to the removal of his respirator. The court, however, found it unnecessary to reach the question whether his rights could be exercised by others since it found the evidence clear and convincing from statements made by the patient when competent that he "did not want to be maintained in a vegetative coma by use of a respirator." *Id.*, at 72. In the companion *Storar* case, a 52-year-old man suffering from bladder cancer had been profoundly retarded during most of his life. Implicitly rejecting the approach taken in *Saikewicz*, supra, the court reasoned that due to such life-long incompetency, "it is unrealistic to attempt to determine whether he would want to continue potentially life prolonging treatment if he were competent." 420 N.E.2d, at 72. As the evidence showed that the patient's required blood transfusions did not involve excessive pain and without them his mental and physical abilities would deteriorate, the court concluded that it should not "allow an incompetent patient to bleed to death because someone, even someone as close as a parent or sibling, feels that this is best for one with an incurable disease." *Id.*, at 73.

The court also rejected certain categorical distinctions that had been drawn in prior refusal-of-treatment cases as lacking substance for decision purposes: the distinction between actively hastening death by terminating treatment and passively allowing a person to die of a disease; between treating individuals as an initial matter versus withdrawing treatment afterwards; between ordinary versus extraordinary treatment; and between treatment by artificial feeding versus other forms of life-sustaining medical procedures. *Id.*, at 1233–1237. As to the last item, the court acknowledged the "emotional significance" of food, but noted that feeding by implanted tubes is a "medical procedur[e] with inherent risks and possible side effects, instituted by skilled health-care providers to compensate for impaired physical functioning" which analytically was equivalent to artificial breathing using a respirator. *Id.*, at 1236.

In contrast to *Conroy*, the Court of Appeals of New York recently refused to accept less than the clearly expressed wishes of a patient before permitting the exercise of her right to refuse treatment by a surrogate decisionmaker. *In re Westchester County Medical Center on behalf of O'Connor*, 531 N.E.2d 607 (1988) (*O'Connor*). There, the court, over the objection of the patient's family members, granted an order to insert a feeding tube into a 77-year-old woman rendered incompetent as a result of several strokes. While continuing to recognize a common-law right to refuse treatment, the court rejected the substituted judgment approach for asserting it "because it is inconsistent with our fundamental commitment to the notion that no person or court should substitute its judgment as to what would be an acceptable quality of life for another. Consequently, we adhere to the view that, despite its pitfalls and inevitable uncertainties, the inquiry must always be narrowed to the patient's expressed intent, with every effort made to minimize the opportunity for error." *Id.*, at 613 (citation omitted). The court held that the record lacked the requisite clear and convincing evidence of the patient's expressed intent to withhold life-sustaining treatment. *Id.*, at 613–615.

The Fourteenth Amendment provides that no State shall "deprive any person of life, liberty, or property, without due process of law." The principle that a competent person has a constitutionally protected liberty interest in refusing unwanted medical treatment may be inferred from our prior decisions. In *Jacobson v. Massachusetts*, 197 U.S. 11, 24–30 (1905), for instance, the Court balanced an individual's liberty interest in declining an unwanted smallpox vaccine against the State's interest in preventing disease. Decisions prior to the incorporation of the Fourth Amendment into the Fourteenth Amendment analyzed searches and seizures involving the body under the Due Process Clause and were thought to implicate substantial liberty interests. See, e.g., *Breithaupt v. Abram*, 352 U.S. 432, 439 (1957) ("As against the right of an individual that his person be held inviolable . . . must be set the interests of society . . . ").

Just this Term, in the course of holding that a State's procedures for administering antipsychotic medication to prisoners were sufficient to satisfy due process concerns, we recognized that prisoners possess "a significant liberty interest in avoiding the unwanted administration of antipsychotic drugs under the Due Process Clause of the Fourteenth Amendment." *Washington v. Harper*, 494 U.S. 210, 221–222 (1990); see also *Id.*, at 229 ("The forcible injection of medication into a nonconsenting person's body represents a substantial interference with that person's liberty").

But determining that a person has a "liberty interest" under the Due Process Clause does not end the inquiry; "whether respondent's constitutional rights have been violated must be determined by balancing his liberty interests against the relevant state interests." *Youngberg v. Romeo*, 457 U.S. 307, 321 (1982). See also *Mills v. Rogers*, 457 U.S. 291, 299 (1982).

Petitioners insist that under the general holdings of our cases, the forced administration of life-sustaining medical treatment, and even of artificially delivered food and water essential to life, would implicate a competent person's liberty interest. Although we think the logic of the cases discussed above would embrace such a liberty interest, the dramatic consequences involved in refusal of such treatment would inform the inquiry as to whether the deprivation of that interest is constitutionally permissible. But for purposes of this case, we assume that the United States Constitution would grant a competent person a constitutionally protected right to refuse lifesaving hydration and nutrition.

Petitioners go on to assert that an incompetent person should possess the same right in this respect as is possessed by a competent person. They rely primarily on our decisions in *Parham v. J.R.*, supra, and *Youngberg v. Romeo*, supra, 102 S.Ct. 2452, (1982). In *Parham*, we held that a mentally disturbed minor child had a liberty interest in "not being confined unnecessarily for medical treatment," 442 U.S., at 600, but we certainly did not intimate that such a minor child, after commitment, would have a liberty interest in refusing treatment. In *Youngberg*, we held that a seriously retarded adult had a liberty interest in safety and freedom from bodily restraint, 457 U.S., at 320. *Youngberg*, however, did not deal with decisions to administer or withhold medical treatment.

The difficulty with petitioners' claim is that in a sense it begs the question: An incompetent person is not able to make an informed and voluntary choice to exercise a hypothetical right to refuse treatment or any other right. Such a "right" must be exercised for her, if at all, by some sort of surrogate. Here, Missouri has in effect recognized that under certain circumstances a surrogate may act for the patient in electing to have hydration and nutrition withdrawn in such a way as to cause death, but it has established a procedural safeguard to assure that the action of the surrogate conforms as best it may to the wishes expressed by the patient while competent. Missouri requires that evidence of the incompetent's wishes as to the withdrawal of treatment be proved by clear and convincing evidence. The question, then, is whether the United States Constitution forbids the establishment of this procedural requirement by the State. We hold that it does not.

Whether or not Missouri's clear and convincing evidence requirement comports with the United States Constitution depends in part on what interests the State may properly seek to protect in this situation. Missouri relies on its interest in the protection and preservation of human life, and there can be no gainsaying this interest. As a general matter, the States— indeed, all civilized nations—demonstrate their commitment to life by treating homicide as a serious crime. Moreover, the majority of States in this country have laws imposing criminal penalties on one who assists another to commit suicide. We do not think a State is required to remain neutral in the face of an informed and voluntary decision by a physically able adult to starve to death.

The Supreme Court of Missouri held that in this case the testimony adduced at trial did not amount to clear and convincing proof of the patient's desire to have hydration and nutrition withdrawn. In so doing, it reversed a decision of the Missouri trial court which had found that the evidence "suggest [ed]" Nancy Cruzan would not have desired to continue such measures, App. to Pet. for Cert. A98, but which had not adopted the standard of "clear and convincing evidence" enunciated by the Supreme Court. The testimony adduced at trial consisted primarily of Nancy Cruzan's statements made to a housemate about a year before her accident that she would not want to live should she face life as a "vegetable," and other observations to the same effect. The observations did not deal in terms with withdrawal of medical treatment or of hydration and nutrition. We cannot say that the Supreme Court of Missouri committed constitutional error in reaching the conclusion that it did.

Petitioners alternatively contend that Missouri must accept the "substituted judgment" of close family members even in the absence of substantial proof that their views reflect the views of the patient. They rely primarily upon our decisions in *Michael H. v. Gerald D.*, 491 U.S. 110 (1989), and *Parham v. J.R.*, 442 U.S. 584 (1979). But we do not think these cases support their claim. In *Michael H.*, we upheld the constitutionality of California's favored treatment of traditional family relationships; such a holding may not be turned around into a constitutional requirement that a State must recognize the primacy of those relationships in a situation like this. And in *Parham*, where the patient was a minor, we also upheld the constitutionality of a state scheme in which parents made certain decisions for mentally ill minors. Here again petitioners would seek to turn a decision which allowed a State to rely on family decisionmaking into a constitutional requirement that the State recognize such decisionmaking. But constitutional law does not work that way.

No doubt is engendered by anything in this record but that Nancy Cruzan's mother and father are loving and caring parents. If the State were required by the United States Constitution to repose a right of "substituted judgment" with anyone, the Cruzans would surely qualify. But we do not think the Due Process Clause requires the State to repose judgment on these matters with anyone but the patient herself. Close family members may have a strong feeling—a feeling not at all ignoble or unworthy, but not entirely disinterested, either—that they do not wish to witness the continuation of the life of a loved one which they regard as hopeless, meaningless, and even degrading. But there is no automatic assurance that the view of close family members will necessarily be the same as the patient's would have been had she been confronted with the prospect of her situation while competent. All of the reasons previously discussed for allowing Missouri to require clear and convincing evidence of the patient's wishes lead us to conclude that the State may choose to defer only to those wishes, rather than confide the decision to close family members.

Petitioners also adumbrate in their brief a claim based on the Equal Protection Clause of the Fourteenth Amendment to the effect that Missouri has impermissibly treated incompetent patients differently from competent ones, citing the statement in *Cleburne v. Cleburne Living Center, Inc.*, 473 U.S. 432, 439 (1985), that the Clause is "essentially a direction that all persons similarly situated should be treated alike." The differences between the choice made by a competent person to refuse medical treatment, and the choice made for an incompetent person by someone else to refuse medical treatment, are so obviously different that the State is warranted in establishing rigorous procedures for the latter class of cases which do not apply to the former class.

The judgment of the Supreme Court of Missouri is Affirmed.

In *O'Connor v. Westchester County Hospital*, 531 N.E.2d 607 (N.Y. 1988), the patient also did not have a written health care proxy, and the court rendered the following decision:

a. A person has the right to decline medical treatment, even lifesaving treatment, absent overriding state interest.

b. No person should be denied essential medical care unless evidence **clearly and convincingly** shows that the person intended to decline treatment under some particular circumstance.

c. A **clear and convincing standard** must be established (and was established herein) in order for a health care provider to terminate artificial life support for the now incompetent patient. The patient's family must produce **clear and convincing evidence** establishing that the patient, while competent, expressed orally a wish not to be kept alive in the event the patient became incapacitated and entered a persistent vegetative state or irreversible coma.

> **Clear and Convincing Evidence**
> The term "clear and convincing evidence" is a standard of proof required in exceptional civil cases. The standard is higher than the "preponderance of the evidence" standard in most civil cases but lower than the "beyond a reasonable doubt" standard required to convict a criminal defendant.

HEALTH CARE PROXY

Written advanced directives provide *clear and convincing evidence* of a patient's wishes. Our legal system currently recognizes four basic advance directive documents involving health care decision making:

1. Health care proxy (durable medical power of attorney)
2. Living will
3. Do not resuscitate order (DNR)
4. Uniform donor instrument (anatomical gifting)

Had Mrs. O'Connor in the above case executed an advance directive permitting surrogate health care decision making, her situation never would have required judicial intervention.

The **health care proxy**, a form of advance decision making, is made while a person is competent and able to make decisions about future health care and treatment. This document operates as a **medical durable power of attorney**, similar to the financial durable power of attorney. It operates under the law of agency; the principal appoints an agent who will act as the patient's (principal's) surrogate in decision making when the patient lacks capacity and competency to make decisions regarding his or her own health care. The principal states in the health care proxy specific wishes regarding treatment or the withholding of treatment. The agent carries out the directives specified in the health care instrument. In the event that issues arise that are not covered in the health care proxy, the agent may use surrogate decision powers and also substituted judgment to fulfill the wishes of the (principal) patient. It is wise for the principal to discuss his or her wishes in detail with the agent beforehand so that when the agent is required to act, the patient's medical treatment philosophy is known. The health care proxy or medical power of attorney is statutory in most states.[5] (Check local statutes.)

The health care proxy is self-explanatory. If the client so directs, it may state the individual's desire not to be kept alive by artificial means or heroic measures if there is no hope of recovery or in the event the patient enters into a persistent vegetative state or becomes comatose. In the alternative, the health care proxy may direct that every effort be made to keep the patient alive.

The Basics of the Health Care Proxy

1. It must be in writing.
2. It must contain the following:
   a. Patient's name and address
   b. Patient's Social Security number
   c. Agent's name and address
   d. Agent's relationship to principal

PRACTICE TIP

It is advisable to appoint a substitute agent in the event that the primary agent is unable to act because of death, incapacity, refusal to act, or mere unavailability. Be sure to include all addresses of multiple agents or substitutes.

---

3. There are restrictions concerning the appointment of an agent. The following parties are usually ineligible:
   a. A nursing home administrator of the facility in which the patient resides
   b. The patient's attending physician
4. The principal (patient) must sign the document. Many states permit another person to officially sign the document on behalf of the principal/patient if the principal/patient is competent but unable to do so. The document should contain language making it durable so that it will survive the patient's incapacity.
5. The document should be notarized, although many states do not require this. Notarization helps to prevent forgery.

6. The document should be witnessed. Most states require the document to have at least two adult witnesses whose addresses should also be stated in the document.
7. The agent is usually prohibited from being a witness due to a potential conflict of interest.
8. Five original documents should be executed and delivered to the following people:
   a. Principal
   b. Agent(s)
   c. Family doctor
   d. Family attorney
   e. Clergy, if applicable.

PRACTICE TIPS

1. Always retain an original document in the files of the law firm for emergency purposes.
2. As with the power of attorney, the health care proxy should be drafted to allow the representative to acquire the principal's medical records and other confidential information with specific reference to the HIPAA provisions.

Expiration Period

Most health care proxy statutes allow the document to remain in effect indefinitely. However, there are exceptions. For example, in Florida a health care proxy expires at the end of seven years. But, even there, if the principal (patient) is incapacitated at the seventh anniversary of the health care proxy, the proxy does not terminate but remains in effect until the patient regains decisional capacity. Should that situation ever arise, the patient could execute a new health care proxy.

Stale Document

If an advance directive is more than 24 to 36 months old, the client should be advised to review it for any possible changes regarding the agent or directions stated in the document. If there are no changes, it could be reaffirmed and redated. Health care providers may not be willing to accept stale, dated advance directives.

Revocation

The principal can accomplish revocation by notifying the agent(s) in writing, certified mail, return receipt requested, or by personal service. It is also necessary to notify the attorney, physician, family members, clergy, and any other interested parties. Oral revocation is often ineffective and not recommended. (Check local statutes.)

IN RE UNIVERSITY HOSP. OF STATE UNIVERSITY OF NEW YORK

754 N.Y.S.2d 153 (2002)

ANTHONY J. PARIS, J.

Petitioner, by Order to Show Cause filed on July 11, 2002, seeks an Order from this Court pursuant to Public Health Law § 2992 determining the validity of a certain Health Care Proxy executed by patient, Yvette Casimiro, on October 31, 1995, and a Living Will/Power of Attorney executed by said patient on April 3, 1997. Petitioner further seeks to remove Respondents, Rosalie and Glenn Karschner, as the agents designated in said Health Care Proxy and Living Will/Power of Attorney, or an Order overriding their refusal to consent to the withholding or withdrawing of life-sustaining treatment on the basis that they are acting contrary to the patient's express intent as set forth in said instruments.

Petitioner has maintained throughout these proceedings that the Health Care Proxy and Living Will/Power of Attorney are validly executed instruments and that the physical condition of the patient satisfies the specified criteria to invoke the patient's expressed wishes that the life sustaining treatment currently in place be terminated. Petitioner further argues that, by their refusal and unwillingness to cooperate with the removal of these life sustaining systems, Respondents are acting in contravention of the patient's directions and intent, and, therefore, they should be removed as health care agents, or, in the alternative, their refusals should be overridden by this Court.

Respondents have argued that their aunt (through marriage and not by blood relation), whom they have known for 40 years, is a devout Catholic who resided with them for five (5) years and did not intend to be removed from life sustaining treatment in the event that same became necessary to sustain her life. Respondents submit that Mrs. Casimiro did not fully understand the nature of the directions set forth in the Health Care Proxy and Living Will/Power of Attorney documents that she executed in 1995 and 1997, respectively. Respondents have further maintained that the Living Will/Power of Attorney which was executed on April 3, 1997, was in fact later revoked by the patient. Kay Ann Linderman, testified that, on October 31, 1995, she witnessed Yvette Casimiro execute the Health Care Proxy that is the subject of this proceeding. Ms. Linderman prepared this document in conjunction with her employment with James A. Travers, M.D., Mrs. Casimiro's treating physician at that time. This congenial witness openly testified that although she did not specifically remember signing this particular Health Care Proxy, the witnessing signature was undoubtedly hers. There was no direct testimony by this witness concerning whether or not Mrs. Casimiro understood the contents of the Health Care Proxy.

Both Respondents testified as to their relationship with Mrs. Casimiro. Yvette Casimiro is Rosalie Karschner's great aunt by marriage. Rosalie Karschner has known Yvette Casimiro for forty (40) years and there is a close and loving relationship between Respondents and Mrs. Casimiro. Yvette Casimiro relied heavily upon Respondent, Glenn Karschner, especially during the period from 1995 to 2000 when she lived with the Respondents. Due to the dementia and the Parkinson's disease which affected Mrs. Casimiro, she left the Respondents' residence and became a resident at Iroquois Nursing Home in 2000. Thereafter, she was admitted to University Hospital in March 2002, at which facility Respondents have been daily visitors.

In April of 1997, Yvette Casimiro visited the law office of Joseph Kelly, Esq. and executed a Living Will/Power of Attorney wherein she designated Respondents as her attorneys-in-fact. Respondents both testified that shortly after the execution of this instrument, when they were reviewing it and other documents with her, Mrs. Casimiro confided to them that she did not realize the implications of this instrument. Mrs. Casimiro further stated that had she fully understood these implications—the disconnection of any life support equipment and the discontinuance of any medical treatment—that she probably would not have signed it.

Respondents also testified that, at Yvette Casimiro's request, Respondent, Glenn Karschner made numerous attempts to contact attorney Kelly for the purpose of Mrs. Casimiro revoking and/or modifying the Living Will/Power of Attorney. However, they were not able to connect with Mr. Kelly for this intended purpose.

The Karschners testified that no conversations were ever had with Mrs. Casimiro regarding the Health Care Proxy she executed on October 31, 1995, and which designated Rosalie Karschner as her agent, because they were never aware of this instrument until it was presented to them at University Hospital in 2002.

Yvette Casimiro, according to Respondents' testimony, is a devout Roman Catholic and believes that only God can take a life. It was the Respondents' testimony that Mrs. Casimiro expressed this sentiment to them on many occasions. It was for this reason and Mrs. Casimiro's expressed intent to revoke the Living Will/Power of Attorney that Respondents refused to execute a Do Not Resuscitate authorization despite being asked to do so by the Ethics Committee of University Hospital.

The issue before this Court is the validity of the Living Will/Power of Attorney and the Health Care Proxy. Both instruments direct the patient's agents, Rosalie Karschner in the Health Care Proxy and both Karschners in the Living Will/Power of Attorney, to essentially authorize the termination of any life sustaining measures. Petitioner has presented evidence that both instruments were validly executed and urges that each remain in force. Respondents, on the other hand, urge the Court to strike the Living Will/Power of Attorney as it was their great aunt's intent to revoke same. They do not contest the validity of the Health Care Proxy, but maintain that by refusing to execute a DNR, they are, pursuant to this instrument, complying with Yvette Casimiro's wishes and desires to stay alive according to her devout Catholic beliefs that only God can take a life.

Both parties in this matter rely heavily on the legal precedent set forth by the Court of Appeals in *Matter of O'Connor*, 72 N.Y.2d 517, . . .* 531 N.E.2d 607 (1988). The Petitioner maintains that by executing a valid Health Care Proxy and Living Will/Power of Attorney, Yvette Casimiro has indicated her legally protected desire, wish and intent to be removed from life sustaining treatment, and that desire and intent should be recognized and implemented by the Court. Respondents Karschner urge that this was not their aunt's intent once she fully realized the implications of the Living Will/Power of Attorney, and that her specified wish was to remain alive, and that is what she and they should allowed to do under the her Health Care Proxy (which document they knew nothing about until 2002).

The patient's wishes must be established by clear and convincing evidence. *Matter of O'Connor*, supra at 531, . . .* In this proceeding, the burden of proof is borne by the Petitioner, University Hospital, which seeks to terminate the life sustaining treatment currently sustaining the life of the patient, Yvette Casimiro. In determining whether or not that quantum of proof has been met, this Court has necessarily considered a number and variety of factors including: the validity of the instruments which purportedly reflect the desire of the patient; the medical and physical condition of the patient both at the time of execution and at present; any intervening factors that may have occurred between the period of execution and the present; the medical testimony and opinions offered as to the patient's existing condition and prognosis concerning her capability of recovery; her expressions of desire and intent; and the patient's expressed religious and moral beliefs.

The Court has reviewed, considered and analyzed all of the evidence in the form of testimony and exhibits, as well as the written memoranda competently and thoroughly presented by the able and experienced attorneys for the parties. Based on this unique and exclusive opportunity, this Court opines that University Hospital has not sustained the burden of proof necessary for this Court to authorize the discontinuation of life sustaining treatment for the benefit of the patient Yvette Casimiro.

There is no question that the Health Care Proxy and the Living Will/Power of Attorney were validly executed by Mrs. Casimiro in 1995 and 1997, respectively. Moreover, there is no question that Mrs. Casimiro's current medical condition is extremely serious and that she cannot express or vocalize her present desire and intent, and may not be able to do so in the foreseeable future.

However, based on the evidence in the record, it appears that the patient's words and actions indicate her desire to remain alive. Other than the execution of the Health Care Proxy and Living Will/Power of Attorney, there was absolutely no evidence offered by Petitioner that the patient vocalized or represented a desire to be removed from life sustaining measures or to have medical treatment discontinued if she was presented with such a circumstance. Moreover, there was no evidence that the patient had any previous family experiences with such a situation, or that she had expressed a strong, firm and persistent opinion that she should not be the beneficiary of such life sustaining measures. On the contrary, Respondents presented ample evidence to allow the Court to formulate an opinion as to the patient's commitment to the termination of life supports—THERE WAS NO SUCH COMMITMENT. While Petitioner did demonstrate that two instruments were executed by Mrs. Casimiro, there was no unequivocal evidence presented that she understood the implications of the language set forth in these instruments which specifically provided for the termination of life supports. Further, the Court finds that any reference to a certain Health Care Survey signed by the patient was inconsequential in determining her true desires. Moreover, there was un-refuted evidence of Mrs. Casimiro's position once she realized the magnitude and permanence of the implications set forth in the Living Will/Power of Attorney that she executed in April of 1997.

A Living Will/Power of Attorney, unlike a Health Care Proxy, is not a creature of statute. Therefore, without statutory guidelines, the Court must necessarily examine the entire record to determine whether or not such an instrument, although validly executed some five (5) years ago, may have been subsequently revoked by the words and/or actions of its signor.

In the present matter, based on the proof presented by Respondents, there is little doubt that Yvette Casimiro, by her actions, revoked the Living Will/Power of Attorney executed on April 3, 1997. At the very least, the record reveals that Mrs. Casimiro intended to do so based on her statements to Respondents as well as the tenets of her religious faith, particularly once Mrs. Casimiro understood the dire implications of the instrument she executed.

Therefore, by reason of the foregoing, the Living Will/Power of Attorney executed by Yvette Casimiro on April 3, 1997 is hereby stricken in its entirety; and it so ordered.

The Health Care Proxy executed by Yvette Casimiro on October 31, 1995 was valid when executed and Respondents do not question its authenticity. Unlike the Living Will/Power of Attorney, there was little testimony concerning conversations between Mrs. Casimiro and

Respondents other than the fact that they knew nothing about the Health Care Proxy until it was presented to them at University Hospital. Their aunt had never indicated to them that she had executed such an instrument. In fact, there was no testimony that a duplicate original or copy of the Health Care Proxy was in Mrs. Casimiro's possession along with other personal papers with which Respondents were familiar while Mrs. Casimiro resided with them from 1995 to 2000.

By comparison, these two instruments, executed separately in 1995 and 1997, are almost identical with the exception of the nutrition provision. By contrast, the Health Care Proxy, unlike the Living Will/Power of Attorney, is a creature of statute and its existence is governed by Article 29-C of the Public Health Law. While created by statutory provision— § 2981 of the Public Health Law—a Health Care Proxy may also be revoked in accord with statutory provisions.

Section 2985 (a) of the Public Health Law reads, in pertinent part, as follows:

§ 2985. REVOCATION

1. Means of revoking proxy. (a) A competent adult may revoke a health care proxy by notifying the agent or health care provider orally or in writing *or by any other act evidencing a specific intent to revoke the proxy*. (Emphasis added).

Insofar as the Health Care Proxy predates the Living Will/Power of Attorney by almost two years, and as the instruments virtually contain the same provisions with the exception of nutrition, the Court finds that the Health Care Proxy executed by Yvette Casimiro on October 31, 1995 has been revoked by implication by virtue of her actions and statements revoking the Living Will/Power of Attorney which was subsequently executed by her.

By reason of the foregoing, the Health Care Proxy executed by Yvette Casimiro on October 31, 1995 is hereby stricken in its entirety.

Petitioner's petition is in all other respects denied.

Federal Patient Self-Determination Act

Highlighting the new emphasis on health care proxies, Congress enacted the federal Patient Self-Determination Act (effective December 1, 1991). It requires every medical facility and nursing home, such as hospitals, nursing homes, hospices, etc., that is a Medicare/Medicaid provider to supply a new patient/resident with written information regarding his or her right to execute a health care proxy and a living will and to make preprinted forms available to them. Under this law the execution of a health care proxy or living will cannot be a condition for admission of a patient to a facility. The patient's chart must note whether the patient has executed a health care proxy or living will.

Use of a Health Care Proxy

Upon entering a hospital, nursing home, or other health care facility, patients should provide the admissions office with a duly executed health care proxy that they have prepared. The patients or their agents should insist that this document be promptly attached to their medical charts.

PATIENT SELF-DETERMINATION ACT OF 1990
Effective December 1, 1991

101-508 ADVANCE DIRECTIVES

1. The requirement of this subsection is that a provider of services or prepaid or eligible organization (as the case may be) maintain written policies and procedures with, respect to all adult individuals receiving medical care by or through the provider or organization—
   A. To provide written information to each such individual concerning—
      i. An individual's rights under State law statutory or as recognized by the courts of the State [to make decisions concerning such medical care, including the right to accept or refuse medical or surgical treatment and the right to formulate advance directives as defined in paragraph (3)], and
      ii. The written policies of the provider or organization respecting the implementation of such rights;
   B. To document in the individual's medical record whether or not the individual has executed an advance directive;
   C. Not to condition the provision of care or otherwise discriminate against an individual based on whether or not the individual has executed an advance directive;
   D. To ensure compliance with requirements of State law (whether statutory or as recognized by the courts of the State) respecting advance directives at facilities of the provider or organization; and
   E. To provide (individually or with others) for education for staff and the community on issues concerning advance directives. Subparagraph (C) shall not be construed as requiring the provision of care, which conflicts with an advance directive.
2. The written information described in paragraph (1)(A) shall be provided to an adult individual—
   A. In the case of a hospital, at the time of the individual's admission as an inpatient;
   B. In the case of a skilled nursing facility, at the time of the individual's admission as a resident;
   C. In the case of a home health agency, in advance of the individual's coming under the care of the agency;
   D. In the case of a hospice program, at the time of initial receipt of hospice care by the individual from the program, and;
   E. In the case of an eligible organization (as defined in section 1876(b)) or an organization provided payment under section 1833 a (1)(A), at the time of enrollment of the individual with the organization.
3. In this subsection, the term "advance directive" means a written instruction, such as a living will or durable power of attorney for health care, recognized under State law (whether statutory or as recognized by the courts of the State) and relating to the provision of such care when the individual is incapacitated.

Often there is no question as to the ability of patients to make health care decisions for themselves. This would not be the case when a patient arrives at the emergency room in an unconscious state. In such circumstances, the emergency medical staff automatically performs all possible life-saving techniques. A family member very often accompanies the unconscious patient to the hospital emergency room or is subsequently notified by the hospital of the patient's arrival at the hospital and the patient's present condition. It is extremely helpful to all if the family member or designated agent of the patient arrives at the hospital with a health care proxy in hand. It eliminates any possible confusion as to what course of action to take under certain life-threatening circumstances. It is the physician's or health care provider's obligation to carry out the directives stated in the health care proxy, and the acceptable medical procedure is as follows:

1. The physician must first consult with the patient as to treatment or withholding of treatment.
2. If the patient is nonresponsive or otherwise lacks legal capacity due to his or her medical condition, then the physician must consult with the designated health care agent(s). Together they must try to carry out the wishes of the patient.
3. If the patient should regain the ability to make health care decisions, then the agent's authority ceases. However, in the event that the patient subsequently loses the cognitive ability to make health care decisions, then the agent resumes his/her active role.

All health care providers have the right not to honor an advance directive and to transfer the patient to a facility that will.

Agent's Rights

The agent usually has the right to:

1. Receive all medical and clinical records
2. Seek a second opinion
3. Discuss treatment options with medical staff

In some states a spouse does not automatically have the right to act as a health care agent, nor does a child. To be agents, they must be named as such in the health care proxy document. In other states, certain family members do have this authority under specified circumstances, as provided for by statute.

One right that agents typically do not have is the right to consent to experimental treatments for the surrogate. However, recent legislation passed in California now allows the health care agents the power to give surrogate informed consent to these experimental treatments so long as the medical experiment relates to the cognitive impairment, lack of capacity, or serious or life-threatening diseases and conditions to which the treatment is targeted.

Failure to Have a Health Care Proxy

The failure to have a health care proxy in place can result in withholding or delaying of treatment. The consequences could be devastating and even fatal. Hospital personnel may be prohibited from carrying out certain medical procedures without the legal authorization of the patient who now lacks the capacity to give such authorization. Directives issued by close family members may be ineffective, depending on state law and whether medical providers choose to follow them. Close family relationships, in and of themselves, may not confer any legal standing. Without a health care proxy legally designating a decision maker, the family members may be required to obtain a court order to enable them to make health care decisions.

Health Care Proxy in New York

The New York State Legislature has enacted an excellent Health Care Proxy Statute.[6] The information below, which has been issued by the New York State Department of Health, will be helpful in understanding the basics.

The form below is recommended for New York and may be adequate in some other states. However, some states have mandatory statutory forms, and in other states formalities of execution differ from this form, such as qualifications of witnesses. Finally, all clients do not share the treatment preferences expressed in this form.

Appointing Your Health Care Agent in New York State

The New York Health Care Proxy Law allows you to appoint someone you trust—for example, a family member or close friend—to make health care decisions for you. By appointing a health care agent, you can make sure that health care providers follow your wishes. Your agent can also decide how your wishes apply as your medical condition changes. Hospitals, doctors, and other health care providers must follow your agent's decisions as if they were your own. You may give the person you select as your health care agent as little or as much authority as you want. You may allow your agent to make all health care decisions or only certain ones. You may also give your agent instructions that he or she has to follow. This form can also be used to document your wishes or instructions with regard to organ and/or tissue donation.

Health Care Proxy Form Instructions

Item (1):   Write the name, home address, and telephone number of the person you are selecting as your agent.

Item (2):   If you want to appoint an alternate agent, write the name, home address, and telephone number of the person you are selecting as your alternate agent.

Item (3):   Your health care proxy will remain valid indefinitely unless you set an expiration date or condition for its expiration. The section is optional and should be filled in only if you want your health care proxy to expire.

Item (4):   If you have special instructions for your agent, write them here. Also, if you wish to limit your agent's authority in any way, you may say so here or discuss them with your health care agent. If you do not state any limitations, your agent will be allowed to make all health decisions that you could have made, including the decision to consent to or refuse life-sustaining treatment.

If you want to give your agent broad authority, you may do so right on the form. Simply write: *I have discussed my wishes with my health care agent and alternate, and they know my wishes including those about artificial nutrition and hydration.*

If you wish to make more specific instructions, you could say:

If I become terminally ill, I do/don't want to receive the following types of treatments . . .

If I am in a coma or have little conscious understanding, with no hope of recovery, then I do/don't want the following types of treatments . . .

If I have brain damage or a brain disease that makes me unable to recognize people or speak and there is no hope that my condition will improve, I do/don't want the following types of treatments . . .

I have discussed with my agent my wishes about _____ , and I want my agent to make all decisions about these measures.

Examples of medical treatments about which you may wish to give your agent special instructions are listed below. This is not a complete list:
- Artificial respiration
- Artificial nutrition and hydration (nourishment and water provided by feeding tube)
- Cardiopulmonary resuscitation (CPR)
- Antipsychotic medication
- Electric shock therapy
- Antibiotics
- Surgical procedures
- Dialysis
- Transplantation
- Blood transfusions
- Abortion
- Sterilization

Item (5): You must date and sign this Health Care Proxy form. If you are unable to sign yourself, you may direct someone else to sign in your presence. Be sure to include your address.

Item (6): You may state wishes or instructions about organ and/or tissue donation on this form. A health care agent cannot make a decision about organ and/or tissue donation because the agent's authority ends upon your death. The law does provide for certain individuals in order of priority to consent to an organ and/or tissue donation on your behalf: your spouse, a son or daughter 18 years of age or older, either of your parents, a brother or sister 18 years of age or older, a guardian appointed by a court prior to the donor's death, or any other legally authorized person.

Item (7): Two witnesses 18 years of age or older must sign this Health Care Proxy form. The person who is appointed your agent or alternate agent cannot sign as witness.

HEALTH CARE PROXY FORM

I, _____

hereby appoint _____

(name, home address, and telephone number)

_____

_____

As my health care agent to make any and all health care decisions for me, except to the extent that I state otherwise. *My agent shall have the power and authority to serve as my personal representative for all purposes of the Health Insurance Portability and Accountability Act (HIPAA). My agent is authorized to execute any and all releases and other documents necessary in order to obtain disclosure of my patient records and other medical information subject to and protected under HIPAA.*

This proxy shall take effect only when and if I become unable to make my own health care decisions.

(1) Optional: Alternate Agent

If the person I appoint is unable, unwilling, or unavailable to act as my health care agent, I hereby appoint
(name, home address, and telephone number)

_____

_____

_____

as my health care agent to make any and all health care decisions for me, except to the extent that I state otherwise.

(2) Unless I revoke it or state an expiration date or circumstances under which it will expire, this proxy shall remain in effect indefinitely. *(Optional: If you want this proxy to expire, state the date or conditions here.)* This proxy shall expire *(specify date or conditions)*: _____

_____

_____

(3) Optional: I direct my health care agent to make health care decisions according to my wishes and limitations, as he or she knows or as stated below. *(If you want to limit your agent's authority to make health care decisions for you or to give specific instructions, you may state your wishes or limitations here.)* I direct my health care agent to make health care decisions in accordance with the following limitations and/ or instructions *(attach additional pages as necessary)*: _____

_____

_____ in order for your agent to make decisions for you about artificial nutrition and hydration (nourishment and water provided by feeding tube and intravenous line), your agent must reasonably know your wishes. You can either tell your agent what your wishes are, or include them in this section. See instructions for sample language that you could use if you choose to include your wishes on this form, including your wishes about artificial nutrition and hydration.

(4) Your Identification *(please print)*

Your Name _____

Your Signature _____ Date _____

Your Address _____

(5) Optional: Organ and/or Tissue Donation
I hereby make an anatomical gift, to be effective upon my death, of:
(check any that apply)

☐   Any needed organs and/or tissues
☐   The following organs and/or tissues _____

_____

☐   Limitations _____

If you do not state your wishes or instructions about organ and/or tissue donation on this form, it will not be taken to mean that you do not wish to make donation or prevent a person, who is otherwise authorized by law, to consent to a donation on your behalf.

Your Signature _____ Date _____

(6) Statement by Witnesses *(Witnesses must be 18 years of age or older and cannot be the health care agent or alternate.)*

I declare that the person who signed this document is personally known to me and appears to be of sound mind and acting of his or her own free will. He or she signed (or asked another to sign for him or her) this document in my presence.

Date _____ Date _____

Name of Witness 1   Name of Witness 2
(print) _____   *(print)* _____

Signature _____   Signature _____

Address _____   Address _____

_____   _____

PRACTICE TIP

Notarizing the health care proxy in New York is not required, but it should be notarized to eliminate any questions as to who executed the document. (Check local statutes for health care proxy forms.)

STATE OF _____ :   )

) ss:

COUNTY OF _____ :   )

         On the day of _____ , 20_____ , before me personally came
_____ , to me known to be the individual
described in and who executed the foregoing instrument, and acknowledged that she/he
executed the same.

Notary Public, State of _____

INITIAL:

PRACTICE TIP

Ask the client to initial the bottom of each page.

The New York Health Care Proxy Form

This is an important legal document. Before signing, you should understand the following facts:

1. This form gives the person you choose as your agent the authority to make all health care decisions for you, including the decision to remove or provide life-sustaining treatment, unless you say otherwise in this form. "Health care" means any treatment, service, or procedure to diagnose or treat your physical or mental condition.
2. Unless your agent reasonably knows your wishes about artificial nutrition and hydration (nourishment and water provided by a feeding tube or intravenous line), he or she will not be allowed to refuse or consent to those measures for you.
3. Your agent will start making decisions for you when your doctor determines that you are not able to make health care decisions for yourself.
4. You may write on this form examples of the types of treatments that you want to make sure you receive. The instructions may be used to limit the decision-making power of the agent. Your agent must follow your instructions when making decisions for you.
5. You do not need a lawyer to fill out this form.
6. You may choose any adult (18 years of age or older), including a family member or close friend, to be your agent. You may select a physician: however, he or she will have to choose between acting as your agent or as your attending doctor because a doctor cannot do both at the same time. Also, if you are a patient or resident of a hospital, nursing home, or mental hygiene facility, there are a special restrictions about naming someone who works for that facility as your agent. Ask staff at the facility to explain those restrictions.

7. Before appointing someone as your health care agent, discuss it with him or her to make sure that he or she is willing to act as your agent. Tell the person you choose that he or she will be your health care agent. Discuss your health care wishes and this form with your agent. Be sure to give him or her a signed copy. Your agent cannot be sued for health care decisions made in good faith.

8. If you named your spouse as your health care agent and you later become divorced or legally separated, your former spouse can no longer be your agent by law, unless you state otherwise. If you would like your former spouse to remain your agent, you may note this on your current form and date it or complete a new form naming your former spouse.

9. Even though you have signed this form, you have the right to make health care decisions for yourself as long as you are able to do so, and treatment cannot be given to you or stopped if you object, nor will your agent have any power to object.

10. You may cancel the authority given to your agent by telling him or her or your health care provider orally or in writing.

11. Appointing a health care agent is voluntary. No one can require you to appoint one.

12. You may express your wishes or instructions regarding organ and/or tissue donation on this form.

Frequently Asked Questions

Why should I choose a health care agent?

If you become unable, even temporarily, to make health care decisions, someone else must decide for you. Health care providers often look to family members for guidance. Family members may express what they think your wishes are related to a particular treatment. However, in New York State, only a duly appointed health care agent you appoint has the legal authority to make treatment decisions if you are unable to decide for yourself. Appointing an agent lets you control your medical treatment by:

- Allowing your agent to make health care decisions on your behalf, as you would want them decided.
- Choosing one person to make health care decisions because you think that person would make the best decisions.
- Choosing one person to avoid conflict or confusion between family members and/or significant others.

You may also appoint an alternate agent to take over if your first choice cannot make decisions for you.

Who can be a health care agent?

Anyone 18 years of age or older can be a health care agent. The person you are appointing as your agent cannot sign as a witness on your health care proxy form.

How do I appoint a health care agent?

All competent adults, 18 years of age or older, can appoint a health care agent by signing a form called a health care proxy. You do not need a lawyer or a notary, just two adult witnesses. Your agent cannot sign as a witness. You can use the form printed here, but you do not have to use this form.

When would my health care agent begin to make health care decisions for me?

Your health care agent would begin to make health care decisions after your doctor decides that you are not able to make your own health care decisions. As long as you are able to make decisions for yourself, you will have the right to do so.

What decisions can my health care agent make?

Unless you limit your health care agent's authority, your agent will be able to make any health care decision that you could have made if you were able to decide for yourself. Your agent can agree that you should receive treatment, choose among different treatments, and decide that treatments should not be provided, in accordance with your wishes and interests. However, your agent can only make decisions about artificial nutrition and hydration (nourishment and water provided by feeding tube or intravenous line) if he or she knows your wishes from what you have said or what you have written. The health care proxy form does not give your agent the power to make nonhealth care decisions for you, such as financial decisions.

Why do I need to appoint a health care agent if I am young and healthy?

Appointing a health care agent is a good idea even though you are not elderly or terminally ill. A health care agent can act on your behalf if you become even temporarily unable to make your own health care decisions (such as might occur if you are under general anesthesia or have become comatose because of an accident). When you again become able to make your own health care decisions, your health care agent will no longer be authorized to act.

How will my health care agent make decisions?

Your agent must follow your wishes, as well as your moral and religious beliefs. You may write instructions on your health care proxy form or simply discuss them with your agent.

How will my health care agent know my wishes?

Having an open and frank discussion about your wishes with your health care agent will put him or her in a better position to serve your wishes or beliefs; your agent is legally required to act in your best interest. Because this is a major responsibility for the person you appoint as your health care agent, you should have a discussion with the person about what types of treatments you would or would not want under different types of circumstances, such as:

- Whether you would want life support initiated/continued/removed if you are in a permanent coma.
- Whether you would want treatments initiated/continued/removed if you have a terminal illness.
- Whether you would want artificial nutrition and hydration initiated/withheld or continued or withdrawn and under what types of circumstances.

Can my health care agent overrule my wishes or prior treatment instructions?

No. Your agent is obligated to make decisions based on your wishes. If you clearly expressed particular wishes or gave particular treatment instructions, your agent has a duty to follow those wishes or instructions unless he or she has a good faith basis for believing that your wishes changed or do not apply to the circumstances.

Who will pay attention to my agent?

All hospitals, nursing homes, doctors, and other health care providers are legally required to provide your health care agent with the same information that would be provided to you and to honor the decisions by your agent as if they were made by you. If a hospital or nursing home objects to some treatment options (such as removing certain treatment), they must tell you or your agent **BEFORE** or upon admission, if reasonably possible.

What if my health care agent is not available when decisions must be made?

You may appoint an alternate agent to decide for you if your health care agent is unavailable, unable, or unwilling to act when decisions must be made. Otherwise, health care providers will make health care decisions for you that follow instructions you gave while you were still able to do so. Any instructions that you write on your health care proxy form will guide health care providers under these circumstances.

What if I change my mind?

It is easy to cancel your health care proxy, to change the person you have chosen as your health care agent, or to change any instructions or limitations you have included on the form. Simply fill out a new form. In addition, you may indicate that your health care proxy expires on a specified date or if certain events occur. Otherwise, the health care proxy will be valid indefinitely. If you choose your spouse as your health care agent or as your alternate and you get divorced or legally separated, the appointment is automatically cancelled. However, if you would like your former spouse to remain your agent, you may note this on your current form and date it or complete a new form naming your former spouse.

Can my health care agent be legally liable for decisions made on my behalf?

No. Your health care agent will not be liable for health care decisions made in good faith on your behalf. Also, he or she cannot be held liable for cost of your care, just because he or she is your agent.

Is a health care proxy the same as a living will?

No. A living will is a document that provides specific instructions about health care decisions. You may put such instructions on your health care proxy form. The health care proxy allows you to choose someone you trust to make health care decisions on your behalf. Unlike a living will, a health care proxy does not require that you know in advance all the decisions that may arise.

Where should I keep my health care proxy form after it is signed?

Give a copy to your agent, your doctor, your attorney, and any other family members or close friends you want. Keep a copy in your wallet or purse or with other important papers, not in a location where no one can access it, like a safe deposit box. Bring a copy if you are admitted to the hospital, even for minor surgery, or if you undergo outpatient surgery.

May I use the health care proxy form to express my wishes about organ and/or tissue donation?

Yes. Use the optional organ and tissue donation section on the health care proxy form and be sure to have the section witnessed by two people. You may specify that your organs and/or tissues be used for transplantation, research, or educational purposes. Any limitation(s) associated with your wishes should be noted in this section of the proxy.

Can my health care agent make decisions for me about organ and/or tissue donation?

No. The power of a health care agent to make health care decisions on your behalf ends upon your death. Noting your wishes on your health care proxy form allows you to clearly state your wishes about organ and tissue donation.

Who can consent to a donation if I choose not to state my wishes at this time?

It is important to note your wishes about organ and/or tissue donation so that family members who will be approached about donation are aware of your wishes. However, New York law provides a list of individuals who are authorized to consent to organ and/or tissue donation on your behalf. They are listed in order of priority: your spouse, a son or daughter 18 years of age or older, either of your parents, a brother or sister 18 years of age or older, a guardian appointed by a court prior to the donor's death, or any other legally authorized person.

DO NOT RESUSCITATE (DNR) ORDER

Hospital/Nursing Home DNR Order

Do Not Resuscitate (DNR) Order
A legal document stating that in the event the patient goes into cardiac or respiratory arrest, the patient requests not be resuscitated or maintained on life support equipment.

A hospital/nursing home **Do Not Resuscitate (DNR) order** is a legal document that an adult patient at a hospital or nursing home signs, usually upon entering the facility, stating that in the event the patient goes into cardiac or respiratory arrest, the patient requests not to be resuscitated. The order is reviewed at least once every week to ascertain if it is still medically appropriate. This type of advance directive is ordinarily used in situations where the patient is terminally ill. The form of the institutional DNR is based on the policy of the individual hospital or nursing home. The contents of the form reflect what the hospital and the physician consider most comfortable in managing terminal cases. It can also be signed by a family member if the patient is unable to do so. The DNR should be signed only after clear communication with the attending physician, who is also required to sign the form. Some localities require witnessing by an independent third party. The family should retain a copy of the signed DNR order.

Non-Hospital DNR Order

A living will or health care proxy will not prevent emergency response teams from resuscitating a patient in the home. Emergency response workers are not lawyers or doctors and are not required to examine the documents before responding to an emergency. A non-hospital DNR will address this concern. Most states have a statutory form which must be used. These forms are conspicuously identifiable, allowing emergency response teams to recognize the document quickly in a crisis situation. In addition to the document itself, New York allows a patient to wear a DNR bracelet which alerts emergency response workers to the existence of a valid DNR.

Before attempting to execute a non-hospital DNR, it is imperative that a person understands the applicable state law. State laws vary greatly on the execution and expiration of a non-hospital DNR. In many states, the document may be executed by any patient with capacity or by their health care agent. In other states, such as Virginia, a patient must be terminally ill before executing the document. New York requires a doctor to execute the document based on a patient's written or oral consent. In addition, states also vary as to technical requirements such as witnessing and notarization. Finally, states differ as to the expiration of a non-hospital DNR. While a nonhospital DNR is effective until revocation in most states, New York requires the document to be reviewed by a physician every 90 days. A sample New York State non-hospital DNR is provided.

Note: Usually, it is those who are terminally or seriously ill with little hope of recovery who execute DNRs. People who are expected to recover from their illnesses generally don't sign DNRs.

SAMPLE NYS HEALTH DEPARTMENT FORM FOR NON-HOSPITAL DNR ORDER

State of New York
Department of Health

Non-Hospital Order Not To Resuscitate
(DNR Order)

Person's Name _____

Date of Birth ____/____/____

Do Not Resuscitate the person named above.

Physician's Signature _____

Print Name _____

License Number _____

Date ____/____/____

It is the responsibility of the physician to determine, at least every 90 days, whether this order continues to be appropriate, and to indicate this by a note in the person's medical chart. The issuance of a new form is **NOT** required, and under the law, this order should be considered valid unless it is known that it has been revoked. This order remains valid and must be followed, even if it has not been reviewed within the 90-day period.

THE LIVING WILL

Definition

The **living will** is another form of advance directive that deals with the removal or with-holding of life support systems, including food, hydration, and curative medication from the patient. This legal instrument differs from the health care proxy in that it need not operate through an agent. It is a direct statement of an individual's wishes regarding terminal

Living Will
An advance directive instrument wherein an individual states that in the event he or she goes into a persistent vegetative state or has a terminal illness, he or she does not wish to be kept alive artificially.

illness, executed when the individual/patient is competent, and put into use when the patient is not.

This legal document has nothing to do with a last will and testament as we think of them. It does not involve testamentary disposition of assets. The only similarity of the living will to the traditional will is that the person who executes the document must be an adult and must be competent at the time of execution.

Uses

The living will becomes effective in the event that the patient loses the capacity to make his or her own medical decisions and becomes:

1. *Terminally ill:* catastrophic illness making life no longer worth living, with no hope of recovery, and death being imminent
2. *Comatose:* no mental capacity and in persistent vegetative state
3. *Brain dead:* flat EEG

The intent of this document is to express the patient's wishes, should the patient ever suffer any of the above medical conditions. It can give specific directions regarding the use of specific forms of life support, including, but not limited to, respirators, ventilators, feeding tubes, etc., designed to keep the patient alive. The patient can also request just the opposite: "If there is no hope for my recovery, do not institute the use of any means of life support to prolong my life. If they are already in place, you may discontinue the use of them."

If a client has no one to appoint as a health care agent or does not wish to execute a health care proxy, yet wishes to make known his or her health care preferences, a living will is an excellent, legally valid method of recording these instructions. This document will provide clear and convincing evidence of the client's wishes in the event that the person becomes incapable of making treatment decisions. Living wills are valid until revoked.

Legal Basis

The living will, similar to the health care proxy, has its derivation in the common law. It protects the individual's right to privacy and unlawful touching as well as the liberty rights guaranteed by the Fourteenth Amendment of the Constitution. Forty-seven states have already enacted living will statutes. (Although the New York State Legislature has not enacted a formal living will statute, pursuant to the doctrine of "clear and convincing evidence," its judicial system will recognize and uphold a written living will or an oral declaration by the patient/client, provided that it can be established by means of the sworn testimony of witnesses at a court hearing to terminate life support systems.)

PRACTICE TIP

Check to see if the client has a living will. See if it was properly executed and witnessed. Determine if it is stale, more than 24 to 36 months old. If it is, ask the client if any changes should be made concerning directives. In any case, if it is stale, have it redated or a new form executed. Living wills should be updated regularly to comply with unforeseen circumstances and new advances in medical technology. Check to see if it is an out-of-state living will. If so, does it comply with local law?

Execution

1. The individual must have capacity.
2. The document must be in writing and signed by the individual (for individuals who are competent but unable to write, an "X" is sufficient, e.g., "X, his mark").
3. The document must be notarized in some states.
4. The document must be witnessed. Certain persons, such as treating physicians or nursing home administrators, are prohibited from being witnesses.
5. Several duplicate original documents should be executed.

Who should receive a duplicate original document?

1. Individual who executed the document
2. Health care provider, *e.g.,* doctor
3. Admissions office of the hospital, nursing home, or rehabilitation facility
4. Trusted family member or close friend (the individual should discuss the contents of the living will with them beforehand.)
5. Law firm, on file.

As with the health care proxy, this document should be immediately attached, in a prominent place, to the patient's medical chart. Some facilities even place an *alert label* on the face of the patient's chart indicating that the patient has a living will. There have been recent cases where the living will was misplaced by the medical facility and the patient was kept alive, contrary to the patient's wishes as outlined in a living will. The medical facility was subsequently and successfully sued by the patient and/or legal representatives. A sample form of the living will can be found on the CD-ROM.

What if the health care provider refuses to honor the living will?

The health care provider has the option of honoring the living will or transferring the individual/patient to another facility that *will* honor it. It is a good idea to find out *before* the patient enters the facility whether the facility to which the client/patient is considering admission will honor the living will. This will spare the client and family unnecessary agony and expense in the patient's final days.

PRACTICE TIP

A living will is not a substitute for a health care proxy. The client should have both a living will and a health care proxy in place. If for any reason the health care proxy fails or the agent fails to act, the living will can be used to indicate the patient's wishes. The health care agent can implement the use of the living will by presenting it to the health care provider.

SUMMARY

The elder law professional must assess the situation of each client and his or her family and formulate answers to the following questions.

1. What is the medical status of the client/patient?
   a. Is the client well? Sick? Hospitalized? Comatose?
   b. If ill, what is the prognosis?
   c. Does the client require rehabilitation?
   d. What type of long-term care, if any, does the client need?
   e. Does the client meet your state Medicaid program's "medical necessity" requirement?
2. What is the client or patient's mental status?
   a. Is the client mentally alert? Competent? Incompetent?
   b. If incompetent or incapacitated, what is the prognosis?
   c. Is treatment required?
3. Does the client already have a health care proxy or living will? If so, arrange to obtain an original from the client for review. Is it current or stale? If there is no health care proxy or living will, determine if the client wishes to execute one.
4. Considerations—Family dynamics:
   a. Is the patient being coerced in any way to execute the proxy or living will, *e.g.,* duress or undue influence?
   b. Is there a consensus of opinion within the family regarding treatment or the withholding of treatment?
   c. Is this a dysfunctional family?
   d. Is there a member of the family who has taken control of the situation?
   e. Is this person the designated agent, or will this person be appointed the designated agent by the client? If the client has no health care proxy or living will and lacks capacity to prepare one at this point in time, will this controlling family member do whatever is necessary to carry out the oral wishes of the client/patient by either testifying before the medical ethics committee of the health care facility or, if necessary, petitioning the court for an order to terminate life support systems, if that is the case?
   f. Conflict of interest within the family: Does any family member or friend stand to gain financially or personally from the withholding of treatment, assuming that withholding treatment would eventually result in the death of the client?

Note: Each hospital and nursing home has a medical ethics committee or advisory board, composed of staff members, a medical ethicist, an attorney, and often a member of the clergy. The function of this committee is to render a decision concerning the withholding or withdrawing of treatment in cases where the patient is terminally ill, comatose, or is in a persistent vegetative state with no hope of recovery and with no health care proxy or living will.

APPOINTMENT OF A GUARDIAN

In the event that an individual becomes incompetent and has not had the foresight to execute a durable power of attorney, that person may be subject to a guardianship or a conservatorship proceeding. If the court decides that the individual is indeed incapacitated, it will appoint a

TERRI SCHIAVO
A CAUTIONARY TALE

In February 1990, Terri Schiavo was a 26-year-old woman in apparent good health. She had told her husband that she did not want to be kept alive by extraordinary means, but *she did not have a living will*. One morning, she collapsed in her home when her heart stopped. Terri entered a persistive vegetative state. Her brain damage was so severe that brain scans showed no higher mental functions, even though her heart and lungs continued to operate. Terri was fed by a feeding tube for eight years.

When it was clear that her condition would not improve, Terri's husband and legal guardian petitioned the court to have the feeding tube removed. The trial court found by "clear and convincing evidence" that Terri would have chosen to withdraw life prolonging procedures if she were capable of expressing her wishes. *Schindler v. Schiavo,* 780 So.2d 176 (F1.2d DCA 2001). A number of appeals, initiated by Terri's parents, all upheld the trial court's determination, but prolonged Ms. Schiavo's life by more than five years. By court order, the feeding tube was removed on October 16, 2003.

After the matter was fully and fairly litigated, Terri's parents then sought relief from the Florida legislature, which passed *"Terri's Law,"* giving Governor Jeb Bush the power to have her feeding tube reinserted. The law was so specific that the governor's power lasted only for 15 days. The law could probably only be applied to one person. Six days after Terri's feeding tube was removed, Governor Bush ordered it reinserted. Terri's husband challenged the constitutionality of "Terri's Law," and the controversy rages on.

Terri's Law has been challenged on three grounds. First, Terri's husband argues that Florida has violated Terri's constitutional right to die under the Federal and Florida Constitutions. Second, that Terri's Law violates the Florida Constitution's separation of powers, which protects the acts of the judiciary from interference by the legislative and executive branches of government. Third, that Terri's Law is a special law written to affect only one person, which is a violation of the Florida Constitution.

At the time of writing, more than $1 million have been spent on attorneys' fees, and Terri Schiavo is still alive despite her expressed wish to exercise her constitutional right to die. The Schiavo case highlights the importance of having a living will to document a person's wishes while the person is still capable of making that difficult decision.

---

guardian or **conservator** to handle the affairs of the individual. Every state has enacted legislation permitting the use of guardians or conservators. Guardianships and conservatorships are basically the same, except that the conservatorship is more restrictive in its control over the incapacitated person. The guardianship tends to be of a shorter duration and more limited. The guardian or the conservator who is appointed by the court may or may not be a trusted family member. Often the court appoints attorneys who are not familiar with the affairs of the incapacitated person, whom they have never met. The court will nevertheless award these guardians and conservators substantial fees for performing their duties. These fees are taken from the assets of the incapacitated person. In order to avoid the possibility of a stranger controlling one's life via a court order, clients should be urged to execute an advance directive for the appointment of a guardian.

The **advance directive for the appointment of a guardian** is a legal document in which an individual who is competent nominates a person to handle the individual's affairs if and when a guardianship or conservatorship is necessary. The court will usually honor the directive, provided that the nominee is a consenting, competent adult capable of handling the ward's affairs. The guardian cannot have a criminal background because guardians/conservators are fiduciaries. The court usually requires the fiduciary to be bonded by a surety company, and a criminal record will prevent an individual from being bonded. In some states, courts distinguish between the guardian of the person and the guardian of the estate; they may be two different people. Guardianship proceedings are discussed in Chapter 5.

Guardian
An individual who has been invested with power by a court of law having jurisdiction and charged with the duty of taking care of a person and managing that individual's property and rights. The person who is the subject of a guardianship is incapable of handling his or her own affairs.

PREDESIGNATION OF A GUARDIAN

1. Must be written.
2. Must be notarized.
3. Must be witnessed.
4. Should be executed in several original counterparts.
5. Law firm should retain one original in its files.

A sample form to predesignate a guardian can be found on the CD-ROM.

ANATOMICAL GIFTING

People are living longer and will do so to an even greater extent in the coming years. While diet, exercise, and a youthful outlook certainly contribute to greater longevity, they are dramatically overshadowed by the incredible advances in modern medical technology in the field of organ transplantation. Heart transplants, kidney transplants, liver transplants, corneal transplants, and bone and skin grafts have become commonplace procedures in modern medical centers throughout the world. As the frequency of these procedures increases and the field of organ transplantation continues to expand, a critical need has arisen for human organs and tissues of all types, which are used not only for saving lives but also for research and development. Media coverage of dramatic organ transplants, celebrity transplants, and reports of unique drugs that prevent organ rejection has resulted in increased public awareness of the great potential of this new field. Note the publicity surrounding baseball star Mickey Mantle's liver transplant and reports of research findings by the National Institutes of Health and the *New England Journal of Medicine*. (Robert Steinbrook, "Allocating Livers—Devising a Fair System," Feb. 6, 1997, p. 436.)

Severe Shortage of Organ Donors

Still, there is a severe shortage of organs for donation in this country. Currently studies indicate that more than 79,000 people are awaiting to receive all types of organs. Federal law prohibits the sale of human organs. There is currently a movement in this country to compensate the family of organ donors to induce donations, but the American Medical Association has not endorsed it. In certain European countries, including Austria, Spain, and Portugal, an individual is presumed to agree to the donation of his or her organs on death unless he or she signs a document refusing to do so. New York State has recently revised its health care proxy statute to permit organ donation. In view of the current situation, clients should be encouraged to enroll in an organ donation plan.

U.S. Department of Health and Human Services

The Health Resources and Services Administration, through its Division of Transplantation, oversees and provides funds for the nation's organ procurement, allocation, and transplantation system and administers the national bone marrow registry program. The division, part of HRSA's Office of Special Programs, also coordinates national organ and tissue donation activities and funds research into expanding organ donation. It also controls the organ transplant program in each state. For example, the New York Regional Transplant Program (NYRTP) is the federally designated organ procurement program in the New York area.

Organ transplants rose 5.4 percent in 2000 compared to 1999. Organ transplants in 2000 totaled 22,827, an increase of 1,172 over the 21,655 transplants that occurred in 1999. The number of living donors rose from 4,747 in 1999 to 5,532 in 2000, an increase of 16.5 percent, the largest one-year jump ever recorded. Donors from cadavers rose from 5,825 in 1999 to 5,984 in 2000, an increase of 2.7 percent.

Kidney transplants are a major part of the organ transplant program. In July 2002, a major research study revealed that kidney transplants from cadavers were just as effective as those from live donors. This will increase the potential number of available kidneys to be used as transplants. Research is ongoing and will improve the quality of life for our elder clients.

When drafting a last will and testament, the elder law attorney should ask about the client's desires concerning organ donation. In addition, the attorney should be familiar with specific advance directives used in anatomical gifting.

THE UNIFORM ANATOMICAL GIFTS ACT

The Uniform Anatomical Gifts Act has been adopted in some form by all 50 states and the District of Columbia. It was originally enacted in 1968 and revised in 1987 to liberalize and clarify the procedures involved therein. The intent of the revised statute was as follows:

1. To simplify gifting procedures.
2. To allow public agencies to use their authority and good offices in arranging for organ donations.
3. To place an affirmative duty upon hospitals to further the cause of organ donations by asking patients near death if they would be willing to be donors and by discussing this possibility with patients' families.
4. To place further duty upon hospitals and public agencies to encourage organ transplants, *e.g.*, the motor vehicle bureau on a license application or renewal form asking whether the applicant wishes to be an organ donor.

The legal professional should be familiar with how the Uniform Anatomical Gifts Act functions. New York State's version of the act is similar to those of other states and merits close examination.

Those Who May Execute an Anatomical Gift[7]

1. *The donor him or herself:* the donor must be a person of sound mind at least 18 years of age.

   Note: Anatomical Gifting by a Minor—Special Provision

   A minor wishing to donate an organ should have his or her parents sign the gift form in the presence of at least two witnesses and should add the following preamble to the form:

   "I am of sound mind and under 18 years of age. I hereby make this anatomical gift to take effect upon my death with the parental consent of the undersigned. The marks in the appropriate brackets and the words filled into the blanks below indicate my desires."

2. *A representative or agent of the donor:* The statute specifies a certain priority of people who have the authority to authorize the anatomical gift in the absence of actual notice or contrary indication by the decedent.

The order of precedence is as follows:

1. Spouse
2. Son or daughter, 18 years or older
3. Brother or sister, 18 years or older
4. Guardian of the donor at the time of death
5. Any other person authorized or under the legal obligation to dispose of the body

For example, in the absence of a specific directive by the decedent, if the spouse is available, then the authority rests with the spouse. If there is no spouse or he/she is not available, the next in line would be the son or daughter 18 years or older, and so on down the line. It is important to note there must be unanimity within a prioritized group, *e.g.*, brother/sister or son/daughter; if the donee has *actual notice* of any opposition to the gift within a prioritized group, then the donee is prohibited from accepting the gift. In addition, if the donee is aware of the fact that the donation of the anatomical gift is in violation of the donor's religious or moral beliefs, then the donee must also *not* accept the gift. It should be noted that the ultimate decision as to whether or not to accept the gift remains with the donee.

The statute was amended in 1990 to provide that if the donee knows upon accepting the gift that it will be used for other than transplantation purposes, the donee, if requested by the donor or the donor's next of kin, shall advise the donor or the donor's next of kin of the following:

1. How the body will be utilized
2. Who will use it
3. The donee's plans for the ultimate disposition of all the remaining body parts

Institutional Involvement

The Transplant Council[8] was created as an advisory board for the New York State Department of Health to oversee this highly complex area of medicine.

Note: New York State Public Health Law 4307 prohibits the sale and purchase of human organs for transplantation. This is currently a misdemeanor but, in view of substantial illegal trafficking of human organs, perhaps should be a Class A felony.

New York Public Health Law 4351 encourages increased institutional involvement in obtaining donor organs. Where a patient is found to be a suitable candidate for organ or transplant donation, the hospital representative *shall*, at the time of death, request the next of kin to make an anatomical donation.

Institutions and Individuals Authorized to Become Donees of Anatomical Gifts and Their Purposes[9]

1. Any hospital, surgeon, or physician, for medical or dental education, research, advancement of medical or dental science, therapy, or transplantation.
2. Any accredited medical or dental school, college or university for education, research, advancement of medical or dental science, or therapy.
3. Any bank or storage facility, for medical or dental science, therapy or transplantation.
4. Any specific donee, for therapy or transplantation.
5. An organ procurement organization

All parties acting in good faith to obtain anatomical gifts are immunized by statute from civil or criminal liability for their actions.

Manner of Executing Anatomical Gifts[10]

An individual may make an effective anatomical gift in the following ways:

1. In a uniform donor instrument known as the Uniform Donor Card (see exhibit on page 84). If the donor chooses to use the Uniform Donor Card, it must be signed by the donor in the presence of two witnesses who must also sign the card in the donor's presence. For the gift to become valid, delivery of the document that creates the gift is not required during the lifetime of the donor. However, it is good practice to inform the donee of the donor's good intentions by giving the donee a copy of the donor card. It is also appropriate to notify donor's and donee's next of kin.

2. As a specific bequest in the donor's last will and testament. The gift is effective immediately upon the death of the testator of the will. Probate does not have to be instituted or completed. The statute clearly states that if the "will is not probated or if it is declared invalid for testamentary purposes, the gift, to the extent that it has been acted upon in good faith, is nevertheless valid and effective."

3. By completing the information concerning anatomical gifts found on the reverse side of a driver's license. (This is an acceptable form of the Uniform Donor Card.)

If a donor chooses to use a driver's license to make a gift, the license must be in force. If the license has expired or has been suspended or revoked, the gift may be declared invalid. Therefore, the driver's license may not be the most effective method of making an anatomical gift.

Anatomical gifts may or may not have specific donees. Therefore, a donor may make a "general" anatomical gift even if the donor has no specific donee in mind.

Timing of Organ Transplantation

In most cases, organs for transplant are removed from the donor's body at the time of death. The statute defines death as "the irreversible cessation of circulatory and respiratory functions of the donor." The time of death must be certified by a physician(s) who is prohibited from participating in the removal for transplantation of any body part.

In special cases such as kidney transplants and bone marrow transplants, where the donor continues to live after donating an organ, the harvesting of the donor's organ must be coordinated with the implantation into the donee.

Revocation of the Anatomical Gift[11]

Anatomical gifts are revocable. Should the donor wish to revoke or amend a donation, the statute provides several relatively simple methods:

- The execution and *delivery* to the donee of a signed statement clearly indicating revocation.
- An oral statement of revocation made before two witnesses, which must then be communicated to the donee.
- A statement during a terminal illness or injury addressed to an attending physician and communicated to the donee.

- A signed card or document found on the donor's person or effects clearly stating the revocation.
- Destroying, canceling, or mutilating the gifting document, provided the document has not been delivered to the donee.

An anatomical gift made in a will can be revoked by executing a codicil to the will or by revoking the will itself.

Safekeeping

As with other important papers and legal documents, advance directives concerning anatomical gifts must be kept in a readily accessible, safe place. Donors should notify their attorney, their physician, and other family members of the location of these papers and of their donative intentions. In addition to the attorney's office, the document can also be deposited or registered with an organ bank or a hospital registry office.

Note: New York State PHL 4360 permits the creation of organ banks and the procurement of organs, tissues, and body parts to be placed into such organ banks.

UNIFORM DONOR INSTRUMENT
UNIFORM ANATOMICAL GIFT ACT
UNIFORM DONOR CARD

I, the undersigned, hereby make this anatomical gift, if medically acceptable, to take effect upon my death. The words and marks below indicate my desires.

I give: (a) _____ any needed organs or parts

(b) only the following organs or parts

_____

(Specify the organ(s) or part(s) for the purposes of transplantation, therapy, medical research or education.)

(c) _____ my body for anatomical study if needed.

Limitations or special wishes if any: _____
(If applicable, list specific donee) _____

Signed by the donor and the following two witnesses in the presence of each other:

_____	_____
Signature of Donor	Date of Birth of Donor
_____	_____
Date signed	City and State
_____	_____
Witness	Witness
_____	_____
Address	Address

NOTE: This is a legal document under the Uniform Anatomical Gifts Act. The following form may be attached to a driver's license.

Pursuant to the Anatomical Gift Act, upon my death, I hereby give (check boxes applicable):

1.   [ ] Any needed organs, tissues, or parts;
2.   [ ] The following organs, tissues, or parts only:

    _____

3.   [ ] For the following purposes only (transplant, therapy, research, education):

    _____

Refusal:

4.   [ ] I refuse to make any anatomical gift.

                _____
                    Signature of Declarant

WILL CLAUSE
DONATION OF EYES TO EYE BANK

I hereby reaffirm my desire to donate my eyes upon my death to the _____ Eye Bank located at _____, with whom I have previously executed an instrument, dated _____, giving my express consent to such donation.

My personal physician, Dr._____, and my wife/husband and executor have been informed of my intention in this matter, and I direct that upon my death they perform any and all acts that may be necessary to effectuate my intention.

ANATOMICAL GIFT BY NEXT OF KIN
OR GUARDIAN OF THE PERSON

Pursuant to the Anatomical Gift Act, upon death, I hereby make this anatomical gift from the body of [name of decedent] who died on [date of death] at [location]. The marks in the appropriate squares and the words filled into the blanks below indicate my relationship to the decedent and my wishes respecting the gift.

I survive the decedent as [ ] spouse; [ ] adult son or daughter; [ ] parent; [ ] adult brother or sister; [ ] grandparent; [ ] guardian of the person.

I hereby give (check boxes applicable):

1.   [ ] Any needed organs, tissues, or parts;
2.   [ ] The following organs, tissues, or parts only:

    _____

3.   [ ] For the following purposes only:

    _____

    _____

_____   _____

Date   Signature of Survivor

_____

Address of Survivor

ANATOMICAL GIFT BY LIVING DONOR

Pursuant to the Anatomical Gift Act, upon my death, I hereby give (check boxes applicable):

1. [ ] Any needed organs, tissues, or parts;

2. [ ] The following organs, tissues, or parts only:

    _____

3. [ ] For the following purposes only (transplant, therapy, research, education):

    _____

_____   _____

Date of Birth   Signature of Declarant

_____   _____

Date of Signing   Address of Declarant

DISPOSITION OF REMAINS

The donor may want to add instructions regarding disposition of remains as follows:

4. After the donated organs or parts are removed, the remains of the body shall be disposed of in the following manner: _____; and at the expense of the following person:_____.

NOTES

1. *Scholendorf v. Society of New York Hospitals,* 105 N.E. 92 (N.Y. 1914).
2. *In Re Quinlan,* 355 A.2d 647 (N.J. 1976).
3. *Cruzan v. Director, Missouri Dept. of Health,* 497 U.S. 261 (1990).
4. *Matter of Westchester County Medical Center on Behalf of O'Connor,* 531 N.E.2d. 607 (N.Y. 1988).
5. Public Law 101-508 (42 U.S.C. 1395 *et seq.*).
6. New York Public Health Law PHL S2981.
7. New York Public Health Law PHL S4301.
8. New York Public Health Law PHL S4361.
9. New York Public Health Law PHL S4302.
10. New York Public Health Law PHL S4303.
11. New York Public Health Law PHL S4305.

REFERENCES

Coalition on Donation
1100 Boulders Parkway, Suite 700
Richmond, VA 23225-8770
Tel 804-330-8620
Fax 804-323-7343

U.S. Dept. of Health and Human Services
Health Resources and Services Administration
Division of Transplantation
www.hrsa.gov/osp/dot

National Marrow Donor Program
Suite 500
3001 Broadway Street NE
Minneapolis, MN 55413-1753
800-627-7692

National Kidney Foundation
30 East Thirty-third St., Suite 1100
New York, NY 10016
800-622-9010

REVIEW QUESTIONS AND EXERCISES

1. Explain and describe the differences between a general power of attorney, a durable power of attorney, and a springing durable power of attorney. What are the advantages and disadvantages of each?

2. Draft a durable power of attorney document.

3. Draft a revocation of a power of attorney. List the parties that should be notified of a revocation.

4. Explain how surrogate health care decision making has changed as a result of the following cases: *Quinlan, Cruzan,* and *O'Connor.* How would the execution of a health care proxy have helped to avoid the problems faced in these three cases?

5. What is the majority opinion in *Cruzan v. Director Missouri Dept. of Health,* 497 U.S. 261 (1990)?

6. Draft a health care proxy. Of what issues should the elder law professional be aware when drafting a health care proxy?

7. What are the rights and duties of the principal and agent after a health care proxy has been executed?

8. Explain and describe the differences between a health care proxy and a living will.

9. Draft a living will. What should you do if the health care provider refuses to honor the living will?

10. Discuss the benefits of anatomical gifting and ways to increase the number of organ donors. Discuss a more equitable system for allocating organs to the people who require them.

CHAPTER 5

Wills

PREVIEW

One of the most important documents that the elder law professional can draft is a last will and testament. The **last will and testament** is defined as a legal instrument by which an individual makes a testamentary disposition of property—real, personal, or intangible. It is revocable during the lifetime of the testator provided the individual is competent. This chapter will discuss in detail all the information that should be included in a last will and testament, as well as the probate process and legal challenges to wills.

LAST WILL AND TESTAMENT

One of the major concerns of the elderly is the disposition of their assets after they die. Therefore, a key function of the elder law attorney is to assist the elderly in their financial planning and to draw up their last will and testament. An experienced elder law attorney can guide the client through the minefield of estate and income taxation and minimize or even eliminate the often enormous tax consequences resulting from the death of the testator, thus permitting the beneficiaries of the estate to receive a larger share of the decedent's assets. An elder law professional is called upon to participate in all stages of the process:

1. The initial will intake: gathering familial and financial information (See the CD-ROM for the Confidential Will Planning Questionnaire.)
2. The actual drafting of the will after the elder law attorney has conferred with the client
3. The execution ceremony of the will
4. The disposition of the document and conformed copies for *safekeeping*

A will is defined as an advance directive allowing a testator (testatrix) to express in writing his or her testamentary plan for the disposition of probatable assets upon death. In some states the legal representative of the estate is known as the personal representative (P.R.), while in others the term *executor (executrix)* is used. In rare circumstances, such as on a battlefield in wartime, oral wills are permitted under strict statutory regulations. Oral declarations created under these circumstances are called **nuncupative wills.** A **holographic will** is a document written solely in the handwriting of the testator. Some states treat this instrument as a valid document without the necessity of the attestation of witnesses.

Last Will and Testament
A true advance directive. A legal instrument by which an individual makes a disposition of property, real and personal, of any kind and nature whatsoever, which is to take effect after his or her death and which by its own nature is completely revocable during the lifetime, provided the individual is competent to make the revocation.

Nuncupative Will
An oral will declared or dictated by a testator who is terminally ill or a soldier on a battlefield about to die. This type of will is valid only in certain states and under certain circumstances.

Holographic Will
A will written by the testator in personal handwriting and not witnessed. Each state has specific laws as to whether it recognizes such a will.

The testator (testatrix) appoints an executor (executrix) in the will to carry out his or her testamentary plan upon death. It is essential that the testator obtain permission beforehand of those whom the testator wishes to name in a fiduciary capacity, *e.g.,* executor, personal representative, trustee, and guardian.

A will may have one or more codicils (little wills). A **codicil** is a legal instrument that modifies some article(s) in the will itself without causing a change to the entire will. It must be executed and witnessed subsequent to the execution of a valid will in the same manner as a will. An individual can attach as many codicils to a will as desired. However, when the will is probated, each individual codicil is subject to the probate process. Unless the document is self-proving, the witnesses have to be located, causing delay and additional expense in the administration of the estate. Therefore, if the will becomes overburdened with multiple codicils, it is advisable to draft a new will encompassing all the changes and revoking the prior will and codicils.

Let us now analyze each article in a basic will that is used in one form or another in every jurisdiction in the United States.

Codicil

A separate legal instrument used to explain, modify, add to, subtract from, qualify, alter, restrain or revoke provisions in an existing last will and testament, acknowledged in the same manner as a will.

Simple Will

LAST WILL AND TESTAMENT
OF

I, _____ , residing at _____ , _____ County, [state], being of sound mind and disposing memory and being mindful of the uncertainties of this life, do hereby make, publish, and declare this instrument to be my Last Will and Testament, hereby revoking all former Wills and Codicils by me at any time heretofore made.

This is the introduction to the will. It usually states the testator's name and address at the time of execution. Some jurisdictions require marital status. Some drafters also include in the preamble a statement of the testator's next of kin and multiple names used by the testator.

- The testator, "being of sound mind and disposing memory."

This refers to the individual's mental ability, or *testamentary capacity*, to execute a will. Testators must know the nature and consequences of their acts. In addition, they have to know what their assets are and the natural objects of their bounty, even if they are not leaving their estate to any or all of them. Testators must be oriented as to time and place and have the cognitive ability to understand what they are doing. If the testator lacks testamentary capacity, the validity of the will is subject to attack.

- The testator must publish the will, or, in other words, state to the witnesses of this document that this is his or her last will and testament and that the testator understands the nature and consequences of these acts.
- Because an individual can have only one valid will at any one time, the preamble must contain terminology revoking any prior wills the testator made. This avoids will contests and delays in the probate process.

ARTICLE I

A. *I hereby direct that my Executor, hereinafter named, arrange for the interment of my last remains in _____ CEMETERY, _____ , [state].*

B. *I hereby direct that my just debts and funeral expenses be paid by my Executor hereinafter named as soon after my death as is practicable, except that the payment of debt secured by a mortgage or pledge of real or personal property may be postponed at the discretion of my Executor.*

If the will provides, the executor may be given the obligation of arranging for the funeral services and the interment of the testator, as well as arranging for the payment of these services from the testator's assets. This may also include arranging for cremation, cryogenics, or even the building of a mausoleum. The executor is required to pay all of the decedent's "just debts," such as medical expenses, expenses of the last illness, administrative expenses of the estate, legal fees, taxes, etc.

The executor is given the power to postpone "any debt secured by a mortgage or a pledge of real or personal property." For example, if there is a mortgage on the testator's residence or on a commercial parcel of real property, the full balance does not have to be paid at the time of death. The executor may continue to make monthly payments until the mortgage is satisfied. Delaying satisfaction of the mortgage will add liquidity to the estate. Inflation also permits the mortgage to be paid off in cheaper dollars.

Article I is a directive by the testator to the executor concerning the early stages of the administration of the estate. It is not a dispositive provision as it does not dispose of property. Article II, discussed below, is the first of the several dispositive articles of the will.

PRACTICE TIP

In addition to directions stated in the will, a testator may also leave written instructions regarding funeral and disposition of remains in a separate document. The will may not be located in time to make the aforesaid arrangements.

ARTICLE II

I hereby give, devise and bequeath any and all articles of tangible personal property to my (Spouse), _____ , provided he/she survives me. If my (Spouse), _____ , shall not survive me, I give all such tangible personal property, in as near equal shares as is practicable, to such of my children _____ , as shall survive me.

In this article, the testator directs the executor to dispose of his personal property, first to his wife, provided she survives; if she does not, then there is an **alternate gift over** to another or other individuals. The beneficiary has to survive the testator if he or she is to inherit. Personal property refers to articles of clothing, jewelry, artwork, silver, coins, antiques, furnishings and household goods, etc. Some testators specify individually each item and its disposition. Any such items may have to be appraised and declared on the estate tax return, if one is required to be filed.

Alternate Gift Over
A stipulation in a will bequeathing property to a secondary beneficiary or beneficiaries, in the event that the primary recipient does not survive testator.

PRACTICE TIP

If the testator does not wish to itemize personal property specifically in the will, a separate letter of instruction can be prepared and delivered to the executor with regard to the specific personal property. Usually, these instructions are carried out by the executor and distributed accordingly, but these instructions are not legally binding.

ARTICLE III

I hereby give, devise and bequeath all the rest, residue and remainder of my estate, real, personal and mixed of whatsoever kind and nature and wheresoever situated, of which I may die possessed or seized or in which I may have any power of appointment or testamentary disposition to my (Spouse) _____ *, provided he/she survives me, (or **per stirpes**).*

Residuary Article
The disposition of the remainder of a testator's estate of which the testator may die possessed.

- Article III is termed the **residuary article**. Whereas Article II only disposes of personal property, specified or otherwise, Article III is a disposition of everything else, "real or personal," of which the testator may die possessed.
- It also includes any assets in which the testator may have any power of appointment or testamentary disposition. If the testator controls assets under a power of appointment, then these assets are considered part of the estate.
- This article also contains an alternate gift over if the primary beneficiary does not survive. If there is no giftover or substitute beneficiary, the gift lapses and is of no effect.

Per Stirpes
The equitable division of the residuary estate amongst the testator's heirs.

- This clause may also state "to my spouse, **per stirpes**." This means that if the spouse predeceases the testator, then the residuary estate will automatically go to the surviving children equally. If one of the children predeceases the testator, leaving surviving children, then his or her share would go equally to his or her children [the testator's grandchildren].
- Specific bequests of money, stock, bonds, securities, interests in real estate or business are also permissible. For example:
  1. "I hereby bequeath 1,000 shares of AT&T to my father Herman Schwartz, provided he survives me."
  2. "I hereby bequeath $10,000 to my brother Darby Schwartz, provided he survives me."
  3. "I bequeath the sum of $20,000 to the American Cancer Society."
  4. "I devise my residence and the contents therein situated at 10 John Street, Brandytown, NY, to my brother Darby Schwartz, provided he survives me."

Bequest
The disposition of personal property.

Devise
The disposition of real property.

These dispositive clauses must be inserted into the will prior to the residuary clause; otherwise, they may be ineffective. The term **bequest** refers to giving personal property, and the term **devise** refers to giving real property.

ARTICLE IV

In the event that my _____ (Spouse) _____ , predeceases me or dies simultaneously with me, then I hereby give, devise and bequeath all the rest, residue and remainder of my estate, real, personal and mixed of whatsoever kind and nature and wheresoever situated, of which I may die possessed or seized or in which I may have any power of appointment or testamentary disposition, to my _____ (Child) _____ , per stirpes. In the event that my beloved _____ (Child) predeceases me, without surviving issue, then I hereby give, devise and bequeath the share of said predeceased child to _____.

Article IV expands on the residuary clause indicating that the testator is leaving assets to his child, *per stirpes,* if his wife predeceases him or dies soon after the testator. However, if the named child predeceases the testator and he or she has no issue, then article IV directs the gift to another.

ARTICLE V

A. *I hereby nominate and appoint my _____ (Spouse) _____ , to be the General Guardian of the person and estate of my children, _____ , during their minority. In the event that my _____ (Spouse) _____ , predeceases me or fails to qualify to act as General Guardian of my said children, or having qualified ceases to act for any reason, then I nominate and appoint my _____ , as Substitute Guardian, such Substitute Guardian to have the same power conferred upon my original Guardian named herein.*

B. *I hereby request that my children, _____ , live with my _____ (Spouse) _____.*

     In the event that my _____ (Spouse) _____ , predeceases me or dies simultaneously with me, then I hereby request that my children, _____ , live with my _____.

Article V is the guardianship clause of the will. If the testator has children who are of minority age, he may nominate in his will a general guardian of the person and the estate of his children during their respective minorities. This is often the spouse, but if the testator is divorced, it may not be. There may be a separate guardian of the property. If the spouse is alive, no guardian of the person is needed because the parents are always the natural guardians. It also provides for a substitute guardian, if the primary guardian fails to qualify as general guardian, *e.g.,* is dead, has a criminal record, does not wish to be guardian, or has qualified to act as guardian but ceases to act for any reason. The substitute is granted the same powers as the original guardian. This clause also permits the testator to request that the children reside with a certain party (parties) in the event of death of both parents. This is always subject to the court's approval.

More Complex Will Clauses

ARTICLE VI

*If at the termination of any **trust** created by this Will all or a portion of the principal of such trust shall vest in absolute ownership in a person who is under the age of twenty-one (21), or if pursuant to this Will any part of my estate, whether principal or income, shall vest in absolute ownership in a person who is under the age of twenty-one (21), I authorize and empower my Executor or Trustee, as the case may be, in his sole and non-reviewable discretion to hold the property so vested in such person, in a separate fund for the benefit of*

Trust
Refers to an agreement between one person called the settler and another person called the trustee, wherein a trustee holds the property received by the settler for the benefit of another in a fiduciary capacity. There are many types of trusts, such as *living trusts, charitable trusts, spendthrift trusts,* etc.

such person and to invest and reinvest the same, collect the income therefrom, and until such person reaches the age of twenty-one (21), to apply so much of the net income therefrom or of the principal thereof for the care, support, maintenance or education (including under-graduate, graduate, and post-graduate), of such person as my Executor or Trustee, as the case may be, shall deem necessary (without any duty to take into account the other resources of such person), either by the payment of bills incurred by or for such person or by making payment or distribution thereof to the Guardian or other legal representative, wherever appointed, of such person or, if a minor, to the person with whom the minor shall reside, the receipt of the person to whom any payment or distribution is so made being a sufficient discharge therefor, even though my Executor or Trustee might be that person; and to accumulate any such income not so paid, if any, and to invest and reinvest the same until said person shall attain the age of twenty-one (21), at which time all accumulated income and unexpended principal shall be paid over to such person. If such person shall die before attaining the age of twenty-one (21), the then principal, together with any accumulated and unexpended income, shall be paid over to the estate of such person. The authority conferred upon my Executor and Trustee by this article shall be construed as a power only and shall not operate to suspend or prevent absolute vesting of any property in such person. My Executor or Trustee, as the case may be, shall not be required to give any bond in any jurisdiction for the performance of his or her duties hereunder.

Articles I–V are representative of a simple will. This article and the following are for far more complex wills. These provisions set up testamentary trusts that will come into effect on the death of the testator. All of the distribution in Article II and Article III are outright **gifts**. Ownership is fixed immediately upon the death of the testator, provided the testator owned these assets at the time of his death. The testator may wish not to do this for many reasons, *e.g.,* he may not wish to place a large sum of money or an asset in the hands of a beneficiary who may squander it very rapidly. He has an option to create a trust so that the assets are devised or bequeathed to a trustee, who becomes the fiduciary owner of the assets. The trustee will distribute them pursuant to the terms of the trust over a specified period of time, *e.g.,* years, to the named beneficiaries or even over the lifetime of the beneficiaries and possibly their **issue**.

It generally is not advisable to permit a beneficiary under the age of 21 to receive any assets directly from an estate. The reasons for this are obvious: to give young people money may inhibit their work ethic, and they may spend the money unwisely. One way to circumvent this situation is to include a provision in the will that does not suspend or prevent absolute vesting of the bequest in the named minor beneficiary. The will would then empower the executor or a trustee in his or her sole and nonreviewable discretion to retain the bequest in a separate fund to be used for the general education, health, and welfare of the minor. This is called the **dipping in power**. It also permits the fiduciary to manage those funds and to collect income until such time as the minor reaches the age of 21.

Dipping in Power
A provision in a will that does not suspend or prevent absolute vesting of the bequest in the named minor beneficiary. The will would then empower the executor or a trustee in his or her sole and nonreviewable discretion to retain the bequest in a separate fund to be used for the general education, health, and welfare of the minor.

PRACTICE TIP

As in the drafting of other articles in the will, it is important to make alternative provisions in the event that the "minor beneficiary" either predeceases the testator or survives, but dies before reaching the majority age of 21.

ARTICLE VII

A. I hereby nominate, constitute and appoint my _____ , _____ , to be the Executor of this, my Last Will and Testament and Trustee of each and every trust created herein.

B. In the event that my _____ predeceases me or dies simultaneously with me, or should my designated executor fail or refuse to accept such office, or is or becomes disqualified to act, or resigns, then, upon the happening of any such events I nominate, constitute and appoint my _____ as substitute Executor and Trustee of and under this, my last Will and Testament, with all the powers and authority he/she would have had if originally so appointed.

C. I direct that no Executor or Trustee shall be entitled to receive any commissions for acting as such.

If a corporate executor or trustee is appointed, he or she will not accept the appointment without receiving commissions and fees. This should be explained in the will.

Article VII provides for the appointments of **executor(s)** and trustee(s). The testator must be judicious in the selection of these **fiduciaries** designated to carry out the testamentary plan. They must be honest, trustworthy, and loyal to the wishes of the testator. It is also advisable that they have money management skills, have time to perform their duties, and are able to withstand pressure from beneficiaries to distribute assets prematurely or contrary to the will. Article VII further provides for an orderly succession of executors or trustees in the event that they are unable to fulfill these obligations for any reason.

Note: It is preferable to appoint fiduciaries who are substantially younger than the testator so as to minimize the possibility of their predeceasing the testator.

Some individuals choose to appoint a corporate fiduciary such as a bank or trust company as primary executor, co-executor, or trustee. This tends to be costly and is not recommended for two reasons:

1. The testator often has no familiarity with the corporate employees who will eventually manage the decedent's personal affairs.
2. The banking industry is constantly undergoing change. As a result, personnel are also changing, and this could lead to a lack of continuity. Some professionals believe that banks are the executors and trustees of choice in that they can provide stable continuous management in complex situations. However, corporate fiduciaries will not accept estates that fall below their minimum asset requirements.

The duties of the testamentary fiduciary can often be arduous and time-consuming and require extensive record keeping. For these reasons, the testator may elect to include a provision providing for (or not providing for, as is sometimes the case with a spouse or other family members) compensation, which is strictly controlled by statute in many jurisdictions. Commissions are usually a percentage of the gross estate subject to many conditions. Because fiduciary commissions are treated as taxable income to the fiduciary (and a deduction to the estate), beneficiaries named as fiduciaries may often choose to waive their right to receive commissions. Corporate fiduciaries, however, always charge commissions.

Executor
A person(s) or corporate entity (bank or trust company) named in a will to carry out the orderly administration of the testator's estate. Also known as the "personal representative" of the estate. See pg. 89.

Fiduciary
A person who acts in a position of trust, *e.g.*, a trustee.

ARTICLE VIII

If any party appointed hereunder or any legatee named under this Will objects to or contests the probate of this will or any part thereof, or attempts to revoke or avoid probate thereof, or attempts to set the same aside, or takes any proceeding whatever with the intended effect of avoiding this Will or any part thereof, then and in that event any devise or bequest or benefit given to or conferred upon such person or beneficiary shall be revoked or annulled, and in that event such person or beneficiary shall receive no part of or benefit of my estate or property.

Interrorem Clause
A clause in a will that states if a named beneficiary contests the will and loses, that beneficiary forfeits any interest the testator provided in the will.

This article, known as the **interrorem clause**, is designed to prevent frivolous will contests, which are costly and divisive. If a named beneficiary contests the will and loses, that beneficiary forfeits any interest the testator provided in the will. A successful contest generally has the effect of nullifying the contested will, and the objectant to the will may receive an amount larger than was provided for in the original will. This article does not pertain to litigants who are not mentioned in the will. This clause is invalid in some states and may not be enforced. Refer to your local statute.

ARTICLE IX

I direct that my Executor, Trustee and any substitutes, are to act as such, in any capacity as aforementioned, without giving bond or security, whether in the State of _____ , or elsewhere, for the faithful performance of their duties.

Bonding
A guarantee by a surety company that protects the assets of the estate from gross negligence, malfeasance, and theft by the fiduciary.

Because executors and trustees act in a fiduciary capacity, the issue of bonding always arises in discussions of wills. **Bonding** is a means of protecting the assets of the estate from gross negligence, malfeasance, and theft by the fiduciary. A bond is a guarantee by a surety company that, if in fact the aforesaid occurs, it will make good to the estate any losses. The bonding company will do this for a premium that is often costly and varies with the size of the estate. Therefore, the testator may wish to save this administrative cost by so indicating, as in Article IX. Waiving of the bond is always subject to the approval of the probate court. Some states always require bonding.

ARTICLE X

The words "Executrix," "Executor," "Trustee" and "Guardian," or any pronoun or adjective referring to such words as used in this, my Will, shall be construed as masculine, feminine, neuter or plural, as the same requires, and shall also be construed to include and apply to any and all successor, alternate or substituted fiduciaries under this, my Will.

This article is grammatically designed to encompass all possible parties named in the will so as to avoid confusion.

ARTICLE XI

I confer upon my Executor and Trustee, if any, with respect to the management and administration of any property, including property held under a power in trust, all of the Powers conferred by Section 11-1.1 of the Estates, Powers and Trusts Law of the State of New York, or comparable statute in effect at my death and, in addition thereto, all the following discretionary powers without limitation or by reason of specification.

A. *To retain any such property; to acquire by purchase or otherwise any kind of property, including common stocks, without being limited to investments authorized for trust funds and without diversification as to kind or amount.*

B. *To sell or otherwise dispose of property at public or private sale for consideration and upon terms, including credit, as they deem advisable, and to grant options for the sale or disposition for a period as they deem advisable.*

C. *To manage and to lease real property for periods beginning presently or in the future without regard to statutory restrictions on leasing.*

D. *To abandon, in any way or for any reason, any property whether or not owned by me at the time of my death, without court order; my Executor and Trustee shall be exonerated from any liability therefor.*

E. *To deposit funds in any bank without limitation as to time or amount.*

F. *To borrow money from any source, including my Executor and Trustee, and to pledge or mortgage any property for any purpose.*

G. *To distribute principal in money or in kind, real or personal, or partly in each, including undivided interests, even though shares be composed differently.*

H. *To delegate powers to agents or others to the extent permitted by law and to pay them for services and reimburse them for expenses; employ and pay the compensation of accountants, custodians, legal and investment counsel.*

I. *To sell or continue to operate, upon such terms and in such forms as to them may seem advisable, any business or enterprise in which I may be interested at the time of my death.*

J. *To determine what is income and what is principal hereunder, and what expenses, costs, taxes shall be charged against principal, and their decision with respect to these matters shall be conclusive.*

This article is traditionally known as the **powers clause**. It grants to the fiduciary the powers necessary to carry out his or her duties when the fiduciary begins to function. The fiduciary literally "steps into the shoes" of the testator and carries forth the testator's wishes. The clause enables the fiduciary to conduct the business affairs of the estate without a court order, which may include the following:

Powers Clause
A clause in a will that grants to the fiduciary the powers necessary to carry out his or her duties.

1. The sale of real estate
2. The sale of securities
3. The sale of personal property
4. The sale of a business
5. The management of funds, real estate, or an ongoing business and banking activities in connection therewith, including the borrowing of funds and committing to mortgaging the assets of the estate

The powers also permit the fiduciary:

1. To use discretion in the manner in which distribution of the assets of the estate are made, *e.g.*, in kind, in cash, etc.
2. To delegate powers by employing professionals such as lawyers, accountants, financial advisors, custodial agents, as seen fit.

Although the fiduciary's powers are traditionally statutory, all states permit the testator to grant the fiduciary additional powers that will facilitate the management of the estate.

Note: The executor must also perform the following tasks in connection with the orderly administration of a decedents' estate:

1. File the original will with the probate court
2. Locate all of the assets of the estate, and clean out decedent's residence, if vacant, *e.g.,* no surviving spouse or other family member
3. Locate and inventory all safe deposit boxes
4. Evaluate all assets, including obtaining appraisals on real, personal, and business property
5. Pay all administration expenses of the estate, including legal fees, court costs, and executors commissions
6. Defend any will contests
7. File the decedent's final income tax return and pay any taxes due
8. File the estate tax and fiduciary returns and pay any taxes due
9. Distribute all the assets to the proper beneficiaries
10. Pay all proper debts of the decedent and of the estate
11. Maintain proper records of all items of principal and income
12. Fulfill court requirements for accounting and distribution of assets in accordance with the will

ARTICLE XII

I direct that all estate, inheritance and succession taxes of every kind imposed by the laws of the United States of America, or by the laws of any state thereof, that shall be assessed against, or that shall be payable in respect of any property disposed of or passing under this my Will, and all interest and penalties, if any, on or in respect of such taxes, shall be paid by my Executor and Trustee as a part of the administration expenses of my estate and shall not be apportioned.

Article XII is often employed by the testator to direct the method of payment of inheritance taxes and administration expenses. This may be helpful to the beneficiaries because the estate is a taxpayer separate from the beneficiaries.

This approach could be problematic if the gift is tangible property rather than cash. An alternative approach would be to assess expenses against the residuary and not against gifts of tangible property.

1. Inheritance taxes and administrative expenses can be paid off the top. For example, inheritance taxes and administrative expenses are paid from the testator's "gross estate." After payment is made, the "net estate" is distributed according to the terms of the will without any further deductions. (This is the most frequently used method.)
2. Inheritance taxes and administrative expenses can be apportioned in accordance with the beneficiary's respective share of the estate, *e.g.,* if the beneficiary receives 10 percent of the estate, 10 percent of the taxes and administrative expenses must be deducted from the beneficiary's "gross share" by the executor before distribution of the "net share."

ARTICLE XIII

If any beneficiary or beneficiaries under this Will and I, or any other person upon whose death such beneficiary or beneficiaries would become entitled to any part of my estate, should die in a common accident or under such circumstances that it is doubtful who died first, then all the provisions of this Will shall take effect in like manner as if such beneficiary or beneficiaries had predeceased me or such other person, as the case may be.

This article is commonly known as the *simultaneous death clause*. The following are examples of when this clause might be of relevance:

1. When a husband and wife die at the same time.
2. When it is difficult to determine whether the husband or wife died first.
3. When the testator wishes to specify the length of time that a beneficiary must survive in order to inherit. Testator can specify, for example, that the beneficiary must survive 30, 60, or 90 days, in order to inherit.

If the beneficiary should die within the specified period of time, then he or she is no longer qualified as a beneficiary. It is important to understand the reasoning behind this simultaneous death clause. The testator may wish to benefit a certain beneficiary during said beneficiary's lifetime so the beneficiary may enjoy the benefit of this gift. However, it may not be the intent for this gift to be passed on intact to the beneficiary's heirs. This enables the testator to control the ultimate disposition of the particular gift, avoid multiplicity of probates, and take advantage of certain tax-saving techniques.

ARTICLE XIV

Should a construction of this, my last Will and Testament, be found necessary, I direct that it be construed under the Laws of the State of _____.

A will should be drafted pursuant to the laws of the testator's domicile. Article XIV is commonly called the **will construction clause**. This clause provides that no matter where the will is probated, whether in another state or in another country, the probate court should apply the laws of the testator's domicile where the will was drafted to determine what the will intended to accomplish. Regardless of the will construction clause, states will follow their own probate requirements in probating the will.

Will Construction Clause
A clause in a will that states that the probate courts should apply the laws of the testator's domicile where the will was drafted.

The Execution of the Will

IN WITNESS WHEREOF, I have hereunto set my hand and affixed my seal this _____ , in the year 20 _____.

_____
, *Testator*

The foregoing instrument consisting of this and _____ (____) other typewritten pages, was subscribed by the above named Testator, and published and declared as the Testator's Last

Will and Testament, and thereupon, we at the Testator's request, and in the presence of each other, did subscribe our names and respective addresses thereto as attesting witnesses, this attestation clause having been read aloud in the presence of said Testator and of each of us.

_____ *residing at* _____

_____ *residing at* _____

_____ *residing at* _____

The testator must date and sign the will at the end of the document in the presence of a minimum of two witnesses. In most states the will formally ends after the signature of the testator; the remainder of the document, is used for subscribing witnesses and a self-proving affidavit. It is not appropriate to have the testator's signature notarized. Each state has its own requirements as to the number of witnesses and formality of execution. It is useful to have three witnesses so that in the event that the will must be proved and the witnesses must be called upon to testify, at least two out of the three can be located. In some states the testator must publish and declare the will to the witnesses and specifically indicate to them that this is the last will and testament of the testator and request the witnesses to sign their names below and to place their addresses next to their names. The testator and witnesses should execute only one original will, the other copies are *conformed*.

Procedure to Conform a Will

After the client has signed the original, the law professional will take copies of the document and print on the testator's signature line the name of the testator and the date of execution. The law professional will then print the witnesses' names and addresses on their respective lines and place next to each line the following symbol: /s/. This symbol indicates that this is a conformed copy of the will and does not contain original signatures. Another method is to photocopy the original (without removing the staples) after execution, with the word *copy* stamped on all pages of the document.

It is common and recommended practice for the attorney-drafter to retain the original document in a safe or vault and give only a conformed copy to the client. The purpose of this procedure is to safeguard and protect the original will. It reduces the possibility of theft, destruction, or tampering by a dissatisfied heir. Though not impossible, it is very difficult to probate a copy of a will. Where a copy is submitted to probate, the proponent must overcome the rebuttable presumption that the testator did in fact revoke the will by intentionally destroying it. This is called a *Lost Will Proceeding*.

If the client desires to retain the original document, have the client execute a dated receipt acknowledging what documents have been received.

Witnesses

In most situations, the attorney's legal staff witnesses legal documents prepared by the office. The staff frequently knows the client and is trained to function in this capacity. If a document is to be executed at a hospital or nursing home, do not expect the facility to provide witnesses or a notary. Most health care facilities have policies that prohibit their employees from witnessing or notarizing any legal documents for a patient or resident. The elder law attorney should be prepared to bring witnesses to the signing ceremony. Witnesses should not be family members who have any financial interest in the matter. Legal staff and close friends of the client have proven to be the best witnesses because they can best determine if the client is of sound mind and acting freely. The witnesses are only present during the execution ceremony to witness the signature of the testator on the will. They are *not* permitted to read the contents of the will.

Revealing the Contents of a Will

One of the most frequently asked questions at the will execution ceremony is whether the testator should disclose the contents of the will to anyone.

The client must decide whether to discuss the terms or contents of the will with family and beneficiaries before the client dies. The attorney will usually advise against this procedure. However, if it is decided by the client to reveal the contents of a will, he or she should be cautioned as to the consequences. If the beneficiaries are not pleased with its contents, they could make the testator's life rather uncomfortable. Clients should be advised to disclose only the following details:

- The existence of the last will and testament.
- The name and location of the law firm that prepared the will.
- The location of the original will if it is with the attorney-draftsman. If the original will cannot be left with the law office, care should be given to prevent the destruction of the will by unhappy relatives after the death of the testator.

Self-Proving Will

Most states permit the use of a procedure allowing the will to be made self-proving. This means that, instead of requiring all of the witnesses to appear at the probate court to testify as to the validity of the will execution procedure, they may execute, in addition to the will itself, an affidavit swearing to the proper execution of the will. This is called a **self-proving affidavit**, which all witnesses must sign before a notary public. It is attached to the end of the will. The law of the potential state of probate must be consulted to determine the statutory requirements for a self-proving affidavit in that state.

The witness's signature on the will is never notarized, but the signature of each witness on the self-proving affidavit *must* be notarized.

PRACTICE TIP

This form varies from state to state. Check local statutes.

THE PROBATE PROCESS

Summary

When the testator dies, the original will is retrieved from safekeeping and is filed in the probate court along with a certified death certificate and petition for probate. The **probate** proceeding is a judicial process involving the authentication of the will, which is not valid

---

Self-Proving Affidavit
An affidavit executed by the witnesses to the will, swearing to the proper execution of the will. This document eliminates the need for the witnesses to appear at the probate court to testify as to the validity of the will. They may be required to testify in a will contest.

Probate
A procedure that takes place in the probate or surrogate's court by which the last will and testament is offered to the court for authentication. The result of the probate proceeding will be the validation of the will and the issuance of letters of testamentary to the executor. The probate court has a general power over the administration of estates. The probate court could also declare the will to be null and void due to improper execution, undue influence, or lack of testamentary capacity.

Self-Proving Affidavit

STATE OF _____)

) *ss:*

COUNTY OF _____)

Each of the undersigned, individually and severally being duly sworn, deposes and says:

The within Will was subscribed in our presence and sight at the end thereof, by, the within named Testator on the day of _____ , 20 ___ at _____.

Said Testator, at the time of making such subscription, declared the instrument so subscribed to be his or her Last Will.

Each of the undersigned thereupon signed his or her name as witnesses at the end of said Will at the request of said Testator and in the testator's presence and sight and in the presence and sight of each other.

Said Testator was, at the time of so executing said Will, over the age of 18 years and, in the respective opinions of the undersigned, of sound mind, memory and understanding and not under any restraint or in any respect incompetent to make a Will.

The Testator, in the respective opinions of the undersigned, could read, write and converse in the English language and was suffering from no defect of sight, hearing, or speech, or from any other physical or mental impairment that would affect the testator's capacity to make a valid Will. The Will was executed as a single, original instrument and was not executed in counterparts.

Each of the undersigned was acquainted with said Testator at such time and makes this affidavit at his request.

The within original Will was shown to the undersigned at the time this affidavit was made and was examined by each of them as to the signature of said Testator and of the undersigned.

The foregoing instrument was executed by the Testator and witnessed by each of the undersigned affiants under the supervision of _____ Esq., an attorney-at-law admitted to the practice in the State of _____.

_____

_____

Severally sworn to before me
this day of _____ , 20 ___

_____
    Notary Public

until approved by the probate court. Once the will is approved, the court issues *letters testamentary* to the person or entity approved as executor or personal representative of the estate. Probate ensures that the testator's wishes will be duly carried out. It protects against fraud by permitting heirs who have been omitted from the will, or provided for minimally, to contest the will on the grounds of lack of testamentary capacity, fraud, or undue influence. Additionally, the probate process requires that all possible heirs who would have inherited had the testator died **intestate** (without a will) be formally notified of the testator's death and of the contents of the will. This is accomplished by service of a notice of

Intestate
One who dies without a will.

probate either personally by mail or by publication in local newspapers pursuant to a court order. This offers them the opportunity to file objections to the will, should they feel they have been treated unfairly.

Intestate Succession

When someone dies without having his or her own will, when the decedent's will is denied probate, or in areas where the will is silent, the estate is subject to the laws of intestate succession. Contrary to popular belief, everyone dies with a will. In effect, the intestacy laws are *a default will* created by the state legislature of the decedent's domicile at death. Because state laws vary significantly, a complete description of intestate succession cannot be provided in the space of this book.

The reader without a will should not feel a false sense of comfort. The intestacy laws may not be appropriate for most people. While one may choose to rely on the intestacy laws to distribute their assets, there are many variables to consider. The question becomes, "do you want the state to decide who gets your money, or do you want to make that decision yourself?"

Generally, the decedent's estate is distributed to his closest relatives under a scheme similar to the following, but each state varies:

- If the decedent has a spouse and no issue, then everything goes to the spouse. *Issue* are all people descended from a common ancestor. A decedent's issue includes her children, grandchildren, and great-grandchildren.
- If the decedent has a spouse and issue, the issue may be entitled to share a percentage of the estate and the spouse may receive a percentage. (In some states, the spouse may get everything.) This is an area that varies greatly from state to state.
- If the decedent has no spouse and issue, then everything goes to the issue.
- If the decedent has no spouse, and no issue, then everything goes to the decedent's parents.
- If the decedent has no spouse, no issue, and no parents, then everything goes to the decedent's siblings and the issue of the decedent's predeceased siblings. A sibling's issue would include the decedent's nieces, nephews, grandnieces, and grandnephews.
- If the decedent has no spouse, no issue, no parents, and no siblings, then everything goes to the decedent's first cousins or their issue.
- When the oldest living relative is more distant than a first cousin, the decedent's estate may *escheat* to the state, meaning the entire estate goes into government coffers. Some states continue the chain of succession to more distant relatives, often referred to as *laughing heirs*. Laughing heirs may have no personal connection to the decedent, but inherit a windfall upon her death.

The following are only a few of the reasons for making a will instead of relying on the government to determine the distribution of your estate:

- The intestacy laws can be very complex. In addition to the order of succession noted above, there are a number of other default rules that can vary by state. These raise questions such as:
  - How should multiple heirs in the same class inherit (*per stirpes* vs. *per capita*)?
  - Who can petition the court to control the estate?

- Who has a right to be the administrator of the estate?
- How are stepchildren and half siblings treated in intestacy?

- Under intestacy, a decedent has no voice in who should become guardian of his minor or disabled children upon his death. In his will, the testator can nominate an appropriate person.

- If a person moves from one state to another, her estate may be distributed differently than she thought when she initially decided not to make a will. The decedent's domicile at death controls which state's law applies, while "a will travels with the testator."

- The intestacy laws result in the estate being distributed only to blood (and adopted in) relatives and the state. Friends, in-laws, and charities cannot inherit under intestacy. Long-term unmarried couples and same sex couples have no right to inherit under intestacy whatsoever.

- Conversely, a person cannot disinherit blood relatives under intestacy. All relatives in the same class take in equal shares.

- Non-marital children must prove their father's paternity in order to inherit, whereas if they are named in a will, that proceeding is avoided.

LEGAL CHALLENGES TO A LAST WILL AND TESTAMENT

Introduction

In most types of litigation, the defendant is alive. In a will contest, the testator is deceased and is not available to appear in court to substantiate the terms of the will and defend his or her interests. However, there is a rebuttable presumption that the testator had testamentary capacity when the will was executed.

Litigation involving a will contest can be presented to the court only after the testator has died. The contestants of the will are required to file with the court their objections to probating the will. The contestants in their legal pleadings accuse the now deceased testator of not having testamentary capacity. They may claim in their objections that the decedent was suffering from dementia or senility or was subject to undue influence. Their objective is to break the will and prevent the distribution of the decedent's assets according to the directions stated in the will. If the contestants are successful, they will benefit from the estate although they were not the intended beneficiaries of the decedent. In view of the fact that the testator is unavailable to protect himself and his intentions, the court will use every legal effort to make certain that the wishes of the now departed testator are carried out.

Legal Capacity

Capacity
An individual's ability to understand the nature, effects, and consequences of his or her acts.

It is essential to understand the concepts of legal **capacity** and competency and their impact upon the validity and enforceability of a last will and testament in the event of a challenge by a family member or other interested party who would eventually benefit if the document offered for probate is judicially declared to be invalid.

Competency is generally defined as the quality of being competent or possession of required skill, qualification or capacity. The law defines competency as the quality or state of being legally competent; legal capacity of qualification based on the meeting of certain minimum requirements of age, soundness of mind, citizenship, or the like. The standard for capacity to make a will is lower than the standard to make a contract or other agreement.

Competence involves a societal judgment of legal capacity. The age of majority in most states is 18. However, this is determined by state law. Upon reaching majority a person can vote, enter into a contract, and partake in the commerce of society.

Decisional capacity involves a person's ability to make a rational decision. It requires a person to (a) have a set of values or standards and (b) the ability to communicate and understand facts and concepts and to process information.

A testator must have sound mind and memory to make a valid will. There are three criteria that a person must possess in order to make a will.

1. *The testator must understand the nature and consequences of the act that he or she is about to perform.* He or she must comprehend that the document about to be executed is his or her last will and testament, and consciously know what the document is, its contents, and the purposes of the will.

2. *The testator must understand the nature and extent of the property he or she possesses.* The testator must understand that upon his or her death, this document will transfer ownership of his or her property to the person(s) or entities named in the will.

3. *The testator must know the names of the persons who are the proper objects of his or her bounty and his or her relation toward them.* For example if the testator is married and has children, the testator must know the names of these individuals and how they are related.

The Uniform Probate Code, which has been adopted by many states in one form or another, codifies the criteria for testing the basic testamentary capacity required making a will.

The testator is required to:

1. Know those persons, such as relatives, who are the natural object of his bounty and understand the nature of their legal claims, and their moral claims, to his bounty
2. Know the nature and extent of his property
3. Comprehend the disposition that his will is making
4. Appreciate the relation of these three elements to each other
5. Form an orderly plan for the disposition of his property

The following case exemplifies the low threshold of cognitive ability required for testamentary capacity.

ESTATE OF KUMSTAR
487 N.E.2d 271 (N.Y. 1985)

The order of the Appellate Division, 105 A.D.2d 747, 481 N.Y.S.2d 646, should be reversed and the matter remitted to Surrogate's Court for entry of a decree granting the petition for probate.

It is the indisputable rule in a will contest that "[t]he proponent has the burden of proving that the testator possessed testamentary capacity and the court must look to the following factors: (1) whether she understood the nature and consequences of executing a will; (2) whether she knew the nature and extent of the property she was disposing of; and (3) whether she knew those who would be considered the natural objects of her bounty and her relations with them" (*Matter of Slade*, 106 A.D.2d 914, 915, 483 N.Y.S.2d 513; see also, *Matter of Delmar*, 243 N.Y. 7, 152 N.E. 448). When there is conflicting evidence or the possibility of drawing conflicting inferences from undisputed evidence, the issue of capacity is one for the jury (Rohan, *Practice Commentary, McKinney's Cons. Laws of N.Y.*, Book 17B, EPTL 3-1.1, p. 275).

Here, there was insufficient evidence adduced at trial to warrant submitting that issue to the jury. The subscribing witnesses and those who were close to decedent when the will was drafted each testified that decedent was alert and capable of understanding the nature of her actions. Decedent's treating physician testified that it was his opinion, based on a reasonable degree of medical certainty, that decedent was competent when she signed the will. By contrast, a physician called by the objectant who reviewed decedent's medical records was unable to state with a degree of medical certainty that decedent was incompetent at the time in question. That the will contained a bequest to a "brother", long since deceased, "in Cuba, Cattaraugus County, New York" does not raise a question of decedent's competence in light of her attorney's testimony that, without knowing of the brother's death, he had assumed that the person referred to was decedent's brother and the fact that decedent's nephew, who along with his two sisters were the sole heirs, bore the same name as decedent's brother and resided in Cuba, Cattaraugus County. Also without significance are the bequests establishing trust funds in relatively small amounts and the omission of a specific devise of certain land to a historical site, contrary to a wish mentioned on several occasions by decedent.

On review of submissions pursuant to section 500.4 of the Rules of the Court of Appeals (22 NYCRR 500.4), order reversed, with costs payable out of the estate to all parties appearing separately and filing separate briefs, and matter remitted to Surrogate's Court, Orange County, for entry of a decree granting the petition for probate, in a memorandum.

N.Y., 1985.

Wachtler, C. J., and Jasen, Meyer, Simons, Kaye, and Alexander, J. J., concur.

Testamentary Capacity and Lucid Intervals

Lucid Interval
A period of time when a person who is known to be confused due to illness has a clear perception and understanding of the nature of his or her acts.

The legal-medical concept of **lucid intervals** is well recognized in American probate jurisprudence. It is a period of time, no matter how brief, when a person who is known to be confused due to illness, has a clear perception and understanding of the nature of his or her acts. It is like being in the eye of a hurricane, clear and calm, for the moment. In order for a will or other testamentary devise to be valid, it must be executed during the period of lucidity. It is important to alert witnesses of the interval of lucidity so that they may carefully observe the testator and be able to testify in court on behalf the testator in the event that the will becomes the subject of a will contest. It is well founded in probate law that a subscribing witness to a will may testify as to facts leading to a conclusion about the testamentary capacity of the testator.

Alzheimer's disease is a devastating disease that causes progressive dementia and eventually leads to death. During the course of the illness, many patients retain enough capacity to execute a valid will. It is critical for the elder law professional to understand that a client diagnosed with Alzheimer's disease is not automatically disqualified from making a will for lack of testamentary capacity. Many cases have held that a testator suffering from mild to moderate stages of the disease still has the legal capacity to make a will. However, in will contest litigation, a physician or psychiatrist may often be called upon as an expert witness to testify on behalf of the objectants to the will. This medical testimony very often indicates that upon examination the patient was suffering from Alzheimer's disease and lacked testamentary capacity. The subscribing witnesses to the will are then called upon to testify that when the will was executed, the testator had a lucid interval and was capable of understanding the nature and consequences of his acts. The court will most likely uphold the will based upon the testimony of the subscribing witnesses. Windows of lucidity present important opportunities for the elder law professional to prepare and assist in the execution of a will or trust for a client stricken with Alzheimer's disease or senile dementia.

If a will or any other advanced directive is being prepared for a person who is suffering from any illness that could affect state of mind, it is important to be prepared to make several visits to accomplish the task of valid execution. A record should be kept of each visit and the questions asked and answered. It should be a rule not to give up trying if there is any hope of a lucid interval. It will be a great service to the client to persist in efforts on his or her behalf.

Insane Delusion

Sometimes a testator has sufficient mental capacity to make a will, but has an *insane delusion* that causes a particular provision of the will to fail for lack of capacity. The delusion must be a belief that a rational person would not hold and the cause of the beneficiary's receiving a lesser distribution.

In one case, the testator irrationally believed that his elderly wife was having an affair and hiding her suitors in the cellar. The court found that he suffered from an insane delusion and would not have disinherited his wife if not for the delusion, *In re Honigman*, 8 N.Y. 2d 244 (1960). Another case involved a man who believed his daughter was kidnapped and replaced with an imposter.

An insane delusion will not be found when the testator had a good reason for disinheriting a beneficiary under a prior will. Due to the high incidence of dementia and the taking of prescribed medications, some elderly persons may believe that their family members are stealing from them or committing other transgressions. The elderly person may decide to disinherit that family member. Considering the prevalence of elder abuse (see Chapter 15), this belief may or may not be well-founded.

Undue Influence—Duress

Legal documents are also subject to challenge on the grounds of undue influence and duress. This occurs when an individual is forced to sign a legal document against his or her will. For example, a close relative, business associate, health care worker, or other interested party may threaten the individual with bodily harm or deprivation of food and other necessities should the individual fail to sign a certain document or include certain terms therein. For example, a daughter will threaten to "throw her mother out of the house" if her mother does not provide her with a substantial bequest in her will. Another common threat is, "You'll never see your grandchildren again unless you do as I request."

There is one exception to the general rule that the court will use its best efforts to enforce a will; bequests or devises of money or property to a lawyer, doctor, nurse, minister, caregiver, or even a close friend who happened to be present during the last illness of the testator are automatically subject to the very close scrutiny of the judiciary. The court will question whether these persons were really the objects of the testator's bounty or did these persons exert undue influence upon the testator to become his or her beneficiaries. In some states the probate court on its own motion may review the will and then conduct hearings into the legal capacity of the decedent. The court will not enforce a will if it finds that the decedent was seriously ill, dependent on pain medications, suffering from senile dementia, organic brain syndrome, or other illnesses or if it suspects undue influence on the part of a confidant. Especially suspicious is a will that provides for a substantial gift to the attorney who drafted it. Check local statutes. The court will determine that under these conditions there exists an increased probability that (a) the testator lacked testamentary capacity, or that (b) the testator was the subject of undue influence at the time the will was made. These named beneficiaries will not receive their devises or bequests from the will.

The following case exemplifies the issue of undue influence.

IN RE PUTNAM'S WILL
177 N.E. 399 (N.Y. 1931)

Crane, J.

The will of Ada W. Putnam, dated the 4th day of October, 1928, has been admitted to probate by the surrogate of New York county, over the objections and contest of Edith I. Smith, a niece of the testatrix. Ada W. Putnam was a widow about 70 years of age, whose only living relative was this niece, for whom she had much affection. By the terms of previous wills, executed under such circumstances that undue influence is not suggested, Mrs. Putnam was consistent in mind and purpose to leave Miss Smith the income of her estate for life. This was the provision in all previous wills as well as the present one. The residuary estate, however, in the previous wills had been left to charity, whereas in this last will and testament it was given to the lawyer who drew the instrument, and in consequence has caused all the trouble. Attorneys for clients who intend to leave them or their families a bequest would do well to have the will drawn by some other lawyer. Any suspicion which may arise of improper influence used under the cover of the confidential relationship may thus be avoided. The law, recognizing the delicacy of the situation, requires the lawyer who drafts himself a bequest to explain the circumstances and to show in the first instance that the gift was freely and willingly made. *Matter of Smith*, 95 N. Y. 516. 'Such wills, when made to the exclusion of the natural objects of the testator's bounty, are viewed with great suspicion by the law, and some proof should be required beside the factum of the will before the will can be sustained.' *Marx v. McGlynn*, 88 N. Y. 357, 371. In the absence of any explanation, a jury may be justified in drawing the inference of undue influence, although the burden of proving it never shifts from the contestant. *Matter of Kindberg's Will*, 207 N.Y. 220, page 228, 100 N.E. 789.

✳ ✳ ✳

Protecting Wills Against Legal Challenges

Legal documents are often challenged on the basis of the client's lack of capacity even though the person appears to be totally competent and you believe that to be the case. For this reason, it is advisable and often invaluable to have the client's file contain the following:

1. A medical evaluation should be conducted shortly before execution of the will, indicating the capacity of the testator, issued by a physician or psychiatrist who would be willing to testify in court.
2. A videotape may be created during the execution ceremony showing that the testator was fully aware of the procedure and met all of the tests of testamentary capacity.
3. Affidavit as to capacity of the testator from family, friends, clergyman, advisors, and other disinterested parties who at that time know the principal intimately can be helpful to prove capacity at the time the will was executed.

In any event, the legal professional must as a matter of routine practice be keenly alert to the indicators that would trigger the need to obtain the above mentioned backup documentation:

1. The client has a known diagnosis of any stage of Alzheimer's disease, Parkinson's disease, senile dementia, stroke, or any other disease or disability that might affect the client's capacity.
2. The client is in a state of extreme emotional stress and upheaval or acts emotionally disturbed.
3. The client is confined to a hospital, nursing home, hospice, rehabilitation facility, or other facility that provides health care.
4. The client is taking "mind altering" psychotropic drugs, *e.g.,* Haldol®, Prozac®, or Zoloft®.
5. The client is terminally ill.
6. The client has relatives who will be disinherited by the will and have the right to sue.

To be forewarned is to be forearmed. A medical report, a videotape, or affidavits may be important to rebut a challenge of incompetence or undue influence at a later time. A detailed record of the interview should be kept on file.

Videotaping the Execution Ceremony: The Practitioner's Dilemma

Anticipating the possibility of a will contest based on lack of testamentary capacity, some attorneys recommend videotaping the will execution ceremony of a testator who may have questionable capacity, believing that the taping will make capacity more credible. Others suggest that videotaping can work against the testator. First, the taping constitutes evidence that even the attorney lacked confidence in the testator's capacity. This can be rebutted by a contention that the testator knew the aggrieved party would sue when he was disinherited so he wanted to show his capacity, but it raises the issue nonetheless. Second, the testator may look terrible on the screen, especially if he is very sick, nonverbal, or in a hospital bed. He may appear to lack testamentary capacity, when he does not. The debate will likely continue until enough cases challenging videotaped wills indicate whether the technique is successful to show capacity.

REFERENCES

Gorman, Warren F., *Testamentary Capacity in Alzheimer's Disease*, Elder Law Journal 4(2) 225–46, (1996).

Robitscher, Jonas B. *Pursuit of Agreement, Psychiatry and the Law*, J.B. Lippincott Company, Philadelphia, 1966.

In re Putnam's Will, 177 N.E. 399, N.Y. 1931.

REVIEW QUESTIONS AND EXERCISES

1. What are the essential elements of a will? If a person drafts a will in New York and then moves to Florida, is this will still a binding legal document?
2. Discuss the rights and duties of the testator and the executor of a last will and testament.
3. What is a holographic will? What are the requirements that make a holographic will a legally binding document? What are the advantages and disadvantages to a holographic will?
4. Draft a sample will.
5. Discuss the residuary article of a will.
6. What is a self-proving will, and what are its benefits?
7. Describe problems that may arise during the probate process.
8. Discuss interrorem clauses. Discuss methods of challenging testamentary capacity. Discuss lucid intervals and their relationship to testamentary capacity.
9. Explain the effects of undue influence on the probate process.
10. What are the ways to protect wills against legal challenges?
11. Discuss the duties of an executor.

CHAPTER 6

Guardianships

PREVIEW

Incapacitation may occur without warning. The elder law professional should prepare clients for this unexpected tragedy by recommending the execution of advanced directives, including a health care proxy, a living will, and a durable power of attorney. Quite often, no advanced directives are in place to handle the incapacitated person's affairs. Although it is commonly believed that a spouse or child will automatically be given authority solely because of his or her marital or filial standing, this is untrue. In order for the incapacitated person's affairs to be handled by family members, advance directives must be executed or judicial intervention will be necessary in the form of a guardianship proceeding. This chapter will discuss the stages of a guardianship hearing, the duties and responsibilities of a guardian, and the termination of the guardianship.

INTRODUCTION

One of the basic cornerstones in life course planning is the preparation of a complete set of advance directives so that clients can maintain control over their lives in the event of their incapacity. Individuals should declare their wishes in legal written documents and appoint someone they trust to handle their affairs and make medical decisions for them in the event that they are unable to do so. The living will and health care proxy enable persons who have suffered a catastrophic illness to direct their care and treatment through medical directives executed prior to their illness by appointing spouses, children, or other trusted persons to act as agent(s).

The elder law professional should be familiar with all types of powers of attorney that, when executed, will enable their clients to have their affairs conducted during the course of an illness or incapacity. Clients can direct and control the distribution of their assets after death by use of the last will and testament, revocable trusts, and other testamentary instruments. But what happens if a client should become ill without the benefit of having these documents in place? One cannot look to the spouse of the ill person if the marital partner has not been given any legal authority to act. Contrary to popular thinking, a spouse or child does not have any such authority solely because of marital or filial standing. They will also not have access to medical information. This is especially true under the new federal privacy laws, especially the Health Insurance Portability and Accountability Act of 1996 (HIPAA).

JUDICIAL INTERVENTION

If an individual fails to plan, judicial intervention may become necessary. In medical decision making, a family member, hospital, or nursing home administrator must petition the court in order to be granted the right to make substituted judgments for the incapacitated person. In financial matters, for example, when assets must be sold in order to finance a catastrophic illness and to support the family during this period of crisis, a family member, or other interested party, must petition the court in order to be granted the right to handle the financial and business matters of the incapacitated person. The procedure of petitioning the court for the appointment of a **guardian** over the person and the property of an incapacitated person is known as a *guardianship proceeding*. In certain states, they are *conservatorship proceedings*.

The court could appoint two separate guardians, one guardian over the person who is responsible for making decisions involving personal affairs, *e.g.,* medical, housing, etc., and another over financial affairs. Alternately, the court could appoint the same person to handle all matters. The guardianship can be unlimited, covering every aspect of the wards' life, or limited to certain matters, *e.g.,* financial. The person over whom a guardianship is judicially imposed is known as the ward or the incapacitated person.

Ultimately, a spouse, other family member, close friend, or business associate may be appointed guardian, but the procedure can be costly, time consuming, and emotionally draining, cause extensive delay in handling pressing matters, and interrupt the flow of income to the family and the ill person. It can also strip the ill individual of all dignity, self-respect, and independence, suspend some or all of their civil rights, and make private affairs a matter of public record.

Thus, judicial intervention should be considered only when there is absolutely no other alternative.

Guardian/ Conservator

An individual who has been vested with power by a court of complete jurisdiction and charged with the duty of taking care of a person and managing that individual's property and personal rights. The person who is the subject of a guardianship has been determined to be incapable of handling his or her own affairs.

SCENARIO

Client (John) sets up an appointment to discuss his brother's affairs. During the initial interview, he discloses the following facts:

John's brother Tom is 72 years old, never married, and lives alone in the one-family house in which Tom grew up and which Tom inherited 20 years ago from their deceased mother. Tom is retired and receives a pension from a state agency that employed him as an auditor. He has no children. Tom's next of kin are his brother John and his other brother Louis, who is an incompetent Medicaid recipient, confined to an out-of-state nursing home. There is a predeceased brother, Arnold, who left two surviving children, Jane and Warren.

Tom never executed a power of attorney, health care proxy, living will, or designation of guardian, though he did execute a last will and testament, a copy of which John produces at the interview (John stated that the original will, the deed to the house, and all of Tom's other papers are locked in a safe deposit box to which only Tom has access). John also produced a list of Tom's assets as follows:

1. *The one-family house in his name only, value $200,000, balance of $40,000 due on the mortgage.*
2. *Two bank accounts in trust for each of his two surviving brothers, each in the sum of $20,000.*
3. *Series E U.S. savings bonds bought between 1955 and 1960, all of which have matured, valued at approximately $80,000, including interest and face value.*
4. *Common stock in General Electric, 500 shares, and 250 shares of ITT, all of which are held jointly in Tom's name and that of his deceased father.*

5. A 1990 Oldsmobile, title in Tom's name, value $1,000.

6. A $25,000 life insurance policy naming his predeceased mother as primary benefi-
ciary and his predeceased father as substitute beneficiary. The cash surrender value
$7,500.

Tom never planned for a catastrophic illness. But three weeks prior to the initial interview,
Tom, unfortunately, suffered a severe stroke. Tom is aphasic, paralyzed on the left side, on
a feeding tube, and ready to be discharged from the hospital to a nursing home.

John wants to know what to do next. He asks the following questions:

1. How will the household and medical bills get paid?

2. Who will pay them and handle the other financial affairs?

3. Because Tom will probably never go back home, can the house be sold? Who will
handle the sale and execute the deed and other transfer documents necessary to close
title?

4. Because Tom's brother Louis, who has been declared incompetent, is the named executor in Tom's will and there is no named substitute, who will be in charge of Tom's estate
when Tom dies?

5. How can access to Tom's safe deposit box be gained?

6. Who will make medical decisions for Tom?

This case is typical of those that the elder law team often faces. It usually results in the
institution of a guardianship proceeding and the ultimate court appointment of a guardian.
Unfortunately, this is the only solution available.

This entire legal nightmare could have and should have been avoided if only Tom had
done some simple planning. He should have executed a durable power of attorney, health care
proxy, living will, and advance designation of guardian. If he had visited an elder law attorney, the counselor would have recommended that Tom execute these documents. Tom would
have been further advised to remove the name of his deceased parents from all securities and
to remove his incompetent brother as the executor of his will. He would have updated his
will, naming a new executor and a substitute executor. He would have made specific provisions for his surviving relatives. But this was not done, so we will now see how a guardianship functions.

Today, every state, territory, and the District of Columbia has passed legislation permitting guardianships and/or conservatorships. There is currently a trend to use **limited
guardianships**, which attempt to maintain some semblance of dignity and independence
for the incapacitated person. The court, using judicial discretion, gives the guardian only
those limited powers that are absolutely necessary for conducting the affairs of the incapacitated person. There is a trend to limit the duration of the guardianship, which can be
subject to the court's review every six months for the purpose of continuing or terminating the guardianship. *Guardianships should be avoided if at all possible*. This is a basic
premise to which every elder law attorney should adhere.

In commencing a guardianship proceeding, the primary concern is to select the
proper venue. The *venue* is the county where the incapacitated person lives, or it may be
the county where the incapacitated person is confined. *Jurisdiction* gives the court with a
venue the right to act and to render valid legal decisions. Once the venue is determined, the
petitioner, a person or institution who desires to initiate a guardianship proceeding, will

**Limited
Guardianship**
Guardianship whereby
the court limits the
powers of the guardian
to those powers that are
absolutely necessary for
conducting the affairs of
the incapacitated person.

prepare documents called *pleadings*, which must first be filed in the court and then served upon the following parties:

1. The alleged incapacitated person
2. The director-administrator of the facility where the alleged incapacitated person resides
3. All next of kin who could inherit from the alleged incapacitated person, and any other persons or agencies who may be designated pursuant to state law

Jurisdiction is obtained once all the above parties are properly served and affidavits of service are filed with the court.

Initial Pleading

Order to Show Cause

In most states, the proceeding is commenced by petition and order to show cause. The order, once signed by the court, appoints a court evaluator, usually an attorney or social worker, whose function is to serve as the "eyes and ears" of the court. The evaluator's task is to evaluate the situation and recommend to the court whether the appointment of a guardian is appropriate. The evaluator will testify at the hearing about his or her findings. The court may also appoint an attorney-ad-litem to represent the proposed ward. The ward may also obtain his own counsel to contest this proceeding. The petitioner and proposed ward cannot be represented by the same attorney because their interests are adverse to one another.

Petition

The petition must accompany the order to show cause and contain the following information:

1. Name and address of petitioner and relationship, if any, to the incapacitated person.
2. Next of kin of the incapacitated person.
3. Jurisdiction and venue.
4. Present medical and mental status. A medical report or affidavit from a physician who has recently examined the alleged incapacitated person is usually attached to the petition as an exhibit. This report must indicate that the alleged incapacitated person is in need of a guardian due to the inability to manage his or her own personal and/or financial affairs. In addition, the report must contain a diagnosis and a prognosis as to the duration of incapacitation.
5. Statement of all assets belonging to the alleged incapacitated person, including cash, stocks, bonds, real estate, etc.
6. Statement containing income per annum and its sources, *e.g.,* Social Security, VA benefits, pensions, dividends, rent, etc.
7. Statement regarding the transfer of any assets by the alleged incapacitated person within the most recent 36 months.

8. Statement as to whether the alleged incapacitated person (AIP) has executed a last will and testament, a durable power of attorney, or a medical power of attorney.
9. Statement of qualifications of the petitioner to become guardian.
10. Statement of ownership of safe deposit box by the incapacitated person.
11. Duration of guardianship applied for—temporary or permanent?
12. Proposed plan of anticipated guardianship.

Hearing

The order to show cause gives notice of the hearing to all necessary parties, including the alleged incapacitated person. The presence of the alleged incapacitated person at the hearing may be waived if the court decides that he or she will not be able to understand the proceedings. Bedside or institutional hearings can be held if deemed appropriate by the court. The court evaluator testifies as to his or her findings and makes a recommendation. The petitioner testifies as to the following:

1. The necessity for the appointment of a guardian
2. The known assets of the AIP
3. The duration of the requested guardianship plan
4. The guardian's willingness to serve in that fiduciary capacity

The petition can be contested. AIPs can retain counsel and claim that a guardianship is not appropriate. In some states appointment of counsel for the proposed ward is required by law. For example, if the family is merely trying to gain control of her assets and put her into a facility against her will, the AIP can produce expert medical testimony to support her position that she does not require the appointment of a guardian. The court may require medical or psychiatric testimony. Testimony may reveal that she only needs a limited guardianship. In a contested proceeding, each side has the right to call other witnesses to establish their respective cases. Acquaintances, bankers, employees—people who have come into daily contact with the AIP—are excellent witnesses. This can result in a full-scale trial. The court makes a decision. If it decides in favor of a guardianship, the court will sign an order authorizing a named guardian to act. The order will contain the following:

1. A list of all powers granted/transferred to the guardian that determine the scope of the guardian's power
2. The duration of the guardianship
3. An amount of the guardian's bond, usually based on twice the value of the assets of the incapacitated person
4. A provision for the payment of fees to the petitioner's attorney, court evaluator, attorney-ad-litem, and examining doctor
5. The due date of the initial guardian's report, often within 90 days of appointment; the due date of the annual accounting required to be filed by the guardian, usually due 90 days after the end of the calendar year
6. If the court rules that there was an inappropriate gift or transfer during incapacity without adequate consideration, the court will sign an order requiring the transfer of property back to the incapacitated person. Check local guardianship statutes.

IN RE GUARDIANSHIP & CONSERVATORSHIP OF HARTWIG
656 N.W.2d 268 (Neb.App. 2003)

HANNON, Judge.

INTRODUCTION

Amelia Hartwig's grandson, Mick Hartwig, filed a petition requesting that he be appointed guardian and conservator of Amelia's estate. John Hartwig, Amelia's attorney in fact and adult son, objected to the proceedings. The county court found that a guardian and conservator needed to be appointed for Amelia, and it appointed Mick. John appeals, alleging that there was not clear and convincing evidence that a guardian or conservator needed to be appointed for Amelia, since he was her attorney in fact, nor was there evidence that he had wasted or dissipated assets so as to warrant appointing a guardian or conservator and bypassing his priority for appointment. The evidence shows Amelia to have few assets, and her durable power of attorney gives John a broad grant of power such that the appointment of a conservator and a guardian is unnecessary. The evidence does not support a finding that John wasted or dissipated Amelia's assets, and we find that John is a suitable and proper person to continue acting as Amelia's attorney in fact. We therefore conclude that the evidence does not disclose the need for the county court's appointment of a guardian and conservator for Amelia. Accordingly, we reverse, and remand with direction to dismiss the proceedings.

BACKGROUND

For most of their lives, Amelia and her husband lived together in their home in Scottsbluff, Nebraska. John, one of their sons, spent the majority of his days from around 1988 to January 1998 visiting and caring for his parents. Amelia and her husband had three other children: Larry Hartwig, Don Hartwig, and Caroline Hughes (Caroline). The evidence showed Caroline and John have a strained and tenuous relationship. Caroline lives in Arizona, but the other children, along with Mick, Larry's son, all reside in Scottsbluff.

In a durable power of attorney dated December 17, 1992, Amelia appointed John as her attorney in fact. The document gives John a broad grant of powers, including but not limited to the power to manage Amelia's affairs; to acquire and dispose of any real or personal property; to open, deposit into, withdraw from, and close any bank accounts; to collect, withdraw, and receive any moneys owing; to add or remove any contents of safe deposit boxes; to apply for and receive any government, insurance, and retirement benefits to which Amelia may be entitled; to employ professionals to render services for and to Amelia and to pay the reasonable fees and compensation of such persons for their services; to give consent for medical treatment to be performed; and to prepare, sign, and file tax returns of all kinds and claims for refunds.

The durable power of attorney contains a clause that states: "If it becomes necessary to appoint a Conservator of my Estate or Guardian of my person, I nominate the following: JOHN E. HARTWIG." The power of attorney stated that it could only be revoked by

(1) the execution by Amelia of a subsequent durable power of attorney, (2) the recordation of her express written revocation, or (3) the lawful revocation by the conservator of her estate. Another clause states that the power shall not be affected by Amelia's disability or incapacity and that the power may be accepted and relied upon by anyone to whom it is presented until that person receives written notice of revocation by Amelia or a conservator of her estate or until that person has actual knowledge of Amelia's death. There is no evidence that Amelia revoked this power of attorney.

On December 3, 1997, Amelia and her husband conveyed their home to John, subject to a joint life estate in the grantors, via a quitclaim deed for $1 "and other good and valuable consideration." John recorded the deed on December 5. At the time of trial, the value of the house was $45,000 to $50,000. Amelia continued living in the home until January 23, 1998, and her husband lived in it until June 2, 2000. Since June 2000, no one has occupied the home, and no one has asserted that the house should be rented. The evidence suggested that the personal property of Amelia and her late husband remained in the house, since John testified that he did not distribute any of his father's personal property, and when asked if such property was still in the house, John testified, "Everything is the same as always." John has continued to pay utilities on the residence from Amelia's accounts.

Amelia was placed in the Heritage Health Care Center (Heritage) in Gering, Nebraska, in 1998, because according to John, her doctor said that John "was unable to take care of her because every time she fell, she broke a bone and she would have to go to a nursing home to recuperate." Her husband was moved into Heritage on June 2, 2000, and he died on February 22, 2001. Virginia Nolan, director of nursing at Heritage, testified that she saw Amelia a minimum of four times a week and that Amelia's medical needs were being cared for. Carol Hintergardt, Heritage's administrator, said that all of Amelia's financial matters with regard to Heritage have been adequately cared for by John since January 1998. Heritage is paid $386 a month from Amelia's account.

Amelia's checking account, for the period ending October 12, 2001, showed that she had an ending balance of $4,503.26. Amelia received $436 per month from Social Security. Amelia's "Interest Checking" account for the period ending September 27, 2001, showed a balance of $3,064.12. The house was Amelia's only asset other than this money in bank accounts.

On or about August 15, 2001, Mick submitted a verified petition in the county court for Scotts Bluff County, alleging that 93-year-old Amelia was incapacitated due to advanced age and senility, and he requested to have a guardian and conservator appointed for Amelia. John contested the action.

A hearing was held on November 8, 2001. John testified that he would be 70 years old in December and that he visited Amelia at Heritage daily. Mick is a 33-year-old teacher at Gering Junior High. Mick testified that prior to the time Amelia went to Heritage, he saw her on average once or twice a week. He guessed that he saw her five or six times in each of the years 1998, 1999, and 2000.

Gail Reznor, an ombudsman for the State of Nebraska, met with Amelia at John's request. Reznor testified that she had asked if John took care of Amelia's needs and that Amelia had said, "'Yes, he's always taken care of me.'" Reznor further testified that she had asked if Amelia would prefer John or Mick to be her guardian and that Amelia had said "'John.'" Reznor testified that the staff at Heritage told her that John took care of Amelia's health care needs and that he always paid the bill on time. Reznor opined that John was adequately caring for Amelia.

Power of Attorney

As stated above, John was appointed as Amelia's attorney in fact in 1992. John testified that the power of attorney was prepared by an attorney. John's father was ill and that social services told John that he should take care of things, including putting his father in a nursing home and signing a power of attorney. John testified that he was chosen to be Amelia's attorney in fact because he was there to help his parents.

John testified that he did not use the power of attorney to have his name placed on Amelia's bank accounts or to sign checks. He testified that he had never used the durable power of attorney to sell any property or make any gifts to third parties from his parents' assets.

John testified that his parents' mental condition was fine in December 1997. Nolan, director of nursing at Heritage, testified that Amelia recognized John and his wife, Gloria Hartwig, when they visited Amelia at Heritage.

Quitclaim Deed

John testified that Amelia requested Denton to prepare a quitclaim deed but that John was not present when that request was made. John testified that Amelia told him, "'You're the only one that cares about and comes to take care of us.' . . . 'So you get the home.'

Visitation of Amelia

Nolan, director of nursing at Heritage, testified that she saw Amelia and John together daily, that they were very happy together, and that she could see Amelia smile and brighten when John arrived. Nolan has never had a problem contacting John and testified that she saw him as much as she saw Amelia. Nolan did not know Mick and did not recognize him as a frequent visitor of Amelia. Hintergardt, administrator at Heritage, saw Amelia usually around 5 days a week. She said that John visited Amelia almost every afternoon. Hintergardt was not aware of ever seeing Mick at Heritage.

County Court's Order

In a journal entry, the trial court ordered, considered, adjudged, and decreed (1) that Amelia is an incompetent person, (2) that the appointment of a guardian and conservator for Amelia is necessary, (3) that Mick is a suitable and proper person to become guardian and conservator, (4) that persons with a higher priority for appointment are passed over, and (5) that John's authority under the durable power of attorney is terminated.

ASSIGNMENTS OF ERROR

John alleges, summarized, that the court erred (1) in finding that a guardian and conservator needed to be appointed for Amelia since he was her attorney in fact and (2) in bypassing the statutory priorities in making that appointment.

John also assigned error to the court's allowing into evidence allegations of conduct which preceded the durable power of attorney, which allegations he asserts should not be considered by the court in a hearing on conservatorship or guardianship. John's brief did not contain an argument regarding this assigned error. Errors assigned but not argued will not be addressed. *Harris v. Harris*, 261 Neb. 75, 621 N.W.2d 491 (2001).

STANDARD OF REVIEW

An appellate court reviews probate cases for error appearing on the record made in the county court. *In re Guardianship & Conservatorship of Donley*, 262 Neb. 282, 631 N.W.2d 839 (2001). When reviewing a judgment for errors appearing on the record, the inquiry is whether the decision conforms to the law, is supported by competent evidence, and is neither arbitrary, capricious, nor unreasonable. *In re Conservatorship of Anderson*, 262 Neb. 51, 628 N.W.2d 233 (2001).

ANALYSIS

The power of a court to appoint a guardian is provided in Neb.Rev.Stat. § 30-2620 (Cum.Supp.2002). In summary, § 30-2620 provides that the court may appoint a guardian if it is satisfied by clear and convincing evidence (1) that the person for whom a guardian is sought is incapacitated and (2) that the appointment is necessary or desirable as the least restrictive alternative available for providing continuing care or supervision of the person alleged to be incapacitated. The statute goes on to provide for the appointment of a limited guardianship unless the court finds by clear and convincing evidence that a full guardianship is necessary.

Neb.Rev.Stat. § 30-2630(2) (Reissue 1995) provides for the appointment of a conservator. It provides that the appointment of a conservator may be made "in relation to the estate and property affairs of a person" if the court is satisfied by clear and convincing evidence that the person (1) is unable to manage his or her property and (2) has property which will be wasted or dissipated unless proper management is provided, or if it is necessary or desirable to obtain funds for the support of the person.

The law is clear that either a conservator or a guardian should be appointed when the need under these statutes is shown to be clear and convincing. With regard to the element justifying the appointment of the guardian and conservator, the court found only that Amelia was incompetent, not that she was incapacitated. It found that a guardian and conservator was necessary, but it did not find that the appointment of a guardian was the least restrictive alternative available for providing for Amelia's continued care and supervision. In view of the undisputed evidence showing that Amelia was being properly cared for in a nursing home, the issue of whether a guardian was needed was clearly before the court. The parties do not dispute that Amelia was unable to manage her property. The trial court found only that a conservator was necessary. It did not find that Amelia's property would be wasted or dissipated without the appointment of a conservator.

The evidence is undisputed that John was Amelia's attorney in fact under a durable power of attorney. Under the Uniform Durable Power of Attorney Act, Neb.Rev.Stat. §§ 30-2665 through 30-2672 (Reissue 1995), a durable power of attorney is not affected by disability or incapacity of the principal designating such attorney, and in the power of attorney, it is specifically provided that it should not be affected by disability or incapacity of the principal. See § 30-2665. A durable power of attorney may be withdrawn through the lawful revocation by the conservator of the estate. Section 30-2667(1) of the act provides that a guardian and conservator of a principal has the same power to revoke a power of attorney as the principal would have if he or she were not disabled or incapacitated. We find nothing that gives the trial court authority to terminate the power of attorney as part of the appointment of a guardian or conservator, but, rather, § 30-2667(1) gives that authority to the guardian and conservator. This is not to say that an appropriate court might not have the authority to cancel the power of attorney upon the grounds of fraud, undue influence, et cetera, as it could with any other document.

In Mick's brief, he argues that since John did not use the power of attorney, it should not give him any authority. It is clear that most powers of attorney are probably not used because the need to use it does not arise. The statute provides for the termination of the power of attorney. There is no statutory provision for termination of a power of attorney by reason of lack of use, nor does Mick cite any authority to support that argument.

Under § 30-2667(2), the principal may nominate, by a durable power of attorney, a conservator or guardian and the court shall make the appointment of the person so nominated except for good cause or disqualification. Neb.Rev.Stat. § 30-2627 (Cum.Supp.2002) provides criteria for who is disqualified and who has a priority to act as a guardian, and Neb.Rev.Stat. § 30-2639 (Cum.Supp.2002) provides criteria for who is disqualified and who has a priority to be appointed a conservator. Both of these statutes give first priority to the person most recently nominated in a power of attorney or a durable power of attorney. John clearly has the right to be appointed the guardian and conservator unless he was disqualified or good cause was shown. The court made no finding that John was disqualified.

The first question is really whether, in view of Amelia's proper care in a nursing home, her limited assets, and the existence of a durable power of attorney, there is any need for a guardian or conservator. In statutory terms, the questions are whether there was clear and convincing evidence that a guardianship is necessary or desirable as the least restrictive alternative to providing for Amelia's care and supervision and whether Amelia's assets would be wasted or dissipated if a conservator is not appointed. In view of the undisputed evidence of John's close attention to his mother and that Amelia is being cared for in the usual manner which elderly and infirm persons are cared for in our society, there simply is no evidence that she is not being properly cared for or that she would be better cared for if someone other than John possessed the power to care for her.

In statutory terms, a conservator should be appointed if the protected person's property will be dissipated or wasted unless proper management is provided. To be blunt, this question comes down to whether there is a reasonable basis for a finding that John will mismanage his mother's limited assets. Mick argues that John wasted Amelia's assets by participating in deeding the house to himself and by using her money to pay the utilities and expenses on a house that he owned. This statement is factually incorrect. There is no evidence that he participated in deeding the house to himself, and the record is clear that he does not own the house, but owns a remainder interest subject to Amelia's life estate. There is evidence that John was paying certain bills for Amelia's home from Amelia's bank account. The payment by a power of attorney of the expenses of a home in which the principal has a life estate and where the principal's personal property is kept is not a dissipation of that person's assets. Amelia still had a life estate in the home, and her personal property was apparently kept therein. There is no evidence which shows it would have been in Amelia's interest to rent the house, and Mick does not argue that John should have rented the house. Since the evidence shows that Amelia was not living in the house and clearly had the right to rent it, at first blush that question arose to us. However, upon reflection, we realize that anyone vaguely familiar with the treatment of the homestead of an aged person on some form of public assistance would not presume that John should be renting the house. The lack of evidence on this issue does not amount to proof that John is breaching his fiduciary duty by not renting the house.

In our society, a great many people can expect to live to an age where they cannot expect to be able to manage their property or affairs or even their persons. A person approaching the age for the need of assistance with these things is allowed to name the persons who will provide for such assistance, and the Uniform Durable Power of Attorney Act was obviously intended to facilitate that right. The act provides that without good cause or disqualification, an elderly person cannot be deprived of the services of a validly appointed attorney in fact. Some of the witnesses testified that their complaints against John were that he would not supply them with information about Amelia's health and did not consult them in making certain decisions. We find nothing in the law that gives the extended family such a right to information about the health of the person, nor do we find any authority for the proposition that an attorney in fact under a power of attorney has the duty to consult the extended family on such issues. The extended family members, of course, have the right to visit that aged person.

CONCLUSION

The evidence shows without dispute that Amelia's interests are being served by John in his capacity as her attorney in fact and that the durable power of attorney gave him the powers that a guardian and conservator would have. Therefore, we conclude as a matter of law that the appointment of a guardian and conservator for Amelia was unnecessary, and we reverse, and remand with direction to dismiss the proceedings.

REVERSED AND REMANDED WITH DIRECTION TO DISMISS.

APPLICATION OF LICHTENSTEIN

646 N.Y.S.2d 94 (N.Y.A.D. 1 Dept. 1996)

MURPHY, Presiding Judge.

Edda Wogelt, a 93-year-old widow of independent means and self-reliant inclination, resided alone in an apartment on Manhattan's Upper West Side until May 1995. At that time, complaining of dizziness, she was admitted to Mount Sinai Hospital. Following consultation with officials from Mount Sinai, Jonathan David Bachrach, an attorney who had drafted Ms. Wogelt's will two years before and upon whom she had thereafter relied for the performance of various minor services, arranged for her admission to the Mosholu Parkway Nursing Home in the Bronx (Mosholu).

In July 1995, petitioner Hanna Lichtenstein, Wogelt's second cousin by marriage, commenced this proceeding, pursuant to Mental Hygiene Law Article 81, seeking to be appointed as guardian of Ms. Wogelt's person and property. The petition alleged that Ms. Wogelt was incapacitated and should be moved to an Orthodox Jewish nursing home in Monsey, New York, in order to satisfy her religious needs and place her close to petitioner. Petitioner's counsel on this petition was Attorney Bachrach.

The court-appointed evaluator presented an affirmation making general observations about Ms. Wogelt's medical condition, noting her financial indebtedness to Mosholu, and expressing some concerns that Attorney Bachrach, having provided various services for Ms. Wogelt in the past, might be acting under a conflict of interest as petitioner's attorney. The evaluator recommended further medical examination "and, possibly, appointment of counsel for [Ms. Wogelt]". On November 23, the evaluator filed a second affirmation with the court, expressing his conclusions that Ms. Wogelt, though suffering from a hearing impediment, was capable of choosing her own residence and appeared satisfied at Mosholu; Ms. Wogelt disliked and distrusted petitioner; there were inconsistencies in the medical opinions of Mosholu staff as to whether Ms. Wogelt suffered from Alzheimer's disease or was able to manage her finances.

At a hearing held at Mosholu on December 1, 1995, the court heard testimony from Dr. Benjamin Rudner, the consulting psychiatrist at Mosholu, that Ms. Wogelt was suffering "mild to moderate dementia"; she was able to recognize and greet people in an appropriate fashion; she was able to communicate in writing, though her deafness impeded oral communication; she had an awareness of her financial situation.

Additional evidence adduced at the hearing included testimony by Helen Sicker, director of social work at Mosholu, that Ms. Wogelt was able to dress, perform light housework in her room, socialize with other residents, participate in religious services, and perform other simple domestic activities. The court evaluator reported, inter alia, his conclusions that Ms. Wogelt did not require appointment of an attorney or a broadly empowered guardian of the person, but did require some assistance in managing her finances. The record also indicates that, after arranging Ms. Wogelt's admission to Mosholu, Attorney Bachrach had received and inventoried valuables from Ms. Wogelt's apartment and maintained them in a safe at his office; he had arranged to have Ms. Wogelt's mail forwarded to his office, in his words, in order to "keep in touch with any important developments and help her with those;" he received seven blank checks signed by Ms. Wogelt, and used six of those checks to pay various bills on her behalf.

In an order and judgment (one paper) entered on or about January 9, 1996, the hearing court, concluding that Ms. Wogelt "has functional limitations which necessitate[ ] [help] with her property management", declined to appoint a guardian of the person, and appointed an independent third party, Marion Stone, as guardian of Ms. Wogelt's property.

Petitioner appealed, arguing that the lower court failed to comply with various requirements of MHL Article 81 and failed to justify its award of fees. Ms. Wogelt, ably represented by Mental Hygiene Legal Services on appeal, has joined in several of petitioner's appellate claims.

By its express terms, Article 81 of the Mental Hygiene Law has as its purpose the establishment of "a guardianship system which is appropriate to satisfy either personal or property management needs of an incapacitated person in a manner tailored to the individual needs of that person, which takes in account the personal wishes, preferences and desires of the person, and which affords the person the greatest amount of independence and self-determination and participation in all the decisions affecting such person's life" (MHL § 81.01). Consistent with this purpose, the article provides that, upon commencement of a proceeding by a qualified party pursuant to MHL § 81.06, the court must undertake a detailed analysis, on the record, of the physical, mental, and financial health of the person alleged to be incapacitated. Although the trial court acted with fairness and acuity in this case, it failed to meet several of the specific and significant statutory requirements in the conduct of its analysis. Consequently, we reverse, and remand this matter for a new hearing.

We note initially that the court evaluator in this matter failed properly to perform the duties set forth in Mental Hygiene Law § 81.09. The evaluator's role under article 81 is that of an independent investigator, empowered to assist the court in independently assessing the totality of circumstances affecting the person alleged to be incapacitated (AIP), determining the AIP's personal capabilities, marshalling the AIP's resources, selecting and empowering an appropriate guardian, and assuring that the due process rights of the AIP are not violated. The evaluator's duties include, inter alia, meeting with the AIP (MHL § 81.09 [c] [1]), explaining the nature and possible consequences of the proceeding and the AIP's right to counsel (MHL § 81.09[c][2]), determining whether legal counsel should be appointed for the AIP (MHL § 81.09[c][3]), interviewing the petitioner (MHL § 81.09[c][4]), and issuing a written report and recommendations to address a lengthy list of specific questions and issues set out in the statute (MHL § 81.09[c][5]). In the matter at bar, the evaluator's investigation and recommendations failed to perform adequately several of the most crucial of these duties, including the personal assessment of Ms. Wogelt's wishes, recommendation on the appointment of counsel, interview with petitioner, report of Ms. Wogelt's physical and financial condition, and analysis of Ms. Wogelt's appreciation of her own limitations. While we do not today hold that an inadequate evaluator's report, standing alone, is sufficient grounds for reversal of a disposition issued after a full and fair hearing, we note that the evaluator's investigatory duties are a crucial aspect of an expeditious article 81 proceeding, and should not be lightly forsaken.

A more critical error in this case was the court's failure to appoint counsel on behalf of Ms. Wogelt. Article 81 requires the court to hold a hearing (MHL § 81.11[a],

Accordingly, the order and judgment of the Supreme Court, Bronx County entered on or about January 9, 1996, which denied petitioner's application for appointment as guardian for the person and property of Edda Wogelt, appointed a third person as guardian of Ms. Wogelt's property, and awarded attorney's fees, should be reversed, on the law, without costs, and the matter remanded for a new hearing.

Order and judgment, Supreme Court, Bronx County, entered on or about January 9, 1996, reversed, on the law, without costs, and the matter remanded for a new hearing.

WALLACH, RUBIN, and WILLIAMS, J. J., concur.

Duties of the Guardian

The guardian's primary responsibility is to manage all of the incapacitated person's assets, to pay bills, and to preserve assets. This management is done in the following ways:

1. The guardian can request the court's permission to make gifts that take advantage of the annual gift exclusion of $11,000 (as of 2002) per donee (split marital gift, $22,000 per donee) and the unified credit of $1,000,000 (as of 2002), and file federal and state gift tax returns to that effect.

2. Many courts are beginning to permit guardians to do financial planning for their wards, including complex estate planning in order to decrease inheritance tax, subject to the court's approval. The guardian may even transfer the ward's assets into an existing irrevocable trust, thereby making the ward eligible for entitlement programs such as Medicaid. As part of Medicaid planning, courts are also allowing guardians to create **special needs trusts** to preserve the assets of the ward. A special needs trust is a trust established for the benefit of a disabled person. The trustee is authorized to use the assets for the beneficiary, but only to the extent that it will not adversely affect the beneficiary's eligibility for public benefits, such as Medicaid.

3. The guardian can petition the court for the power to transfer real property from the incapacitated person to an adult child of the incapacitated person who has been living in the incapacitated person's home for two or more years and who has assisted the incapacitated person during the past two years. This transfer, permitted by Medicaid, makes the residence exempt as a Medicaid resource. Some judges will permit this transfer under certain circumstances, if state law allows it.

4. The guardian can arrange for the sale of the incapacitated person's real property, subject to the court's approval. In some states, this requires the filing of a separate petition with the court. After the sale, the guardian must report back to the court as to the receipt of the proceeds. Then the court directs the distribution of proceeds and approval of brokers' fees and legal fees.

5. There are ongoing duties such as an annual accounting and inventory.

The attorney who filed the initial guardianship proceeding on behalf of the petitioner is entitled to compensation for services rendered in connection with the proceeding. The court will set the fee based on the filing of an affidavit itemizing professional services rendered and in accordance with court standards. Legal fees can also be paid privately by the family members from their own funds. Under those circumstances, most courts will not set the fee. Guardians themselves receive compensation annually for their services, usually in the amount of two percent of funds received and two percent of funds spent. This varies from state to state.

Death or Resignation of a Guardian

In the event that the guardian predeceases the incapacitated person, his or her legal representative must file a final accounting as of the date of death of the guardian. The court will then appoint a new guardian. Should the guardian resign for any reason before the guardianship is terminated by the court or the death of the incapacitated person, a final accounting must also be filed, and the court will also appoint a new guardian.

Malfeasance of the Guardian

In the event that the guardian has committed acts of malfeasance, the court has the power to remove the guardian and compel a final accounting and to appoint a new guardian, who will then be instructed by the court to file a claim with the bonding company for any loss of funds.

DISCIPLINARY COUNSEL V. CLIFTON
684 N.E.2d 33 (Ohio, 1997)

PER CURIAM.
The respondent undertook the dual roles of guardian and attorney for the guardianship of both the person and the estate of an incompetent woman who it appears had no close relatives. As the record indicates, respondent failed miserably in the performance of his duties in both roles. Over a six-year period respondent wasted his ward's considerable estate

through both negligence and design. Just as important, over those same six years, respondent failed to provide adequately for the care and comfort of his ward.

A guardian of the estate is required by R.C. 2111.14(B) to manage the estate for the best interest of the ward. The duty of management requires that the guardian attend to the assets of the ward as a prudent person would attend to his or her own assets. The record here indicates that respondent, filling the dual role of guardian and attorney to the guardian, not only allowed assets of Cawein's estate to dissipate but also appropriated funds of the estate to his own use.

A guardian of the person is required by R.C. 2111.13(A) to protect the person of the ward and to provide suitable maintenance as the amount of her estate justifies. Thus, the guardian of an elderly woman has a duty to provide care and maintenance according to her means and position in life. *Tonge v. Salisbury* (1934), 54 R.I. 170, 171 A. 372. The successor guardian found Cawein poorly dressed in a crowded, shabby room with no curtains, a broken television, and an inadequate wheelchair. Under those circumstances, respondent failed to maintain Cawein according to the means of a woman with an estate initially valued at over $500,000. The successor trustee in this case took the kind of responsible action that should have been taken by respondent.

A guardian of the person of an elderly incompetent must take steps to see that the ward, however incapacitated, has the comfort and care that he or she could afford were the ward personally able to order such care. Frankly, we find respondent's actions as the guardian of the person and estate of Cawein to be despicable and contemptuous.

As to respondent's responsibility as attorney for the guardianship, we said in *Disciplinary Counsel v. Lucey* (1984), . . . 470 N.E.2d 888, 890, "'There are few ethical breaches which impact more negatively on the integrity of the legal profession than the misuse of a client's funds.'" Recently we said, "Public trust in the legal profession is tested daily in the service provided by each individual lawyer to his or her clients. When a lawyer, who has taken responsibility for a client's papers or property, commingles client funds or dissipates that property, the lawyer not only ill serves the client but also contributes to the erosion of public trust in the profession." *Miami Cty. Bar Assn. v. Hallows* (1997), 78 Ohio St.3d 75, 77, 676 N.E.2d 517, 518. In that case and in *Cleveland Bar Assn. v. Armon* (1997), 78 Ohio St.3d 497, 678 N.E.2d 1371, we noted that the appropriate sanction for the misuse of client funds is disbarment.

In this case, unlike *Miami Cty. Bar Assn. v. Hallows*, we find no mitigating circumstances whatever. Respondent is permanently disbarred from the practice of law in Ohio. Costs taxed to respondent.

Judgment accordingly.

MOYER, C. J., and DOUGLAS, RESNICK, FRANCIS E. SWEENEY, Sr., PFEIFER, COOK, and LUNDBERG STRATTON, J. J., concur.

Termination of Guardianships by the Court

Guardianships can be terminated by the court under the following circumstances:

1. The incapacitated person recovers sufficiently to handle his or her own affairs. A petition must be filed with the court indicating said recovery. Medical proof must be submitted in the petition to substantiate the recovery.

2. The initial guardianship was limited to a specific period of time. The court will review it at the termination of that period and determine whether to renew or terminate.

3. The depletion of the incapacitated person's funds will result in the termination of the guardianship over the property; the guardianship may continue over the person.

Termination of Guardianships by the Death of the Incapacitated Person

a. The powers of the guardian are automatically terminated upon the death of the incapacitated person, but funeral expenses may be paid by the guardian.
b. The guardian must immediately notify the court of the death of the ward.
c. The guardian must file a final accounting that will include the decedent's funeral expenses.
d. The court, upon review and approval of the final accounting, will determine final guardianship fees and legal fees. It will then issue an order requiring the payment of all court-awarded fees and discharging the guardian and the bonding company from further legal responsibility. In its order, the court will also require the guardian to turn over all net proceeds of the guardianship to the executor/administrator of the incapacitated person's estate.

A sample Guardianship Intake Questionnaire is located on the CD-ROM.

REVIEW QUESTIONS AND EXERCISES

1. What are the ways to avoid a guardianship proceeding?
2. Discuss situations that require guardianship proceedings. Discuss a limited guardianship and the traditional guardianship appointment.
3. Discuss the disadvantages of a guardianship proceeding.
4. Draft a petition for a guardianship proceeding.
5. What are a guardian's duties and responsibilities in a guardianship proceeding?
6. Discuss the procedure for terminating a guardianship.

CHAPTER 7
Financial and Estate Planning

PREVIEW

There are three things that are certain in life: uncertainty, death, and taxes. This chapter explores taxes by discussing how the elder law professional can help clients to do estate planning to provide for maximum inheritance for their heirs. This chapter discusses in depth financial and estate planning, focusing on the new federal estate tax legislation, state legislation, gift taxes, income taxes, and ways to avoid or minimize tax liability through the creation of life estates and trusts. Reverse mortgages are also discussed as a method of maintaining an elder person at home.

ESTATE TAX

Introduction

All of a person's assets, including real and personal property of any kind, are subject to a special tax upon the death of the owner. This tax is referred to as inheritance tax, **estate tax**, or succession tax; the terms are used interchangeably. Assets are taxed by the federal government and also by some states. The concept of estate tax is not unique to the United States; it is found in most of the Western world. Only 2 percent of the estates of people who died in 1999 were subject to federal estate tax. IRS data indicated that fewer than 100,000 estate tax returns were filed in 1999. The 3,300 largest estates, valued at more that $5 million each, paid more that 50 percent of all estate taxes collected in 1999. Thus, this tax affects a very small percentage of the population.

Estate Tax
A tax levied by the federal government or a state on the assets of a decedent as they are transferred to the heirs of the decedent.

New Tax Legislation

The federal estate tax laws were substantially changed by the Economic Growth and Tax Relief Reconciliation Act of 2001 (Act). Prior to this law, the estate and gift taxes were known as the unified credit. Estate taxes and gift taxes, were combined for a maximum credit. Under the Act, the amounts exempt from estate tax (plus gift tax) will gradually increase from $1 million to $3.5 million in 2009, before the tax is completely eliminated in 2010. The gift tax exemption however, remains at $1 million. The Act includes a "sunset" provision that returns the estate tax exemption to pre-2001 levels.

There has been a heated debate over whether Congress should pass legislation permanently repealing the estate tax. Those against a permanent repeal argue that it will cost the U.S. Treasury $55.8 billion in 2012 and $740 billion in the next 10 years, and that only the wealthiest Americans will benefit from a permanent repeal. They contend that the government needs the tax revenues the estate tax produces to cover the cost of benefits that will be demanded by the baby boomers in the decades to come. The opposition claims that it is a death tax and constitutes an unfair levy.

Estate and Gift Tax Provisions in the Economic Growth and Tax Relief Reconciliation Act of 2001

Generation-Skipping Transfer Tax (GST)
An additional federal tax imposed upon assets transferred by a donor to a donee at least two generations removed, *e.g.,* a grandparent to a grandchild.

- *Phase out of the estate.* The estate tax including the 5 percent surcharge on estates between $10 million and $17,184,000, began to decrease in 2002 and will be completely eliminated by 2010. (See Transfer Tax Exemptions and Rates on p. 129.)

- *Repeal of* **generation-skipping transfer taxes** *(GST).* This tax is generally levied upon a *direct skip*, which is defined as a transfer directly to a grandchild, or in trust for the grandchild, while the parent is living—$1 million is exempt. It will be repealed in 2010.

- *Increase in transfer tax exemption for estate taxes.* The transfer tax exemption for estate taxes gradually increased after 2002. It reaches a maximum exemption of $3.5 million in 2009 and completely disappears in 2010. (See Transfer Tax Exemptions and Rates on p. 129.)

- *Reduction in the top gift tax rate.* The top gift tax rate of 50 percent will gradually decrease until it reaches 35 percent in 2010. It will then be the same as the highest income tax rate. (See Transfer Tax Exemptions and Rates on p. 129.)

- *Gift tax transfer exemptions are increased.* The gift tax exemption increased from $675,000 in 2001 to $1 million in 2002. It will not increase any further and has not been repealed. After the repeal of the estate tax in 2010, it will be the same as the tax rates then in effect.

- *The step-up rule for inherited property will be repealed concurrent with the repeal of the estate tax law.* Under the present law, all assets in a decedent's estate are entitled to a step-up in basis to the fair market value at death or, if the executor/personal representative of the estate chooses the alternative value, at six months after the date of death (whichever results in a lower tax). When the beneficiaries of the estate sell inherited property, they will avoid capital gains tax on the appreciation that occurred prior to decedent's death.

  For example, if the decedent purchased a house for $100,000 and spent $50,000 in improvements, the cost bases for capital gains taxes would be $150,000. If it were sold during the decedent's lifetime for $300,000, the capital gain would be $150,000. If the house passed to a beneficiary as a result of death of the owner, the beneficiary's cost basis would be the fair market value on the date of death, not the original cost basis.

  Effective in 2010, this step-up in basis to fair market value will also be repealed. After 2010, the decedent's pre-death gains tax basis will be transferred to the beneficiaries. The executor/personal representative of the estate will be permitted to increase the stepped-up basis to $1.3 million plus an additional $3 million for assets that are inherited by the surviving spouse. The total step-up in basis for a surviving spouse could go as high as $4.3 million. The legislation provides that the aforementioned basis will be adjusted for inflation. These limits are also to be adjusted for built-in losses and loss carryover amounts.

- *Reporting requirements.* There will be special requirements on reporting of the tax basis of all inherited property. Clients (donors and executors/personal representatives) should be advised to keep meticulous records regarding the cost basis of assets. This law is complex and should be studied carefully.

- *Sale of principal residence.* The new law extends to beneficiaries and estates of decedents dying on or after January 1, 2002, the income tax capital gains exemption up to $250,000 gain on the sale of a principal residence (See p. 148 for further discussion.)
- *Family-owned business deduction.* The family-owned business deduction is repealed in 2004. The special deduction for qualified family-owned businesses effective under the 1997 tax reform act is repealed for estates of decedents dying after December 31, 2003.

Transfer Tax Exemptions and Rates

Year	Gift Tax Transfer Exemption	Estate and GST Tax Transfer Exemption	Highest Estate, GST, And Gift Tax Rates
2002	$1 million	$1 million	50%
2003	$1 million	$1 million	49%
2004	$1 million	$1.5 million	48%
2005	$1 million	$1.5 million	47%
2006	$1 million	$2 million	46%
2007	$1 million	$2 million	45%
2008	$1 million	$2 million	45%
2009	$1 million	$3.5 million	45%
2010	$1 million	NA	35% (gift tax only)
2011	$1 million	$1 million	50%

Estate Tax Filing Requirements

U.S. citizens who die after December 31, 2001, and who own property in the United States must file an estate tax return if the estate assets exceed $1 million, no matter how old they were, no matter where they died. Foreign residents must also file estate tax returns if their estates have assets in the United States in excess of $1 million. The estate tax return, IRS Form 706, is a highly complex document. The deadline to file the return is nine months from the date of death, but an extension for an additional six months can be obtained without any difficulty.

There are several acceptable methods of filing:

- Mail the return to the IRS using the U.S. Postal Service. The date of mailing is legally considered the date of filing.

PRACTICE TIP

All mail or correspondence to the Internal Revenue Service (IRS) should be sent via *certified mail*, return receipt requested.

- Hand-deliver the return to a local IRS office. A copy of the return should also be presented to the cashier's office to be date-stamped as proof of filing.
- Pursuant to IRS notice 97-26, IRB 1997-17,1, delivery of the return to certain private carriers will receive the same treatment as if delivered to the U.S. Postal Service. The date that the IRS Form 706 is delivered into the custody of the authorized private delivery service and entered into its electronic database, or the date that a notation is entered on the cover sheet of the delivery envelope, is considered the legal date of mailing. The acceptable private services are:

  - DHL Worldwide Express (DHL Same Day Service and DHL USA Overnight)
  - Federal Express (FedEx Priority Overnight, FedEx Standard Overnight, and FedEx 2 Day)
  - United Parcel Service (UPS Next Day Air, UPS Next Day Air Saver, UPS 2nd Day Air, and UPS 2nd Day Air A.M.)

Any filing after the expiration of the statute of limitations is considered late and subject to penalties and interest. In order to obtain an extension, the legal representative of the estate must file IRS Form 4768 requesting an extension and must also attach to the form a written statement detailing why it is not possible or is impracticable to file a return within the required nine months. The tax return must be signed by the executor or administrator of the decedent's estate, as well as by the preparer. If there is more than one legal representative, then all must sign the return.

To avoid the payment of interest and any possible penalties, the estate tax should be paid when filing the extension.[1]

Estate Defined

Gross Estate: The **gross estate** of a decedent consists of all the property owned by the decedent at the time of death, whether or not subject to probate.

Taxable Estate: The **taxable estate** is determined by subtracting allowable deductions from the gross estate.

The gross estate includes:

1. Real estate
2. Cooperative apartments
3. Condominiums
4. Stocks and bonds
5. Cash, mortgages, bank accounts
6. Life insurance
7. Jointly held assets
8. Powers of appointment
9. Annuities
10. Miscellaneous assets, *e.g.,* automobiles, boats, airplanes, art objects, jewelry, limited partnerships
11. All business interests
12. Gifts made within three years of death

Gross Estate
Any type of property, real and personal, of any kind or nature, that was owned by a decedent and will be the subject of federal estate tax.

Taxable Estate
The total assets of a decedent, minus all allowable deductions, that can be taxed by the state.

13. Gifts of:
   a. life insurance, *e.g.,* life insurance trust
   b. release of a retained life estate
   c. power to revoke a revocable trust

These gifts are all includable in the donor's estate. All gift taxes paid by decedent or spouse within three years of the death of the decedent must also be included in the gross estate.

PRACTICE TIP

When reviewing a decedent's estate, obtain all copies of gift tax returns filed within three years of the date of death.

Question 11

The estate taxpayer is entitled to receive certain deductions from the gross estate as follows:

1. Funeral expenses
2. Probate and administration fees
3. Legal fees
4. Medical expenses in connection with the decedent's last illness
5. Executor's commissions
6. Broker's commissions
7. Unlimited marital deduction for qualifying property passing to the decedent's surviving spouse
8. Losses from casualties or theft
9. Unpaid taxes of decedent
10. Unpaid debts of decedent
11. Balance on mortgages
12. Charitable bequests, *e.g.,* value of property passing to a charity, public institution, or to the federal, state, or local government
13. Tax credit for state death taxes paid
14. Credit for foreign estate taxes paid
15. Unified credit, deducted from estate tax liability
16. Credit for estate taxes paid on prior transfers under certain circumstances

Responding to Change

In response to the tax law changes, elder law professionals should:

1. Review all estate plans that have been set up for clients.
2. Review all wills and trusts that have been previously prepared for clients.
3. Make certain that all assets are set up properly to take advantage of the credit shelter trusts permitted under current and future law. The unlimited marital deduction is

continued and allows unlimited transfers upon death to a surviving spouse. One million dollars per individual taxpayer can also pass to children or other heirs before estate taxes are levied. To shelter $3 million, a testamentary credit shelter trust (bypass trust) must be created, and the $1.5 million must be transferred to this trust upon the death of the first spouse. When the second spouse dies, this $1.5 million (corpus of the credit shelter trust) will pass to the children or other heirs tax free. The second spouse to die will also be permitted to transfer $1.5 million to children or other named heirs. Thus, upon the death of the second spouse, $3 million will be transferred free of any inheritance tax; $1.5 million from the testamentary credit shelter trust and $1.5 million from the personal exemption. This exemption will increase to $3.5 million in 2009. Therefore in 2009, a married couple can shelter $7 million from estate taxes.

4. See that all wills that contain a credit shelter (bypass trust) specifying the $1.5 million exemption passing into the trust are reviewed carefully in the light of the new tax law. Disclaimer trusts may be required. This will give the surviving spouse control of the amount passing into the credit shelter trust. The full unified credit does not have to be placed in the credit shelter trust, only the portion that is disclaimed. In addition, assets being held jointly by a married couple will have to be adjusted and transferred to one or the other spouse or split in some proportion to take advantage of the increased exemptions.

5. Examine carefully ownership of small family businesses and family farms in order to take full advantage of the $3 million exemption, which could save up to $277,000 in estate taxes. Consideration should be given permitting spousal ownership of business shares, so that upon the death of the second spouse, the shares will be transferred to the children of the marriage tax free, up to the $2.6 million exemption. (This exemption will be repealed as of 2004.)

STATE DEATH TAXES

Following the lead of the federal government, many states levy an inheritance tax. In general, their *death tax* is equal to the maximum amount of federal credit allowed on the federal estate tax return (Form 706). Currently, any state inheritance tax paid by an estate is treated as a credit on the federal estate tax. Effectively, there is no additional charge against the estate for paying state death tax. Many states receive tax revenues under this procedure. The state tax credit is an amount equal to the lesser of:

1. The amount actually paid by the estate for state death tax.
2. The amount stated in the table in the Internal Revenue Code (IRC) 2011.

New Legislation

Beginning in 2002, the state inheritance tax credit is reduced by 25 percent per year until it is completely eliminated in 2005. In 2005, the estate will only be entitled to claim a federal tax deduction of the estate tax actually paid. This may result in a higher estate tax burden. The state tax credit will be fully reinstated in 2011. Many states will suffer as a result of the new law because there will be a decline in the tax revenue they receive. Legal professionals should be cognizant of the fact that states adversely effected will no doubt enact new legislation to overcome this revenue shortfall. The following chart summarizes the changes.

Year	State Death Tax Credit
2001	100% credit allowed
2002	25% reduction
2003	50% reduction
2004	75% reduction
2005	No estate tax deduction credit
2006	No estate tax deduction credit
2007	No estate tax deduction credit
2008	No estate tax deduction credit
2009	No estate tax deduction credit
2010	No estate tax deduction credit
2011	100% credit allowed

New York Estate Tax

Elder law professionals in New York have an unusual problem. The New York estate tax is based on the federal state tax credit in effect on July 22, 1998, because New York estate tax legislation does not automatically conform to federal tax laws. New York estates will continue to be subjected to a state inheritance tax up to 16 percent. Practitioners doing estate planning under the new law must consider the fact that the combined federal and state tax bracket for a New York estate after 2002 could reach 63 percent. It is hoped the New York legislature will act to change the current law.

State Inheritance Tax

Some states differentiate between residents and nonresidents in imposing inheritance tax.

> *State Domiciliary:* The resident who has a **domicile** in the state (one who makes a home for more than six months of the year and votes and files taxes in that state) is required to pay inheritance tax on all real property and personal property no matter where the assets are located.
>
> *Nondomiciliary (Nonresident):* If the decedent is a nonresident, only the real property located within the state is subject to taxation.

Domicile
A place where an individual has a fixed permanent home to which he or she always has the intention of returning when absent. An individual may have more than one residence, but only one domicile.

States vary regarding the imposition of inheritance tax. The elder law professional should check local tax codes for specific regulations.

The Sponge Tax ("Pick-Up" Tax)

The sponge tax is a typical inheritance tax imposed by some states (*i.e.,* New York and Florida). The tax will be paid to the state, but that exact amount will be deducted from the actual tax due to the federal government. The decedent's estate pays no additional tax because of the sponge tax.

GIFT TAX

Financial planning is essential for elder law clients. They should consult with their lawyers and accountants to ensure that they have sufficient assets to provide for their spouses and families after death. Estate and gift taxes are imposed upon assets transferred during lifetime or after death. Clients naturally want to find legal methods to minimize or to even avoid these enormous taxes, which could amount to as much as 70 percent of their assets when federal and state taxes are combined. They worked hard to accumulate assets during their lifetime, paid income and capital gain tax on their assets over the years, and now they want to preserve these assets for their families.

Today, a major part of the elder law practice is devoted to preservation of assets for the elderly of all income levels and to estate and gift tax planning for elderly individuals with substantial net worth. Medicaid asset preservation planning is very important for clients who fall into the middle and lower income brackets, in order to qualify them for benefits from the Medicaid entitlement program.

The elder law professional must have a basic understanding of how the federal and state gift tax laws operate because every asset transfer has tax implications and impacts upon the Medicaid eligibility of the donor.

New Federal Tax Legislation

The Economic Growth and Tax Relief Reconciliation Act of 2001 gradually reduces the estate tax and generating-skipping tax until they are completely repealed in 2010. The law does not repeal the gift tax. Effective January 1, 2002, the lifetime gift tax exemption for U.S. citizens and residents was increased to $1 million from the 2001 level of $675,000. Since then, the gift tax credit has remained at that level. In 2010, the gift tax rate is then set at the highest income tax rate in effect at the time. It appears unlikely that Congress will ever repeal the gift tax. (See p. 139 for a discussion of the unified credit.)

Transfers (Gifts)

A transfer is a change of ownership, operation, and control of any type of asset, *e.g.,* cash, securities, real estate, personal property, from a donor (transferor) who is the current legal owner to a donee (transferee), the recipient new owner. The donee may be an individual, a corporation, a charitable foundation, a trust, or any other entity. The donor, in order to make an effective transfer that would not be questioned at a later date by governmental authorities such as the Internal Revenue Service or Medicaid or by potential heirs, must be competent at the time of the transfer. Donors must be fully aware of the nature and consequences of their acts at the time of the transfer. A donor who has carefully engaged in financial planning would also have executed a durable power of attorney with specific gifting powers in order to make an effective transfer that could not be successfully challenged at a later date.

Many situations have occurred wherein a durable power of attorney has been executed without specific gifting powers and the donor's agent has made a transfer in order to reduce income tax, inheritance taxes, or to qualify for Medicaid. The IRS has challenged these gifts on the grounds that the agent has acted in an ***ultra vires*** capacity (without authority) and has subsequently included the gifts in the gross taxable estate of the deceased donor, making the gifts ineffective for estate tax planning purposes. Medicaid, as it becomes more aggressive, may also challenge these transfers, which could result in a denial of Medicaid benefits. In both instances, it is recommended that the donor have medical documentation to substanti-

Ultra Vires Acts
Acts beyond the scope of the powers granted to an agent. The agent acts without the authority to bind the principal. The act may not be binding upon the principal.

ate competency at the time of the transfer of assets or execution of the durable power of attorney.

SCENARIO

A man, married for the second time, with most of his business and personal assets in his own name, has a stroke, leaving him incompetent. He has not executed a durable power of attorney.

When the donor is incompetent and no durable power of attorney has been executed, guardianship proceedings may be used for transfers, if permitted by state law. Whether Medicaid-motivated transfers can and will be approved in a guardianship proceeding is a hot issue, varying from state to state and case to case.

Once appointed, however, a guardian should attempt to obtain special permission from the court to do Medicaid asset planning and make transfers. Judicial intervention is a costly and time-consuming procedure that could be avoided with some basic estate planning.

Frequently Asked Questions

What is a gift?

A gift is a transfer of an asset for less than fair market value. Internal Revenue Service Reg. Section 2511-1(a) 1(g)(1), 2(b) defines a gift as follows:

> When a donor transfers all right, title, and interest in and to a piece of property, personal or real, to the donee, and the donee now has possession of it, the donor no longer has any power to change its disposition.

When is a gift complete?

A gift is complete when the donor has parted with dominion and control so as to leave the donor without any power to change its disposition.

Are gifts or transfers taxable?

Yes. The federal gift tax applies to all transfers of real or personal property, tangible or intangible, wheresoever situated in the world. For example, if a donor who is a U.S. citizen owns a parcel of real property in France and gives it to a donee who resides here in the United States, or anywhere in the world for that matter, that transfer is subject to U.S. gift tax. Some states also impose gift taxes.

Who is required to file the gift tax return?

The donor files the tax return and pays the tax.

Is a nonresident alien subject to gift tax?

Gifts made by nonresident aliens are subject to gift and generation-skipping transfer (GST) taxes for gifts of tangible property situated in the United States. Under certain circumstances, they are also subject to gift and generation-skipping taxes for gifts of intangible property. (See Section 2501(a) of the IRS Code.)

A nonresident alien who makes a gift subject to gift tax must file a gift tax return reporting:

- Gifts of future interests
- Gifts of present interest totaling more than $11,000 to any donee other than a spouse
- Outright gifts totaling more than $100,000 to a spouse who is not a U.S. citizen

What form is to be used, and where should it be filed?

IRS Form 709, which is to be filed in the same place where the donor files his or her federal income tax returns.

Can a donor obtain an extension for filing a gift tax return?

There are two methods of extending the time to file the gift tax return. Neither method extends the time to pay the gift or generation-skipping transfer (GST) taxes.

An extension of time to pay the gift or GST taxes must be requested separately. (See Regulations Section 25.6161-1 of the IRS Code.)

By Letter. The donor can request an extension of time to file a gift tax return by writing to the district director or service center for the appropriate area. The letter must explain the reasons for the delay. A letter *must* be used to request an extension of time to file a gift tax return, unless the donor is also requesting an extension to file an income tax return.

PRACTICE TIP

All correspondence and filing of returns should be done by certified mail, return receipt requested. This provides proof of mailing or filing.

By Form. Any extension of time granted for filing a calendar year federal income tax return will also extend the time to file any gift tax return. Income tax extensions are made by using IRS Forms 4868, 2688, or 2350, which have check boxes for IRS Form 709. The taxpayer may only use one of these forms to extend the time for filing a gift tax return if also requesting an extension of time to file an income tax return.

When should the gift tax return be filed?

On April 15 of the year following the gift. For example, any gifts made in the year 2003 are reportable on IRS Form 709, which must be filed by April 15, 2004.

What is the maximum federal gift tax rate?

The maximum tax rate as of 2003 is 49 percent. The rates are the same as the estate tax rates (unified rate).

What is the donee's responsibility?

The donee is not required to report the gift to the Internal Revenue Service on an income tax return and does not have to file a gift tax return. However, the donee *is* required to report any interest, distributions, etc., generated by the gift as income on the federal income tax return in the year in which the income was received. For example, a donee received a gift of 100 shares of IBM stock on December 15, 2004. The donee received the first dividend check on January 15, 2005. This and all subsequent dividends received in 2005 must be declared on the 2005 federal income tax return (and state return, if applicable), which is due for filing on April 15, 2006. The donee is not required to declare any prior dividends received by the donor. If the donee receives a cash gift and deposits it in an interest-bearing account, the donee will declare only the interest earned on the cash deposit, never the principal.

On the subsequent sale of a gift by the donee, how does the donee determine the tax basis?

The donee must first determine the value of the gifted asset as of the date that the donor obtained the asset. This can be accomplished by inspecting the donor's gift tax return, which requires the donor to report the cost basis, if available. If the return is not available and values cannot easily be obtained, as in the case of real estate or art, then the donee must obtain an appraisal fixing the value of the gift as of the date of transfer. This value is known as the **donee's tax basis**. The basic rule here is: *The donee's tax basis is the donor's tax basis at the date of transfer* (IRS Code Section 1015). If the donor transfers stock with a cost basis of $10, when the donee subsequently sells the stock for $30, the donee will be subject to a capital gains tax on the profit of $20. In the case of the sale of gifted real property, capital improvements made by the donor or donee are added to the original cost basis of the donor in the calculation of the donee tax basis. For example, if the subject of the gift is a one-family dwelling that the donor purchased for $50,000, spending an additional $25,000 on capital improvement, the donor's basis will be $75,000 at the time of gift. If the donee subsequently sells the improved one-family dwelling for $175,000, having made no further improvements, the profit of $100,000 will be subject to capital gains tax. *Remember that there is no capital gains treatment of cash gifts.*

Are transfers to trusts subject to gift taxation?

Irrevocable Trusts. Transfers to an irrevocable trust are fully taxable because the donor has given up all dominion and control of those funds.

Revocable Trusts. Transfers to revocable trusts are not subject to gift tax. They do not have to be reported because the donor has retained dominion and control over these assets and can recall them at any time.

Are gifts subject to any state taxation?

Most, but not all, states have followed the lead of the federal government and have enacted gift tax legislation. The donor's individual state's tax laws must be reviewed to ascertain the tax liability and the date of filing, which may differ from the federal filing date.

Does establishing a joint bank account create a gift tax situation?

If the donor creates a joint bank account for the donor and the donee (or similar kind of ownership by which the donor can retrieve the entire fund without the donee's consent), a gift by the donor to the donee occurs only when the donee draws on the account for his or her own benefit. The amount of the gift is the amount that the donee withdraws without any obligation to repay the donor. If the donor buys a U.S. savings bond registered as payable to him- or herself and the donee, there is a gift to the donee only when the donee redeems the bond without any obligation to account to the donor.

When must a spouse sign a gift tax return?

To have gifts and generation-skipping transfers treated as if made one-half by each spouse, one will sign the tax return and the other will sign the consent form in the tax return.

When must the consenting spouse also file a gift tax return?

If the spouses elect gift splitting, then both the donor spouse and the consenting spouse must each file separate gift tax returns, unless all the requirements of either Exception 1 or 2 below are met.

> *Exception 1.* During the calendar year:
> * Only one spouse made any gifts
> * The total value of these gifts to each third-party donee does not exceed $22,000
> * All of the gifts were of present interests

> *Exception 2.* During the calendar year:
> * Only one spouse (the donor spouse) made gifts of more than $11,000 but not more than $22,000 to any third-party donee
> * The only gifts made by the other spouse (the consenting spouse) were gifts of not more than $11,000 to third-party donees other than those to whom the donor spouse made gifts
> * All of the gifts by both spouses were of present interests

>   If either Exception 1 or 2 is met, only the donor spouse must file a return, and the consenting spouse signifies consent on that return. This return may be made on Form 709-A, United States Short Form Gift Tax Return. This form is much easier to complete than Form 709 and should be used whenever gifts to each third-party donee made by both spouses total not more than $22,000 for the year and consist entirely of present interests in tangible personal property, cash, U.S. savings bonds, or stocks and bonds listed on a stock exchange.

Are gifts to spouses reportable on IRS Form 709?

No tax return is required to be filed in connection with any gifts made to a spouse.

May a married couple file a joint gift tax return?

The IRS Code indicates that a married couple is prohibited from filing a joint gift tax return unless the spouse is not a U.S. citizen. (See below.)

GIFT AND ESTATE TAX EXEMPTIONS

Annual Exemption

Under current law, the donor is entitled to an annual gift tax exemption of $11,000 per donee for gifts of a present interest [IRC Section 2503(b)]. The gift can be made to any person, related or unrelated, to a charity, or to a trust during the calendar year. For example, a donor can give a total of $110,000 to 10 related or unrelated persons and not be subject to any gift tax or be required to file a gift tax return, provided that no one person or trust receives more than $11,000 within the calendar year. The IRS requires that the transfer be completed by the end of the taxable year. Therefore, a gift check must clear the donor's account on or before December 31, of the tax year.

Under the Taxpayer Relief Act of 1997, signed by President Clinton on August 5, 1997, the $10,000 limit was indexed to inflation starting in 1998, with increases in increments of $1,000. In 2002, it reached $11,000.

There is an unlimited gift tax exemption between married couples, *e.g.,* a wife can give her husband $10 million and pay no tax on the transfer and have no filing requirements, provided both spouses are U.S. citizens. This annual exemption is indexed to inflation and may rise as inflation occurs. In 2002, the annual gift tax exemption for spouses *who are not U.S. citizens* also rose from $100,000 to $110,000.

Gift Splitting

A donor may, with the consent of a legal spouse, split a gift so that the gift will be treated as having been made one-half by each spouse. This enables a couple to give away $22,000 per year regardless of which donor's assets are the subject of the gift. For example, a married couple can give away $220,000 to 10 persons in one year, provided no individual gift is in excess of $22,000. This type of transfer will not be considered a taxable event, and no gift tax return is required. A married couple making gifts in excess of $22,000 per donee are required to file gift tax returns.

Gift Tax Credit

The gift tax laws have changed substantially under Economic Growth and Tax Relief Reconciliation Act of 2001. For many years the estate and gift taxes have been levied under a unified credit system. The tax credit was the same, and it could be used during one's lifetime as a credit for a gift tax or for estate tax. The unified credit stops operating in 2004. In 2004 and 2005, the federal estate tax exemption increases to $1.5 million; however, for the first time, the gift tax exemption will not rise. It will remain $1 million until 2010, when the federal estate tax is repealed. The gift tax will remain in full force and effect, but the rate will be reduced to 35 percent. The $1 million exemption will also remain. The gift tax rates will continue to decline along with the estate taxes rates until 2010. See the table on New Gift Tax Rates and Exemptions.

New Gift Tax Rates and Exemptions

Year	Exemption Amount (Unified Credit)	Maximum Tax Rate
2001 (prior law)	$675,000	55%
2002	$1 million	50%
2003	$1 million	49%
2004	$1 million	48%
2005	$1 million	47%
2006	$1 million	46%
2007	$1 million	45%
2008	$1 million	45%
2009	$1 million	45%
2010	$1 million	35%

Marital Transfers (Gifts)

Unlimited transfers are permitted between legally married spouses. This provision is continued in the tax legislation of 2001. The Internal Revenue Code provides that such transfers are not subject to federal gift and estate taxation laws. With regard to the individual states, if the state has enacted gift and estate laws, it tends to follow the federal law in this regard. Marital transfers, regardless of amount, do not have to be reported in any way.

Gifts to Charitable Organizations

Gifts made to qualified charitable institutions, local state and federal governments, veterans' organizations, etc., are generally not subject to gift tax (IRC, Sec. 2522(a)). However, they may be used as deductible items on income and estate tax returns, subject to certain restrictions.

Special Gift Tax Exemption for Grandparents

1. *Education:* The IRS Code, Section 25.250-6 provides grandparents with an unlimited gift tax exemption for any tuition paid directly to educational institutions on behalf of their grandchildren. The grandchild must be a natural or *legally adopted grandchild, not a step-grandchild.* With multiple remarriages quite common among grandparents these days, situations may arise wherein one *grandparent spouse* may have insufficient funds to make such an educational gift on behalf of a natural grandchild. In that event, the other *grandparent spouse* may transfer unlimited funds to a spouse by means of the marital exemption. The natural grandparent may then pay the tuition directly to the educational institution. This exemption applies to tuition only and not to room, board, books, etc.

2. *Medical:* This unlimited gift tax exemption is also applicable where payment is made by a grandparent on behalf of a natural or adopted grandchild donee to a health care provider for medical services rendered to the said donee. Payment of medical expenses as described above, no matter the amount, is not subject to a gift tax, provided that the funds are paid directly to the health care provider (IRS Code Section 2503(E)).

Uniform Transfers to Minors Act (UTMA)

People, including grandparents, can elect to make annual gifts up to $11,000 per person, or split marital gifts of $22,000, into a custodial account for the benefit of minors. The use of this type of account avoids the necessity and cost of setting up a formal trust for the benefit of a minor.

A potential problem may arise when the minor beneficiary attains the age of 18. At that point, the beneficiary can access the account and withdraw the entire principal without accounting to any person. This could result in the money being wasted or squandered.

In a trust, the age limit to receive principal or income is totally at the discretion of the grantor of the trust. This may be the method of choice in certain circumstances, especially where it is anticipated that the gifts over a period of time will be substantial.

Life Insurance Transfers

The proceeds of a life insurance policy owned by an individual at the time of death are includable in the gross estate and are, therefore, subject to estate taxation. Life insurance transfers are an important estate planning and tax savings technique because the beneficiary of these proceeds is not required to pay any tax upon them. It is the obligation of the owner's estate. To avoid estate taxation of the proceeds of face value of the policy, the owner may transfer ownership of the policy to another individual such as a spouse or a child or to a life insurance trust, tax-free, provided that the owner (donor) survives three years from the date of transfer. If the donor does not survive the three-year period, then the gross proceeds of the policy are included in the donor's estate for estate tax purposes. It is permissible for the owner of the policy and the beneficiary to be one and the same person.

The parties of a life insurance policy are:

1. The insurer
2. One that is insured under the policy, *i.e.,* the insured
3. Beneficiary of the proceeds of the policy when the insured dies
4. The owner of the policy, who can be a trust, the insured, or a beneficiary

In other words, if a transfer of a life insurance policy is made more than three years prior to the owner's death, the proceeds of the policy are not includable in the owner's gross taxable estate. However, if a transfer of ownership of the policy falls *within* three years of the date of the owner's death, this will result in the inclusion of the proceeds in the owner's (decedent's) gross estate.

The transfer of the face value of the policy is not subject to the gift tax. However, the cash surrender value at the time of the transfer is subject to the gift tax. This is usually substantially less than the face value of the policy. If the transfer involves a term life insurance policy with no cash surrender value, there is nothing to report for gift tax purposes.

INCOME TAX AND THE ELDERLY CLIENT

Introduction

The federal personal income tax was introduced in the United States early in the 20th century. Today, it probably takes the largest cut out of most people's earnings. The tax rate is applied to all kinds of personal income including wages, self-employment income, and investment income. The tax rate as of 2004 is progressive, starting at 0 percent below $14,300 and rising to the top rate of 35 percent for income over $319,000. In determining the net amount of income that is subject to income tax, a variety of factors comes into play:

- Marital status
- Number of dependents
- Itemized deductions
- Contributions to retirement accounts (IRAs, 401(k)s, self-employment plans, etc.)

Most states also impose income taxes, except Alaska, Florida, Nevada, South Dakota, Texas, Washington, and Wyoming.

Legislation Effective 2002

The Economic Growth and Tax Relief Act of 2001 (The Act) produced tax savings to nearly all Americans. The only complication is that The Act has a sunset provision that will cause all the beneficial changes to terminate as of 2010. We must wait to see if Congress passes additional changes to eliminate this provision.

- *Tax Rate Cuts:* The Act provides for a 10 percent tax rate bracket that applies to a portion of income that was previously taxed at 15 percent. Beginning in 2002, there was a decrease in overall tax rates. See the table, Income Tax Rate Reductions.
- *Itemized Deductions:* Taxpayers will see a gradual phaseout of the familiar itemized deductions. After 2009, itemized deductions will be completely repealed.
- *Personal Exemptions:* Taxpayers will also experience the phaseout of the personal exemption. It will be totally repealed after 2009.

Income Tax Rate Reductions

Calendar Year	28% Rate Reduced to	31% Rate Reduced to	36% Rate Reduced to	39.6% Rate Reduced to
2002–2003	27%	30%	35%	38.6%
2004–2005	26%	29%	34%	37.6%
2006 and after	25%	28%	33%	35%

Filing Requirements

Regardless of age, every person must file an income tax return if gross income exceeds the total of the individual personal exemptions and the standard deductions. These last two items vary from year to year and must be checked annually to determine the necessity of filing income tax returns. Income tax returns must be filed for any year that gross income, including Social Security benefits, exceeds $7,450 for a single person or $13,400 for a married couple. Returns are to be filed between January 1 and April 15 of the year following the end of the tax year on December 31.

Extensions of time to file can automatically be obtained until August 15 (four months late) by filing Form 4868, but this is not an extension to pay tax. An estimate of the tax due should be filed with Form 4868, and a payment should be made to avoid interest charges and possible penalties. A copy of the extension issued by the IRS must be attached to the return when filed. If a taxpayer needs more time, another extension may be requested by filing Form 2688 before August 15. This form requires a valid excuse, such as missing records or illness. If the IRS consents, the taxpayer can get an extension of an additional two months. All correspondence regarding returns should be filed by certified mail, return receipt requested. (See the table, when to File a Federal Income Tax Return.)

When to File a Federal Income Tax Return

IF your filing status is . . .	AND at the end of 2003 You were* . . .	THEN file a return if your gross income** was at least . . .
Single	under 65	7,800
	65 or older	8,950
Married filing jointly***	under 65 (both spouses)	15,600
	65 or older (one spouse)	16,550
Married filing separately	any age	3,050
Head of household	under 65	10,500
	65 or older	11,200
Qualifying widow(er) with Dependent child	under 65	12,550
	65 or older	13,500

*If you turned 65 on January 1, 2003, you are considered to be age 65 at the end of 2002.
**Gross Income means all income you received in the form of money, goods, property, and services that is not exempt from tax, including any income from sources outside the United States (even if you may exclude part or all of it). *Do not* include Social Security benefits unless you are married filing a separate return and you lived with your spouse at any time in 2002.
***If you did not live with your spouse at the end of 2002 (or on the date your spouse died) and your gross income was at least $3,000, you must file a return regardless of your age.

Payment of Taxes

The payment of income tax must be made upon filing of the return, which is due on or before April 15. Failure to pay will result in interest and penalties for late filing. Penalties can be waived at the discretion of the IRS for good cause. Although the IRS does not permit waiving of interest, under the Taxpayer Relief Act of 1997 the federal government will accept credit, debit, or charge cards for the payment of federal income taxes. Thus, a taxpayer can now get frequent-flier miles as an incentive to pay taxes. As of 2002, the IRS accepts payment from American Express®, MasterCard®, Discover®, and Visa® credit cards. It is not clear if estimated taxes or withholding taxes may also be paid in this fashion.

Estimated Tax (Form 1040ES)

The majority of the clients of the elder law attorney are retired and/or elderly and are not working. They do not receive wages. Their income is primarily from investments, stocks, bonds, Social Security benefits, etc. There is usually no withholding on these types of income. Therefore, they may have to file quarterly estimated tax returns on April 15, June 15,

September 15, and January 15 of the next year. It is important to become familiar with estimated tax rules and regulations concerning both federal and state where required. They were substantially changed under the Taxpayer Relief Act of 1997.

Standard Deductions (Form 1040)

People over 65 receive special increased personal deductions according to current IRS rules and regulations. The amount changes annually. Blind people over 65 get additional deductions. This rule should also be checked annually. (The standard deduction will be eliminated in 2010.)

Moving Expenses (Form 1040)

Moving expenses of the elderly in connection with retirement are not generally deductible from income taxes.

Medical and Dental Expenses (Form 1040, Schedule A) (IRC Section 213)

Medical, dental, and drug expenses in excess of 7.5 percent of adjusted gross income are deductible, provided they are used in the diagnosis, care, treatment, cure, and prevention of illness of the taxpayer. For a specific list of deductions, it is recommended that elderly clients consult their accountants. These expenses can include transportation, durable medical equipment, prescription drugs, bandages, etc.

Some of the most common deductible medical expenses are:

- Alcoholism treatment
- Acupuncture
- Chiropractors
- Contact lenses
- Cosmetic surgery—limited
- Crutches
- Dental treatment
- Drugs
- Durable medical equipment
- Eyeglasses
- False teeth
- Guide dog
- Hearing aids and batteries
- Lab fees
- Lifetime care payment—limited
- Medical insurance
- Nursing care services
- Nursing home

- Oxygen
- Organ transplant
- Prosthetic devices
- Psychiatry
- Surgery
- Therapy
- Wheelchairs

Nursing Home Expenses (Form 1040, Schedule A)

The Internal Revenue Code permits the costs of skilled nursing facilities to be deductible as a medical expense. No deductions are permitted for assisted-living or independent living facilities. The facility must provide *care and treatment* for the elderly person in order for the payment to such facility to be treated as tax-deductible.

Long-Term Care Insurance (Form 1040, Schedule A)

In 1997, premiums paid for long-term care insurance became deductible for the first time as a medical expense. The deductible amount depends upon the age of the taxpayer. (See the section on long-term care insurance in Chapter 12 for specifics.)

Marriage Penalty

Traditionally, married couples file a joint tax return resulting in their joint income being taxed as one taxpayer. The Internal Revenue Code creates a *marriage penalty* when the joint tax liability of a married couple filing a joint tax return is greater than the total amount of their tax liabilities calculated as if they were filing as two unmarried tax filers. When married couples file separately, the taxes that are due are usually greater than if they filed jointly. The marriage penalty that currently exists will be reduced for the lower income brackets under the tax act passed in 2001 and will take effect in 2005.

Third-Party Designation

As of 2002, the Internal Revenue Service provided a new feature designed to assist the elderly and disabled taxpayer. If a taxpayer wants to permit the IRS to discuss his or her tax returns with a family member, friend, or any other person, they may check the *Yes* box in the *third-party designee* area of the return, and provide the requested information. If the tax preparer is to be the designated party, only the word *Preparer* must be entered. The designation authorizes the designee to do the following:

- Give the IRS any information that may be missing from the return
- Call the IRS regarding the processing of the return, including status of refunds or payment(s)
- Respond to certain IRS notices that have been received by the taxpayer

The designated party has no authority to receive refund checks, bind the taxpayer to any additional tax liability, or otherwise represent the taxpayer before the IRS. Further authority can be given only by the taxpayer executing a Form 2848, Power of Attorney and Declaration of Representative.

The authorization cannot be revoked by the taxpayer. It will automatically terminate no later than the due date (without regard to extensions) for filing the tax return. The return for the year 2004 is due on April 15, 2005, and the delegation will cease as of that date.

Innocent Spouse Relief

If a married couple files a joint tax return, both spouses are jointly and severely liable for any tax due, including any interest and penalties. Therefore, if one spouse refuses to pay the tax due, the other may have to pay. Recently the IRS has been somewhat kinder to spouses caught up in this situation. The *innocent spouse* may qualify for relief from liability for tax on a joint return under the following circumstances:

- If there is an understatement of tax because the errant spouse omitted income or claimed false deduction or credits.
- If the innocent spouse is divorced, separated, or no longer living with the errant spouse.
- If it would not be fair to hold the innocent spouse liable, given all the facts and circumstances surrounding the particular case.

Death of a Taxpayer—Filing Instructions

If a taxpayer dies before filing a return for the calendar year of death, the taxpayer's spouse or legally appointed personal representative, executor, or administrator may file and sign the tax return for the deceased taxpayer, and in the case of a legally appointed representative, attach a certificate of authority issued by the probate court. IRC Section 6012(b)(1).

If the deceased taxpayer was not required to file a return but had tax withheld, a return must be filed to obtain the refund within three years of the due date of filing. The return must indicate that the taxpayer is deceased and his or her date of death.

If the taxpayer's spouse died and the surviving spouse did not remarry in the calendar year of death, then the surviving spouse can file a joint tax return for the year of death of the spouse. The surviving spouse may also file a joint return for the following year if the deceased spouse died before filing a return for the year of death. For example, if a spouse died in 2003 and did not remarry in 2003, a joint tax return can be filed for 2003. If a spouse died in 2003 before filing a return for 2002, a joint return for 2002 and 2003 can be filed. Indicate on the return *"Filing as a Surviving Spouse."* Sections IRC 6013(a)(2); 6013(b)(1).

A deceased taxpayer's Social Security number should not be used for any tax years after the year of death, except for estate tax return purposes.

Claiming a Refund for a Deceased Taxpayer

If filing a joint return as a surviving spouse, file the tax return only to claim the refund (filing within three years of the date due is required in order to claim the refund). If the filer is a court-appointed representative (personal representative, executor, or administrator), attach a copy of the certificate of appointment issued by a court of competent jurisdiction. The IRS requires that all others that file returns on behalf of a decedent attach a Form 1310 to obtain the refund.

Filing Requirements for Incompetent Taxpayers

Internal Revenue Code Regulation 6012(b)(2) provides that if a taxpayer is under a disability and unable to file a required tax return, the return should be filed by the individual's duly authorized agent, committee, guardian, conservator, fiduciary, or other person charged with the care of the disabled person's property and affairs.

Internal Revenue Code Regulation 1.6012-1(a)(5) states that in the case of a taxpayer who is unable to file a tax return as a result of disease or injury, the return may be prepared, signed, and filed by an authorized agent pursuant to validly executed IRS Power of Attorney (Form 2848), which must be attached to the filed return. The agent signing the return for the ill taxpayer should sign the taxpayer's name on the return and write "*By Brandy Schwartz as attorney in fact for Hermann Taxpayer.*"

Internal Revenue Code Regulation 1.6012-1(a)(4) provides for the filing of a tax return for a minor with taxable income. The tax return should be filed, if possible, by the minor himself/herself or by his/her parent, court-appointed guardian, or other person who is charged with the care of the minor's person and property. The authorized person would sign the child's name, "*By Brandy Schwartz, as guardian.*"

Filing an Amended Return

A tax return generally can be amended within *three years* after the original date of filing or within *two years* after the date the tax was paid, whichever is later. The IRS will grant additional time to file an amended return if the taxpayer can establish physical or mental inability to manage financial affairs, *e.g.,* taxpayer is the subject of a guardianship, conservatorship, or is incapacitated. Usually a physician's certificate is required.

PRACTICE TIP

Legal professionals are frequently asked by their clients, "How long should I keep my financial and tax records?"

The statute of limitations for a tax return audit is three years from the date the return was due or filed or two years from the date the tax was paid, whichever is later. There is no statute of limitations if the return has not been filed.

Generally, it is recommended that all records be kept for seven years and records pertaining to property, real or personal, be retained as long as they are needed to calculate the cost basis of the original or replacement property. This is critical in determining capital gains tax liability or losses when the property is eventually sold.

Sale of Residence—Capital Gains Exemption (Form 1040, Schedule D)

1. Since May 6, 1997, a homeowner may exclude up to $250,000 of home sale profits (net capital gains). The exemption is doubled to $500,000 for homeowners who file joint tax returns. Under the 1997 law, a house that sells for $700,000 with a cost basis of $200,000 would not be subject to any capital gains tax. There are no longer any age limitations. However, the homeowner must have lived in the premises two out of the last five years to qualify for the $250,000 or $500,000 if married.

   Example:

$700,000	*proceeds*
−$200,000	*basis*
−$500,000	*exemption*
0	*taxable gain*

2. Schedule D, Form 1040, is used to report capital gains. Different tax rates will apply to capital gains depending upon how long the capital asset was held before it was sold.

The 1997 Tax Law and its effect on the Sale of a Primary Residence

Under the law in effect prior to May 6, 1997, the profits from the sale of a primary residence could be rolled over within 18 months without the payment of capital gains tax, provided the homeowner complied with the IRS Code and purchased a new primary residence costing at least the same amount as the residence that was just sold.

1. The 1997 law permits homeowners to avoid paying capital gains taxes on the first $250,000 in profits for a single filer and $500,000 for a married taxpayer filing jointly.

   The exception as described above is not a one-time credit; it can be used over and over again. The only qualification is that the taxpayer resides in each residence for at least two of the five years prior to sale. The law is designed in such a way that the average American homeowner will never have to pay capital gains tax in connection with the sale of a residence so long as the profit is $500,000 or less. Wealthier taxpayers will, of course, pay capital gains tax if they sell their residence and the profits are in excess of $500,000.

   The 1997 law terminated the provision that exempted $125,000 capital gains profit for homeowners age 55 and older when they sold their principal residence.

2. Married taxpayers who have expensive houses and realize substantial profits upon the sale of their residences are in a better tax situation than single taxpayers in the same position. A married taxpayer with an $800,000 profit from the sale of a residence reports $300,000 in gains, while a single taxpayer reports $550,000. At a 20 percent rate, the married taxpayer pays $60,000 in taxes, the single taxpayer pays $110,000. Marital status is important.

3. To obtain the $500,000 exemption, the residence must be sold during a tax year when the taxpayer can file a joint return. The year that the seller's spouse dies is included.

   The tax act of 2002 extends to beneficiaries and estates of people dying after January 1, 2002, the income tax capital gains exemption up to a $250,000 gain on the sale of a principal residence, provided the decedent occupied the residence for three out of the last five years before the sale of the residence.

   Example: If a seller's spouse died on February 1, the surviving spouse would have until December 31 to sell the residence and get the $500,000 exemption. But if the spouse died on December 15, the house would have to be sold by December 31 (15 days) to get that exemption.

4. The tax law still permits the surviving spouse to obtain the stepped-up basis on the one-half of the residence the surviving spouse inherits as a result of the other spouse's death. This stepped-up basis will also serve to reduce the capital profits from the sale of the residence. The automatic step-up in basis is still allowed for any other heirs who might inherit the residence upon the death of the owner.

5. The 1997 tax law requires that only one of the spouses reside in the residence to obtain the capital gains exemption. An unmarried person who buys a residence could get married before the sale and benefit from the increased exemption. Divorce after the sale does disqualify the 500,000 exemption

6. The 1997 law protects most Americans from capital gains tax on the sale of their homes. The tax adversely affects people who continually rolled over their profits and now have gains in excess of $500,000. They cannot sell their houses unless they are willing to pay a substantial tax to the government. The law repealed the rollover provisions that allowed a homeowner to defer taxes by rolling over home sales gains by a new home purchasing within 18 months of the sale of their old.

7. The pre-1997 law remains in effect regarding losses. If a residence is sold at a loss, the seller is not entitled to a tax deduction for the loss.

8. The 1997 law eliminated the record-keeping requirement for nearly everyone who sells a principal residence, except when profits are in excess of $500,000.

9. A person with several homes can take full advantage of the law as follows:

   Example: Suppose Jane is single and owns four houses in Palm Beach, Florida. She could live in each one of them, one at a time for at least two years, and then sell each property. The law tends to benefit a person who has the flexibility of moving from house to house. Every time Jane sells, she can avoid paying taxes on profits up to $250,000. She can readily buy run-down properties, live there for two years, fix them up, and sell, and not pay any taxes on sale profits up to $250,000 ($500,000 if she were married.)

10. The 1997 law also allows for the use of a portion of the exemption if the homeowner is unable to fully meet the two-year requirement. The amount of the exemption would be based upon the fraction of the two years that the residence was occupied by the taxpayer.

Capital Gains Tax on the Sale of Stock

The current top federal tax on long-term capital gains is 15 percent. **Capital gains** are defined as the profits made on the sale of stocks, bonds, property, and other investments or assets. Long-term capital gain involves the tax on profits received from the sale of stock held for more than one year. If the stock were held for less than one year, the gain would be taxed at ordinary income.

Capital Gains
The profits made on the sale of stocks, bonds, property, and other capital investments or assets.

Charitable Contributions (Form 1040, Schedule A)

The elderly taxpayer does not receive any special benefits because of age when making charitable gifts. However, the contributions serve to reduce income tax liability and the size of the taxable estate. Special rules govern charitable donations and specify how much of a gift can be deducted.

Because tax laws change periodically, the elder law firm is urged to keep up with the changes that affect the elderly client. It is a good idea to develop a relationship with a tax accountant who can be consulted as questions arise.

Social Security Benefits

Social Security benefits are subject to taxation to a limited extent. See p. 218 for a more detailed explanation.

Tax Credits for Elderly, Disabled, or Blind Persons

An individual must be 65, disabled, or blind with very low income to qualify for these tax credits. The following qualify:

- Single filers, income below $5,600
- Married filers, filing joint returns, income below $8,500
- Married filers, filing separately, income below $4,700

Form 1040EZ must be filed to obtain the credit. Certain states also provide similar tax credits for state income tax.

Individual Retirement Accounts (IRAs)

Individual
Retirement Account
(IRA)
An account that allows a person the opportunity to save for the future on a tax-sheltered basis.

Individual Retirement Accounts provide opportunities to save for the future in tax-sheltered accounts. Contributions are tax deductible and are currently limited to $3,000 per year per individual. Joint filers can contribute $6,000. This amount increases to $4,000 per individual in 2004, and $5,000 per individual in 2005. Additionally, the current law has a provision to index the maximum contribution limit to the annual cost of living adjustments. This will allow for further increases per individual after 2008 in $500 increments. The limits apply for both traditional IRAs and Roth IRAs.

A tax law signed by President Clinton on August 5, 1997, created a tax-free retirement account. It is known as the **Roth IRA**, after Senate Finance Committee Chairman William V. Roth, Jr., or the **IRA-Plus account**. Contributions are not tax-deductible, but earnings are tax free after five years. Eligibility for Roth IRAs phases out for upper-income taxpayers ($150,000 to $160,000 for couples; $95,000 to $110,000 for individuals). The law gradually raises income limits for those eligible to make tax-deductible contributions to the traditional IRAs (to $80,000 from $40,000 for full contributions for couples and to $50,000 from $25,000 for full contribution for singles). It adds penalty-free withdrawals before age $59\frac{1}{2}$ for educational purposes and first-time homebuyers. This latter benefit applies to all IRAs, the traditional as well as the Roth.

Roth IRA/IRA-Plus
Account
An individual retirement account that allows withdrawals without tax penalties.

The Roth IRA has some additional features:

- Contributors can withdraw an amount up to their original contributions at any time without being subject to any penalty.
- No requirement exists for distribution to begin at age $70\frac{1}{2}$, as occurs with the traditional deductible IRA.

- Conversion of funds from an existing IRA to the Roth IRA is permitted. Only taxpayers with an adjusted gross income below $100,000, on either a joint or individual return, can move money from an existing IRA to a Roth IRA without incurring tax penalties. However, tax is due on some or all of the money being withdrawn from an existing IRA. The tax depends on whether the IRA was funded with deductible or nondeductible contributions. If a person is considering conversion, careful planning is important. The transfer could result in shifting the taxpayer into a much higher bracket.
- Changes were included in tax-deferred retirement savings plans. Under the old law, there was a *success tax* in the amount of 15 percent levied against withdrawals from retirement accounts if the withdrawal in a single year was above $160,000 or above $800,000 for taxpayers who withdraw their balance in one lump sum. This penalty was removed under the 1997 tax law.

The current law also permits deferment of taxes on withdrawals from retirement savings account. Retirees with $1 million or more in retirement savings accounts are not subject to the 15 percent tax. Contributors with large balances in their retirement accounts can leave their savings where they are. Retirees must begin making minimum withdrawals based on life expectancy after age $70\frac{1}{2}$. But taxpayers who continue to work after age $70\frac{1}{2}$ can leave their full balance in retirement plans until the year following their retirement. The new tax law makes some changes in Roth IRAs effective 2005. Check the law itself for detailed information (EGTRRA).

Individual Retirement Contribution Limits

Provision	Years	Amount
IRA—both Traditional and Roth	2002–2004	$3,000
	2005–2008	$4,000
	2008 and beyond	$5,000, indexed in $500 increments based on cost of living adjustment
IRA catch up for individuals over 50	2002–2005	$500
	2006	$1,000
Simple IRA	2002	$7,000
	2003	$8,000
	2004	$9,000
	2005	$10,000
	2006 and beyond	$500 increments based on cost of living adjustment increase
Education IRA	2002	$2,000
401(k) and 403(b)	2002	$11,500
	2003	$12,500
	2004	$13,500
	2005	$14,500
	2006	$15,500
	2007 and beyond	$1,000 increments based on cost of living adjustment increase

LIFE ESTATES AND THEIR USES

Protecting the Homestead

Life Estate
An interest in real property that allows the life tenant the right to live in the residence and the interest of the life tenant ceases upon his or her death, and the remainder owns the property in fee simple absolute.

One of the most popular methods of asset preservation is the creation of a **life estate**. It is often used in the areas of estate planning and Medicaid planning. Life estates allow elderly homeowners to transfer while they are alive, rather than at the time of their death, a principal residence to children, other family members, or any other person. This involves transferring a residence by a donor to a donee, with the donor reserving the right in the deed to reside in that residence for the rest of his or her life. This procedure removes the residence from the probate estate. In most states, creating a life estate avoids estate recovery by the Medicaid program. As discussed in the section on Medicaid above, this transfer is subject to the current 36-month look-back rule. No Medicaid penalty period is created if the residence is transferred to a spouse or a child living in the premises for two or more years. Additional penalty exemptions can be found in the chapter on Medicaid. The fair market value of the residence is the amount treated by Medicaid as a transfer of resources and will usually result in the creation of an ineligibility period, if transferred during the look-back period.

A life estate is created by a simple deed transfer by the owner (grantor-donor) to the new owner (grantee-donee). The life estate is established by inserting the following language into the standard deed: "The grantor hereby retains a life estate in the subject premises." The deed must be recorded.

If the house is owned by husband and wife, they can retain joint life estates. If only one spouse owns it, the grantor can retain a life estate for himself and his spouse.

PRACTICE TIP

When executing the deed, the grantor should initial the clause creating the life estate. This is a backup that further reinforces the intent of the grantor(s).

Whether or not the life estate will be beneficial to a particular client deserves careful consideration by the elder law attorney.

When to Use a Life Estate

The Type of Property to be Transferred

It should be or will become the domicile of the client.

The Financial Status of the Client

Life estates tend to work in situations where the residence is one of the principal assets of the client. In order to preserve this asset, make the transfer as soon as possible to avoid the 36-month look-back rule, especially if the transfer is by an aging donor who has a good probability of applying for Medicaid in the next three to five years.

The Tax Advantage of Life Estates

Under normal circumstances, if the donor transfers the residence to the donee without reserving a life estate, then when the donee sells the property, the tax basis will be that of the donor, and the donee will probably pay a high capital gains tax. If, however, a life estate has been created and the donee waits until the death of the donor, he or she will get a *stepped-up basis*, which is defined as the fair market value of the residence on the date of the death of the donor. (Remember, it is critical to have the property appraised as of the date of transfer and as of the date of the life tenant's death.) It is also necessary for the donee to have an estate tax return filed on behalf of the decedent's estate (life tenant). It must include the property subject to the life estate as an asset of the decedent in order to take advantage of the stepped-up basis. A federal gift tax return must be filed when the transfer is made and the life estate is created. Check to see if state tax law also requires filing of gift or estate tax returns.

The estate and gift tax provisions enacted in the Economic Growth and Tax Relief Act of 2001 eliminated the step-up-in-basis rule. After 2010, the decedent's pre-death income tax basis will be transferred to the donee of the life estate. The executor/personal representative of the estate will be permitted to increase the stepped-up basis to $1.3 million.

The Restriction on Sale and Potential Loss of the Capital Gains Exclusion

According to law, the entire title to the transferred property cannot be sold by the donee (now referred to as the *remainderman*) during the lifetime of the donor (life tenant) unless the life tenant consents, thereby extinguishing the life estate. This is perfectly legal except that there are adverse tax consequences: the donee's basis of sale is the donor's original purchase price plus capital improvements, usually resulting in a high capital gains tax to the donee. In view of this, if the owner anticipates selling the residence within three to five years, a life estate transfer should not be considered. However, if a transfer of property has already been made and the donor is considering selling, it is recommended that the premises be rented to avoid the potential capital gains tax. (See "The New Tax Law and How It Will Affect the Client's Sale of a Primary Residence," p. 148.)

Transfer of a Residence Reserving a Life Estate in Medicaid Planning

Special consideration must be given when the elder law attorney is representing a single person, widow, or widower. Transferring a residence and reserving a life estate will not make the donor automatically eligible for Medicaid unless it involves an "*exempt*" transfer to a specified class of donees. (Medicaid will also treat the residence as an exempt resource if the donee signs a statement indicating intent to return to the home after a nursing home stay. In this situation, a remainder interest in the residence does not need to be conveyed, unless there is a desire to avoid probate and possible estate recovery from the Medicaid program.)

However, if the residence is transferred, reserving a life estate, it is important to understand how Medicaid will treat this transaction. The value of the life estate and the remainder are determined actuarially according to tables found in the CMS state Medicaid manual based on the age of the transferor. The value of the remainder is less than the fair market value of the entire residence. Therefore, a shorter ineligibility period will be created in a life estate transfer than if the residence was transferred in fee without the reservation of a life estate.

The net rental income on the residence, if any, is counted as "*income*" by Medicaid. However, most states allow the residence to remain vacant or to be rented for only the cost of taxes, insurance, maintenance, etc. These rules vary from state to state. Medicaid does not treat the life estate itself as a resource asset.

If no transfer is made of the residence and a person applies and is accepted by Medicaid, the following may occur:

1. If an intent to return to the residence is filed with Medicaid, the residence is treated as exempt until the death of the Medicaid recipient, or the sale of the residence, whichever occurs first. Then Medicaid will force the sale of the residence through its estate recovery program.

2. If no intent to return has been filed, Medicaid will file its lien and force the sale of the residence and use the proceeds to pay nursing home bills as part of the spend-down process until the patient becomes Medicaid eligible again. (If a patient receives resources, Medicaid will normally be suspended until such resources are spent down.) Many local Medicaid programs will not grant benefits if the applicant owns a residence when the application is filed. Medicaid may require that the residence be sold first and the proceeds spent down to eligibility level. Check local Medicaid regulations for more information.

TRUSTS

Definition

A **trust** is a written, contractual agreement wherein a party, known as a trustee, possesses legal title to property, real or personal, and manages the property for the benefit of another party, known as the beneficiary. It is a financial planning tool. The trust agreement should be signed by the creator of the trust, as well as the trustee, before a notary public. It is good practice to have the signatures witnessed as well.

Key Elements of a Trust

Settlor of Trust
The individual who creates the trust and signs the trust agreement.

Trustee
Fiduciary who holds the property in trust.

1. *Settlor:* The **Settlor of the Trust**, also known as the creator or grantor of the trust, executes the trust agreement and transfers assets to the trust.

2. *Trustee:* Title to the Trust *Res* (property) vests in the **trustee**, who is responsible for the following:

   a. Managing the trust corpus while acting in a fiduciary capacity.

   b. Preserving the trust's assets, making prudent investments so that the income beneficiary as well as the residuary beneficiary will be protected.

   c. Filing the annual trust income tax return Form 1041 and state tax returns, if required, and also for paying the fiduciary income tax.

- The trustee will customarily receive a commission for services. These commissions are usually controlled by statute and are a deductible expense when filing a gift tax return.
- Maintaining proper records and distributing assets in accordance with the terms of the trust.
- Mismanagement of the trust can result in liability for malfeasance in office.

3. *Beneficiary:*

   a. **Income Beneficiary**—This party is named in the trust to receive the income from the trust in predesignated distributions.

   b. **Residuary (Remainder) Beneficiary**—This is the named party who will eventually receive the corpus of the trust. The beneficiary receives his or her interest in the trust upon the termination of the trust.

   The income beneficiary and the residuary beneficiary can be one and the same party, or they can be two different parties. This depends upon the settlor's intent.

4. *Trust* Res: The **Trust *Res*** is the actual corpus, principal, or body of the trust. It represents the assets transferred by the settlor to the trust, as well as any accretions to the principal. Most trusts have provisions allowing the addition of assets in the future from any source. Subsequent transfers are also subject to gift tax. The principal of the trust when it is initially created is usually found on a schedule attached to the trust agreement.

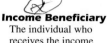

Income Beneficiary
The individual who receives the income from a trust.

Residuary Beneficiary
The individual who receives the remaining corpus of a trust at the time it terminates, or one who receives the residuary of an estate.

Trust Res
Property transferred by the settlor of the trust to the trustee. Refers to the subject matter of a trust.

Consequences of Reserving Certain Powers

The grantor of the trust may intend to retain some or all control over the trust after having created it. Some of the commonly retained powers are:

- The right to terminate or revoke the trust
- The right to be named the trustee
- The power to change beneficiaries
- The power to change the trustees
- The power to invade the corpus for any reason
- The power to control the investment procedures employed by the trustee
- The power to add to the corpus of the trust

The direct result of the settlor retaining some or all of the above-mentioned rights and powers will be the inclusion of the principal of the trust into the settlor's estate upon death. The income from the trust will also be taxable to the settlor. The general rule is that the more control the settlor retains, the more likely the assets and income from the trust will be treated as his or hers for tax purposes.

Inter Vivos Trust

An *inter vivos* **trust,** by its nature, is created during the lifetime of the creator, *e.g., among the living*. It is a private agreement and is not usually filed as a public document. It is customarily funded during the lifetime of the creator. This type of trust may be revocable or irrevocable by its terms.

Inter Vivos Trust
A trust created during the lifetime of the creator.

Testamentary Trust

Testamentary Trust
A trust created in a last will and testament.

A **testamentary trust** is a trust created in a last will and testament of the testor. The trust can only be changed or withdrawn during the lifetime of the creator by changing the will. Thus, this trust becomes irrevocable on the date of death of the creator. It is funded on the death of the creator from the assets in the creator's estate and comes into existence upon the probate of the creator's will. The trust becomes a matter of public record after the will is probated.

Irrevocable Trust

Irrevocable Trust
A trust that cannot be revoked after it has been created by the settlor.

stepping down

An **irrevocable trust**, once established by the creator, cannot be revoked. The creator has fully divested all right, title, and interest in the property of the trust and has not retained any power to revoke the trust. The income from the trust is not taxable to the creator. It is taxable to the income beneficiary to the extent the income is distributed to the beneficiary during the tax year. Undistributed income is taxable to the trust. Tax rates may be higher for a trust than for individuals. The assets held by the irrevocable trust are not part of the creator's estate, nor are they subject to probate. If the trust has the necessary tax clauses, a transfer of gifts or assets to the trust will benefit from the annual gift tax exemption of $11,000 or $22,000 if it is a split gift (2002). Current law permits a grantor to transfer to any trust up to $1 million free of gift tax. Excess amounts are subject to a gift tax.

Revocable Trust (Living Trust)

Revocable Trust
A trust agreement wherein the settlor reserves the right to revoke the trust at any time.

Living Trust
Trust agreement-*inter vivos* trust created by the settlor and operating during the lifetime of the settlor, usually for his or her benefit and that of his or her spouse. It becomes irrevocable on the death of the settlor.

A **revocable trust** can be altered, collapsed, or revoked by the creator at any time during his or her lifetime. The creator has reserved the power to revoke the trust at will. The so-called **living trust** is a revocable trust. A revocable trust is often used to avoid probate. It will be discussed later in this section. The income from the revocable trust is fully taxable to the creator, and the assets are treated as part of the creator's estate upon death. Transfers are not subject to a gift tax.

One of the most commonly used estate planning techniques is the *living trust*. It has gained a substantial amount of popularity among seniors because its use can avoid the probate process and reduce the costs of handling the decedent's affairs. This is its main redeeming feature. However, it was not designed to protect against the adverse effects of estate taxation, except to the extent that it may provide for creation of a *credit shelter* trust on the death of one grantor, which can be done just as effectively by will.

The living trust (also known as the *loving trust*) is a revocable *inter vivos* trust. The grantor retains all powers and is usually the primary trustee, with the spouse or a child as substitute or alternate trustees. The grantor is the income beneficiary. In view of the fact that the grantor retains control and receives the income generated by the trust, the corpus and income are treated for tax purposes as solely belonging to the grantor. This trust can be revoked at any time by the grantor for any reason. The trust becomes irrevocable upon the death of the grantor.

Advantages

1. Its primary feature is the ability to avoid the costs and delays of probate proceedings. No due diligence search is required to locate the whereabouts of missing or unknown heirs.

2. No conservatorship or guardianship will be required in the event that the grantor becomes incapacitated or incompetent. As a result, there will be no interruption in the flow of income to the necessary parties.

3. If the grantor owns real estate in several states, the use of the *living trust* can avoid ancillary probate in the other states. These probates can be expensive and time-consuming. Under a living trust, title to the real estate is vested in the trustee, and therefore, no probate will be required.

4. The grantor can retain control of the assets for investment purposes and does not have to rely upon the judgment of a newly appointed trustee.

5. It reduces, but does not completely eliminate, the risk that the trust will be attacked by disinherited heirs on grounds of the grantor's lack of capacity, fraud, or undue influence exerted upon the grantor.

6. Because the living trust is an *inter vivos* creation and not set up as the result of a will being probated (testamentary trust), there is very little, if any, judicial intervention in the operation of the trust after the death of the grantor. Accounting and administrative procedures are more informal than in estates.

7. No fiduciary tax return is required. The income is reported on the personal 1040 income tax return of the grantor.

8. No federal tax identification number is required. The Social Security number of the grantor is used.

9. It creates a rapid transfer of assets on death.

10. The *living trust* is a private document and is not usually filed in public records.

PRACTICE TIP

A good estate planning technique is to prepare a revocable trust for a person who has missing, unknown, or no heirs. Setting up a revocable trust avoids the costly and time-consuming due diligence search for heirs that is required in a probate proceeding.

Disadvantages

1. Income from the trust is taxable to the settlor.

2. The assets of the trust are included in the settlor's gross taxable estate.

3. Upon the death of the settlor, a named substitute will assume the role of trustee, and trustee commissions may have to be paid.

4. A fiduciary income tax return (1041) must be prepared every year after the death of the settlor.

Credit Shelter Trust (Bypass Trust)

A credit shelter trust is a testamentary trust created in a last will and testament or in a revocable trust of a decedent and is available for use only between married couples. Because it only goes into effect upon the death of the testator, it can be revoked or the terms can be modified during lifetime. The funding of the trust takes place after the death of the testamentary settlor. Therefore, no assets are tied up or transferred during lifetime. The trust becomes irrevocable after death. Trust income tax returns (Form1041) must be filed after the death of the testator.

Advantages

The credit shelter trust utilizes the estate tax credit and permits a married couple to transfer $3 million tax (2004) free to beneficiaries such as children or any other designated beneficiaries. The amount that a married couple can transfer tax free will increase gradually to $7 million by 2009.

Operation

The terms of the trust are specified in the last will and testament of the grantor. The basic procedure is to transfer the unified credit exemption (currently $1.5 million) to a trust that will not be included as part of the gross estate of the surviving spouse. In order to accomplish this, the assets qualifying for the unified credit exemption must be owned by the testator/grantor of this testamentary trust. Upon death, the unified credit exemption will, as probate assets, pass into a credit shelter trust of which the surviving spouse is beneficiary. Jointly held assets or assets that have named beneficiaries will pass outside the will and, therefore, cannot qualify to be part of the credit shelter trust.

The surviving spouse should not be the sole trustee. There should be at least one other trustee, perhaps a child of the decedent. A third trustee should also be appointed to act as a backup trustee in the event the any of the other named trustees fail to act.

Tenants by the Entirety
Joint tenancy of real property between spouses whereby the surviving spouse retains complete possession of the entire property.

The credit shelter trust can be funded with the family residence. A house owned both by husband and wife as **tenants by the entirety** will pass directly to the surviving spouse on the death of the other spouse, as a non-probate asset. Therefore, it would not be available to fund the trust. If the title to the real estate were changed to a tenancy in common, during the estate planning process, then upon death of the first spouse, ownership would not pass to the surviving spouse. The decedent's share would pass into the probate estate and be available for funding the credit shelter trust.

Typical Example of a Credit Shelter (Bypass) Trusts

Both husband and wife prepare individual wills that contain provisions transferring, upon the death of the first spouse, in this case the husband, a sum equal to the maximum amount of assets that can pass free of federal estate tax into a credit shelter trust. The terms of the trust are specified in the will. The surviving spouse is named as the income beneficiary for life; the children (the issue of the marriage) are named the residuary beneficiaries of the trust. The surviving parent and at least one child are named as cotrustees. The surviving spouse will receive income from the trust during her entire lifetime. Upon her death, the corpus of the trust will pass to the residuary beneficiaries tax free because the wife had no ownership in the corpus of the trust. As a result, when she dies, the corpus will not be treated as part of her estate.

In her will, the surviving spouse, can leave the maximum amount to pass free of federal estate taxes to her children outright. Currently, this sum is equal to $1.5 million. In essence, the husband leaves $1.5 million to the wife in trust. The principal of the trust passes to the children upon her death, and she, in turn, in her will leaves her own $1.5 million outright to the children. Thus, $3 million can pass tax free. Under the tax act of 2001, a married couple can shelter as much as $7 million by 2009. Care must be taken in drafting these trusts. If the maximum exemption credit is used, then the corpus of the trust could be funded with a maximum of $3 million. The testator and/or the testator's spouse may be unwilling to tie up the entire exemption in the credit shelter trust of the first spouse to die. To control the amount flowing into the credit shelter trust, a disclaimer credit shelter trust could be used.

The credit shelter trust in the surviving spouse's will for the benefit of the husband does not come into existence due to the fact that he predeceased her. Good practice would be to advise her to execute a new will soon after the husband's death.

It is important to consult local state tax laws to see how each state treats credit shelter trusts. Most follow the federal rules.

Since 1998, small businesses and family farms have an immediate exemption of $1.3 million that can be transferred to a credit shelter trust.

PRACTICE TIP

Use of Disclaimer Credit Shelter Trusts: A testamentary trust employed to control the amount of assets flowing into a credit shelter trust. If the will states that the full exemption flows into the credit shelter trust, it could result in the surviving spouse receiving minimal, if any, outright assets. To avoid this possible scenario, the will should permit the surviving spouse to disclaim any amount up to the maximum amount of the exemption. The disclaimed amount will be used to fund the credit shelter trust. The disclaimer must be executed by the surviving spouse and filed with the probate court and the IRS within nine months of death of the decedent. This planning technique provides an excellent method of controlling the funding of the credit shelter trust based on the financial circumstances of the surviving spouse at the time of the death of the other spouse.

Life Insurance Trust

A **life insurance trust** is an *inter vivos* irrevocable trust. The settlor creates this trust to avoid paying estate inheritance tax on the proceeds of a life insurance policy. The trustee owns the policy, and the trust is named as beneficiary to receive the proceeds of the policy upon death of the insured. Because the insured does not own the policy, and the trust is irrevocable (IRS Code Section 2042), the proceeds are not subject to inheritance tax. The beneficiaries are usually the insured's children, but may be any other individual. Upon the death of the settlor, the beneficiaries of the trust may loan some or all of the proceeds of the life insurance policy to the estate to pay any estate tax liability in exchange for non-liquid assets of the estate. The funds going into the trust from the life insurance policy are free from any estate tax because the policy was owned by the trust and not by the deceased insured. This is a wonderful tax-planning technique for large estates.

The trust is funded most commonly during the lifetime of the settlor by making gifts to the trust. The annual exemption is also available to the settlor. Thus, the settlor can transfer up to $11,000 (or up to $22,000 if a split marital gift) to the trust without paying any gift tax (2004). The funds are then used by the trustee to pay the annual premium on the life insurance policy.

Life Insurance Trust
An *inter vivos,* irrevocable trust employed to create tax-free assets that can be used to pay inheritance tax.

In most situations after the initial gift is made, the trustee applies for life insurance on the life of the settlor, naming the trustee as the owner of the policy and the trust as its beneficiary. Existing policies can be transferred to the trust, but the insured must survive for 36 months after the transfer. Otherwise, the proceeds will be treated as taxable to the estate of the insured settlor.

PET AS A TRUST BENEFICARY

Introduction

There are more than 140 million pet dogs and cats in the United States. Medical studies have proven that pets are able to lower blood pressure of their owners and reduce their stress levels. Many nursing homes have resident cats and dogs that provide love and affection to the elderly residents. I have a friend who provides volunteer work at a local nursing facility by bringing her two golden labs every week to visit with the residents. Everyone benefits from these weekly visits.

When my mother died, my father was 82 years old. He no longer had any interest in creating new relationships with other women. I knew that pets provided unconditional love and affection. My father was working in my office as a paralegal, but I knew that he was lonely. One day I took him to lunch, and we stopped to visit a local animal shelter. There we both fell in love with an eight-week-old bundle of tan and white fur. My father adopted this sheltie–collie cross on the spot and named him Brandy. They ate, lived, and slept together in the same bed for 15 years until my father died at the age of $97\frac{1}{2}$. My father retired from the practice at the age of 94 and moved with Brandy to an independent living facility in Florida. As my father aged, he wanted to be certain that Brandy would be taken care of in the event he predeceased his much-loved pet. I assured him that his loyal friend and companion would always have a home with me. Upon my father's death, I arranged to fly Brandy back to New York to live with me. I took care of him until I sadly had to put him to sleep at the age of $17\frac{1}{2}$, one of the hardest tasks that I have ever performed in my life.

Many elderly clients are concerned about what would happen to their pets if they became ill or died. They assume that family and friends will be there to take them in and provide loving care for their best friend, as I did for Brandy. This is not always the case. Alternative provisions should be made in the event that no one is willing to provide a home for the pet. If this is not done, many of the pets owned by the elderly will be abandoned, run away, or be put into pet shelters and eventually euthanized. Pet ownership brings with it the responsibility of providing long-term care in the event the owner predeceases the pet, which is often the case with the elderly. The elder law attorney will be called upon to represent clients who are pet owners and to provide compassionate solutions for the long-term care of their loving friends. The *pet trust* is a wonderful planning tool that can be employed to accomplish the task.

Historically, gifts to pets were invalid for two legal reasons. First, the trust did not provide for a human beneficiary who could be identified in definite and certain terms to enforce the trust. Second, the gift violated the **rule against perpetuities.** This ancient common law legal principle is still in effect today in many states. It requires that a trust have a finite life. No interest in property is valid unless it vests, if at all, no later than 21 years plus a period of gestation, after some measuring life-in-being at the time of the creation of the interest. In order for a pet trust to be valid, the disposition of the trust property must be settled no later

Rule Against Perpetuities
A common-law rule stating that in order for a future interest to be good, it must vest after its creation (as at the death of a testator) within a life in being or lives in being plus 21 years plus the period of gestation of any beneficiary conceived but not yet born.

than 21 years after the death of the measuring life that was alive at the time the trust was created, funded, or became irrevocable. The rule against perpetuities did not permit an animal's life to be used as the measuring life.

There are other issues involved in setting up pet trusts. Property law has traditionally held that pets are personal property, and personal property cannot own property. Leaving a monetary bequest to a pet may create the potential for estate litigation. The mental status of the decedent could be questioned as well as the amount of the bequest.

The first so-called pet trusts were really honorary trusts. These trusts were not legally enforceable, and it was totally discretionary on the part of the trustee to carry out the terms of the trust. If the trustee did not honor the wishes of the decedent, the funds set aside to provide care of the pet would fall into the residuary of the estate and be distributed accordingly.

Many states recognize that America is aging and that there exists a large segment of the elderly population who are avid pet owners. Pets are treated as a member of the family and must be provided for in case of the elderly owner's death. The Uniform Probate Code (UPC), which permits pet trusts, has been adopted by many states, and a substantial number of states have enacted legislation changing the rule against perpetuities, making a pet trust an exception to the rule so that no measuring life is required to legally establish this form of trust. Many state laws now specifically permit the creation of a legally enforceable pet trust. The trustee is required to carry out the terms of the trust and has no discretion as to enforceability. In the event that the trustee fails to adhere to the terms of the trust for the benefit of the pet beneficiary, courts have the authority to remove the noncompliant trustee and appoint a successor fiduciary.

The Pet Trust

There are several planning issues when considering a **pet trust**:

Pet Trust
A trust usually created in a pet owner's will for the future care and benefit of a beloved pet.

1. Check state statutes to see if legislation has been enacted permitting the establishment of pet trusts. Many states consider pets a property and therefore cannot be direct beneficiaries of trusts.
2. A caregiver for the pet must be identified.
3. A plan of compensation must be established for the caregiver.
4. Long-term housing must be arranged.
5. The availability of pet insurance should be investigated.
6. Medical treatment and long-term illness.
7. Burial of the pet, *e.g.,* memorial services, cremation, or traditional burial.
8. Disposition of the funds remaining in the trust after the pet's life ends, *e.g.,* does the remaining principal go to the caregiver, to animal charities, or to other named beneficiaries?
9. Drafting considerations, such as using a traditional will to create the pet trust or a revocable trust that becomes a private document, and so less likely to be the subject of litigation.
10. Selecting a trustee, co-trustee, and a substitute trustee, choosing the caregiver as the trustee or having independent financial control.
11. Investing the principal of the trust.
12. Provisions must be made for the viability of the trust drafted in one state and eventually enforced in another jurisdiction. If a client executes her will that contains a pet trust

in New York and years later retires in Arizona, the will should clearly state the intent of the testatrix and provide for alternative solutions if the trust is not enforceable in another jurisdiction.

EXAMPLE

TESTAMENTARY CLAUSE FOR A PET TRUST

I hereby give and bequeath the sum of $100,000 to my friend Elizabeth Smith, as trustee, pursuant to [State] Probate Code Section [   ]. In the event that Elizabeth predeceases me or is unable or unwilling to serve as trustee, then I hereby nominate and appoint John Smith as substitute trustee with the same powers as the original trustee.

The trustee named herein shall apply as much of the net income and principal of this trust as the trustee determines in her or his sole discretion to be necessary and appropriate for the lifetime care and maintenance of my beloved sheltie "BRANDY," provided he survives me. In the event that _____ predeceases me, this trust shall have no force and effect.

Upon the death of "Brandy," the trust shall terminate or if for any other reason the said trust terminates or fails, any principal remaining in the trust shall be distributed to the Society for the Prevention of Cruelty to Animals.

This example provides an excellent guide to drafting a pet trust. It provides for a substitute trustee so that there will not be a vacancy in office if the primary fiduciary fails to serve, while in office is unable to continue, or dies in office. The trustee is given the discretion to use the principal of the trust as she or he sees fit for the best interests of the ward. One hopes the trustee will act in the pet's best interest. It also contains provisions for an orderly distribution of the remaining trust corpus upon the termination of the trust for any reason. Pet trusts must be drafted carefully considering all of the issues listed above.

New York Estate. Powers & Trusts Law § 7-6.1 Honorary trusts for pets.

A trust can be established with the income and principal to be used for the benefit of a pet or pets. The trust must terminate upon the death of the pet or pets or at the end of 21 years, whichever occurs sooner. An earlier trust termination date can be specified by the settlor of the trust. Upon termination of the trust, the corpus will be distributed in accordance with the terms of the trust, and if no residuary beneficiary has been designated, then the corpus will revert to the settlor's estate for ultimate distribution. The courts in New York State have the authority to reduce the amount to be transferred to the trust if the court determines that amount intended by the settlor to fund the trust substantially exceeds the amount required for the long-term care and maintenance of the pet.

The Internal Revenue Code does not recognize the validity of pet trusts. There is currently a bill pending in Congress that would allow animal guardians to establish a charitable remainder trust to care for their companion animals (Charitable Pet Trust Bill, H.R 176). It would provide for care and maintenance for millions of pets whose households consider them members of the family.

PRACTICE TIP

To minimize challenges to pet trusts, the following should be considered:

1. A donor leaving a bequest to a pet should advise family and friends of his or her intent.

2. The bequest should be a reasonable amount, sufficient to provide long term care for the pet. Excessive amounts could be challenged by heirs of the decedent and/or the court.

3. Videotaping the creator of the pet trust will go a long way in establishing competency. Competency and capacity can also be established by asking questions relating to the client's orientation as to time and place. Does the client know who is the current president of the United States? What season is it? What is the name of the pet? How long have you owned this pet, etc?

4. Obtain medical records from treating physicians as to the mental capacity and general health of the donor. This will help in establishing the soundness of mind of the donor.

References:

Heller, Bette. *Trusts for Pets*, 26 Colorado Law 71, 1997.

Shipley, Gerhard. *Pet Trusts: Providing for Pets*, available at www.keln.org/bibs/shipley.html

www.estateplanningforpets.org

REVERSE MORTGAGES

Introduction

Most seniors wish to grow old in the community rather than in an assisted-living facility or another type of communal residence. My clients try every possible way to avoid giving up their homes when they are in financial difficulties. A new financial planning tool has come to their aid. The **reverse mortgage** allows the elderly to draw out the cash equity from their homes without having to sell their cherished residence. They continue to own their homes and do not have the expense of repaying a *forward mortgage*. The reverse mortgage loan does not have to be paid back to the lender during the time that the homeowner resides there. The loan is repaid in the future upon the death of the borrower, the sale of the home, or when the home is permanently vacated (the mortgagee goes to a nursing home). Short-term reverse mortgages can be very expensive, with the cost decreasing in the event the elderly mortgagee lives beyond life expectancy as calculated in government life expectancy tables. With the careful use of this new financial planning technique, the elderly can remain in their homes, pay all their own bills, and avoid enlisting the support of their children and other family members.

Reverse Mortgage A mortgage used for people over 65 who are living at home and who wish to access the equity in their homes so that they can use these funds to pay their bills and remain at home. Repayment of the mortgage is due upon the death of the owner or sale of the residence.

In this manner, the elderly can maintain their dignity, self-respect, and independence while remaining in their own homes.

Eligibility Requirements for a Reverse Mortgage

- All applicants must be at least 62 years of age.
- All record owners appearing on the deed of ownership must also be applicants for the reverse mortgage.
- The real property subject to the reverse mortgage must be the principal residence of the applicant.
- The dwellings must be one of the following types to qualify for reverse mortgages: single-family residence, condominiums, planned unit developments, two- to four-unit owner residences, and prefabricated homes.
- Cooperative apartments and mobile homes do not qualify.
- The applicant is not required to have an income to qualify.
- A real estate appraisal is completed by the lending institution, which will use it to determine the amount of the loan to be approved.

The Mortgage Application Process

First, a credit report is prepared. The mortgage lending institution conducts a title search to verify ownership, easements, mortgage bankruptcy proceedings, certificate of occupancy, and liens or judgments against the subject property. A tax search must also be conducted to see if all real estate, water, or sewer charges and school taxes and assessments are current.

If the search reveals any liens, judgments, tax arrears, or open mortgages, they all must be paid off and satisfied prior to or at the time of mortgage closing. Proceeds of the mortgage loan closing are often used to pay off any or all of the aforesaid liens, mortgages, etc. The borrower cannot receive any funds until all of the liens and mortgages are satisfied.

When the mortgage lender is satisfied that the title is clear, a mortgage closing is scheduled either at the lender's office or at the residence of the applicant. The documents signed at the closing are a first mortgage, which will be recorded as a first lien against the subject premises, and a promissory note stating the terms of repayment of the mortgage. Title insurance maybe required by the lender, with the premium charged to the borrower.

Reverse Mortgage Lenders

There are two classes of lenders. State and local governmental authorities are often mortgage lenders, but their loans have certain restrictions. Governmental loans often require that the proceeds of the mortgage be used to make immediate home repairs, *e.g.,* a new roof or heating system or to pay off real estate tax arrears. Private sector lenders include banks, mortgage companies, savings and loan associations, and private pension plans. Proceeds from the private lending institutions have no restrictions as to their use.

Financial Implications

The Amount of the Loan

Lending institutions consider the following factors in making a loan: age of borrower, appraised value of the subject property, and the cost factor of the loan. The older the borrower or the more valuable the real property, the greater the cash that will be made available to the applicant. Careful investigation of the many plans available is necessary to obtain the maximum loan.

Costs

- Points, placement, or origination fees
- State mortgage tax
- Legal fees
- Homeowners insurance
- Monthly servicing fees
- Title insurance
- Notary fees
- Satisfaction of mortgage fees
- Recording fees

Tax and Entitlement Program Consequences

The Internal Revenue Service does not treat payments received from a reverse mortgage as income.

If the elderly reverse mortgage recipient is on Medicaid, SSI, or any other public benefit entitlement program, the loan proceeds are only considered countable assets if the funds are retained in the recipients' account past the end of the calendar month in which they are received. They must be spent down, otherwise the individual could become ineligibile for the entitlement program.

Types of Payout Plans

- *Fixed Term:* The owner receives a set monthly payment for a certain number of years, *e.g.,* $300 per month for 10 years.
- *Open-Ended Term:* The owner receives a monthly payment for as long as the owner lives in the residence.
- *Lines of Credit: Payments are* made by the lender only upon specific request of the borrower, similar to a home equity loan.

Borrower Rights of Recission

Federal law protects the reverse mortgage applicant, granting a three-day period to reconsider the loan. The borrower can cancel the loan for any reason within three business days of the mortgage closing. Funds are not released until the recission period has expired. The following are the strict rules regarding the recission procedure:

- The recission must be *in writing,* addressed to the lender.
- It can be in the form of a letter, fax, telegram, or a pre-approved form provided to the borrower at the closing.

- Delivery can only be made by fax, telegram, or a mailed or hand-delivered letter.
- *Oral recission in any form is not acceptable.*

Repayment

- Upon the sale of the subject residence
- When the borrower vacates the premises for a period of one continuous year
- Failure to keep the subject premises fully insured
- Failure to properly maintain and repair the subject premises
- Failure to pay all levied property taxes and assessments
- Declaration of bankruptcy
- Institution of eminent domain or condemnation proceedings against the subject premises
- Any type of fraud or misrepresentation made in connection with obtaining the reverse mortgage loan
- Donation of the home to a charity
- When the owner abandons the home

A Reverse Mortgage Acceleration Clause

Most mortgages have a provision that makes the mortgage callable prior to its regular expiration date if the actions of the borrower put the lender's interest in jeopardy, or defeats the purpose of the mortgage, for example:

- Placing a second mortgage against the subject premises
- Change in usage from residential to commercial
- Addition of a new owner to the deed
- Rental of all or part of the subject premises

Ordinary forward mortgages and reverse *mortgages* are different. Mortgage payments made pursuant to the forward terms of an ordinary mortgage increase the equity of the homeowner. By contrast, in a reverse mortgage, the equity of the homeowner is reduced as the lender continues to make payments to the homeowner. Laws applying to reverse mortgages vary greatly from state to state.

PRACTICE TIP

Clients should be advised to retain an attorney when obtaining a reverse mortgage and carefully review the costs, interest rate charges, and the benefits. Reverse mortgages can be very costly to the unwary borrower.

NOTES

1. See Kess, "*Statute of Limitations for Estates*," 44 *N.Y. L. J.*, 318 (1997).
2. See IRS Code Sections 2035 & 2036; 42 U.S.C.A. § 1396p (c).

REVIEW QUESTIONS AND EXERCISES

1. What is estate tax? How has the *Economic Growth and Tax Relief Reconciliation Act of 2001* affected estate tax? What are the advantages and disadvantages to this tax law? What should the elder law professional do to protect client's estates under this tax law?

2. Discuss the concept of the taxable estate and the gross estate. Discuss deductions from the gross estate.

3. What is a generation-skipping transfer tax?

4. What is a gift tax? What are the responsibilities for the donor, and what are the responsibilities for the donee of a gift? What are the gift tax exemptions? How have the gift tax laws changed since the creation of the Economic Growth and Tax Relief Reconciliation Act of 2001?

5. What is income tax? What exemptions are available to income tax that may be especially useful for the elderly client?

6. What are IRAs? How can IRAs help avoid taxes? What are the advantages and disadvantages of the IRA? What are the differences between a Roth IRA and a traditional IRA?

7. What is a life estate? What is its use in estate planning? How is a life estate created? What are its advantages and disadvantages?

8. What is a trust? What are the different types of trusts that can be created? What are the advantages and disadvantages among different types of trusts? What are the responsibilities of the settlor, trustee, and beneficiaries of the trusts? What is the difference between an income beneficiary and a residuary beneficiary?

9. What is a disclaimer trust?

10. What is a pet trust? What issues should the elder law professional be aware of before creating a pet trust? Draft a sample pet trust.

11. What is a reverse mortgage? Who is eligible for a reverse mortgage? What are its advantages and disadvantages? What advice should the elder law professional provide to a client who wants to obtain a reverse mortgage?

CHAPTER 8

Love and Marriage Among the Elderly: When Granny Ties the Knot

PREVIEW

There is a significant increase in the rate of marriage between members of the older generation, and this will continue as the baby boomers age. Half of all marriages in America end in divorce. There is an increased frequency in divorce among those over fifty. Marriages that have lasted 30 to 50 years now end in divorce. This age group includes widows, widowers, divorced people, and the never married. They remarry and may get divorced. Studies indicate that the rate of divorce in second marriages is even higher than that of first marriages.

Living alone in the later years of life is usually not an acceptable option. Avoiding the problems that often come with a life of loneliness such as depression, alcoholism, and other medical problems is a major concern to seniors. Some opt to cohabit without the benefit of marriage, and others decide to follow the route of traditional marriage. Whichever path they embark on, legal challenges and financial problems will be encountered.

Elder law practitioners must be prepared to represent aging clients as they enter into new romantic and financial relationships in their "golden years." The advice and counsel of a knowledgeable and compassionate elder law attorney and her staff is indispensable to these clients. Some of the issues that commonly confront the elderly when contemplating marriage or cohabitation are: wealth preservation, pension benefits, debt protection, health-related matters, Medicaid eligibility, Medicare benefits, life insurance, estate tax consequences, children of prior marriages, living arrangements, wills, trusts, health care proxies, and durable powers of attorney.

This chapter studies in depth the issues that may complicate love and marriage among the elderly. It talks about marriage, cohabitation, common law marriages, and prenuptial agreements.

PRENUPTIAL AGREEMENTS

Marriage is a legal contract, and as such, it is subject to judicial interpretation and statutory regulation. Prenuptial agreements are designed to provide a basis for harmony, thereby eliminating and/or minimizing the potential legal entanglements that elderly couples may encounter during their marriage.

Prenuptial agreements are also known as antenuptial agreements or marital agreements. They have been in existence since the Middle Ages and will continue to be employed as an important financial planning tool for the foreseeable future. The law treats properly written or executed agreements that are executed by the parties before the marriage ceremony as legally binding contracts. Legal rights, interests, and obligations of the bride and groom must be carefully documented in the agreement. The prenuptial agreement will have controlling effects on the couple during their lifetimes, and upon their heirs after death. The issues of waivers of the

> **Prenuptial Agreement**
> Legal agreement executed by two individuals who are contemplating marriage. It sets forth their respective rights into each other's properties in the event of separation, divorce, or death.

right of election, appreciation of after-acquired property, debts of the parties, property distribution for children of prior marriages, and support after the dissolution of the marriage are some of the topics encompassed by the usual agreement. The prenuptial agreement is also designed to protect against claims made by "unhappy marital partners" against the professional practices, retirement benefits, pension rights, family enterprises, life insurance and questions of support, alimony, and property rights should there be a divorce.

Elderly clients have also begun to address the financing of long-term catastrophic illness in prenuptial agreements. Who will be liable for the high cost of a nursing home in the event one of the marital partners suffers a catastrophic illness and is confined to a skilled nursing facility? The issue of Medicaid eligibility is also frequently addressed in premarital planning. Prenuptial agreements are an important financial planning tool, and elder law professionals must be familiar with this area of law.

Validity

Prenuptial agreements are valid in all the states. Statutes have been enacted to enforce these agreements. They are not considered in violation of public policy and are commonly used in first and subsequent marriages, especially where there are substantial financial differences between the parties.

Many (24) states have adopted some form of the **Uniform Premarital Agreement Act**. In the interpretation of these agreements, courts generally apply the applicable law of the state where the agreement was executed. Federal law regarding spousal rights must also be considered when drafting agreements involving an individual's qualified pension plan under the Employee Retirement Security Act (ERISA).

PRACTICE TIP

Courts tend to construe prenuptial agreements strictly. Therefore, elder law practitioners are cautioned to review local statutes before preparing pre- and post-marital agreements in order to comply fully with all legal requirements.

Essential Elements

The prenuptial agreement must be in *writing* and conform to the Statute of Frauds. Oral agreements are unenforceable.

Full and complete financial disclosure in writing prior to the execution of the agreement is critical. A common reason for creating a prenuptial agreement is to obtain a waiver from a proposed spouse to some or all assets of the other proposed spouse. The waiver is usually mutual. The only method of obtaining a legally enforceable waiver is by full disclosure of all financial matters. The consenting party then has full knowledge and understanding of the amount and nature of the assets he or she is agreeing to waive. If the agreement is ever the subject of enforcement, the defense of fraud or coercion can be defeated by complete disclosure. Full and complete financial disclosure is evidenced by attaching financial schedules and exhibits to the prenuptial agreement, including copies of tax returns, pay stubs, bank and brokerage statements, profit and loss statements, and any other pertinent financial information.

PRACTICE TIP

The client should sign and date each financial statement attached to the prenuptial agreement. This helps to insure the completeness, accuracy, and fairness of financial disclosure. A certified statement, accompanied by an affidavit that there has been full and complete disclaimer by the affiant, is usually a good idea.

Independent legal counsel must represent each party. *One attorney cannot, and should not, represent both parties under any circumstances.* Each party must pay legal fees of his or her own independent counsel. This will prevent or minimize any fraud, overreaching, or undue influence in the negotiations and execution of the agreement. One of the parties should not recommend an attorney or offer to pay for the legal fees of the other party, no matter how innocent the intent is. The defense of undue influence or overreaching will be defeated if this basic rule of fairness is *not* complied with. In the event one of the parties refuses to obtain his or her own counsel, the prenuptial agreement should state that the party has been informed of his or her right to an attorney and waived it. If possible, this should be stated in front of disinterested witnesses.

PRACTICE TIP

The elder law attorney representing one party should not refer the other party to an attorney. The other party must be advised to obtain independent legal counsel of his or her own choosing. The appearance of any type of undue influence or impropriety must be avoided at all cost.

Timing

The validity of the agreement is subject to attack if the prenuptial agreement is signed on the eve of the wedding day because it may be an indicator of some undue influence exerted by one party upon the other. For example, the day before the wedding the groom/bride demands, "You sign on the dotted line now, or we call the whole wedding off."

The element of fairness must be present. The agreement can be declared void on the grounds that the parties did not have enough time to completely review the contents of the agreement and verify the completeness of the financial disclosure. Ideally, the meeting between the parties, their independent counsel, and the execution of the agreement should take place at least several weeks prior to the wedding. This document should not be signed in the limousine on the way to the wedding ceremony!

Terms

The agreement will be reviewed for fairness at the time of execution, as well as at the time of enforcement. Each state has its own interpretation on this. The attorney drafting the document must take this into consideration in order to protect the validity of the agreement. Provisions should be included to encompass the changes in asset structure and income as the party's age. What may appear to be reasonable at the date of execution may not be fair when future enforcement is sought. Economic hardship may occur, and this may result in unnecessary litigation. When enforcing an agreement, the courts will take into consideration the length of the marriage. Was it a short-term relationship, or did the marital couple live together for many years?

Proper Execution

Many states require that the signatures of all parties to the agreement be acknowledged before a notary public in the same form that a deed is acknowledged.

Elder law professionals are advised to refer to local statutes for more information on the entire subject of prenuptial agreements.

Initial Consultation on a Prenuptial Agreement

 Documents Needed
- Any existing agreements affecting distribution of property
- Income tax returns for the most recent three years
- Gift tax returns for the most recent three years
- Recent bank statements
- Current brokerage statements
- Pay stubs
- Complete financial statement listing all stocks, bonds, notes, CDs, bank and savings accounts, and other financial records, preferably prepared by an accountant
- Inventory of all artwork, jewelry, and other collectibles
- Inventory of safe deposit box
- Current statements from pension plans, IRAs, and annuities
- Deeds and closing statements to all real estate, including primary residence, vacation homes, and business property, jointly or otherwise owned
- Leases
- Life insurance policies
- Casualty insurance policies
- Health care insurance policies
- Long-term care insurance policies
- Cooperative apartment shares of stock and proprietary leases
- Condominium documents
- Divorce or annulment decree
- Property settlement agreements
- Proof of citizenship
- Birth certificates of any children of a prior marriage
- Adoption papers of children adopted during a previous marriage
- Death certificates of prior spouses
- Documentation in connection with any pending or future litigation
- Statement of all debts and obligations, including unpaid tax bills of any nature

- Statements of private business interests, partnerships, or shareholders agreements in which a party has an interest
- All legal documents, including last will and testament, power of attorney, and health care proxy

The Initial Prenuptial Consultation

There are a number of issues that must be examined with the client prior to drafting a prenuptial agreement.

Often, the elder law attorney is initially consulted by both parties, but counsel can represent only one party. The other party must be advised gently but firmly to obtain independent counsel. It is imperative that meetings take place with only the client present. If the client is accompanied by an adult child of a prior marriage, it must be made clear that the attorney represents the parent and will carry out only the wishes and directions of the client. The elder law attorney must be aware of undue influence and overreaching by an adult child. The author has personally experienced enormous pressure placed upon a parent, resulting in the cancellation of wedding plans two days before the ceremony.

SCENARIO

A widower plans to marry a widow. He owns a home, and she owns a condominium. She has agreed to sell her residence and move into his larger residence. They have agreed that he would provide her with a life estate in his residence in the event that he predeceased her. The widower is accompanied by his daughter during the initial visit to the attorney's office to discuss a prenuptial agreement. The daughter strongly indicates that she does not want this other woman to live in "mommy's house." She has controlling influence on her father, and the potential marriage fails.

Issues

- Living arrangements, lifestyles, and financial support agreements must be reviewed.
- Co-mingling of assets in the creation of joint accounts or "in trust for accounts" between spouses, and their implications in the event of a divorce or death, must be discussed.
- Provisions for the surviving spouse should be considered, including financial support and housing after the death of a spouse.
- The detailed financial statements of each party, including all current debts, should be reviewed.
- Provisions for catastrophic illness and preservation of assets must be addressed.
- Consideration should be given to asset preservation in case of divorce or death.
- Protecting assets for the benefit of children of a prior marriage may be necessary.
- Review existing wills and revocable trusts to see if they conform to the new marital relationship. Should stepchildren be included in the new will? Dying intestate must be avoided at all costs. Intestate succession can result in having up to one half of the decedent's assets go to a surviving spouse with the remainder going to children of a previous marriage.
- Review all durable powers of attorney, health care proxies, and living wills.
- Review all life insurance policies as to the current beneficiaries.

- Pension benefits must be ascertained. Private pensions are controlled by federal legislation under ERISA. Pensions governed by ERISA are required to offer spousal benefits for couples married for at least one year before retirement or death, unless there is a written waiver executed by the married couple.
- Consider estate tax implications that may result from the forthcoming marriage.
- Estate planning should be reviewed, and credit shelter/by-pass and disclaimer trusts should be considered if the estate assets of either part qualifies.
- Review all divorce and annulment decrees and ascertain their validity.
- The relationships of the adult children of a prior marriage must be explored. Their concerns should be addressed. It may be prudent, if there are issues, to suggest a family meeting to discuss the children's concerns. Is legitimate concern being exhibited by the children for the welfare of the parent, or are they motivated by the preservation of their inheritance? The elder law professional should be guided by the decisions of the client. This is a very delicate area. I have seen children destroy any chance at a second marriage that an elderly parent might have just to protect their own selfish financial interest.

ANALYSIS OF A PRENUPTIAL AGREEMENT

Let us now analyze a basic prenuptial agreement that is commonly used, in one form or another, in all jurisdictions of the United States. This discussion is designed to provide the legal professional a clear understanding of the terms of this important document.

The prenuptial agreement that is discussed in the following section is valid under New York State law. Consult your local statutes for more information.

AGREEMENT made this _____ day of _____, 2004 in the County of Queens, City and State of New York, by and between _____, residing at _____ AND, residing at _____.

> *This clause, the preamble, is the introduction to the agreement. It usually states the names and address of the prospective bride and bridegroom and the date the agreement was entered into. Next are what is commonly termed the "WHEREAS" clauses, which outline the intent of the contracting parties.*

WITNESSETH:

WHEREAS, the parties hereto are about to marry, intending to spend the rest of their lives together, and out of mutual love and respect for one another, they wish to honor and implement each other's wishes and intentions concerning the financial security of each other: and

> *This clause states that the intent of the parties is to enter into a marriage. This agreement will be void if the parties do not marry.*

WHEREAS, the parties hereto desire to fix and determine by antenuptial agreement the rights and claims that will accrue to each of them in the estate and property of the other by reason of the marriage, and to accept the provisions of this agreement in lieu of and in full discharge, settlement, and satisfaction of all such rights and claims, including the right of election to take against any last Will and Testament of the other, and including the right to share in property acquired during the marriage by the other spouse, and the right to be supported, except as set forth herein; and

This clause is the prepatory language. It specifically outlines the intention of the parties to future obligations, legal rights, and benefits during the lifetime and upon the death of one of the parties after marriage. No legal rights or benefits accrue until the marriage takes place.

WHEREAS, each of the parties represents that he or she understands the provisions of Section 5-1.1 and 5-1.1A of the Estates, Powers, and Trusts Law of the State of New York, providing among other things that in the event a Testator dies and leaves a Will and leaves surviving a husband or wife, a personal right of election is given to the surviving spouse to take his or her share of the Estate as in intestacy, subject to the limitations, conditions, and exceptions contained in said Section; and

*In the event that a deceased spouse fails to provide in his or her last will and testament for the minimum share that a surviving spouse would be entitled to under the intestacy law of a specific jurisdiction, each state has enacted statutes granting the surviving spouse the personal right to file a **right of election** against the decedent's estate in order to legally obtain the survivor's statutory minimum share. Both parties, in order to effectuate asset preservation and permit distribution of the estate assets to the children of a prior marriage and other family members of the deceased spouse, usually waive this personal right of election and any rights under intestacy if there is no will.*

Right of Election
A surviving spouse's statutory right to choose either the gifts given by the deceased spouse in the will or a forced share of the estate as defined in the probate statute.

The forced share in MY is 1/3

WHEREAS, each of the parties further represents that he or she understand the provision of Section 4-1.1 of the Estates, Powers, and Trusts Law of the State of New York, setting forth, among other things, the manner of distributing a decedent's property, if not devised or bequeathed, and more particularly as the same relates to a surviving spouse; and

If a spouse dies intestate, each jurisdiction has statutes providing for the distribution of assets to the surviving spouse and issue of a prior and/or current marriage. Both parties to the agreement usually waive their rights to any inheritance as a result of the intestacy of a deceased spouse. This mutual waiver is also another method of asset preservation, and is designed to keep estate assets out of the hands of a second spouse.

WHEREAS, each of the parties further represents that he or she understands the provisions of Section 236 of the Domestic Relations Law of the State of New York, setting forth, among other things, the manner of awarding an equitable distribution of marital property acquired during the marriage and fixing the respective obligation to support the other spouse; and

Each state has laws pertaining to the distribution of assets in the event a divorce ensues. Some states adhere to the equitable distribution procedure, while others are community property states. Check your local statutes.

WHEREAS, each of the parties represents that he or she has been given the opportunity to consult an attorney as to the legal consequences and results of the execution of this Agreement; and

To ensure the fairness of the agreement, and to avoid undue influence, overreaching, fraud, and the appearance of impropriety, each party must obtain legal counsel of his or her choice.

WHEREAS, the bride has two children from a prior marriage to wit: Mary Jones and Jane Jones, and the groom has two children from a prior marriage to wit: Hermann Smith and Leonard Smith; and

The issue of the parties must be identified at the time the agreement is created.

WHEREAS, each party enters into this agreement with full knowledge of the extent and approximate present value of the property and assets of the other, and of all the rights and privileges in and to such property and assets that may be conferred by law upon each in the property and assets of the other by virtue of their marriage but for the execution of this Agreement,

> *Full financial disclosure by both parties of all assets, properties, and income provide the essential element of fairness to the agreement. Schedules listing all assets must be attached to the document. Both parties usually waive their rights to each other's assets. In order to have a valid mutual waiver, each party must know what he or she is giving up.*

WHEREAS, each of the parties hereto recognize that in the event of the death of the other and providing the survivor shall first marry, the survivor, without this Agreement, might be entitled to share in such decedent's Estate; and

WHEREAS, as a condition of marrying, the parties desire to enter into an agreement before marriage, by which each waives the right of election to take against the other's last will and testament and the right to take an intestate share of the other's Estate; each waiving any and all other rights in and with respect to the property as owned by the other's Estate, except as to those rights that are now or may hereafter be specifically set forth in a Will for the benefit of the other or are otherwise designated by the other as property that will pass to the other at death, by virtue of an "in trust for" or beneficiary designation; and

> *This clause contains the mutual agreement of both parties to waive their respective rights in and to each other's estates in the event of the death of the other party. The waiver includes intestate and testate estates. There is no mutual waiver of any specific rights set forth in a subsequent last will and testament providing benefits for the other spouse. Even though a wife/husband waives her/his interest in and to her husband's/his wife's estate, he/she may provide for her/him in his/her will and he/she does not waive such a bequest or devise in this agreement. He/She may also create a joint account or acquire a home and put his wife's/her husband's name on the deed. Upon death she/he will inherit the property by operation of law. This agreement does not provide the waiver of any rights to property that may pass to her/him in this manner.*

WHEREAS, each party desires to voluntarily and irrevocably waive, renounce, and surrender all rights, title, and interest, legal, equitable, or otherwise, which each may have in the "Separate Property" of the other as set forth in Schedules "A" and "B" annexed hereto and as further defined in "Article III of this Agreement," whether real, personal, or mixed, of the other, in the event of the dissolution of their prospective marriage including any rights of equitable distribution of Separate Property as set forth in Schedules A and B and as further defined in Article III of the Agreement; and

> *In this clause, the parties agree to irrevocably waive all their rights in and to the property of the other. This is a key element of the agreement. There must be full and fair disclosure for this waiver to be enforceable.*

NOW, THEREFORE, in consideration of the contemplated marriage of the parties, and the mutual transfers of property and release of property rights herein provided, the parties do hereby mutually agree as follows:

ARTICLE I—GENERAL STATEMENT OF INTENTIONS

This Agreement is made in consideration of the contemplated marriage of the parties, and shall not become effective unless and until such marriage is celebrated.

The marriage must take place for this agreement to be enforceable. If the marriage does not occur, then the agreement is null and void, and no rights accrue to either party.

ARTICLE II—BINDING EFFECT OF AGREEMENT

The parties do hereby adopt as part of their agreement each of the recitals contained above in the WHEREAS clauses, and agree that they shall be binding upon the parties hereto by way of contract and not merely by way of recital or inducement: and such clauses are hereby confirmed and ratified as being true and accurate by each party.

ARTICLE III—SEPARATE PROPERTY

Except as set forth in Article IV below, all property owned by either of the parties at the time of their marriage and all property owned by either party after their marriage including, without limitation, the assets of each party as set forth in Schedules A and B annexed hereto, whether real, personal, or mixed, including, but not limited to, interests in any business enterprise, professional practice, license to engage in a particular field of endeavor, graduate degrees, bank accounts, brokerage accounts, stock trading accounts, certificate of deposit, stock, bonds, treasury bills, or like financial instruments, wheresoever situated, whether vested, contingent, or inchoate, together with the rents, issues, proceeds, dividends, interest and profits thereof, and increment in the value thereto, and the proceeds of the sale thereof and the investment and reinvestment thereof and the rents, issues, proceeds, dividends interest in any pension plan, profit sharing plan, 401(k) Plan, Keogh, IRA, or similar retirement plans or accounts (excepting Social Security benefits) in existence as of the date of their marriage or thereafter shall be the "Separate Property" and Estate of the respective parties now owning, or hereafter acquiring, such property, free and clear of any rights, interests, claims, or demands of the other, and the other hereby covenants and agrees to make no claim or demand on the Separate Property of the other, regardless of any claim of a direct or indirect contribution to the appreciation of such Separate Property, in the event of the divorce or legal separation of the parties or the annulment or other termination of the marriage.

*This clause provides an exact definition of what the parties consider **Separate Property**.*

ARTICLE IV—JOINT MARITAL PROPERTY

The parties agree that only property to which they take joint title, or which is specifically designated by them as "joint property," shall be deemed **Marital Property**, and any and all other property owned now or hereafter by either party shall remain the Separate Property of the person who holds title or ownership of it.

*This article defines what the parties treat as **Joint Marital Property**.*

ARTICLE V—NON-MARITAL SEPARATE PROPERTY

The parties agree that the following shall remain his or her Separate Property under his or her control and ownership, including all increases in value (due to the efforts or contributing of either party or otherwise), and shall at no time become Joint Marital Property.

Each party essentially agrees to waive any and all interest in and to the appreciation of their separate property. If the husband's house (deed only in his name) appreciates in value by $100,000, the wife is not entitled any portion of the appreciation. Earnings and property derived from earnings are clearly defined as separate property. All non-marital assets are clearly defined separate property. The elder law attorney should make every effort to be certain that the client has made full disclosure in completing the financial schedules. The issue of fraud, duress, undue influence, and concealment can always be raised at a later date if enforcement of this agreement is ever required.

All prior financial obligations, unless the parties so agree, are not treated as a marital debt. After the inception of the marriage, the respective parties must pay these obligations from their own separate assets.

A purchase of a marital residence by a married couple in joint name is considered marital property. However, upon the sale of the residence, each party will receive the exact amount they contributed to the purchase, and any appreciation will be divided equally.

(A) EARNINGS AND PROPERTY DERIVED FROM EARNINGS

BRIDE _____ and GROOM _____ mutually agree that the earnings and all sums of money accumulated as a result of a party's skill, effort, education, background, personal services, and other work, together with all property acquired or income derived from such labors will be the **Separate Property** of that party who earned the income or through whose income that property was obtained. Each party hereto acknowledges that, but for this agreement, the earnings and accumulations from the services, skills, and efforts of one of the parties would constitute marital property, and that by this agreement such earnings and other accumulated properties are specifically designated as the Separate Property of the person to whom the earnings and accumulations are attributable.

Past earnings of a party and property obtained from earnings are treated as separate property.

(B) ASSETS: FURTHER STATEMENT OF SEPARATE PROPERTY

Each of the parties agree that the property described in his or her respective Schedule of Assets annexed hereto as Exhibits A and B respectively, shall remain the Separate Property of the other as well as:

(i)   All property, whether real or personal, belonging to the other party at the commencement of their marriage, including assets acquired for each of them in their separate names while living together outside their marital relationships.

(ii)   All property acquired by the other party out of the proceeds or income from property owned at the commencement of their marriage, or attributable to appreciation in value of said property, whether the increase is due to the market condition or to the services, skills, or efforts of either party to this agreement: and

(iii)   **INHERITANCE OR GIFTS FROM THIRD PARTIES**

Notwithstanding any provision contained herein to the contrary, any and all properties acquired during the marriage by either party by way of gift or inheritance from a third party shall be deemed Separate Property and in the event of a separation or dissolution of marriage, shall remain the Separate Property of the said party including earned income, increments, accretions, or increase in value of such Separate Property.

(iv)   **JOINT GIFTS TO BOTH PARTIES**

The parties agree that any property given to them jointly during the marriage, including, without limitation, wedding gifts, to the extent the gifts are existent at the time of a prospective distribution, shall be distributed equally upon separation, dissolution of marriage, or annulment.

(C) NON-INCURRING DEBT

Each of the parties agrees that any and all debts incurred by him or her, either prior to the marriage or subsequent thereto, shall remain the separate liability of the party incurring the debt.

(D) SALE OF MARITAL RESIDENCE

If the parties purchase a residence to be used as a marital residence, and title to such residence is taken jointly by the parties, then upon any subsequent sale of such residence, each party shall receive from the "net sale proceeds" (gross sale proceeds after payment of any mortgages, liens, broker's commissions, and closing costs) the amount he or she contributed toward the purchase price, (the "Separate Portion"). Any appreciation to said residence shall be shared by the parties equally.

ARTICLE VI—WAIVER OF SPOUSAL SUPPORT

Each party represents to the other that he or she is presently employed and/or is capable of being self-supporting. Consequently, each agrees that in the event of a divorce or legal separation of the parties or the annulment or other termination of the marriage, they will each waive maintenance and support from the other, whether temporary support or permanent support, except as provided herein.

Each party agrees to waive maintenance, alimony, and support in the event the marriage is dissolved. In the case of the elderly, many no longer work, and this article may not be adequate.

ARTICLE VII—PROPERTY ACQUIRED DURING THE MARRIAGE

The parties agree that any marital property as defined in Article IV of this Agreement shall be shared equally upon divorce.

ARTICLE VIII—WAIVER OF RIGHTS IN THE EVENT OF DEATH

Except as otherwise provided herein, each of the parties hereto, does hereby waive any and all rights accruing under any section of the Estate, Powers, and Trust Law of the State of New York, or that may hereafter accrue under such Estate, Powers, and Trusts Law or under any other law of the State or any state, Territory, or Possession of the United States of America or under any other law of any foreign nation in reference to the property set forth in Schedules A and B of this Agreement, the appreciation of exchange of said property, and in any and all property hereafter acquired, and does particularly, but without limitation, waive any and all rights that have accrued or that may hereafter accrue to the other by reason of Sections 5-1.1, 5-1.1A and 4-1.1 of the said Estates, Powers and Trusts Law of the State of New York, or by an amendment thereto or extension thereof, or any other law conferring rights to or in the other's Estate or any part thereof in reference to the Property set forth in Schedules A and B of this Agreement, the appreciation or exchange of said property, and in any and all property hereafter acquired; and each of the parties hereto does hereby specifically waive any and all rights of claim of election that he/she may at any time have taken any share of that portion of the other's estate that constitutes property set forth in Schedules A and B of this Agreement and the appreciation or exchange of said property with the same force and effect as though there has never been a marriage one to the other.

> *The article sets forth the critical waivers of the right of election and inheritance to the other party's assets in the event of death. This is essential to wealth preservation of the respective parties. Check local statutes.*

ARTICLE IX—INTERSPOUSAL TRANSFERS DEVISES REQUESTS BY AND BETWEEN THE PARTNER

Nothing herein contained shall prevent either party from voluntarily providing for the other by *inter vivos* gift or testamentary bequest, nor shall this Agreement be deemed a waiver of any interest voluntarily granted to the other party pursuant to the terms of a valid Will executed by the deceased spouse.

> *Regardless of all the waivers contained in this prenuptial agreement, any of the parties may at any time after the consummation of the marriage make gifts to the other party during lifetime. Either party may execute a will making provisions for the surviving spouse.*

ARTICLE X—WAIVER OF STATUTORY ALLOWANCES

Each of the parties hereto hereby waives all statutory allowances of any kind under Section 5-3.1 of the Estates, Powers, and Trusts law of the State of New York, as said section now exists or may hereafter be amended, or any similar or subsequently enacted statute of the State of New York or of any other state of jurisdiction with respect to the property set forth in Schedules A and B of this Agreement, the appreciation for exchange of said property, and in any and all property hereafter acquired. This provision shall not be construed as preventing either party from appointing the other as Executor or Executrix of his or her Estate.

This is an additional mutual waiver of any benefits from their respective estates.

ARTICLE XI—CONTRIBUTION TO A MARITAL FUND

The parties agree to make equal periodic contributions to a "**marital fund**" for the maintenance of their household and purchases of joint marital property. Each party shall have equal rights to the management and control of the marital fund. In the event of the parties' separation or the annulment or dissolution of the party's marriage, the marital fund shall be considered joint marital property and be distributed as set forth in Article IV of this agreement.

ARTICLE XII—INCOME TAX RETURNS PARTIES TO FILE JOINTLY–ALLOCATION OF LIABILITY

The parties acknowledge that they will file joint income tax returns with the appropriate federal and state taxing authorities after their marriage. All liabilities on any such joint income tax returns, whether heretofore or hereafter filed, shall be borne by the parties in the same proportion that their respective incomes (less their respective deductions) bear to the taxable income reported on such returns, except that, in no event, shall the bride be obligated to pay, or contribute, on account of any taxes or tax liability, any amount in excess of the amount that she would have been required to pay had she filed a tax return separately from the groom for the tax year in question. Any and all tax refunds shall be divided between the parties in accordance with the same proportion as is utilized for dividing liabilities for the income tax return in question. If any claim is made or liability imposed on account of additional tax, interest or penalty, or adjustment arising out of any joint return that may be hereafter filed, that liability is attributable to understated income and/ or overstated deductions of one of the parties hereto, that was not known to the other, then such claim or liability shall be the responsibility of the party whose understated income or overstated deductions resulted in the claim or liability and that party hereby agree to indemnify and hold the other party harmless from any loss, expense (including reasonable attorney's fees and disbursements), and damage on account thereof.

The parties further agree that they will cooperate with each other if any audit, claim, tax deficiency, or other proceeding is brought by the relevant taxing authorities against the parties, or either of them, on account of any joint return heretofore or hereafter filed.

(OR)

PARTIES TO FILE INDIVIDUALLY

The parties agree that each shall file separate income tax returns during their marriage. Each party shall be solely responsible to pay any taxes owed and shall be solely entitled to any refund due as a result of such filing.

ARTICLE XIII—RECONCILIATION

If the parties shall separate and then, prior to a divorce, reconcile, the parties agree that the terms of this Agreement shall not be affected by such reconciliation and each shall retain his or her rights and interests as set forth in the Agreement, unless the parties otherwise agree in writing. If any transfer of property has been effected during the period of separation, upon a subsequent reconciliation the parties shall perform such acts and execute any and all documents necessary to put the parties back in the same situation they would have been in had no separation occurred.

ARTICLE XIV—GET

The parties intend to be married in accordance with the laws of the Jewish faith. The groom agrees that in the event of the dissolution of marriage, he will agree to give the bride a *Get* pursuant to the laws of the Jewish faith.

ARTICLE XV—PETS

The parties represent that the bride/groom presently has possession of a pet named _____, which shall remain in the bride's/groom's possession, in the event of the parties' separation or dissolution of marriage.

ARTICLE XVI—LONG-TERM ILLNESS DISABILITY

The parties hereby agree that if either party suffers a prolonged illness and/or disability (hereinafter "disability"), then any and all medical and health-related expenses (hereinafter "medical expenses") incurred in connection with the disability shall be paid out of the separate property of the infirmed and/or disabled party (hereinafter "disabled party") as set forth on the attached schedules, whichever the case may be. It is the understanding and intention of each party that the separate property of the party who is not disabled shall under no circumstances be used to pay the medical expenses of the disabled party if said disabled party's assets shall prove insufficient. Not withstanding any provisions herein contained to the contrary, either party may expend the separate property of the other party for the health, maintenance, and welfare of such other party if authorized to do so under a Power of Attorney duly executed in accordance with the laws of the State of _____.

> *This clause could be unenforceable if the ill spouse applied for public assistance or Medicaid. A spouse is liable for the medical expenses of the other spouse in the event the ill spouse has no funds.*

ARTICLE XVII—ANNULMENT

In the event either of the parties desires to obtain an Annulment under the doctrines of the _____ faith, the other party shall reasonably cooperate in obtaining such as Annulment. The costs for obtaining such an Annulment shall be shared equally by the parties.

ARTICLE XVIII—SOCIAL SECURITY NUMBERS

The groom represents and warrants that his Social Security number is _____. The bride represents and warrants that her Social Security number is _____.

ARTICLE XIX—CONFIDENTIALITY

The parties shall not disclose the terms and conditions of this Agreement to any third parties, except to the court, to governmental agencies such as the Internal Revenue Service, or to the extent necessary for their financial planning (*i.e.,* to accountants). Except with respect to the Court and governmental agencies, disclosure shall be permitted only if the third parties agree in writing to the confidentiality terms of this Agreement. Either party breaching this provision further agrees to exonerate and indemnify the other party against and hold the other party harmless from any damages resulting from this breach. Each party acknowledges that the other party has advised him/her that, in the opinion of the other party, unauthorized disclosure of the terms and conditions of this Agreement to unauthorized third parties may result in irreparable harm to the non-disclosing party.

ARTICLE XX—PRIMARY RESIDENCE

In the event that the husband should predecease the wife during the time that they are married (as "married" is hereinafter defined), the wife shall have the right to continue to reside in their primary residence until the occurrence of the remarriage of the wife (as "remarriage" is hereinafter defined); provided, however, that the wife shall pay all expenses of every kind and nature in connection with said residence (including but not limited to all repairs, whether ordinary, extraordinary, structural or otherwise), except only for the payment of real estate taxes and, if the primary residence is a condominium or cooperative apartment, the maintenance or common charges, as the case may be, which real estate taxes and maintenance charges or common charges, as applicable, shall be paid for by the husband's estate as an obligation of the estate. If the primary residence is rented and occupied by the parties under a lease (not a proprietary lease of a cooperative apartment), the wife shall have the right to cause said lease to be transferred to her sole name, including any rent security deposited under said lease, without payment to the husband's estate, provided that said request is made in writing to the husband's estate representatives within ninety (90) days after his death. This paragraph shall apply only to the primary residence of the parties and not to any other residence that they or either of them may own at the time of the husband's death.

ARTICLE XXI—MEDICAL AND HEALTH INSURANCE

The husband at his sole expense shall provide to the wife and also for himself for as long as they are married (as "married" is hereinafter defined) Medicare Part B insurance plus AARP-sponsored Medigap insurance and also AARP-sponsored long-term health care insurance with the broadest coverage and minimal deductible available, said obligation to continue for as long as and to the extent necessary for either or both of them, as the case may be, shall qualify and be eligible for Medicaid entitlements. At the reasonable request of the wife, the husband shall provide documentation to her of his compliance with the foregoing obligation, and the wife, in addition, is hereby authorized to obtain direct confirmation from any insurer.

ARTICLE XXII—DEFINITIONS

The following definitions shall apply to the respective expressions whenever used in this agreement:

(a) "Remarriage" as used everywhere in this agreement shall be deemed a remarriage of the wife, regardless of whether said remarriage shall be voided or voidable or terminated by divorce or terminated by divorce or annulment or otherwise and shall also be deemed to include circumstances whereby the wife shall live with an unrelated person in a husband-wife relationship (irrespective of whether or not they hold themselves out as such) for a continuous period of 60 days or for periods of time aggregating 120 days or more on a non-continuous or interrupted basis in any 18-month period.

(b) The time during which the parties are "married," or the period of the "marriage" of the parties, as used everywhere in this agreement shall be deemed for the purposes of this agreement to constitute the period of time commencing with ceremonial marriage of the parties to each other and continuing until the earliest happening of any of the following events: (i) the commencement of a matrimonial action; (ii) the divorce or legal separation (by decree, judgment, or by agreement) of the parties; or (iii) the physical separation of the parties wherein either or both of the parties have commenced to live separate and apart from the other with the intent not thereafter to live together, regardless of whether that intent is expressed in writing, orally, or otherwise; or (iv) the death of either party. "Matrimonial action" as used everywhere in this agreement shall be as it is presently or may be hereafter defined by the Civil Practice Law of the State of New York, Section 105(p).

Situs
The location of an event for the purposes of legal jurisdiction.

ARTICLE XXIII—SITUS

This Agreement shall be deemed to be made under, and shall be governed by the laws of the State of New York applicable to Agreements made and to be performed entirely within the State of New York.

ARTICLE XXIV—ENTIRE AGREEMENT

This Agreement contains the entire understanding of the parties. There are no representations, warranties, promises, covenants, or undertakings, oral or otherwise, other than those expressly set forth herein.

ARTICLE XXV—BINDING EFFECT

This Agreement shall insure to the benefit of and shall be binding upon the heirs, executors, and administrators of the parties.

ARTICLE XXVI—WAIVER OF RIGHTS TO SHARE IN RETIREMENT BENEFITS

Each of the parties hereto agrees, upon the request of the other, to execute, acknowledge, and deliver such further documents and all such other things as may be necessary, useful, or desirable to carry out the objectives of this Agreement, including but not limited to any consents required by Section 417 of the Internal Revenue Code of the Employee Retirement Income Security Act of 1974 ('ERISA').

> *This article involves waiving of pension rights under federal law and must be in every prenuptial agreement.*

ARTICLE XXVII—RECEIPT OF ORIGINAL DOCUMENT

Each of the parties hereto acknowledges receipt of a signed original or duplicate original counterpart of this Agreement.

ARTICLE XXVIII—SEVERABILITY

If any provision of this Agreement shall, for any reason, be invalid, illegal, or unenforceable, the remaining provisions of this Agreement shall nonetheless continue in full force and effect.

ARTICLE XXIX—NON-MERGER OF AGREEMENT

In the event that either party commences an action for absolute divorce, annulment, or judicial separation, it is the intention of the parties that the provision contained herein shall be incorporated by the Court by reference in any judgment rendered by the Court and that the provisions of this Agreement shall not merge but shall survive as an Agreement between the parties.

ARTICLE XXX—MODIFICATION OF AGREEMENT

This Agreement shall not be deemed to be amended or modified by any act of a party of commission or omission. This Agreement may be modified only in writing duly subscribed and acknowledged by the parties.

ARTICLE XXXI—WAIVER OF PROVISIONS OF AGREEMENT

Any waiver by either party of any provision of this Agreement or any right hereunder shall not be deemed a continuing waiver, and shall not prevent or stop such party from thereafter enforcing such provision or right, and the failure of either party to insist in any one or more instances upon the strict performance of any of the terms or provision of this Agreement by the other party shall not be construed as a waiver or relinquishment for the future of any such term or provision, but the same shall continue in full force and effect.

ARTICLE XXXII—ONE PARTY DRAFTED THIS AGREEMENT

The parties acknowledge and represent that each has procured and been advised as to all aspects this Agreement by independent counsel of his or her own choice. The fact that the bride's attorney actually prepared this agreement has no bearing whatsoever on either party's decision to execute same, and each party is satisfied that he or she has freely negotiated the contents hereof free from the persuasion or influence of the other or any third party.

ARTICLE XXXIII—EACH PARTY PAYS HER/HIS OWN LEGAL FEES

Each party shall be solely responsible for the payment of his or her own attorney fees for services rendered in connection with the negotiation, preparation, and review of this agreement.

ARTICLE XXXIV—FULL DISCLOSURE STATEMENT AND FAIRNESS OF AGREEMENT

Both the legal and practical effect of this Agreement in each and every respect and the financial status of the parties have been fully explained to both parties, and both parties acknowledge that it is a fair Agreement and is not the result of any fraud, duress, coercion, pressure, or undue influence exercised by either party upon the other or by any other person or person upon either; that each party has been advised to seek and to obtain legal advice from counsel of his or her own selection, and has been afforded an opportunity to do so. (CLIENT) _____ has been represented herein by (ATTORNEY) _____, whose office address is, and _____ (CLIENT) has been represented by _____ (ATTORNEY), whose office address is _____.

> *This article is employed to insure that the parties have acted in a full and fair manner and that full disclosure has been accomplished, and each party is represented by independent counsel. The names and addresses of the respective attorneys should be included in this article.*

ARTICLE XXXV—TIMING OF EXECUTION OF AGREEMENT

The parties recognize and understand that this agreement is being executed _____ days prior to their scheduled wedding date of _____, 20 _____. The parties acknowledge that each has had sufficient opportunity prior to executing this Agreement to consult with counsel, reschedule the wedding date if necessary, and/or to not proceed with the marriage, but each nonetheless agrees that the timing of the execution of this Agreement relative to their wedding date has no effect upon their decision to execute same. Each party further waives his or her right to, at any time in the future, argue that he or she had insufficient time to make an informed and calculated decision to execute same. The parties further state that they had ample time to make an informed and calculated decision between them prior to the date hereof. The execution of this Agreement at this time is only as a result of their deliberations and thoughtful consideration of the provisions herein contained.

IN WITNESS WHEREOF, the parties have hereunto set their hands the day and year first above written.

_____
CLIENT

_____
CLIENT

STATE OF   )

COUNTY OF   )

On _____, before me, the undersigned, personally appeared, personally known to me to be or proved to me on the basis of satisfactory evidence to be the individuals whose names are subscribed to the within Instrument and _____ acknowledged to me that they executed the same in their capacity, and that by their signatures on the instrument, the individuals or the person upon behalf of

_____
NOTARY PUBLIC

STATE OF   )

COUNTY OF   )

On _____, before me, the undersigned, personally appeared, personally known to me to be or proved to me on the basis of satisfactory evidence to be the individuals whose names are subscribed to the within Instrument and the individuals acted executed the instrument.

_____
NOTARY PUBLIC

The document must be properly executed and acknowledged by both parties before a notary public.

This document was prepared by: Ronald J. Schwartz
LAW OFFICE OF RONALD J. SCHWARTZ, P.C.
Member of the New York and Florida Bar
246-16 Union Turnpike
Bellerose, New York 11426
718-347-6100

In conclusion, the prenuptial agreement must be drafted to meet the special needs and concerns of the bride and groom. Boilerplate clauses should be modified to meet specific circumstances of the clients.

COHABITATION BETWEEN UNMARRIED COUPLES

Cohabitation
The act of living with a partner without being legally married. Cohabiting couples are not entitled to the same benefits from the state as married couples.

Lifestyles have changed in America. It is now quite common for couples of all ages to live together without marriage until death finally separates them. Many relationships that occur later in life often result in cohabitation without the benefit of marital bliss. Society has been very tolerant of such living arrangements, but the state has not. Unmarried couples are not entitled to the statutory benefits provided by the state. Joint tax returns may not be filed, and no health care decision can be made for their "*significant other*." Inheritance by intestacy is not permitted between an unmarried couple. Each person certainly can make a will, power of attorney, or health care proxy naming his or her "live-in friend," but no automatic marital rights are available under the law.

Parties may enter into a written cohabitation agreement to establish certain rights and living arrangements. These are enforceable contracts if they are properly executed and are fair and reasonable, the consideration provided by either party is not solely "meretricious sexual services," and there is no proof of undue influence, fraud, or overreaching.

Written or oral contracts are called express contracts. Only California recognizes a cohabitating partner's rights based on an implied contract. An implied contract is an unspoken but mutually understood agreement that the cohabitators would share their earnings.

Elderly couples often decide to live together and not marry for many significant reasons:

1. Social Security benefits may decrease. Pensions are a primary source of income to the elderly, and any reduction could drastically affect their lifestyle.
2. There is no liability for the debt of a partner if the couple is not married.

MARVIN V. MARVIN

The famous case of *Marvin v. Marvin,* 18 Cal3d. 600 (1976), involved the Actor Lee Marvin and his live-in girlfriend, who sued him for palimony. Ultimately, the court found that there was no implied agreement to share in Mr. Marvin's property, but if there had been, he would have been required to give Ms. Marvin "palimony," financially supporting her after their breakup.

VALIDITY AND INVALIDITY OF PRENUPTIAL AGREEMENTS

BLOOMFIELD V. BLOOMFIELD
764 N.E.2d 950 (2001)
New York State Court of Appeals

OPINION OF THE COURT

Smith, J.

This case requires us to determine the scope and enforceability of a prenuptial agreement executed over 30 years ago. For reasons that follow, we hold that the agreement does not constitute a waiver of maintenance but must be reviewed by the trial court as to whether it is unconscionable.

The facts concerning the prenuptial agreement are largely undisputed. Plaintiff husband, now a 62-year-old practicing attorney, and defendant wife, a 55-year-old self-employed antiques dealer, were married on May 30, 1969. The parties separated in January 1995. Before the parties married, plaintiff drafted, and requested that defendant sign, a prenuptial agreement in which she waived her spousal property and elective rights. Specifically, in pertinent part, defendant agreed to "WAIVE AND RENOUNCE ANY AND ALL RIGHTS that, and to which, [she] would otherwise be entitled to because of such marriage, whether present or future rights, to any and all property which [plaintiff] has now, or which he may acquire in the future, whether the same be real, personal, [or] mixed property, or of any kind or nature and wherever situated."

At the time the agreement was executed, plaintiff was 30 years old, a practicing attorney, and the son of a practicing attorney who owned various real estate properties that he placed in plaintiff's name. Defendant was 24 years old and had completed one year of college. Defendant claims that the parties were alone in her apartment when she signed the agreement. Plaintiff claims they were at his father's office with a notary present. Notably, the parties do not dispute that defendant was not represented by counsel in the negotiating, drafting or signing of the document, nor that she signed the document.

Twenty-five years later, in 1995, plaintiff initiated divorce proceedings. Defendant answered and counterclaimed demanding equitable distribution. Two years into the discovery phase of the action, plaintiff first raised the existence of the prenuptial agreement and asserted his intent to rely on that agreement as a defense to defendant's claim for equitable distribution.

Supreme Court adjudged the prenuptial agreement void on its face both because it violated the 1969 version of General Obligations Law § 5-311, which prohibited a wife from waiving her entitlement to support, and because it lacked compliance with the execution formalities under the current Domestic Relations Law § 236(B)(3). The Appellate Division affirmed, finding that the agreement contained broad waiver language that necessarily constituted an impermissible waiver of support. The Appellate Division further found that even if the agreement were not void on its face, the parties' marriage would toll the Statute of Limitations, thus allowing defendant to challenge the validity of the agreement on other grounds.

Because we conclude that the agreement does not encompass a waiver of support, we reverse. However, we remit the case to Supreme Court for a determination of whether the agreement is unconscionable.

Initially, we note that defendant is not time-barred from challenging the validity of the prenuptial agreement because this particular argument arises from, and directly relates to, plaintiff's claim that the agreement precludes equitable distribution of his assets. It is axiomatic that claims and defenses that arise out of the same transaction as a claim asserted in the complaint are not barred by the Statute of Limitations, even though an independent action by defendant might have been time-barred at the time the action was commenced (CPLR 203[d]; 118 E. 60th *Owners v. Bonner Props.*, 677 F.2d 200, 202–204; *Rebeil Consulting Corp. v. Levine*, 208 A.D.2d 819, 820, 617 N.Y.S.2d 830; *Maders v. Lawrence*, 2 N.Y.S. 159, 49 Hun 360; see generally, 1 Weinstein-Korn-Miller, *N.Y. Civ Prac* ¶ 203.25, at 2-140-2-142).

Duly executed prenuptial agreements are accorded the same presumption of legality as any other contract (*Matter of Sunshine*, 40 N.Y.2d 875, 389 N.Y.S.2d 344, 357 N.E.2d 999, affg. 51 A.D.2d 326, 381 N.Y.S.2d 260). Indeed, there is a "strong public policy favoring individuals ordering and deciding their own interests through contractual arrangements" (*Matter of Greiff*, 92 N.Y.2d 341, 344, 680 N.Y.S.2d 894, 703 N.E.2d 752). Thus, as with all contracts, we assume a deliberately prepared and executed agreement reflects the intention of the parties. Further, while we must be concerned with what the parties intended, we generally may consider their intent only to the extent that it is evidenced by their writing (*Rodolitz v. Neptune Paper Prods.*, 22 N.Y.2d 383, 386–387, 292 N.Y.S.2d 878, 239 N.E.2d 628). When evidence is lacking that both parties intended to violate the law, a contract that may be construed both lawfully and unlawfully should be construed in favor of its legality (*Galuth Realty Corp. v. Greenfield*, 103 A.D.2d 819, 478 N.Y.S.2d 51; see also *Great N. Ry. Co. v. Delmar Co.*, 283 U.S. 686, 691, 51 S.Ct. 579, 75 L.Ed. 1349 [concluding, " where two constructions of a written contract are possible, preference will be given to that which does not result in violation of law"]).

Applying these settled principles to the instant appeal, we find that the plain language of the agreement indicates that defendant waived only her right to distribution of property either then owned or later acquired. The agreement neither expressly nor implicitly refers to a release of plaintiff's support obligations to defendant. A waiver of rights to present and future interests in plaintiff's property, without more, does not constitute a waiver of the right to receive support. The courts below incorrectly construed the provision to be a waiver of the right to receive support, which would have invalidated the agreement under the 1969 version of the General Obligations Law § 5-311. This construction, however, belies the intent of the parties, who never contested plaintiff's duty to provide support until the courts below voided the agreement by grafting into the property waiver an additional waiver of support.

Mindful of the fact that, under New York law, wives had no legal interest in their husbands' property in 1969, we read the agreement to state defendant simply waived any present interest she may have had in plaintiff's property when the agreement was executed and also waived any future property rights she might acquire through subsequent changes in the law.

Even if the Appellate Division correctly concluded that defendant's waiver encompassed her right to receive support, the validity of support waivers in marital agreements is governed by the newly enacted version of General Obligations Law § 5-311, not the version of General Obligations Law § 5-311 that was repealed by the New York State Legislature. The general principle that the validity of a contract depends upon the law that existed at the time the contract was made does not appertain to variations of the law that are made due to changes in public policy (*Goldfarb v. Goldfarb*, 86 A.D.2d 459, 461–462, 450 N.Y.S.2d 212; see also, *Compania de Inversions Internacionales v. Industrial Mtge. Bank*, 269 N.Y. 22, 26, 198 N.E. 617). We would have applied the version of General Obligations Law § 5-311 that was in effect at the time plaintiff attempted to enforce the agreement. This version, which still exists today, allows either spouse to contract to relieve the other of a requirement of support except to the extent that the spouse may become a public charge, and represents a change in the public policy of this State. We further note that noncompliance with the execution formalities contained in Domestic Relations Law § 236(B)(3) does not invalidate the prenuptial agreement, given that the agreement was made prior to the effective date of that subdivision (see, Domestic Relations Law § 236[B][3]).

Supreme Court did not address the issue of unconscionability. While the Appellate Division concluded that "it also appears that the agreement could be held unconscionable" and was "manifestly unfair" (281 A.D.2d 301, 305, 723 N.Y.S.2d 143), these considerations were not essential to its ruling. Defendant should now be permitted to contest the conscionability of the agreement before the trial court. Accordingly, the order of the Appellate Division should be reversed, with costs, the matter remitted to Supreme Court for further proceedings in accordance with this opinion and the certified question answered in the negative.

Chief Judge KAYE and Judges LEVINE, CIPARICK, WESLEY, ROSENBLATT and GRAFFEO concur.
Order reversed, etc.

BLUE V. BLUE

60 S.W.3d 585 (Ky.App., 2001)

OPINION

Knopf, Judge:

By orders entered October 25, 1999, and November 10, 1999, the Jefferson Family Court upheld a premarital property agreement between David Blue and Pamela Blue. The trial court erred, Pamela contends, by failing to recognize that a large increase in the value of the property has rendered the agreement unconscionably favorable to David and hence unenforceable. Pamela further asserts that the trial court evaluated the agreement according to an incorrect standard of validity and failed to demand from David a sufficiently detailed statement of his holdings and net worth. Although we agree with Pamela that the trial court's scrutiny of the agreement seems to have been unduly limited, we are persuaded that the error was harmless. Accordingly, we affirm.

David and Pamela married each other for the second time on May 2, 1988. They had previously married in March 1982. That marriage ended in divorce in November 1987. During the pendency of the first divorce, David and Pamela considered reconciling, and those considerations led to their remarriage the next year. They both had children during earlier marriages, but no children were born during their marriages to each other.

Among the couple's concerns as they contemplated reconciling and remarrying was a property settlement. David was president of Louisville Scrap Material Company, Inc., with extensive ownership interests in that company and in other assets. His net worth immediately following the 1987 divorce was estimated to be in excess of five million dollars. Pamela's estate at that time was approximately $190,000.00, including what had been awarded to her in the divorce.

The settlement agreement the parties had entered prior to their 1982 marriage needed to be revised, so in February 1988 Pamela's attorney began preparing a new agreement. After some negotiations, David and Pamela reached a consensus on the terms of their new prenuptial agreement, which they both signed on May 2, 1988. Under their agreement, only property acquired in their joint names or expressly designated during the marriage as "joint" would, in the event of divorce, be subject to division. Otherwise, [a]ll property owned by each party on the date of the marriage shall be deemed to be the owner's separate property and shall remain his or her separate property after the marriage unless converted to joint property. . . . Any appreciation, improvements to or income earned by separate property shall be separate property and belong to the owner of the property which produced it. Any purchase, exchange or acquisition of other property from the proceeds or exchange of either party's separate property shall be deemed the separate property of that party who exchanges, sells or otherwise converts his or her separate property. All income earned by the parties after the marriage shall be the separate property of the party who earned the income. Any gift, inheritance, bequest, or devise shall be the separate property of the party who received it.

In essence, the agreement provides that in lieu of the statutory provisions with respect to marital property, David and Pamela's separate holdings and incomes will remain separate and, in the event of divorce, Pamela will receive a vehicle, furniture, certain personal effects, and cash in an amount reflecting the length of the marriage—here, according to Pamela, about $650,000.00.

In February 1999, David filed a petition for dissolution of the marriage. About two months later, he moved for a declaration of rights holding that the May 1988 property agreement is valid and enforceable. The trial court granted David's motion. The court noted that Pamela does not allege that the agreement was obtained through fraud, duress, mistake, or nondisclosure of material facts. The trial court further found that the agreement was not unconscionable when it was executed. Pamela argued that circumstances had changed since 1988 when she and David executed the agreement, to the extent that the agreement has now become manifestly unfair and thus unenforceable. In particular, she notes that David's net worth has increased substantially, to as much as twenty-four million dollars according to one of his discovery responses and possibly even more, inasmuch as another late-filed discovery response indicates that in 1998 David sold his interest in Louisville Scrap Material Company for a gross amount in the neighborhood of seventy-seven million dollars. Because as David's wife Pamela contributed various homemaker services to David's business ventures and did not pursue an outside career of her own, she contends that it would now be unconscionable to enforce the prenuptial agreement strictly according to its terms and to deny her any share of what, absent the agreement, would be her and David's very large marital estate.

Since 1972, Kentucky's version of the Uniform Marriage and Divorce Act, KRS Chapter 403, has provided as a general rule that the property a husband and wife acquire during the course of their marriage shall be subject to equitable division between them in the event of divorce. By virtue of the prenuptial agreement executed May 2, 1988, Pamela and David agreed to forego this right of equitable division. Under the agreement, Pamela has no rights to much of the property acquired during the marriage, or to the increase in value of David's nonmarital assets.

Traditionally, in such cases as *Stratton v. Wilson* and its progeny, Kentucky courts recognized the validity of prenuptial agreements only so far as they were intended to take effect upon death. But to the extent that any provisions of a prenuptial agreement contemplated divorce or separation, our courts held that they were against public policy and therefore void. In 1990, the Kentucky Supreme Court specifically overruled *Stratton*, and held that premarital contracts which provide for the disposition of property in the event of divorce may be enforced. However, in *Gentry v. Gentry*, our Supreme Court stated that enforcement of such agreements is subject to three limitations:

> [T]he trial judge should employ basically three criteria in determining whether to enforce . . . [a prenuptial] agreement in a particular case: (1) Was the agreement obtained through fraud, duress or mistake, or through misrepresentation or non-disclosure of material facts? (2) Is the agreement unconscionable? (3) Have the facts and circumstances changed since the agreement was executed so as to make its enforcement unfair and unreasonable?

We agree with Pamela that prenuptial contracts are subject to review for conscionability at the time enforcement is sought. Unlike parties who execute a property settlement agreement at the end of a marriage, parties entering into a prenuptial agreement at the beginning of a marriage are sometimes not as likely to exercise the fullest degree of vigilance in protecting their respective interests. Often there will be many years between the execution of a prenuptial agreement and the time of its enforcement. It is, therefore, appropriate that the court review such agreements at the time of termination of the marriage, whether by death or by divorce, to ensure that facts and circumstances have not changed since the agreement was executed to such an extent as to render its enforcement unconscionable.

Nevertheless, the definition of the word "unconscionable" remains the same for both separation and prenuptial agreements. An agreement is unconscionable and must be set aside if the court determines that it is manifestly unfair and unreasonable. The opponent of the agreement has the burden of proving the agreement is invalid or should be modified.

After reviewing cases from other jurisdictions, the Indiana court noted the general rule among states which consider the validity of prenuptial agreements at the time enforcement is sought:

> [a] court may decline to enforce an antenuptial agreement, but only where enforcement would leave a spouse in the position where he would be unable to support himself. At that point, the state's interest in not having the spouse become a public charge outweighs the parties' freedom to contract.

Turning to the facts of the case before it, the Indiana Court agreed that there was evidence to support the trial court's finding that the husband had suffered drastic financial reversals. However, the trial court there did not make any findings concerning his ability to support himself. The Indiana Court of Appeals concluded that the husband could only be relieved of his obligations under the agreement if there was evidence that he would be unable to provide for himself if the prenuptial agreement was enforced.

Following the same reasoning, the trial court in this case took note of the fact that while David's net worth increased substantially during the marriage, Pamela's financial condition has either remained the same or improved slightly. Since David and Pamela's financial conditions were already disparate when they married in 1988, the trial court concluded that an increase in David's assets, by whatever percentage, does not render the agreement unconscionable to Pamela in the absence of some negative change in her financial situation.

We agree with Pamela that a finding of unconscionability requires a comparison of the situations of the two parties, and that a gross disparity between the parties' resources may render a prenuptial agreement unconscionable. However, the emphasis of this inquiry relates to the reasonable expectations of the parties as contemplated by the agreement. As noted by the trial court, the parties' financial situations were already disparate when they entered into the agreement.

Pamela agreed to forego any share in the increase in value of Donald's assets. She took the risk that Donald's assets could appreciate substantially. The trial court further found that Pamela's contributions to the increase in value of David's nonmarital property were not beyond the contemplation of the parties in the agreement. Furthermore, Pamela will receive about the same amount of assets as she bargained to receive, and she remains eligible to receive maintenance from David should the trial court determine that maintenance is justified.

Given these circumstances, the mere increase in the value of David's nonmarital property, by whatever percentage, does not render the prenuptial agreement unconscionable as to Pamela. Additional discovery with respect to David's assets would therefore serve no purpose. To set aside the agreement, Pamela must show more than that David's position has improved. She must also show that her position has suffered in a manner which was beyond the contemplation of the parties when they signed the agreement. In the alternative, Pamela must establish that the agreement is oppressive or manifestly unfair to her at the time of dissolution. Despite the limited scope of the trial court's consideration of the issue of unconscionability, Pamela did not present any evidence to support such findings. Consequently, we find that the trial court was correct in holding that the prenuptial agreement is not unconscionable and may be enforced.

Accordingly, the judgment of the Jefferson Family Court is affirmed.

DOIG V. DOIG

787 So.2d 100 (Fla.App. 2 Dist., 2001)

Fulmer, Acting Chief Judge.

Derek Doig ("the Husband") appeals the final judgment dissolving his marriage to Richelle Doig ("the Wife"). He argues that the trial court erred in invalidating a prenuptial agreement and awarding the Wife $28,500 as one-half of the enhancement value of the marital home. He also argues that the trial court erred in determining the Wife's entitlement to attorney's fees and costs. We reverse the trial court's ruling that the agreement was invalid. Nevertheless, we uphold the trial court's conclusion that the Wife was entitled to a share of the enhancement value of the marital home, but we remand for entry of an amended judgment. We dismiss for lack of jurisdiction the challenge to the Wife's award of attorney's fees.

In the final judgment of dissolution, the trial court invalidated the parties' prenuptial agreement based on the following four findings: (1) The Husband presented the agreement to the Wife ten days before the wedding, and the Wife was advised not to sign the agreement by a lawyer she consulted; (2) the Husband did not fully disclose his financial condition to the Wife such that she could make an informed decision about the agreement; (3) although the parties had discussed the possibility of an agreement a reasonable time before the wedding, the Wife was given no time to ask sufficient questions of the Husband or make her own investigation because the written agreement was presented to her after all the wedding and travel arrangements had been made; and, (4) the agreement unfairly limited the Wife's share of marital assets and was executed under duress given the circumstances set forth above.

When considering the validity of an antenuptial agreement, a trial court must determine whether the agreement contains fair and reasonable provisions for the spouse waiving his or her rights or else whether the spouse obtaining the waiver of rights made a full and fair disclosure of assets to the other spouse. *Del Vecchio v. Del Vecchio*, 143 So.2d 17, 20 (Fla.1962).

Inadequacy of provision for the wife does not in itself vitiate an antenuptial agreement. If, when she signed the contract freely and voluntarily, she had some understanding of her rights and had been fully informed by the husband as to his property or if, notwithstanding the husband's failure to disclose, she had or reasonably should have had a general and approximate knowledge of the character and extent of his property, she will be bound. *Id.* at 20.

The evidence at trial showed that the Husband and Wife resided together approximately five years prior to the marriage and the Husband did fully disclose his financial condition by affidavit at the time the agreement was signed. At no time did the Wife testify or even raise as an issue at trial that the Husband failed to fully disclose his financial condition.

The Wife also never testified that she had insufficient time to ask questions or make her own investigation regarding the agreement. Her testimony was essentially that, when asked by her counsel whether she signed the agreement freely and voluntarily, she answered, "No." When asked if she signed the agreement under duress, she answered, "Yes." The only testimony the Wife ever presented to explain why she signed the agreement or why she felt that she had no choice but to sign was that the Husband would not marry her unless she signed the agreement. It is undisputed that the Husband made it clear that without the agreement there would be no wedding. However, this ultimatum does not, in itself, constitute duress.

With respect to the trial court's finding that the agreement unfairly limited the Wife's share of marital assets, the only marital asset at issue was the enhancement in value of the marital residence, which was titled in the Husband's name and which the parties stipulated was a nonmarital asset. The Husband argues that the Wife was not entitled to any enhancement value in the residence, relying on the prenuptial agreement, which states: "Neither party shall make any claim or acquire any interest in the other party's separate property if it increases in value during the marriage." We construe this provision of the agreement to address passive appreciation. Therefore, the agreement does not preclude the application of section 61.075(5)(a)(2), Florida Statutes (1999), which provides that increases in value of a nonmarital asset that are attributable to marital labor or funds are subject to equitable distribution.

The trial court found: "Both parties contributed to the maintenance and the improvement of the residence which resulted in the increase in value which is a marital asset subject to distribution. . . ." We agree with this finding and, therefore, affirm the trial court's determination that the Wife was entitled to be awarded one-half the enhancement value of the marital residence. See *Pfleger v. Pfleger*, 558 So.2d 198 (Fla. 2d DCA 1990). We reject, however, the trial court's valuation of the enhancement. The trial court found that the home had a stipulated fair market value of $110,000. Based on the cost of repairs ($41,500) and the purchase price ($94,400), the trial court arrived at an enhancement value of $57,000. Although it is unclear how the court arrived at this valuation, if the court took into account the amount spent on repairs, as the Husband speculates, this was error. We, therefore, direct the trial court to reduce the award to the Wife to reflect her share of the enhancement value which should be one-half of the difference between the fair market value of $110,000 and the purchase price of $94,400, which we calculate to be $7,800.

As for the Husband's challenge to the trial court's award of attorney's fees and costs, we do not address this issue because the trial court did not set the amount of the award in the final judgment, but simply stated that the Husband shall pay to the Wife an amount to be heard later. An order that establishes attorney's fees and costs, but not the amount of fees and costs, is a nonfinal and nonappealable order. See *Ritter v. Ritter*, 690 So.2d 1372, 1376 (Fla.2d DCA 1997). We, therefore, dismiss the attorney's fee and cost issue for lack of jurisdiction.

Affirmed in part, reversed in part, dismissed in part, and remanded with directions.

SALCINES, J., and CAMPBELL, MONTEREY, (Senior) Judge, concur.

3. If one of the unmarried parties develops a catastrophic illness such as Alzheimer's disease or has a stroke and is permanently confined to a skilled nursing facility with no long-term care insurance, the costs would be astronomical. A married spouse is responsible for the medical costs of his or her ill spouse. This is not the case if the parties are not married. Many elderly couples refuse to marry because of the potential financial liability.
4. Living together usually allows each member of the relationship to keep his or her assets separate, unless they decide to have a joint operating account for the household expenses.
5. No right of election against a partner's estate is granted to unmarried couples. The surviving partner cannot file any claim against the estate.

Common Law Marriage
A marriage that takes legal effect, without license or ceremony, when a couple live together as husband and wife, intend to be married, and hold themselves out to others as a married couple.

Common Law Marriages

Elderly couples live together in common law marriages. They hold each other out as husband and wife, but have never obtained a valid marriage certificate and complied with the marital laws of their respective states for formal marriages. If the state of their domicile recognizes common law marriage, then the couple is treated as though they were legally married under the traditional state laws governing marriage. Common law couples and legally married couples are entitled to the same legal benefits, *e.g.*, inheritance, distribution of assets, and all property rights. Only the following states recognize common law marriage: *Alabama, Colorado, District of Columbia, Georgia (if created before 1/1/97),*

Idaho (if created before 1/1/96), Iowa, Kansas, Montana, New Hampshire (for inheritance only), Ohio (if created before 10/10/91),Oklahoma, Pennsylvania, Rhode Island, South Carolina, Texas, and Utah.

In determining the validity of a common law marriage, the judicial system will examine the relationship of the parties. The burden of proof is upon the party desiring to enforce the marriage. Proof includes the fact that the couple, in fact, acted as a married couple—if, for example, they shared joint bank accounts, joint ownership of real and personal property, joint brokerage accounts, joint business transactions, living together as husband and wife, and there is evidence that there were children born during the relationship.

Medical decisions cannot be made by a common law partner unless he or she has executed health care proxies or medical durable powers of attorney. Financial decisions cannot be made unless durable powers of attorney have been executed.

The elderly find that common law marriage may not be the best form of a relationship. It is difficult to establish the long-term relationship between parties as required under common law because their life expectancy is short.

Note: There is a trend among elderly people (friends, siblings, cousins) of moving in together to share resources and provide care for one another.

Key elements of a common law marriage
- An agreement to be married (oral is acceptable).
- Continuation of the marital agreement for a period of time. The relationship between the parties must be exclusive.
- Holding each other out to the general public as husband and wife.

DOMESTIC PARTNERSHIP REGISTRIES

A minority of states and municipalities offer domestic partnership registration to unmarried couples. Domestic partnerships provide some of the incidents of marriage to unmarried couples. Unlike a common law marriage, partnership recognition is not automatic and a couple must register with the state or municipality in order to be eligible. This option may be limited to same-sex couples, but others include opposite-sex partnerships. People who do not have a romantic relationship may also be able to benefit from domestic partnership registries including same-sex roommates.

New York City's Domestic Partnership Registry allows unmarried opposite- or same-sex couples who register with the city, visitation rights in hospitals and jails that are otherwise limited to immediate family members. In addition, registration allows for succession rights in rent-regulated housing. The rights granted by the law are limited to those controlled by New York City.

Because many incidents of marriage are governed by state law, state domestic partnership laws can offer partners more expansive rights and obligations. California's Domestic Partnership Law allows opposite-sex senior couples (62 years and over) and same-sex couples of any age a broad array of state rights. "Registered domestic partners shall have the same rights, protections, and benefits, and shall be subject to the same responsibilities, obligations, and duties under law, whether they derive from statutes, administrative regulations, court rules, government policies, common law, or any other provisions or sources of law, as are granted to and imposed upon spouses" (CA Family Code § 297.5[a]). The specific rights included have been expanding since the law was enacted in 2002. As of July 2003, California domestic partners were able to inherit in intestacy as though they were married to their pre-deceased partner. In 2004 rights to paid employment leave to care for a partner or the child of a partner will be added.

State laws vary significantly as to the rights offered. For example, New Jersey's domestic partnership law does not grant intestacy rights, while Hawaii's law does. Domestic Partnership Registration may be easier to enter into and easier to terminate than a traditional marriage, but it is an undertaking that should not be considered lightly. While the California law provides certain benefits to cohabiting partners, it also creates the same financial liability obligation as married partners. The fact that the opposite-sex partnerships are available only to seniors can be both a blessing and a curse. Should one partner become ill, registration will allow the well partner to visit his or her partner in an intensive care unit. However, should the ill partner require Medicaid, the state can seek reimbursement from the well partner, just as it would a community spouse.

SAME-SEX MARRIAGE AND CIVIL UNIONS

Domestic partnership registries are the result of an effort to provide some of the rights of married couples to homosexual couples to whom marriage had previously been unavailable.

For years same-sex couples have attempted to gain some spousal or familial rights. Absent a domestic partnership law, elderly couples who had spent most of their lives together could be precluded from hospital visitation rights when one partner became ill. Until recently, attempts to acquire partnership rights have been unsuccessful. For example, in New York, a man attempted to adopt his homosexual partner in order to give him the rights of a family member. A court ruled that even though adoption of adults is generally allowed, the adoption in question was invalid because it was an attempt to create a legal family relationship between homosexuals. This trend of denying rights to homosexuals seems to be reversing.

Recently, legal challenges to the traditional notion of marriage as being limited to opposite-sex couples have begun a maelstrom of controversy and may soon make domestic partnership registries a thing of the past. The issue raises a variety of interesting legal arguments. To understand the debate, keep these legal principles in mind. The Federal Constitution is the Supreme Law of the Land as interpreted by the Federal Supreme Court. Federal law supersedes state law. A state's constitution supersedes state law. A state's highest court is the final arbiter of its own constitution. An amendment to a constitution supersedes any previous constitutional provisions.

The following is a timeline of events and a description of the legal issues involved in this highly contentious debate:

- In the 1990s a series of Hawaii court cases determined that recognition of homosexual marriage was required under the state constitution because to ban gay marriage was unlawful gender discrimination. (A later amendment to the Hawaii Constitution changed the law on that issue.)
- 1996—Congress realized that a marriage valid in one state is generally valid in all states and recognized by the federal government. Because they were concerned that Hawaii same-sex marriages would be recognized in all fifty states, they passed the Defense of Marriage Act (DOMA), defining marriage as "a legal union between one man and one woman as husband and wife" for federal purposes and indicating that no

state was required to recognize gay marriages from other states. More than thirty state legislatures followed suit with similar laws.

- The constitutionality or the necessity of DOMA remains questionable. The federal Constitution provides that "[f]ull faith and credit shall be given in each state to the public acts, records, and judicial proceedings of every other state." This means, for example, that a driver's license or a marriage certificate issued in Alaska is valid in Alabama. However, the Full Faith and Credit Clause has been interpreted to include an exception when a marriage violates the strong public policy of the state. This argument has been used to support bans on interracial marriage (now unconstitutional) and marriages between close relatives (*e.g.,* nieces and uncles). Critics from the left and the right argue that the application of DOMA to state recognition of marriage is either unconstitutional because the public policy exception is not written into the federal Constitution or unnecessary because the public policy exception applies without a federal law on the subject.

- 1998—New Hampshire's highest court found that precluding homosexual couples from having marital rights was unconstitutional based on their state constitution.

- 2000—The New Hampshire legislature then passed this country's first and only civil union law. Civil unions grant most of the rights of marriage but avoid the constitutional problems of interstate recognition and eligibility for federal spousal benefits because it is not deemed a true marriage. Similar civil unions have been recognized in a number of European countries as an alternative to marriage.

- 2003—The Massachusetts Supreme Court ruled that homosexuals have the right to marry under its state constitution. The Court ruled that civil unions were not an acceptable alternative to full marital recognition.

- 2004—Officials in California, New Mexico, Oregon, New York, New Jersey and Washington State have interpreted their state constitutions as permitting gay marriage and have begun performing marriage ceremonies for same-sex couples. In San Francisco, City Hall stayed open around the clock on Valentine's day weekend and deputized recently married partners in order to marry as many couples as possible. In the ultimate photo-op, comedian Rosie O'Donnell flew to San Francisco and married her longtime partner. The mayor of New Paltz, New York, was indicted for solemnizing marriages of same-sex couples who had no marriage license. The validity of these marriages will have to be determined by the courts of their respective states.

- 2004—President George W. Bush held a press conference calling for a federal constitutional amendment to prevent any state from recognizing same-sex marriage or "the incidents of marriage." This provision could be interpreted to include a ban on domestic partnerships and civil unions. An alternate version of the amendment would allow civil unions to be recognized under state law, but not under a state's constitution. The amendment is opposed by both liberals and some conservatives who believe that a measure as drastic as a constitutional amendment is unwarranted.

The process to pass a constitutional amendment can take several years. It must pass both houses of Congress by a two-thirds vote and be ratified by thirty-eight states. The constitutionality of DOMA remains a question. In the meantime, attitudes about gay marriage may be changing. When Vermont's Civil Union Law was passed, more than two-thirds of Vermont's citizen's were opposed to it. Since the law has been enacted, a majority of residents support the law. Similarly, 59 percent of Massachusetts citizens now support civil marriage for same-sex couples. Like the future of DOMA and the constitutional amendment, the future of gay marriage is uncertain.

REFERENCES

DaSilva, Willard H., "Changing Population Trends Spur New Interest in Prenuptial Agreements for Love Money and Security", *New York State Bar Association Journal* 74(2) 8–18 (2002).

Grama, Lyn Joanna, "The New Newlyweds: Marriage Among the Elderly, Suggestions to the Elder Law Practitioner," *The Elder Law Journal* 7(2) 379–407 (1999).

West's Legal Forms, Second Edition, Volume 7, Chapter 4: *Antenuptual Agreements*, 274–338 (providing model clauses for use in antenuptial agreements to supplement this chapter).

REVIEW QUESTIONS AND EXERCISES

1. In what ways can the elder law professional protect the assets and interests of the elderly client who is planning marriage?
2. What are the essential elements of a valid prenuptial agreement?
3. With what issues must the elder care professional be concerned with in drafting a prenuptial agreement?
4. Why would an elderly couple choose to cohabit without marrying?
5. Discuss the advantages and disadvantages of cohabiting without marriage versus marriage.
6. What is a common law marriage, and what are the elements of a common law marriage? How does a common law marriage differ from a traditional marriage?
7. Draft a prenuptial agreement.

CHAPTER 9

Entitlement Programs Part I:
Social Security
Social Security Disability
Supplemental Security Income

PREVIEW

Social Security began in 1935 as part of President Franklin D. Roosevelt's New Deal. Although everyone is familiar with the mandatory Social Security deductions that regularly appear on their paycheck stubs, most Americans do not know what Social Security benefits are or how and when to access them. With the rapid approach of retirement for the baby boomer generation, much debate has arisen regarding the future of Social Security. Can this system that immediately transfers money paid into the system by current employed workers to current retired workers, their dependents, survivors, etc., continue to survive?

This chapter explores in detail the Social Security system—its historical background, its problems, its benefits, and the process to access benefits.

THE SOCIAL SECURITY SYSTEM

Introduction and Historical Background

Working Americans are very familiar with the mandatory Social Security deductions, but they may not know exactly what these Social Security benefits are or how to access them. Many believe that Social Security benefits will be ample enough to sustain them in their older years, which probably will not be the case.

Social security is not unique to the United States. Actually, it originated in the industrialized nations of Europe. Germany, one of the first nations to become industrialized, enacted social security for retired workers long before the United States. German Chancellor Otto Von Bismarck assisted in creating the system in the 1880s based on a retirement age of 65, knowing full well that the life expectancy of the average German was 42. Because most people did not live to attain the age of 65, he anticipated few claims for benefits.

In the United States, August 14, 1935, marked the beginning of the system with the passage of the Social Security Act. The first check was issued in January 1940 in the sum of $22.54. One of the significant components of President Roosevelt's New Deal, this far-reaching legislation was designed to provide a safety net for old age. The plan was to have the government, under the newly formed Social Security Administration (SSA), pay out monthly sums ranging from $10 to $85 to retired workers. The funds to pay these benefits were to come from a payroll tax levied on each employee and employer. In years to come, the Social Security Act was expanded, and it currently covers the following categories:

- Children of retired or disabled workers
- Survivors of workers
- Self-employed
- Farm owners and workers
- Household workers

In addition, the Social Security Act was further expanded to include:

- Medicare—hospital and medical insurance
- Supplemental Security Income (SSI)—assistance for elderly, blind, and disabled people with minimal income and assets

Social Security Today

Today, almost every worker in the United States, including all state and federal employees, is required by law to be a member of the Social Security system. The only workers who are not eligible are federal employees hired before January 1, 1984, and railroad workers. They are covered under a separate retirement system.

Nationally, benefits were paid to 45.4 million people in December 2000. This number included 28.5 million retired workers, 5.1 million widows and widowers, 5 million disabled workers, 3 million wives and husbands, and 3.8 million children. Social Security beneficiaries represented 15.7 percent of the total population, and 91.5 percent of the population 65 or older.

Monthly benefits averaged $845 for retired workers; $810 for non-disabled widows and widowers; $787 for disabled workers; and $417 for wives and husbands of retired and disabled workers. Average payments for children of deceased workers were $549; for children of retired workers, $396; and for children of disabled workers, $228.

Monthly payments in December 2000 totaled $34.9 billion. Of this amount, $25.5 billion was paid to retired workers and their dependents, $5.1 billion to survivors, and $4.3 billion to disabled workers and their dependents. Average benefits and total monthly payment included a 3.5 percent cost of living increase effective December 2000.

Federal Insurance Contributions Act (FICA)
The vehicle by which mandatory contributions are made into the Social Security system.

The **Federal Insurance Contributions Act (FICA)** is the vehicle by which mandatory contributions are made into the Social Security system. FICA is a payroll tax borne equally by the employer and the employee, collected by the Internal Revenue Service, and then paid to the United States Treasury for redistribution. Legislation enacted in 1997 requires each party to contribute 7.65 percent, for a total of 15.30 percent by employee and employer. The 7.65 percent contribution from each party is actually distributed as follows:

1. 5.26 percent goes to the Federal Old Age and Survivors Insurance Trust Fund, which is used by the government for retirement and survivor's benefits and benefits for dependents of retirees.
2. 0.94 percent goes to the Federal Disability Insurance Trust Fund. The government uses these funds for disability benefits.
3. 1.45 percent goes to the Hospital Insurance Trust Fund, which the government uses for Medicare Part A, hospital coverage.

In 2002, the maximum salary subject to 6.2 percent of FICA is $84,900, which increases annually. There is no salary cap on the remaining 1.45 percent for the hospital insurance trust fund. Whereas the employee will benefit in years to come as a result of paying into the system (provided he or she meets the eligibility requirements for monthly payments), the employer receives no other benefit from the contribution than to declare it as a tax-deductible operating expense.

In 1983, Congress took a second look at the Social Security system and found that it had begun to fail. Legislation was passed to prevent the system from collapsing. It increased payroll taxes, raised the level of earnings subject to payroll tax, increased retirement age from 65 to 66 by the year 2005, and to age 67 in the year 2022. The amendment further provided that all employed federal workers hired after January 1, 1984, and workers employed by non-profit corporations after January 1, 1984, were required to be covered by Social Security. For the first time, it made Social Security benefits subject to federal income tax, depending upon the income of the beneficiary.

The legislation known as the *Social Security Act* is located in Title 42 of the United States Code. The Social Security regulations can be found in Title 20 of the Code of Federal Regulations, Part 404, *et seq*. The Social Security Administration regularly issues Social Security rulings, Program Operations Manual Systems (POMS), and a Hearings, Appeals, Litigation and Law (HALLEX) manual. These government publications will provide useful information regarding current decisions, interpretations of rules, and regulations for the elder care law firm involved in Social Security matters.

Conceptual Problems

The concept of the Social Security system is based on the transfer of funds from current employed workers via a payroll tax to current retired workers, their dependents, survivors, etc. The money is paid into the system and immediately paid out. It is not designed as a savings plan.

What actually occurs is that any money not used to pay benefits and administrative expenses is invested in U.S. government bonds (Social Security Trust Fund). In effect, the government borrows the excess money and issues U.S. savings bonds as security for the loan. The money is then used by the government to cover operating expenses for government projects, etc. The government must make good on these bonds (IOU notes), as the Social Security Administration requires their repayment to pay out its benefits to *its* beneficiaries. This concept continues to work so long as there are enough employees (and therefore enough resulting funds) to make contributions to the Social Security fund. But what if there are economic reversals and the number of gainfully employed Americans decreases? Where will the funds come from to pay the currently retired employees?

Critics of the manner in which the Social Security system operates compare it to a monumental "Ponzi scheme," wherein the government promises to pay employees who have contributed their fair share into the fund at a future date.

The problem is that current retirees are drawing their benefits exclusively from funds that are being paid in by current employees. The critics are greatly concerned about where the money will come from to pay the benefits of current employees who will retire in the future. The influx of baby boomers, born between 1946 and 1964, into the retired segment of the population is an especially serious problem. They will begin to collect benefits in 2008. Fiscal and social catastrophe looms on the horizon. It is anticipated that by 2012, Social Security will spend more than it receives. The Social Security system will then have to take money from the trust fund, which is predicted to be empty by 2029. Reforms will be necessary in order to protect the system from collapse. Chairman of the Federal Reserve, Alan Greenspan, has proposed reducing annual cost of living adjustments and raising the retirement age even further as two methods of keeping the program's costs down.

Privatization of Social Security has emerged as an issue in the last few years as a result of the above problems. Rather than lending surplus funds to the United States Treasury for operating expenses, the funds would be reinvested responsibly and securely in the private sector of the economy, *e.g.,* in blue chip stocks and bonds. Wall Street favors this idea. The popularity of this concept, however, has all but disappeared due to the decline in the stock market in 2000 and the unethical business practices of certain firms like Enron.

Another concept suggested to prevent the collapse of Social Security is to permit the employee to create his or her own Social Security fund, a private-sector, mandatory personal savings account. Under such a system, the FICA taxes paid by the employer and the employee would be deposited into an employee's individual account. The funds could only be withdrawn upon retirement or disability, subject to Social Security laws. The individual could self-direct the investment of this fund, as in an IRA or Keogh account.

The U.S. Social Security system has begun to study Chile's privatized retirement system. Argentina, Peru, Columbia, Uruguay, Bolivia, Mexico, El Salvador, and Hungary have all already adopted Chile's model to some degree. In 1981, Chile created the pension savings account (PSA) system of private retirement accounts funded from compulsory contributions by employees via payroll deductions. These funds are managed by private-sector retirement plan administrators who function under tight governmental regulations. Currently five million people receive benefits, and 3.2 million employees make regular contributions. A mandatory 13 percent payroll deduction of monthly salaries goes into these private savings accounts administered by the private sector. The system provides that the accounts are portable and, therefore, travel with the employee from job to job. Upon retirement, a member of the system has the option of converting the savings account to an annuity or to arrange for scheduled withdrawals.

An integral part of the plan is a guarantee by the Chilean government that all its retirees will receive a minimum pension. The government has agreed to make up any shortfall in the event the mandatory savings accounts provide benefits that fall below the guaranteed minimum pension.

Unfortunately, Chile's 21-year-old private pension system is beginning to have some problems. It is now suffering from declining long-term returns, soaring costs, and unethical practices. If this system were used in the United States, we could face similar problems.

There are other suggested reforms of the Social Security system, including raising the retirement age or increasing the tax. Currently the law provides for the retirement age to receive full Social Security benefits to rise to 67 over a 24-year period commencing in 2003. Age 62 would remain for qualifying for reduced benefits, but the reduced benefit would be lowered from 80 percent to about 70 percent. Therefore, a person who desires to retire early will only receive about 70 percent of full benefits. This will occur simultaneously with the increase in the normal retirement age to 67. One proposal is to raise the normal retirement age to 70 over a period of years.

In 2002, the first $84,900 of wages is subject to a payroll tax of 12.4 percent. The employer and the employee pay it equally. Proposals have been presented to raise both the tax rate and the taxable wage base. The real test of a pension system is how it performs over generations without creating deficits. Our system has worked since its inception. Hopefully, it will continue to do so with proper reform.

Planning for Retirement

Eligibility for Retirement Benefits

In order for a member of the Social Security system to become eligible to receive retirement benefits, the applicant must have paid into the Social Security system for a specific period of time. An individual who works and pays Social Security taxes earns Social

Year of Birth	Quarters Required
1922	33
1923	34
1924	35
1925	36
1926	37
1927	38
1928	39
after 1929	40

Security credits called **quarters**. The number of quarters required to receive retirement benefits depends upon the worker's date of birth.

For example, if a person was born after 1929, 40 quarters (10 years) are required to obtain retirement benefits. The quarters are not lost by stopping work; they remain credited to the employee's permanent account. Quarters do not have to be consecutive. The Social Security Administration (SSA) will not pay out benefits unless the required number of quarters is in the account. The worker with the required number of quarters is considered fully insured for life. Most persons will earn substantially more than their required number of quarters. The surplus quarters will not increase Social Security benefits, but the income earned while accumulating these excess quarters will increase benefits.

Quarters
The credits a working individual earns in order to qualify for Social Security benefits. The Social Security Administration will not pay out benefits unless the required number of quarters is in the account (40 quarters, or 10 years, if the individual was born after 1929).

Employees' Earnings Records

To determine an employee's earning record, obtain Form SSA 7004SM, Request for Earnings and Benefit Estimate Statement, from:

1. The local Social Security office
2. The toll-free Social Security number 800-772-1213, 24 hours per day, seven days a week
3. The toll-free number for the deaf or the hard of hearing 800-325-0778, between 7 a.m. and 7 p.m. on regular business days

Complete the form SSA 7004-SM and mail to:

Social Security Administration
Wilkes Barre Data Operations Center
P.O. Box 7004
Wilkes Barre, PA 18767-7004

The Social Security Administration will return a statement to the applicant that will provide the following basic information:

- Total wages credited to the earnings record each year
- Number of work credits (earned-quarters)
- Estimated monthly retirement and disability benefits available
- Estimate of Social Security taxes paid into the system
- Estimate of family's benefits if applicant dies

It is a good practice to advise all clients to file requests to verify their earnings every three years to see if the entries into their account are correct. There have been many cases where the Social Security Administration has made substantial errors, and there is a time limit to correct these errors of which very few people are aware. The deadline for correcting earnings records is April 15th of the fourth year following the year in which the employee made the earnings. Further basic information can be obtained via the Internet at http://www.ssa.gov.

Determination of Retirement Benefits

Primary Insurance Amount (PIA)
The benefit amount received from Social Security.

The benefit amount is called the **Primary Insurance Amount (PIA),** which is based upon the worker's earnings averaged over the working career, or **Average Indexed Monthly Earnings** (AIME). Generally, the greater the lifetime earnings, the higher the retirement benefits. Lower benefits will result from some years of no earnings or low earnings in contrast with the higher earnings of a person who worked steadily. The benefit amount is also controlled by the person's age at the time retirement takes place and benefits commence. The person who elects to retire at 62, the earliest possible retirement age, will receive benefits lower than the person who works until 65 or 70. Social Security law now provides for automatic cost of living adjustments (COLA), which increase income of the already retired. Another reform is to lower the COLA.

Collecting Benefits

The full retirement age will be gradually increased from 65 to 67 starting after December 31, 1999. This increase will have a direct impact upon persons born in 1937 and later. This change is designed to increase the surplus in payroll tax collections, thereby increasing the income of the Social Security fund.

The minimum age to obtain Social Security benefits is age 62. However, the benefit amount will be permanently reduced according to the number of months prior to the applicant's

AGE TO RECEIVE FULL SOCIAL SECURITY BENEFITS	
Year of Birth	**Full Retirement Age**
1937 or earlier	65
1938	65 and 2 months
1939	65 and 4 months
1940	65 and 6 months
1941	65 and 8 months
1942	65 and 10 months
1943–1954	66
1955	66 and 2 months
1956	66 and 4 months
1957	66 and 6 months
1958	66 and 8 months
1959	66 and 10 months
1960 and later	67

attaining his or her 65th birthday. The benefits will actually be reduced by 4/5th of 1 percent for each month prior to 65 that retirement occurs.

If a person retires after age 65, increased benefits are available up to age 70. Each additional year beyond age 65 that a person continues to work adds another year of earnings to his or her PIA. The benefit is increased by a certain percentage as indicated in the table on Delayed Retirement.

BENEFIT INCREASES FOR DELAYED RETIREMENT

Year of Birth	Yearly Rate of Increase
1917–1924	3%
1925–1926	3.5%
1927–1928	4%
1929–1930	4.5%
1931–1932	5%
1933–1934	5.5%
1935–1936	6%
1937–1938	6.5%
1939–1940	7%
1941–1942	7.5%
1943 or later	8%

Medicare coverage is available at age 65, even if the worker continues employment past 65. If delayed retirement is chosen, it is recommended that Medicare still be obtained at age 65.

Benefits are paid monthly as follows:

SCHEDULE OF SOCIAL SECURITY BENEFIT PAYMENTS 2002

	Social Security Benefits paid on	If birth date on
Supplemental Security Income (SSI) Benefits	Second Wednesday	1st-10th
All Social Security Beneficiaries receiving benefits prior to May 1997	Third Wednesday	11th-20th
	Fourth Wednesday	21st-31st

Representative Payee

The Social Security Act provides for a procedure allowing a representative payee to be appointed for a Social Security beneficiary if it is determined that the interest of the beneficiary will be served by representative payment rather than direct payment. The beneficiary must be incapable of handling his or her own benefit payment in order to qualify for the appointment of a representative payee. This can be accomplished without going through a formal conservatorship or guardianship proceeding. The SSA will request medical proof of competency and capacity. If a legal guardian or conservator is appointed by the court, then filing the order of appointment with the SSA will facilitate the appointment of the legal guardian or conservator as the representative payee. (File Form SSA-11BK). If no legal representative exists, then the SSA will consider appointing a close family member, friend, a public nonprofit group, or a private profit group who currently has custody of the beneficiary (*e.g.,* nursing home, adult home, etc.). Once appointed, the representative payee will receive the Social Security benefits and must use them for the benefit of the beneficiary to:

- Purchase food, clothing, shelter, medical care
- Pay debts and expenses
- Invest any surplus not used for the beneficiary
- Report to SSA any changes that might affect the beneficiary's right to payment
- File an annual account with the SSA on SSA form 623-F6

The representative payee's appointment can be terminated by the SSA if it concludes that there has been a misuse of funds or if the beneficiary has regained the capacity to handle his or her own affairs. Termination also occurs upon the death of the beneficiary.

Overpayment of Social Security Benefits

An overpayment occurs whenever the Social Security Administration (SSA) issues a payment of more than the amount due to the beneficiary. The overpayment may be caused by an error on the part of the SSA or by the beneficiary because of failing to report information properly to the SSA. A common form of overage occurs when a beneficiary dies, the SSA is not notified, and benefits continue to be paid to the decedent's account by electronic transfer.

When the problem of overpayment confronts a beneficiary or his or her estate, several options are provided in the regulations:

1. Refund the overage or arrange to pay it off in installments.
2. Appeal the overage charge (reconsideration).
3. Request a waiver of the overpayment.

The SSA often settles these overpayments and reduces the amount due. It also has the right to deduct overpayments from the beneficiary's future payments. Before the SSA can act to recover an overage, it must provide adequate notice to the beneficiary of its intentions and advise beneficiary of his or her rights under the law. If the beneficiary refuses to act, the SSA then is entitled to full recovery.

If an elder care attorney is retained to represent a person in a Social Security matter, the SSA and the federal courts set the legal fees. The fee is usually set at 25 percent of past due benefits, and a fee request form (SSA-1560) must be filed by counsel stating the services rendered on behalf of the client.

Social Security Direct Deposit Program

Direct deposit delivers Social Security or Supplemental Security Income (SSI) benefits into the beneficiary's bank, savings and loan, or credit union account quickly and safely. The U.S. Treasury sends an electronic message to the financial institution crediting the account with the exact amount of the Social Security or SSI benefit. Once the funds are posted to the account, the beneficiary can access the account and use the funds in any desired

Direct Deposit
Allows for the Social Security or Supplemental Security Income to be deposited into a specified bank account electronically. This procedure eliminates the possibility of theft or loss of the check, and guarantees a quick and safe deposit.

manner. This procedure eliminates the possibility of theft or loss of the check. **Electronic Direct Deposit should be recommended to all clients**.

Social Security strongly encourages all beneficiaries to receive their monthly benefits by direct deposit. As of January 1999, 75 percent of all Social Security and SSI beneficiaries received their benefits by direct deposit. Social Security indicates that they will continue to mail checks to beneficiaries but direct deposit produces substantial savings to the government. In the future, all payments will probably be made electronically.

If the beneficiary has an existing account at a financial institution, it will assist in implementing the direct deposit program. Form SSA-SF-1199a must be completed by the individual and the financial institution and then sent to the Social Security Administration. It takes approximately 90 days for direct deposit to be put into effect. However, if the beneficiary arranges this transfer directly through a local Social Security office, the procedure can be accomplished much more quickly.

Benefits for Family Members

Social Security not only pays benefits to insured workers who retire but also to certain family members, as follows:

- Spouse age 62 or older
- Spouse below age 62 if he or she is taking care of a dependent child under age 16 or who is disabled
- Divorced spouse age 62 or older
- Children up to age 18
- Children age 18–19 if they are full-time students through grade 12
- Children over age 18 if they are disabled

Spousal Benefits

The spouse of a retired Social Security beneficiary is entitled to receive one half of the full benefit of the spouse, unless the spouse has chosen to receive his or her benefits below age 65. If that is the case, then the spousal benefits are permanently reduced by a specific percentage based on the number of months before he or she becomes 65. However, the regulations provide that the spouse must be age 62 or older. The spouse is entitled to full benefits regardless of his age if he is caring for a child who is either disabled and receiving Social Security benefits or under 16 years of age.

To qualify as a legal spouse, there must be a valid marriage under state law between the insured Social Security beneficiary and the spouse who is applying for benefits under his or her spouse's account. The Social Security Act provides for an exception to this rule under what is termed as a ***deemed-valid marriage.*** A person can be considered a *deemed* spouse under the Social Security Act if the spouse in good faith participated in a marriage ceremony that would have under state law been considered valid except for a legal impediment. A common example of this is an insured worker who failed to obtain a valid divorce or annulment from a first spouse and then married his current second spouse. The second spouse, now claiming benefits under a spouse's account, must not have known of the legal impediment at the time of marriage.

Eligibility benefits for divorced spouse

- The marriage must be valid.
- The marriage must have lasted more than 10 years.
- The divorced spouse must be age 62 or older.
- The divorced spouse must not be remarried.
- If the spouse has been divorced for at least two years, he or she can qualify to obtain benefits even if the insured worker has not retired. However, the worker must have accumulated enough quarters in the account for the divorced spouse to qualify for benefits, and the spouse must be age 62 or older. The amount of benefits received by a divorced spouse has no effect upon the amount of benefits to which a current spouse is entitled.
- There is no two-year waiting period if the respective spouses were each receiving benefits prior to the dissolution of their marriage.

Benefits for Children

Qualifications for children's benefits

- Natural children
- Legitimate children
- Illegitimate children
- Stepchildren
- Adopted children
- Grandchildren
- Step-grandchildren

Eligibility requirements

- The child must be under the age of 18, or be 18 or older, with a disability that commenced before age 22, and remain disabled.
- The child's age could be up to 19 if he or she is a full-time student.
- The child must be dependent.
- The child must be unmarried.

Survivor Benefits

Part of the FICA is used for survivor's insurance, which is similar to life insurance. When a qualified insured worker dies, his or her survivors are entitled to *survivor's benefits*. Survivors are classified as:

- Widows
- Widowers
- Divorced widows
- Divorced widowers

- Unmarried dependent children
- Dependent parents

Eligibility benefits for widows or widowers:

- The marriage to the deceased insured worker must have lasted at least nine months in duration immediately prior to the death of the insured worker.
- The nine-month spousal requirement is waived if the spouse's death was the result of an accident, occurred when on active military duty, or the spouse was married to the spousal applicant for nine months at a previous time.
- Full benefits are available at age 65 or older.
- Reduced benefits are available at age 62.
- Disabled widow or widower at a minimum age of 50.
- A widow or widower can receive benefits at any age if he or she takes care of a dependent under 16 or a disabled child who received benefits.

If an insured worker has been divorced, the ex-spouse is eligible for survivor's benefits with the same requirements as the worker's widow or widower, provided the marriage lasted 10 years or more. The former spouse is exempt from the 10-year length-of-marriage rule if he or she is caring for the deceased worker's dependent child who is younger than 16 or disabled and receiving benefits on the deceased worker's Social Security account. However, the child must be the worker's former spouse's natural or legally adopted child.

Benefits paid to a surviving divorced spouse age 60 or older (50–60 if disabled) will not have any effect upon the benefits received by other survivors of the deceased worker.

Survivor's benefits rules

- Benefits begin in the first month during which a full and complete application is filed and approved.
- Benefits terminate if there is a remarriage, unless the spouse is over age 60 at the date of the remarriage.
- If the spouse becomes entitled for any reason, to equal or larger Social Security benefits, the survivor benefits will terminate.

A parent of a deceased fully insured worker is entitled to benefits under the following conditions:

- The parent must be age 62 or older.
- The parent must not have remarried since the death of the insured child.
- The parent must be the natural mother or father of the deceased worker or must have adopted the deceased worker before age 16 or become a stepparent before the insured child attained age 16.

The Social Security Act provides for the payment of a lump sum of $255 to the surviving spouse, provided the deceased worker and his or her spouse were living together in the same household. This payment can also be made to children of the deceased worker if there is no surviving spouse, provided that the children are receiving benefits on record.

Cost of Living Adjustment (COLA)

Cost of living adjustments (COLAs) are annual increases in Social Security benefits to offset the effects of inflation on fixed incomes. Automatic benefit increases have been in effect since 1975. Based on the increase in the consumer price index (CPI-W) from the third quarter of 2000 through the third quarter of 2001, Social Security beneficiaries and Supplemental Security Income (SSI) recipients received a 2.6 percent COLA for 2002.

Estimated Average Monthly Social Security Benefits	Before and after the 12/2001 COLA	
	Before 2.6% COLA	After 2.6% COLA
All retired workers	$852	$874
Aged couple, both receiving benefits	$1,418	$1,454
Widowed mother and two children	$1,719	$1,764
Aged widow(er) alone	$820	$841
Disabled worker, spouse and one or more children	$1,325	$1,360
All disabled workers	$794	$815

Other important Social Security adjustments include:

Tax Rate	2003
Employee	7.65%
Self-Employed	15.30%

The 7.65 percent tax rate is the combined rate for Social Security and Medicare. The Social Security portion (OASDI) is 6.20 percent on earnings up to the applicable taxable maximum amount ($87,000 in 2003). The Medicare portion (HI) is 1.45 percent on all earnings.

Social Security Disability Thresholds	2003
Substantial Gainful Activity (SGA)	
Non-Blind	$800/mo.
Blind	$1,300/mo.
Trial Work Period (TWP)	$570/mo.

Maximum Social Security Benefit Worker Retiring at Age 65 in January	2002
	$1,660/mo.

SSI Federal Payment Standard	2003
Individual	$552/mo.
Couple	$829/mo.

SSI Resources Limits	2003
Individual	$2,000
Couple	$3,000

SSI Student Exclusion Limits	2003
Individual	$1,320
Couple	$5,327

Applications for Social Security Retirement Benefits

Applications should be filed several months before actual eligibility because it takes several months for processing claims. If a person files late, *e.g.*, after his or her 65th birthday, retroactive benefits are available for up to six months from the date of filing the application.

Apply by:

1. Call 800-772-1213
2. The deaf or hard of hearing may call 800-325-0778
3. Go in person to any local district office

Documents required by the applicant

- Social Security number
- Birth certificate
- W-2 forms for last 12 months
- Tax return for last year if self-employed
- Spouse's birth certificate and Social Security number, if he or she is applying for benefits
- Children's birth certificates and Social Security numbers, if applying for children's benefits
- Proof of U.S. citizenship or lawful alien status if applicant was not born in the United States. Spouse and all children must also produce proof of citizenship or lawful alien status if they are applying for benefits
- The name of applicant's bank and account number for electronic deposit of benefits into bank account

Original documents or certified copies are required, but they will be returned to the applicant.

Right to Appeal

If the applicant received a decision denying benefits, an appeal process can be initiated. The applicant has only 60 days after receipt of the initial determination to file for reconsideration (appeal). The claimant has a right to be represented by counsel.

If the reconsideration results in a denial of benefits, the claimant has the right to demand a formal hearing before an administrative law judge (ALJ). Counsel may represent the claimant and be present at the hearing. The request for the hearing again must be made within 60 days of receipt of the notice of denial. If the hearing decision is not favorable to the claimant, the next step in the administrative process is to file an appeal with the Appeals Counsel Review. This new appeal must also be filed within 60 days of the decision of the ALJ.

If all else fails and the claimant has exhausted all administrative remedies, he or she may seek help within 60 days of the receipt of the decision from the appeals counsel. An action must be commenced within the 60-day period in the local federal district court having jurisdiction. Judicial review will then be forthcoming.

SOCIAL SECURITY DISABILITY BENEFITS

Social Security provides the insured with monthly cash benefits in the event of disability. An applicant is considered disabled if unable to do any kind of work ("to perform substantial gainful activity") for which he or she is suited and the disability is expected to last for at least one year or to result in death. This is a very confined definition of disability and is strictly adhered to by the SSA. It is really designed to provide continuing income when the qualified worker cannot do so. Benefits are required to continue for the period of disability and will cease upon recovery or death.

Eligibility

- A fully insured worker at any age
- Certain members of the worker's family may also qualify for benefits on his or her account
- Unmarried sons or daughters including adopted children, stepchildren or grandchildren. The children must be under age 18 or under age 19 if in school full-time
- Unmarried sons or daughters 18 or older who became disabled before age 22
- Spouse age 62 or older, or at any age if he or she is caring for a child of the worker who is under 16 or disabled and also receiving benefits
- Disabled widow or widower 50 or older. Disability must have started prior to death of the worker's spouse or within seven years after the worker's death. If the widow or widower caring for the deceased worker's children received Social Security benefits, he or she is eligible if he or she becomes disabled before those payments end or within seven years after they end

A person receiving disability benefits at age 65 will have his or her benefits converted to retirement benefits. Social Security disability benefits may be taxable. A person who receives Social Security disability benefits will automatically be enrolled and entitled to Medicare benefits after receiving benefits for two years. Benefits are not paid for partial disability.

Important Regulations

- There is a five-month waiting period before disability benefits are paid.

- Twelve months of retroactive benefits prior to application filing are available if all other requirements are met.
- Disability ends at age 65.
- Upon return to work, disability ends.

Other Grounds for Disability Benefits

People with AIDS (HIV infection) are eligible for disability benefits when they become disabled and unable to work. For further information, refer to *A Guide to Social Security and SSI Disability Benefits for People with HIV Infection* (SSA Pub. 05-10020).

Drug addiction and alcoholism are grounds for benefits. The disabled person must enter rehabilitation treatment to qualify for benefits. If the person fails to obtain treatment, benefits will be suspended. If the suspension continues for 12 consecutive months, the benefits will automatically terminate. Benefits are payable only for a maximum period of 36 months.

Blindness is also a qualification. An applicant is considered blind under the Social Security rules if vision cannot be corrected to better than 20/200 in the better eye or if the visual field is 20 degrees or less, even with corrective lenses. There are special rules for the determination of eligibility for blindness benefits. The Social Security Act issues a leaflet entitled *If You Are Blind—How We Can Help* (No. 05-10052). The Code of Federal Regulations 404.154 & 1584 should be consulted.

Number of Social Security quarters to qualify

1. *Before age 24:* Workers may qualify if they have six quarters earned in the three-year period ending when the disability starts.
2. *Age 24 to 31:* Workers may qualify if they have credits for having worked half the time between age 21 and the time they became disabled.
3. *Age 31 or older:* In general, workers will be required to have the number of work credits shown in the following chart. Unless a worker is blind, at least 20 of the credits must have been earned in the 10 years immediately before he or she became disabled.

Born After 1929, Disabled At Age	Quarters Required
31 through 42	20
44	22
46	24
48	26
50	28
52	30
54	32
56	34
58	36
60	38
62 or older	40

Applications

It takes about 90 days for claims to be processed, and no benefits will be issued until the sixth full month of disability has been completed.

Apply by:

- Going in person to any local Social Security office as soon as a person becomes disabled
- Telephone, using the telephone numbers aforementioned
- Certified mail, return receipt requested

Necessary Documents

- Social Security number
- Proof of age, a birth certificate for each applicant
- Names, addresses, and telephone numbers of each treating physician, hospital, clinic, and institution, as well as specific dates of treatment
- List of all medications used by the applicant
- All medical records from physicians, therapists, hospital clinics, and case workers
- Laboratory results
- A job history for preceding 15 years (specify the type of work performed)
- Copy of the most recent W-2 form
- Most recently filed federal tax return, if self-employed
- If spouse is applying, dates of all his/her prior marriages

The applicant should contact all treating physicians, advise them that an application has been filed for Social Security disability, and request that they cooperate by supplying any information required by the Social Security Administration.

The Decision Process

The Social Security office will review the application to see if the applicant meets the eligibility requirements, *e.g.,* necessary quarters, age, etc. The application will then be forwarded to the Disability Determination Services (DDS) office in the state wherein the applicant resides. That agency will make the final decision as to whether or not the applicant is disabled under Social Security law by reviewing all medical reports and documents originally filed with the application, as well as any reports they have subsequently obtained. The applicant may be required to undergo additional medical exams and medical tests, all of which are paid for by the Social Security Agency, including travel expenses.

If the claim is denied or the applicant disagrees with the decision, an appeal can be filed. The appeals process is the same as discussed earlier in this chapter. There are four levels of appeal. The last level of appeal is to institute a suit in the local federal district court. Timing at all levels is critical in the appellate process. All appeals must be filed within 60 days of the time the applicant receives the decision that he or she is appealing. See Social Security Administration Publication *The Appeals Process* (No. 05-10041).

Recertification of Disability

The Social Security Act provides that benefits are to continue as long as a person is actually disabled. However, the claimant's case will be reviewed based on the probability of recovery.

- If medical improvement is expected, the case will normally be reviewed within six to 18 months.
- If medical improvement is possible, the case will normally be reviewed sooner than three years.
- If medical improvement is not expected, the case may be reviewed no sooner than seven years.

Ending benefits

The Social Security Administration can decide that the beneficiary is no longer disabled and terminate the benefits under the following circumstances:

- The beneficiary is working and has average earnings of $500 or more per month. These are considered "substantial" earnings.
- The medical condition has improved so that the person is no longer considered disabled.
- There are reporting requirements to which the disabled person must strictly adhere, *e.g.,* improvement in medical condition or return to work, etc. Failure to do so can result in suspension or termination of benefits.

Disability benefits can be paid for the full duration of an insured worker's life provided the disabled worker continues to meet all the eligibility requirements (except the 36-month maximum benefit available for disability resulting from alcoholism or drug abuse).

- Earnings are adjusted each year for inflation.
- Earnings do not include income from savings accounts, dividends, investments, insurance annuities, or pensions.
- The reduction of benefits also affects the dependent's benefits.

WORKING AND RECEIVING SOCIAL SECURITY AT THE SAME TIME

A person can work while receiving Social Security benefits. This could mean higher benefits in future years and can be very important later in life. It also could increase the future benefit amounts available to the beneficiary's family and survivors.

Reduction of Social Security Benefits based on Earned Income: The Retirement Earnings Test

The Retirement Earnings Test (RET) reduces the Social Security benefits of beneficiaries who have earned income above a threshold amount ($11,520 in 2003) and are between 62 and 64 years of age.

Social Security beneficiaries who are not of full retirement age (currently 65) will have to give up $1 in benefits for every $2 they earn in excess of $11,520 in 2003 (up from $11,280 in 2002).

For those individuals that reach full retirement age in 2003, $1 in benefits will be withheld for every $3 they earn over $30,720 in 2003 (up from $30,000 in 2002). The retirement earnings test does not apply to people who have reached full retirement age by the beginning of the year, who can earn any amount without reducing their Social Security benefits.

In 2000, the law affecting working Social Security beneficiaries was amended. While working, the benefit amount will now be reduced only when a person reaches full retirement age. The Social Security Administration has developed a formula to determine how much the benefit must be reduced:

Taxation of Social Security Benefits

Social Security benefits became subject to income tax in 1984. The tax varies according to the recipient's income:

- Retired persons with little or no income will not be taxed on their Social Security benefits.
- Persons in higher income brackets who may also be employed will be taxed on the Social Security benefits they receive.

Rules for Determining Taxability of Social Security

The Fifty-Percent Rule

If the taxpayer's provisional income for the year exceeds the base amount, the amount of Social Security benefits that must be included by the taxpayer in gross income for the year is the lesser of:

1. One-half of the Social Security benefit received by the taxpayer that year
2. One-half of the above excess

The statutory base amount is $32,000 for married couples filing a joint return and $25,000 for singles in 2003. Provisional income is defined as the total of modified adjusted gross income plus one-half of the Social Security benefits received during that tax year.

The Eighty-Five Percent Rule

If the taxpayer's provisional income exceeds an adjusted base amount, then gross income is determined to include the lesser of:

1. 85 percent of the Social Security benefits received
2. The sum of the smaller of the amount included under the 50 percent rule or one-half of the difference between the adjusted base amount and the base amount of the taxpayer plus 85 percent of the excess of the provisional income over the adjusted base amount. For married individuals filing a joint return, the adjusted base amount is $44,000 and for single individuals, $34,000. In 2003, if a married taxpayer files separately, gross income shall include the lesser of 85 percent of the taxpayer's Social Security benefits or 85 percent of the taxpayer's provisional income

Social Security Benefits Worksheet

The calculations involved determining the taxability of Social Security benefits is complex, but the following worksheet will assist the taxpayer.

SUPPLEMENTAL SECURITY INCOME PROGRAMS

Congress passed legislation in 1973 establishing the **Supplemental Security Income Program (SSI)**. The statute can be found in title XVI of the Social Security Act. (42 USC

Supplemental Security Income (SSI)
Benefits to people who are 65 or older, blind, or disabled, and who have minimal income.

SOCIAL SECURITY BENEFITS WORKSHEET

1. Enter the total amount from box 5 of ALL your Forms SSA–1099 and RRB–1099 ... 1. ____
   Note: *If line 1 is zero or less, stop here; none of your benefits are taxable. Otherwise, go to line 2.*
2. Enter one-half of line 1 ... 2. ____
3. Enter the total of the amounts from:
   Form 1040: Lines 7, 8a, 8b, 9a, 10–13a, 14, 15b, 16b, 17–19, and 21
   Form 1040A: Lines 7, 8a, 8b, 9a, 10a, 11b, 12b, and 13 ... 3. ____
4. *Form 1040 filers*: Enter the total of any exclusions/adjustments for:
   • Qualified U.S. savings bond interest (Form 8815, line 14)
   • Adoption benefits (Form 8839, line 30)
   • Foreign earned income or housing (Form 2555, lines 43 and 48, or Form 2555–EZ, line 18), and
   • Certain income of bona fide residents of American Samoa (Form 4563, line 15) or Puerto Rico
   Form 1040A filers: Enter the total of any exclusions for:
   • Qualified U.S. savings bond interest (Form 8815, line 14)
   • Adoption benefits (Form 8839, line 30) ... 4. ____
5. Add lines 2,3, and 4 ... 5. ____
6. *Form 1040 filers*: Enter the amount from Form 1040, line 33, minus any amounts on Form 1040, lines 25 and 26.
   Form 1040A filers: Enter the amount from Form 1040A, line 20, minus any amounts on Form 1040A, lines 18 and 19 ... 6. ____
7. Is the amount on line 6 less than the amount on line 5?
   No. None of your social security benefits are taxable.
   Yes. Subtract line 6 from line 5 ... 7. ____

8. If you are:
   - Married filing jointly, enter $32,000
   - Single, head of household, qualifying widow(er), or married filing separately and you **lived apart** from your spouse for all of 2003, enter $25,000 .... 8. _____

   Note: If you are married filing separately and you lived with your spouse at any time in 2003, skip lines 8 through 15; multiply line 7 by 85% (.85) and enter the result on line 16. Then go to line 17.

9. Is the amount on line 8 less than the amount on line 7?
   - **No.**   None of your benefits are taxable. Do not enter any amounts on Form 1040, line 20a or 20b, or on Form 1040A, line 14a or 14b. But if you are married filing separately and you lived apart from your spouse for all of 2003, enter -0- on Form 1040, line 20b, or on Form 1040A, line 14b.
   - **Yes.**   Subtract line 8 from line 7 .... 9. _____

10. Enter $12,000 if married filing jointly; $9,000 if single, head of household, qualifying widow(er), or married filing separately and you **lived apart** from your spouse for all of 2003 .... 10. _____
11. Subtract line 10 from line 9. If zero or less, enter -0- .... 11. _____
12. Enter the **smaller** of line 9 or line 10 .... 12. _____
13. Enter one-half of line 12 .... 13. _____
14. Enter the **smaller** of line 2 or line 13 .... 14. _____
15. Multiply line 11 by 85% (.85). If line 11 is zero, enter -0- .... 15. _____
16. Add lines 14 and 15 .... 16. _____
17. Multiply line 1 by 85% (.85) .... 17. _____
18. **Taxable benefits.** Enter the **smaller** of line 16 or line 17 .... 18. _____
    - Enter the amount from line 1 above on Form 1040, line 20a, or on Form 1040A, line 14a.
    - Enter the amount from line 18 above on Form 1040, line 20b, or on Form 1040A, line 14b.

    Note: *If you received a lump-sum payment in this year that was for an earlier year, also complete Worksheet 2 or 3 and Worksheet 4 to see whether you can report a lower taxable benefit.*

PRACTICE TIP

If part of the benefits are taxable for 2001 and they include benefits paid in 2001 that were for an earlier year, it may be possible to reduce the taxable amount shown on the worksheet. (See I.R.S. Pub. 915 for details.)

§ 1381 *et seq.* [1982].) It provides monthly benefits to people who are 65 or older, blind, or disabled, and who have minimal income. The program provides benefits for adults as well as for disabled and blind children. People who qualify for Supplemental Security Income (SSI) usually qualify for food stamps and Medicaid. The maximum federal benefit changes yearly. Effective January 1, 2002, the federal benefit rate is $545 for an individual and $817 for a couple.

In December 2000, more than 6.6 million people received federally administered SSI payments, including about 1.3 million aged and 5.3 million who were disabled or blind. About two million recipients were aged 65 or older, about 3.7 million were 18–64, and about .85 million were under age 18.

Qualifications for SSI

Applicant must be:

- 65 or older and must provide proof of age such as a birth certificate or baptismal record
- Blind, with central visual acuity of 20/200 or less in the better eye with the use of a correcting lens or extremely severe limitation in the field of vision
- Disabled, that is, the applicant has physical or mental problems that keeps him or her from active gainful employment and that is expected to last at least a year or to result in death

Residency and Citizenship Requirements

The applicant must provide proof of residency and citizenship status.

Residency

1. The law defines a resident as a person who resides in one of the 50 states, the District of Columbia, or the Northern Mariana Islands. Residents of Puerto Rico are excluded from receiving SSI benefits.
2. The applicant must establish residency in the U.S. for 30 consecutive days. The following documents can be used to establish residency:
   a. Tax returns
   b. Rent receipts
   c. Telephone and electricity bills

Citizenship

Citizenship can be established by the production of any one of the following documents:

1. Certified birth certificate showing birth in the U.S.
2. Baptism birth records
3. U.S. passport
4. Certificate of naturalization

Qualified Alien

The Welfare Reform Legislation passed in August 1986 has drastically restricted the rights of immigrants to obtain SSI benefits:

1. No illegal immigrant can receive SSI benefits.
2. Qualified aliens may receive SSI benefits. The statute defines a "qualified alien" as a permanent resident, an asylee, a refugee, a person paroled into the United States for at

least a year, a person whose deportation is withheld for certain statutory purposes, or a person who is granted conditional entry into the United States.

Further restrictions include the following categories of qualified aliens eligible for SSI benefits:

1. The qualified alien who has received status as an asylee, refugee, or person whose deportation has been withheld is eligible to receive benefits for only the first five years after status has been granted
2. The qualified alien who has received an honorable discharge or who is on active duty in the military and his or her spouse and unmarried children

If disabled, the applicant must accept occupational rehabilitation services if they are offered.

Income Eligibility

In order to be eligible for SSI, the applicant must have a minimal income. The income threshold is determined by the state in which the individual resides. To obtain this information, the applicant can call the SSA at the toll-free number 800-772-1213.

Exempt Income

- $20 per month of general income
- The first $65 of earned income and half of the remaining earned income over $65 in any month
- Food stamps
- Food, clothing, or shelter obtained from nonprofit organizations
- Most home energy assistance
- Student scholarships, grants, and fellowships, with certain limitations
- Wages used to pay for items or services the applicant needs for work because of disability, *e.g.,* wheelchair if applicant needs to work
- Wages used to pay expenses that are caused by working, *e.g.,* wages to pay transportation to and from work, if applicant is blind

People who live in city or county rest homes, halfway homes, or other public institutions will usually not qualify for SSI, with the following exemptions:

- If the applicant lives in a publically operated community residence that provides housing for no more than 16 people
- If the applicant lives in a public institution mainly to attend approved educational or job training
- If applicant lives in a public emergency shelter for the homeless
- If the applicant resides in a public or private institution and Medicaid is paying half the cost of the applicant's care

Eligibility is also based upon assets that the applicant owns, such as real estate, personal property, bank accounts, savings bonds, etc. A single person may possess up to $2,000 in assets, and a married couple up to $3,000. The following items are exempt:

- Personal residence and the land on which it is situated
- Personal and household goods and personal effects up to $2,000—wedding rings, engagement rings, etc.,
- Life insurance policies with up to $1,500 cash surrender value
- Automobile—if necessary, no value limits; if nonessential, maximum value $4,500
- Burial plot for the applicant and members of the immediate family
- Up to $1,500 in burial funds for the applicant
- Up to $1,500 in burial funds for the applicant's spouse
- Trusts, only if irrevocable and the principal cannot be obtained by the claimant

The total number of persons receiving a Social Security payment, a federally administered SSI payment, or both was 49 million. Federally administered payments totaled nearly $2.7 billion in December 2000: $2.4 billion in federal SSI payments and $293 million in state supplements. The average federally administered payment was $379. Aged persons received an average of $300; the disabled and blind received an average of $398.

In addition 683 thousand people in 30 states received state-administered payments of $75.8 million in December 2000.

Applications

Application must be made directly to the Social Security office.

The documents required are:
1. Social Security number
2. Birth certificate or other proof of age
3. Proof of residence
4. Financial information

Right to Appeal

If an application for SSI is denied, the applicant has a right to appeal for an administrative hearing as well as commence an action in federal court for judicial review. The rules are like those relating to other Social Security appeals.

REVIEW QUESTIONS AND EXERCISES

1. What is Social Security? How does the system operate? How is the system funded?
2. What is the inherent problem with the Social Security system as it exists today? With the imminent retirement of the baby boomer generation, how can the Social Security system be revised to ensure its continued survival?

3.   Discuss the plan to privatize the Social Security system. What are the advantages and disadvantages to this concept?

4.   Who is eligible to receive Social Security benefits? How are they calculated?

5.   What are the ages at which people can retire? What are the advantages and disadvantages of early retirement as compared to a delayed retirement?

6.   What family members are entitled to receive an insured retired worker's Social Security benefits? Are divorced spouses entitled to receive the retired worker's Social Security benefits?

7.   Discuss Social Security disability benefits. Who is eligible to receive them? What can cause Social Security disability benefits to cease?

8.   What is Supplemental Security Income (SSI)? Who is eligible to receive it?

CHAPTER 10

Entitlement Programs Part II: Medicare and Medicaid Assistance Programs

PREVIEW

With the graying of the United States, entitlement programs have a greater impact. From the continual discussion of reforms to the increasing usage of the system, Medicare and Medicaid have become a common discussion point. This chapter is devoted to providing the legal professional with a basic knowledge of federal and state entitlement programs available to the elderly client. These programs are designed to assist the elderly in meeting their medical and long-term care expenses. The reader will be provided with a detailed account of Medicare and the Medicaid Assistance Program, including what is and is not covered, how to spend down a client's assets, and a thorough understanding of the Medicaid look-back rule. Additionally, this chapter discusses rights under the Federal Family and Medical Leave Act and its effect on the elderly client and family members.

INTRODUCTION

The majority of the clients in the practice of elder law are over the age of 65. Statistics currently indicate that 50 percent of Americans who reach that age are apt to require some form of long-term skilled care at some time during their lives; 20 percent will spend a year or more in a skilled nursing facility, never to return to the community.

As discussed previously, demographic studies indicate that Americans are now living longer. The longer the elderly live, the greater the probability that they will develop long-term catastrophic illness, such as Alzheimer's disease, Parkinson's disease, senile dementia or organic brain syndrome, or suffer a stroke. Currently four million Americans suffer from the devastation of Alzheimer's disease. This dreaded illness is expected to grow in epidemic proportions in the coming years due to the changing demographics in aging. All of these illnesses at some time will require long-term care, and patients will need to access the entitlement programs of Medicare and Medicaid.

This chapter is devoted to providing the legal professional with a basic knowledge of the federal and state entitlement programs available to elderly clients. These programs are designed to assist the elderly in meeting their medical and long-term care expenses. Unfortunately the government is making these programs increasingly difficult to access due to ever more restrictive legislation and a lack of publicity. By being familiar with these programs, however, the legal professional can help eligible clients to obtain the benefits to which they are legally entitled.

There are two basic programs: **Medicare** and **Medicaid**. Forty million elderly or disabled Americans are currently enrolled in Medicare, and approximately 36 million low-income Americans are Medicaid recipients. Both programs are administered by the **Centers for Medicare and Medicaid Services**, formerly known as the **Health Care Finance**

Medicare
A federal program based on age designed to provide hospital medical insurance for people over 65 years of age, established under the Social Security Act.

Medicaid
A federal program administered by the states to provide medical assistance, nursing home care, and home care, etc., for poor, indigent people. It is a needs-based program, not based on age.

Administration (HCFA), a federal agency within the Department of Health and Human Services, the largest federal agency in the United States government.

MEDICARE

Medicare is a national health insurance program. It has two parts:

Medicare Part A
Hospital insurance that helps to pay for care in a hospital, skilled nursing facility, home health care, and hospice care.

Medicare Part B
Medical insurance that helps to pay for doctor's bills, outpatient hospital care, and other medical services not covered by Part A.

Part A: Hospital insurance that helps pay for care in a hospital, skilled nursing facility, home health care, and hospice care.

Part B: Medical insurance that helps pay for doctor's bills, outpatient hospital care, and other medical services not covered by Part A.

Eligibility

To qualify for Medicare, one must normally meet the following eligibility requirements:

1. The individual must be a United States citizen or a permanent resident of the United States.
2. The individual must be at least 65 years of age with the following exceptions:
   - A disabled person of any age after two years from the date of onset of the disability
   - A person of any age with end stage renal disease (permanent kidney failure requiring dialysis or a kidney transplant)
3. The individual or a spouse must have worked at least 10 years in Medicare-covered employment, *e.g.,* payroll deductions have been paid into Medicare fund

Other Avenues

All those individuals who meet the following eligibility requirements are entitled to Part A benefits without having to pay premiums.

1. Individuals already receiving retirement benefits from Social Security or the Railroad Retirement Board
2. Individuals eligible to receive Social Security or Railroad Retirement benefits who have not already filed for them
3. Individuals or spouses who had Medicare-covered government employment
4. Individuals under age 65 who:
   - Have received Social Security or Railroad Retirement Board disability benefits for 24 months
   - Are kidney dialysis or transplant patients

Premiums

The individual who meets the above criteria does not have to pay a premium for Part A benefits. However, if an applicant wishes to be covered under Part B, that person must pay a monthly health premium of $66.60 (2004). Premium usually increases annually. The premium is automatically deducted from the individual's Social Security, Railroad Retirement, or Civil Service benefits check. A person may have only Part A. There is no requirement to have Part B.

Payments

Medicare is not always the primary payer. Medicare is the secondary payer if the applicant is entitled to:

- Workers' compensation benefits
- Federal Black Lung benefits
- No-fault liability insurance
- Group health care, under certain circumstances
- V.A. benefits

The health care provider is required to submit Medicare claim forms on behalf of the patient.

MEDICARE PART A COVERAGE

The Medicare Hospital Funded Insurance Program is funded by the Medicare tax as a payroll deduction.

Benefit Periods

The Medicare program sets up benefit periods as a measurement of coverage in hospitals and skilled nursing homes. The designated benefit period allows the Medicare recipient a specific number of days of coverage in each of the above types of facilities.

The benefit period commences on the day of admission to a hospital and ends upon discharge; coverage is for 60 days.

Upon every admission to a hospital, a person is entitled to a new benefit period, and the Part A benefits are renewed. It is important to note that there are no limits to the number of benefit periods a Medicare recipient can receive during his or her lifetime, provided there is a 60-day uninterrupted period when no hospitalization is required.

Specific Coverage

Inpatient Hospital Care

Medicare Part A pays as follows if the patient is admitted to a Medicare-certified hospital within a benefit period:

1. Patient pays the first $876, as of 2004. This is known as the patient's deductible. This increases every year. The deductible is paid only once during a benefit period.
2. Medicare pays all other hospital expenses for the first 60 days of admission.

Medi-Gap Insurance Policy
Medicare supplement insurance policy sold by private insurance companies to fill gaps in Medicare coverage. They must be issued in accordance with strict federal and state regulations.

3. From the 61st day through the 90th day, Medicare pays all covered expenses except for a co-insurance deductible of $219 *per* day (2004), which is the responsibility of the insured. (The patient may obtain a **medi-gap insurance policy** to pay for the deductibles incurred by the patient. These policies are sold by private insurance companies.)

4. After 90 days, there are reserve days. Every Medicare recipient has a lifetime reserve of 60 days. If a patient is hospitalized for more than 90 days in a benefit period, the patient can draw on the reserve days to help pay for the excess cost. In each reserve day, there is a co-insurance cost to the patient of $438 (2004). Medicare pays costs above the co-insurance amount. (It should be noted that all of the deductibles mentioned above usually increase annually.)

Covered Services

1. Semi-private room
2. Meals (special diets)
3. Regular nursing services
4. Rehabilitation services
5. Drugs
6. Medical supplies
7. Lab tests
8. X-rays
9. Operating rooms
10. Recovery rooms
11. Intensive care units (ICU)
12. Coronary care units (CCU)
13. All other medically necessary services and supplies

Services Not Covered

1. Telephone
2. Television
3. Private room, unless medically necessary, *e.g.,* quarantine
4. Private-duty nursing

Qualifications for Hospital Care Part A

1. A physician orders inpatient hospital care for illness or injury.
2. The care required can only be provided in a hospital.
3. The facility is a Medicare participant.
4. The facility's Utilization Review Committee or Peer Review Committee does not issue a notice disallowing the hospital stay.

Psychiatric Hospital Coverage

Lifetime maximum coverage limited to 190 days.

Note: Psychiatric care provided in a general hospital is not subject to the 190-day rule.

Skilled Nursing Facility (SNF)

Medicare coverage in a **skilled nursing facility (SNF)** is provided if the recipient meets the following five criteria:

1. Patient requires daily skilled nursing or rehabilitation services that can only be provided in an SNF.
2. Prior to admission to the SNF, the patient must have been confined to a hospital for a minimum of three days (72 hours).
3. Admission to the SNF occurs within 30 days of hospital discharge after a three-day hospital stay.
4. The medical condition for which the patient is receiving skilled care was just treated in the hospital or actually arose while hospitalized.
5. A medical professional certifies to Medicare that skilled nursing care is medically necessary.

Skilled Nursing Facility (SNF)
Facility providing skilled nursing care, a subacute care facility for patients who do not require hospitalization but cannot be cared for at home.

Medicare does not pay for custodial care in an SNF, *i.e.,* where the patient receives no skilled care.

Blood Coverage

1. Each Medicare Part A recipient has a three-pint deductible per year. This is called the *annual blood deductible*.
2. The patient or family member can replace the blood deductible by a donation, or it can be paid for directly by the patient.
3. Both Part A & B cover blood transfusion. The maximum deductible for both parts is only the three pints specified above.

Home Health Care

Limited home health care is provided by Medicare if the following criteria are met:

1. Patient requires *intermittent* (not full-time) skilled nursing care, physical therapy or speech therapy, tube-feeding, monitoring of blood sugars with insulin injections, sterile dressing changes, or injections of intravenous fluids.
2. Patient is confined to the home.
3. The physician certifies that home health care is required and organizes a plan to deliver it.
4. The home health care agency is a qualified Medicare provider.
5. No prior hospital stay is required.

6. There is no deductible.
7. Medicare covers 80 percent of the approved amount of durable medical equipment—wheelchairs, hospital beds, oxygen supplies, and walkers. The patient pays 20 percent. Custodial needs and homemaker services are not covered by Medicare.

Hospice Care

Hospice Care
A freestanding health care facility caring for terminally ill individuals. Hospice care is also provided at home for terminally ill individuals and is covered under Medicare for up to six months.

palative care

Limited **hospice care** is provided if all of the following criteria are met:

1. A physician issues a certification of terminal illness (life expectancy six months or less).
2. Patient elects to receive hospice care instead of standard Medicare benefits.
3. Hospice program must be a Medicare-approved provider.
4. Maximum coverage in most cases is 210 days.
5. Hospice care can be provided at home or in a facility as an inpatient.
6. Hospice coverage can extend to include homemaker services, counseling, and certain prescription drugs (not used for curative purposes—drugs used for providing comfort and relief are usually covered).
7. There is a $5 deductible for each drug prescription and $5 deductible per day for respite care (provides temporary relief to the persons who regularly assist with home care, *e.g.,* family members).
8. If the hospice patient does not die within the covered period, the hospice may discharge the patient from the facility, and coverage for home care can also be terminated.

Medicare coverage is not available to cover health care services received outside the United States and its territories. There are certain exceptions for treatment in Canada and Mexico.

MEDICARE PART B COVERAGE

Medicare Part B provides the following non-hospital medical coverage:

1. Medically necessary services of a physician—at home or in doctors' offices, clinic (outpatient), SNF, or hospital, provided the services rendered are performed within the U.S. and its territories (See note above.)
2. Outpatient hospital services
3. X-rays, MRIs, CAT scans, EKGs, and lab tests
4. Ambulances—coverage is limited, provided it meets Medicare standards and only if transportation by any other type of vehicle would endanger life.
   Transportation covered includes:
   a. Between patient's home and hospital
   b. Home to SNF
   c. SNF to home or hospital
5. Breast prostheses following a mastectomy
6. Services of certain specially qualified practitioners who are not physicians (*e.g.,* a chiropractor, podiatrist, dentist, optometrist—coverage is very limited)

7. Physical and occupational therapy
8. Speech therapy
9. Home health care, if no coverage for Part A of Medicare
10. Blood, three-pint deduction
11. Injections that inoculate against the flu, pneumonia, and hepatitis B
12. Pap smears used to detect cervical cancer, once every two years
13. Mammograms used in screening for breast cancer, every 12 months
14. Outpatient mental health services
15. Prostheses for limbs and eyes
16. Braces for arms, legs, and back
17. Durable medical equipment, *e.g.,* wheelchairs, walkers, hospital beds, and oxygen equipment authorized by a physician for home care
18. Kidney dialysis and kidney transplants
19. Heart and liver transplant in a Medicare-approved facility
20. Medical supplies, *e.g.,* osteotomy bags, surgical dressing, splints, and casts
21. Eyeglasses, covered only if patient needs corrective lenses after cataract surgery
22. Bone mass measurements
23. Colorectal cancer screening—fecal occult blood test once every 12 months, flexible sigmoidoscopy or barium enema once every 48 months and colonscopy once every 24 months
24. Diabetes services and supplies
25. Glaucoma screening, once every 12 months .
26. Prostate cancer screening once every 12 months

Medicare now provides coverage for the treatment of Alzheimer's disease. New research shows that Alzheimer's patients respond to physical therapy, psychotherapy, and other forms of treatment. The quality of their lives significantly improves, and admissions of Alzheimer's patients to long-term care facilities is reduced. This new coverage by the **Centers for Medicare and Medicaid Services** began in December 2001 and is currently being implemented throughout the country. In the past, Medicare claims for the treatment of Alzheimer's were routinely denied. Previously, Medicare provided no coverage for mental health care, hospice, or home health care if the diagnosis was Alzheimer's.

Medical Services and Items Not Covered by Part A or B

1. Routine physical
2. Most dental care and dentures
3. Routine foot care
4. Hearing aids
5. Most prescription drugs
6. Acupuncture
7. Cosmetic surgery
8. Custodial care (help with activities of daily living) at home or in an SNF
9. Health care received while traveling outside the U.S. (except in limited cases—emergencies in Mexico and Canada)

Part B Deductible

The annual deductible is $100. After the deductible is met, Medicare pays 80 percent of covered services. The patient pays the remaining 20 percent (usually covered by private medigap policy). This is called co-insurance. The patient's share of the bill could amount to more than 20 percent of the Medicare-approved amount, for example:

1. The patient who receives **hospital outpatient services** is responsible for paying 20 percent of whatever the hospital *actually* charges, not 20 percent of the Medicare-approved amount.
2. The patient who receives **outpatient mental health services** must pay 50 percent of the Medicare-approved amount.

The Medicare-approved amount is the fee which Medicare deems to be fair and reasonable for the services rendered to the patient.

Medicare Part A: 2004

Services	Benefit	Medicare Pays	Patient Pays[1]
HOSPITALIZATION Semi-private room and board, general nursing, and other hospital services and supplies.	First 60 days 61st to 90th day 91st to 150th day Beyond 150 days	All but $876 All but $219 a day All but $438 a day -0-	$876 $219 a day $438 a day All costs
SKILLED NURSING FACILITY CARE (SNF) Semi-private room and board, skilled nursing and rehabilitative services, and other services and supplies.	First 20 days Additional 80 days Beyond 100 days	100% of approved amount All but $109.50 a day -0-	-0- Up to $109.50 a day Entire cost
HOME HEALTH CARE Part-time or intermittent skilled care, home health aide services, durable medical equipment, and supplies and other services.	Unlimited as long as Medicare requirements are met.	100% of approved amount; 80% of approved amount for durable medical equipment.	Nothing for services; 20% of approved amount for durable medical equipment.
HOSPICE CARE Pain relief, symptom management, and support services for the terminally ill.	For as long as doctor certifies need, usually up to 210 days.	All except limited costs for outpatient drugs and inpatient respite care.	Limited costs for outpatient drugs and inpatient respite care. ($5 deductible)
BLOOD[2] When furnished by a hospital or skilled nursing facility during a covered stay.	Unlimited if medically necessary.	All except for first three pints per calendar year.	Only for first three pints.

Medicare Part B: 2004

Services	Benefit	Medicare Pays	Patient Pays[1]
MEDICAL EXPENSES Doctors' services, inpatient and outpatient medical and surgical services and supplies, physical and speech therapy, diagnostic tests, durable medical equipment, and other services.	Unlimited if medically necessary.	80% of approved amount (after $100 deductible); reduced to 50% for most outpatient mental health services.	$100 deductible, plus 20% of approved amount and limited charges above approved amount.
CLINICAL LABORATORY SERVICES Blood tests, urinalyses, and more.	Unlimited if medically necessary.	Generally 100% of approved amount.	-0-
HOME HEALTH CARE Part-time or intermittent skilled care, home health aide services, durable medical equipment and supplies, and other services.	Unlimited as long as you meet Medicare conditions.	100% of approved amount; 80% of approved amount for durable medical equipment.	Nothing for services; 20% of approved amount for durable medical equipment.
OUTPATIENT HOSPITAL TREATMENT Services for the diagnosis or treatment of illness or injury.	Unlimited if medically necessary.	Medicare payment to hospital based on hospital cost.	20% of whatever the hospital charges (after $100 deductible).
BLOOD[2]	Unlimited if medically necessary.	80% of approved amount (after $100 deductible and starting with 4th pint).	First three pints plus 20% of approved amount for additional pints (after $100 deductible).
AMBULATORY SURGICAL SERVICES	Unlimited if medically necessary.	80% of predetermined amount (after $100 deductible).	$100 deductible, plus 20% of predetermined amount.

[1]Either you or your insurance company is responsible for paying the amounts in the Patient Pays column.
[2]Blood paid for or replaced under Part A of Medicare during the calendar year does not have to be paid for or replaced under Part B.

MEDICARE PARTICIPATION PROGRAM

Assignment of Medicare Benefits

Assignment of Medicare Benefit is a procedure where the physician, health care provider, and medical suppliers agree to accept the Medicare-approved amount as payment in full and do not charge the patient the 20 percent co-insurance. Medicare usually pays 80 percent of the approved amount directly to the doctor or supplier.

Limitation of Medical Fees

Federal law prohibits a doctor who does not accept assignment from charging more than 15 percent above the Medicare-approved amount for services provided to a Medicare beneficiary.

Doctors who refuse to accept assignment for elective surgery are required by law to provide the patient with a written estimate of costs before the surgery, if the total fee will exceed $500. Without a written estimate, the patient is protected and is entitled to a refund of money paid in excess of the Medicare-approved amount for the surgical procedure.

If a physician who does not participate in the federal Medicare program provides medical services believing that Medicare will ultimately deem them unnecessary, the physician must so inform the patient before rendering the service. If these requirements are not met, the patient cannot be held liable for the resulting fees.

Claims

Private insurance companies have contracts with **Centers for Medicare and Medicaid (CMS)** to process Medicare claims. They actually make the payments to the Medicare beneficiaries. The health care provider must file the Medicare claim with the insurance company on behalf of the patient, who is required to receive notice of the filing.

Second Opinion

A patient may wish to consult another physician for a second or third medical opinion. Medicare pays for second opinions of medical conditions covered by Medicare. Third opinions are also covered if the first two opinions contradict each other.

Peer Review Organization (PRO)

Peer Review Organization (PRO)
Physician-sponsored organizations that review services provided to individual beneficiaries to determine whether or not the care given meets community and professionally recognized standards of quality.

A Peer Review Organization (PRO) is a physician-sponsored organizations under contract to **CMS**. Its mission is to improve the quality of care provided to Medicare beneficiaries and ensure that they receive health care services that are medically necessary, reasonable, and provided in an appropriate setting, whether in the hospital or as an outpatient. PRO review of services provided to individual beneficiaries determines whether or not the care given meets community and professionally recognized standards of quality.

PROs are groups of doctors who are paid by the federal government to review medical necessity, appropriateness, and quality of hospital treatment furnished to Medicare patients.

They assist with complaints about premature discharge from a hospital, and patient complaints about quality of care received in hospitals, outpatient departments and skilled nursing facilities, and complaints about care provided by home health agencies and Medicare managed care plans.

MEDICARE BENEFICIARY'S RIGHTS

The following is a list of all the basic rights granted to a Medicare beneficiary:

- Good quality medical care, including the right to make informed decisions concerning the treatment received in hospitals, nursing homes, and outpatient centers and from home health care agencies and Medicare Health Maintenance Organizations
- Nondiscrimination—no religious or cultural discrimination is permitted

- Culturally competent services
- Written notice of any decision made by a hospital or peer review organization denying Medicare coverage for hospital services
- Reconsideration by a PRO of a denial decision for hospital services
- Notification and explanation of the final decision rendered by the PRO
- Written statement about further appeal rights, including information on proper procedures to effectuate the appeal
- Privacy of personal information
- Privacy of health information

Hospital Patient's Rights under Medicare

The following lists all of a Medicare patient's rights while hospitalized:

- The patient has the right to receive all the hospital care that is necessary for the proper diagnosis and treatment of illness or injury. According to federal law, the discharge date must be determined solely by medical needs, not by diagnostic related groups (DRGs) or Medicare payments.
- The patient has the right to be fully informed about decisions affecting Medicare coverage and payment for hospital stay and for any post-hospital services.
- The patient has the right to request a review by a PRO of any written **Notice of Noncoverage** that is received from the hospital stating that Medicare will no longer pay for hospital care.

Notice of Noncoverage
A written explanation for why a Medicare beneficiary is denied medical services. A patient must have this in order to exercise the right to request a review by the PRO.

Medicare Beneficiary's Rights If Subject to Premature Discharge

If the Medicare beneficiary believes that he or she is being discharged from a hospital prematurely, the patient or a representative should:

- Immediately discuss concerns with doctor, patient representatives, social worker, discharge planner, and elder law attorney.
- Demand written status that indicates when the patient will become personally responsible for hospital charges if the patient decides to remain in the hospital and refuse discharge.
- Immediately telephone the local PRO, and further consult with the elder law attorney if necessary.
- Ask a hospital representative for a written notice of explanation immediately. This notice is called a *Notice of Noncoverage*. A patient must have this Notice of Noncoverage in order to exercise the right to request a review by the PRO.

Other considerations are:

- The Notice of Noncoverage will state either that the doctor or the PRO agrees with the hospital's decision that Medicare will no longer pay for the patient's hospital care.

- If the hospital and patient's doctor agree, the PRO will not review the case before a Notice of Noncoverage is issued. The PRO will respond to a patient's request for a review of the Notice of Noncoverage and seek the patient's opinion.
- Provided the patient requests a PRO review by noon of the first work day after receipt of the Notice of Noncoverage, the patient cannot be compelled to pay for hospital care until the PRO makes its decision.
- If the hospital and the doctor disagree, the hospital may request the PRO to review the case. If it does make such a request, the hospital is required to send the patient a notice to that effect. In this situation, the PRO must agree with the hospital, or the hospital cannot issue a Notice of Noncoverage.
- The patient may request that the PRO reconsider the case after receipt of a Notice of Noncoverage, but because the PRO has already reviewed the case once, the patient may have to pay for at least one day of hospital care before the PRO completes this reconsideration.

If the patient does not request a review, the hospital may bill the patient for all the costs of stay beginning with the third day after receipt of the Notice of Noncoverage. The hospital, however, cannot charge the patient for care unless it provides the patient with a Notice of Noncoverage.

Requesting a Review of the Notice of Noncoverage

If the Notice of Noncoverage states that the physician agrees with the hospital's decision:

- The patient may make a request for review to the PRO by noon of the first working day after receipt of the Notice of Noncoverage by contacting the PRO by phone or in writing.
- The PRO must ask for the patient's views about the case before making its decision. The PRO will inform the patient by phone or in writing of its decision on the review.
- If the PRO agrees with the Notice of Noncoverage, the patient may be billed for all costs of stay beginning at noon of the day after receipt of the PRO's decision.
- The patient will not be responsible for the cost of hospital care before receipt of the PRO's decision.

If the Notice of Noncoverage states that the PRO agrees with the hospital's decision:

- The patient should make a request for reconsideration to the PRO immediately upon receipt of the Notice of Noncoverage by contacting the PRO by phone or in writing.
- The PRO can take up to three working days from receipt of the request to complete the review. The PRO will inform the patient in writing of its decision on the review.
- Because the PRO has already reviewed the case once prior to the issuance of the Notice of Noncoverage, the hospital is permitted to begin billing for the cost of stay beginning with the third calendar day after receipt of Notice of Noncoverage, even if the PRO has not completed its review.
- Thus, if the PRO continues to agree with the Notice of Noncoverage, the patient may have to pay for at least one day of hospital care.

The process described above is called **immediate review**. If the patient misses the deadline for this immediate review while in the hospital, at any point during the hospital stay the patient may still request a review of Medicare's decision to no longer pay. The request can also be made after the patient has left the hospital. The Notice of Noncoverage will indicate how to request this review.

Immediate Review
A review by the PRO of a Notice of Noncoverage. The Medicare beneficiary is not responsible for paying the costs of any hospital stay until after the immediate review.

Post-Hospital Care

When the doctor determines that the patient no longer needs all the specialized services provided in a hospital but still requires medical care, he or she may discharge the patient to a skilled nursing facility or home care. The discharge planner at the hospital will help arrange for the services needed after discharge. Medicare and supplemental insurance policies have limited coverage for skilled nursing facility care and home health care. Therefore, the patient should find out which services will or will not be covered and how payment will be made. The elder law professional should be a part of this process and consult with the doctor, hospital discharge planner, patient representative, and family members in making preparations for care after discharge from the hospital.

Appealing Medicare Payments

If a Medicare beneficiary does not agree with the Medicare-assigned payment for services rendered, the beneficiary has a right to appeal the decision. The appeal must be made within six months of the notice of payment to the provider. The time to file an appeal can be extended for good reason (for example, an extended illness that prevents the Medicare beneficiary from being able to file). If the appeal is denied, the Medicare beneficiary must pay the billed amount.

SPECIAL MEDICARE ENTITLEMENT PROGRAMS FOR LOW-INCOME BENEFICIARIES

The Qualified Medicare Beneficiary program (QMB), Specified Low-Income Medicare Beneficiary program (SLMB), and Qualified Individual program (QI), assist the poorest Medicare beneficiaries by paying all or some of Medicare's cost sharing amounts (*i.e.,* premiums, deductibles and co-payments). To qualify, an individual must be eligible for Medicare and must meet certain income guidelines that change annually.

The **Qualified Medicare Beneficiary program** (QMB) is available to people whose income does not exceed 100% of the poverty level and resources do not exceed $4,000 for individuals and $6,000 for couples. Under current poverty guidelines individuals with monthly income up to $796 ($1,061 for couples) are eligible. This program pays for a beneficiary's Medicare premiums, deductibles, and coinsurance.

The **Specified Low-Income Medicare Beneficiary program** (SLMB) is available to people whose income is between 100–120 percent of the poverty level and resources do not exceed $4,000 for individuals and $6,000 for couples. Under current poverty guidelines individuals with monthly income up to $951 ($1,269 for couples) are eligible. This program pays for a beneficiary's Medicare Part B premium ($66.60).

SPECIAL MEDICARE ENTITLEMENT PROGRAMS FOR LOW-INCOME BENEFICIARIES

These programs pay Medicare premiums, deductibles, copayments, etc., for elderly and disabled persons entitled to Medicare Part A whose income is below the national poverty level:

1. Qualified Medicare Beneficiary Program (QMB).
   A. Income must be at or below the national poverty level.*

2002	Monthly Income Limits
*48 States * (Alaska and Hawaii are slightly higher)*	
Individuals	$1,273
Couples	$1,714

   B. Assets:

Individuals	$4,000
Couples	$6,000

2. Specified Low-Income Medicare Beneficiaries program (SLMB).

2002	Monthly Income Limits
*48 States * (Alaska and Hawaii are slightly higher)*	
Individuals	$789
Couples	$1,061

* These limits change annually

The Qualified Individual Program-1 (QI-1) is available to Medicare beneficiaries with income between 120 percent and 135 percent of the federal poverty level. Under current poverty guidelines, individuals with monthly income up to $1,068 ($1,426 for couples) are eligible. There is no limit on resources. This program pays for a beneficiary's Medicare Part B premium ($66.60).

OTHER HEALTH CARE COVERAGES

The elder law professional should be aware of the existence of other insurance and ways to pay health care costs. Medicare may not be the only health care coverage for your clients. The following should also be considered:

1. *Employer or union coverage.* Health care coverage may be available based on prior employment of an individual or his or her spouse.
2. *Veterans benefits.* Contact the U.S. Department of Veterans Affairs at 800-827-1000.
3. *Military benefits.* TRICARE For Life (TFL) provides expanded medical coverage for Medicare-eligible retirees, including retired National Guard members, reservists, and their family members.
4. *Medicare savings program.* There are state programs for people with limited income and resources that are designed to pay some or all of Medicare's premiums, deductibles, and co-insurance. Check your state programs.
5. *Medicaid.* This program is discussed later in this chapter.

6. *Medi-gap insurance.* This is Medicare supplement insurance sold by private insurance companies to fill gaps in Medicare coverage, which must be issued in accordance with strict federal and state regulations.

7. *Long-term care insurance.* This insurance is sold by private insurance companies to cover medical care and non-medical care in connection with the activities of daily living at home, in an assisted living facility, or in a skilled nursing facility. This is discussed in detail in Chapter 8.

THE MEDICARE PRESCRIPTION DRUG MODERNIZATION ACT OF 2003

With this law, we're giving older Americans better choices and more control over their health care, so they can receive the modern medical care they deserve.

—President George W. Bush

Many people will wake up and discover that the Medicare bill is a cruel hoax. It does not provide the kind of benefits that they had hoped for. . . .

—Senator Hillary Rodham Clinton

On December 8, 2003, President Bush signed the Medicare Prescription Drug Modernization Act. The signing of the $400 billion bill marked the largest expansion of the Medicare program since its creation in 1965 and is the result of recent efforts to privitize the Medicare program. The bill itself is more than 1,100 pages long, but the major provisions are provided below.

Prescription Drug Coverage:

- *Transitional Discount Drug Card:* In 2004 and 2005, seniors will be able to purchase a drug benefit discount card for approximately $30 per year and receive a 10–25 percent discount on prescription drugs.
  - The card will be available to all seniors in the Medicare program who do not already receive prescription drug coverage through Medicaid.
  - Seniors in the program must choose a private sponsor upon enrollment in the program. The cards will be sponsored by Pharmacy Benefit Managers (PBMs), wholesalers, retail pharmacies, insurers, or Medicare + Choice plans. The idea is that these companies will be able to use their collective bargaining power in negotiating with the pharmaceutical industries and attain lower prices for seniors than they would receive individually.
- *Comprehensive Coverage:* Beginning in 2006, more comprehensive coverage will be provided.
  - *Initial Coverage:* Beneficiaries will pay approximately $35 per month for coverage with an annual deductible of $250. The government then pays 75 percent of prescription drug costs until those costs reach $2,250 in any calendar year.
  - *"The Donut Hole":* Beneficiaries in the program will be responsible for 100 percent of drug costs from $2,250 to $5,100 in any calendar year.
  - *Catastrophic Coverage:* The program pays 95 percent of prescription drug costs above $5,100 in any calendar year while the beneficiary is responsible for a modest co-payment.

- *Low-Income Beneficiaries:*
  - In 2004 and 2005, low-income beneficiaries, individual seniors with income less than $12,123 per year and less than $6,000 in assets (thresholds for married couples are slightly higher), will receive a $600 subsidy toward prescription drugs applied to their discount card.
  - After 2006, the program waives the premium, deductible, and the "donut hole" gap in coverage for low-income seniors. For individuals with income above $12,123, the premiums and deductible are phased in. Seniors with income exceeding $13,500 pay the full premium and deductibles.
- *Employer Prescription Plans:* The law provides for $70 billion in tax-free subsidies to employers who provide prescription coverage for retirees.

Critics, including many grassroots senior organizations, argue that the law does more to subsidize drug companies, private insurance companies, and the wealthy than to help poor and middle class seniors. The following provisions highlight some of the complaints:

- *Pharmaceutical Companies:* The law limits the government's ability to negotiate lower prices for prescription drugs, which has been a major reason for the success of Canada's prescription coverage. At the same time, the law continues the ban on importation of prescription drugs from Canada without approval from the Department of Health and Human Services. The department has consistently refused to approve importation of any prescription drugs from Canada.
- *Private Insurers:* In addition to the privately sponsored discount card program, the law provides subsidies to private insurance companies and allows them to compete with Medicare for coverage. The pilot program begins in 2010 in six metropolitan areas. Critics claim that the private insurers will be able to "cherrypick" only the healthiest seniors for coverage.
- *Medical Savings Plans:* The law allows workers under 65 with high insurance deductibles to save money by establishing a medical savings account. Earnings can be withdrawn tax free provided the money is used to pay medical expenses. Critics argue that only the wealthiest Americans will be in a financial position to establish these plans.

Because many provisions do not take effect for several years, only time will tell whether the Medicare Prescription Drug Modernization Act will be a boon or a bust for our nation's seniors.

MEDICAID ASSISTANCE PROGRAM

The Medicaid program, passed by Congress in 1965, is designed to assist people of all ages who are poor and unable to afford health care. In contrast to Medicare, which is an age-based program, Medicaid is based on financial need. The majority of the Medicaid budget provided for by Congress is spent on financing nursing home care and home care for the elderly.

Medicaid is a joint federal and state program primarily funded by the federal government with some state contribution and is administered by the **Centers for**

Medicare and Medicaid. The federal government sets the standards, permitting the states to modify them to a certain degree and to opt out of certain programs, provided they obtain government approval.

The Medicaid program covers catastrophic illness for the poor, blind, and disabled regardless of age. It is the largest program providing medical and health-related services to America's poorest people. It is a third-party payment system, and the state pays the bill. The federal enabling statute can be found in the United States Code Annotated 42 USC., Sec. 1396 *et seq.*, and *Code of Federal Regulations* (CFR 430) *et seq.* (refer to individual state codes, rules, and regulations). It is the largest federal entitlement program providing medical and health related services to America's poorest citizens.

The Medicaid program permits each state to:

this is not a national ligestlestion MN standard.

1. Establish its own eligibility standards
2. Determine the type, amount, duration, and scope of services
3. Set the rate of payment for services
4. Administer its own program

The elder law professional should obtain local Medicaid regulations for more specific information.

Common Questions

The legal professional must be able to respond to the following questions often asked by elder law clients:

1. What is Medicaid?
2. What is Medicare? Is there a difference?
3. How do I become eligible for Medicare/Medicaid?
4. Will Medicaid pay for nursing homes?
5. Will Medicaid pay for home care?
6. Will Medicaid pay for hospice care?
7. If I enter a nursing home, will Medicaid seize my assets?
8. If I own a house, will Medicaid put a lien on it?
9. Am I entitled to use my annual gift exclusion permitted by the Internal Revenue Service Code estate and gift tax provisions and still qualify for Medicaid benefits?
10. Can Medicaid seek reimbursement from the estate of a Medicaid recipient after his/her death?
11. If I transfer my home to my disabled child, will I still qualify for Medicaid?
12. Can I transfer my home to a child who has been living with me for two or more years and still qualify for Medicaid?
13. Does Medicaid pay me directly, or does it pay the nursing home facility?
14. Can I transfer my assets to a trust in order to shield them from becoming a Medicaid resource?
15. Is the law restricting transfer of assets, enacted as of January 1, 1997, still in effect?

Basic Benefits

1. Nursing home coverage—long-term care
2. Home care
3. Hospital and physician services for eligible recipients of any age

Residency Requirements

1. Applicant must be a U.S. citizen, or
2. Applicant must be a lawful permanent resident of the United States—a legal alien.
3. Applicant must be a resident of the state and county in which the application is filed.

Mandatory Goods and Services

- Inpatient and outpatient hospital services
- Laboratory and x-ray services
- Physician services, including dental services if they could be provided by a physician
- Nurse midwife services; family planning services; certified pediatric and family nurse practitioners
- Early and periodic screening, diagnosis, and treatment for individuals under age 21

Optional Medicaid Services

- Nursing facility services
- Nursing facility services for the mentally retarded
- Dental services
- Clinic services
- Private duty nursing services
- Pediatric services
- Optometrist services
- Chiropractic services
- Physical, occupational, and speech therapy; hearing and language disorder services
- Prescription drugs
- Medical devices, including dentures, prosthetics, or eyeglasses
- Diagnostic, screening, preventive, and rehabilitative services
- Hospice services
- Case management services
- Respiratory care services, inpatient hospital services, skilled nursing facility services, and nursing facility services for aged individuals in institutions for mental disorders.
- Any other appropriate medical and remedial care recognized under state law, specified by the HHS [42 U.S.C. Sec 1346 p(d)(A)].

These services depend upon the individual state programs

Medicaid Resource Limits (Exempt Resources)

Medicaid resource limits refer to the maximum amount of "countable resources" (not including the residences and certain other exemptions) that an individual can have in order to be eligible to qualify for the Medical Assistance Program (2004). Note that these resource limits usually increase annually by rather small amounts. What follows is a brief summary of resource limits in New York State. The elder law professional should be thoroughly familiar with Medicaid resource limits in his or her states.

Medicaid Resource Limits
The maximum amount of countable resources that an individual can have in order to be eligible to qualify for the Medical Assistance Program.

1. *Single person:* Maximum of $3,950 in New York ($2,000 in most states).
2. *Married couple:* Where one spouse is institutionalized (the ill spouse), the spouse living in the community (the well spouse) may retain a maximum of $92,760, and the institutionalized spouse can retain only the maximum for a single person. In most states, the actual "protected resource allowance" is determined by a complex formula designed to require "spending down" half the couple's assets, but this can often be avoided with careful planning. In New York, a spouse with excess resources may file a *spousal refusal letter* and retain those excess resources. Medicaid will sue the community spouse to obtain the excess resources and is usually successful in the litigation. However, the community spouse will be required to pay the Medicaid nursing home rate, not the private pay rate which is much higher. New York is the only state to date that permits the use of *spousal refusal.*
3. *Income:* The community spouse can retain up to $2,319 per month from the income of both spouses, the minimum monthly maintenance needs allowance (MMMNA). This amount can be increased in hardship cases. In the event that the MMMNA of the community spouse does exceed $2,319, Medicaid will request that the community spouse contribute 25 percent of the excess income for the care of the institutionalized spouse. In New York, a spouse may refuse to comply with Medicaid's request and file a spousal refusal letter with the Medicaid agency. Medicaid benefits will still be granted, but Medicaid will retain the right to commence a court action against the refusing spouse to obtain the excess income. The institutionalized spouse (or single individual) can retain from her or his monthly income a *personal needs allowance* in an amount determined by state law ($50 in New York). The remaining balance of the Medicaid beneficiary's income, known as the *net available monthly income (NAMI)* is paid to the nursing home. The nursing home resident receiving Medicaid benefits is required to sign an authorization permitting the facility to collect the NAMI directly from the payor (*e.g.,* Social Security or pension benefits).

   The rules are different for community-based Medicaid. Married couples may have a combined resource level of $5,700. The monthly income that can be retained by a single person receiving Medicaid benefits is $659. An additional $20 is also allowed to be retained from monthly income if the Medicaid beneficiary is elderly, blind, or disabled. Married couples may retain $950 from their monthly income. Excess resources must be spent down in order to qualify for Medicaid.
4. *Life insurance:* Life insurance policies with maximum total face values of $1,500, provided total cash surrender values do not exceed $1,500, are allowed.

   Term life insurance with no upper limit, provided the policy has no cash surrender value.
5. *Homestead:* The **homestead** is the family residence and surrounding land in which the Medicaid applicant, spouse, child under the age of 21, the applicant's blind or disabled child of any age, or the applicant's other dependent relatives resides. The exempt

Homestead
The family residence and surrounding land in which the Medicaid applicant resides.

status of the homestead continues in effect for as long as the Medicaid recipient or one of the above-mentioned individuals resides in the residence. The statutory definition of a homestead or residence includes a cooperative apartment, condominium, or a one- to three-family house. No dollar limit is placed upon the value of the homestead. In New York and some other states, the homestead will continue to remain an exempt resource even after the individual becomes institutionalized, provided the homeowner files a statement with Medicaid declaring an intent to return to the homestead. This remains an exempt resource even if the premises are temporarily vacant.

Because the homestead cannot be considered a Medicaid resource, its sale cannot be forced. However, in some states Medicaid still has the right to file a lien against the vacant premises if none of the relatives listed above reside there. In some states, upon the death of the Medicaid recipient, Medicaid can force its sale and can make a claim for monies it advanced on behalf of the recipient. An additional exception applies to a sibling of the Medicaid recipient who has an equity interest in the homestead that existed for at least a year before institutionalization took place. This sibling has a continual right to use the homestead without having title to it. Check the local state's Medicaid lien and estate recovery laws, which vary widely at this writing.

Medicaid Transfer Rules

Medicaid has enacted specific rules and regulations regarding the transferring of assets by a Medicaid applicant. In general, these rules are designed to discourage advance planning and to penalize Medicaid applicants for transferring their assets to become eligible for Medicaid assistance. (See pp. 256 for restrictions regarding asset transfer effective January 1, 1997, and amendments effective August 5, 1997, which are currently not being enforced by the government.)

Medicaid Look-Back Rule

Medicaid Look-Back Rule
In order to obtain Medicaid assistance, the applicant must provide an asset trail (financial information for a period immediately before the date of the application [currently 36 months]).

The procedure for obtaining Medicaid assistance requires the filing of a detailed application listing the applicant's entire assets and income, as well as those of the spouse. The application is designed to compel the applicant to provide financial information regarding the 36-month period immediately prior to the date of application. This is known as an *asset trail*. When Medicaid first was enacted, the "look-back period" was only 12 months. As the government began to spend more money on this program, it decided to make it more difficult for citizens to qualify. In order to effectuate its plan, the **Medicaid look-back rule** was increased from 12 to 18 months, then subsequently to 24 months, then to 30 months, and finally to 36 months on August 10, 1993.

The exception to this 36-month rule is transactions involving transfers of assets to and from trusts, which from August 10, 1993, have had a look-back period of 60 months. It is anticipated that Congress will continue to make it more difficult to obtain Medicaid benefits and further extend this look-back period.

The Look-Back Period

The Medicaid applicant must reveal on the application, what, if any, transfers of assets have been made during the 36-month period (or 60-month period if a trust is involved) prior to the filing of the Medicaid application. Basically, every transfer of assets to a third party (a transfer without consideration—a gift) will create a penalty period. The penalty period is defined as the time during which no Medicaid benefits can be obtained due to the transfer of assets. A denial of benefits will result if an application is made before the penalty period expires. If the penalty period has expired, then benefits will be granted if all other eligibility requirements have been met.

Calculation of Penalty Period

The penalty period is calculated by dividing the total uncompensated value of assets transferred by the statewide average or, at the option of the state, the local community average, the monthly private pay rate for nursing facilities. The penalty period is unlimited and usually runs from into first day of the following month of transfer. If there are multiple transfers, their penalty periods run consecutively. Transfers are penalized only if they are motivated, at least in part, by intent to qualify for Medicaid.

EXAMPLE: On December 1, 2002, a healthy person, age 81, transfers all of her assets ($100,000) to her son as part of an estate plan. On December 3, 2002, she falls down a flight of stairs at home, fractures her hip, and becomes totally incapacitated, requiring long-term care at a nursing facility. If she applies for Medicaid on January 1, 2003, no penalty period can be assessed because the transferor at the time of the transfer did not intend to qualify for Medicaid. If the transfer were to be challenged by Medicaid, then the applicant will request a fair hearing. The applicant must prove that the transfer was not made to qualify for Medicaid.

EXAMPLE: If A, who is a widow, transfers $60,000 to her niece as a gift in order to qualify for Medicaid, then the total uncompensated value of the assets transferred is $60,000. The formula for determining the penalty period is as follows: Divide the total uncompensated value of assets transferred, which is $60,000, by the statewide average or local community average monthly private pay rate for nursing home facilities. (See figure.)

Formula to Determine Medicaid Penalty Period

$$\frac{\text{The Total Uncompensated Value of Assets Transferred}}{\substack{\text{Average Cost of Nursing Home} \\ \text{in the Community—Private Pay}}} = \text{Medicaid Penalty Period}$$

For example:

$$\frac{\$60,000 \text{ (Gift Transfer)}}{\$6,000 \text{ (Average Cost of Nursing Home)}} = \text{10-Month Medicaid Penalty Period}$$

In the example above, the penalty period created by the transfer now makes the transferor ineligible for institutional Medicaid assistance for 10 months.

The penalty period becomes unlimited if the Medicaid applicant applies for Medicaid during the penalty period. Moreover, the premature application triggers "imposition of a period of ineligibility." Therefore, the applicant must wait out the penalty period and then apply for Medicaid. Provided the applicant has reached the statutory resource levels and meets all other requirements, Medicaid coverage should be granted.

EXAMPLE: If the applicant transfers $600,000 under the above formula, the penalty period will be 100 months. That period will not be enforced (it will remain at 36 months, or 60 months if a trust is involved) provided the applicant does not apply for Medicaid within the 36-month penalty period. If the applicant applies within the 36-month period, then the penalty period is unlimited and extends to the full 100 months.

It is critical to understand that the look-back period is only 36 or 60 months, but the penalty period is unlimited. Therefore, it is crucial to advise clients not to apply for any Medicaid benefits during the look-back period if the transfer penalty period is in excess of 36 or 60 months. If it is under 36 or 60 months, they can apply at the end of the penalty period.

Certain transfers do not affect Medicaid eligibility:

1. All transfers to the spouse of the applicant of any amount at any time.
2. Transfers to blind or disabled children of the applicant and to children of the applicant below the age of 21, at any time.
3. Transfer of title in a residence by Medicaid applicant to a sibling possessing an equity interest in that real property, providing the sibling has resided in those premises for at least one year prior to the institutionalization of the Medicaid applicant.
4. Transfers of title by a Medicaid applicant in a residence to a child of the applicant who has resided in the home of the Medicaid applicant for a minimum of two years prior to institutionalization and has cared for that person for at least the past two years, thereby enabling the ill parent to remain at home until the time of institutionalization. Extensive proof of residence, such as income tax returns, driver's licenses, mailing address, and other documentation, must be presented to establish that the child actually lived there for the two-year statutory period.
5. Transfers made entirely for some purpose other than Medicaid eligibility, *e.g.,* tax planning, probate avoidance, etc.
6. Transfers where imposing a penalty would cause undue hardship, *i.e.,* assets were unlawfully taken by a relative from the Medicaid applicant. This may occur in undue influence cases or illegal transfers by an attorney-in-fact.

Income Cap States

Federal Medicaid regulations permit individual states to create more restrictive financial requirements in order to qualify for Medicaid. One method is to lower the income levels of the Medicaid applicant. If the applicant's monthly income is in excess of the prescribed level, the application will automatically be denied. Florida, a low tax-based state with no income tax and no inheritance tax, has limited resources to spend on Medicaid programs.

Consequently, it has enacted income cap regulations that, in effect, disqualify many residents from receiving Medicaid assistance. Any individual residing in Florida with a monthly income of more than $1,656 (2003) will *not* qualify for Medicaid without the help of an attorney. The source of income is irrelevant. However, an attorney can always solve the income "problem" with a **Miller trust**, which effectively makes the income cap go away. See page 253.

The following is a list of income cap states:

1. Alabama	8. Florida	15. Oklahoma
2. Alaska	9. Idaho	16. Oregon
3. Arizona	10. Iowa	17. South Carolina
4. Arkansas	11. Louisiana	18. South Dakota
5. Colorado	12. Mississippi	19. Texas
6. Connecticut	13. Nevada	20. Wyoming
7. Delaware	14. New Mexico	

It is critical to note that one should consult with an attorney to determine the current status of a state's income rules and whether it is considered a spend-down or income cap state.

Non-Income Cap States

The State of New York does not follow the income cap rules. In contrast to Florida, an individual residing in New York with a monthly income in excess of $1,656 (2003), who meets the other financial criteria, *will* qualify for Medicaid. New York uses the budget method whereby an individual with excess income transfers the excess income to the skilled nursing facility as partial payment of the nursing bill and Medicaid picks up the difference. In New York, excess income will not disqualify a Medicaid applicant in and of itself. New York has had a higher tax base and more funds to use for Medicaid benefits; now, however, New York is beginning to feel the budgetary crunch of the general economic downtrend in the United States and is also beginning to institute stricter Medicaid requirements.

Planning Technique—The Florida/New York Connection

If a client resides in Florida and has relatives in New York, the client can be transferred from Florida to New York in order to qualify for Medicaid. If the patient is ill, transportation arrangements can be made for a transfer by Medivac. The cost might be $7,000 to $10,000, but once the patient is on Medicaid, the benefits are far in excess of any costs of transfer. If the patient has excess resources at the time of entering the skilled nursing facility, he or she will pay as a private patient until the funds are exhausted, whereupon the patient will qualify for New York Medicaid, regardless of income level. New York has no residency requirement; twenty-four hours establishes residency. If the family wishes to keep the ill relative in Florida and there is an issue of excess income that might result in ineligibility for Medicaid in this income cap state, the use of the qualified income trust should be considered. The excess income could be placed in a qualified income trust and Medicaid eligibility would probably be granted, provided the applicant qualified in all other respects.

Frequently Asked Questions

Is a nursing home legally permitted to provide different services and levels of care for private paying patients and Medicaid recipients?

Federal law specifically requires all nursing home operators to treat their residents equally. The policies concerning transfer and discharge of residents must be "identical . . . for all individuals regardless of their source of payment [42 U.S.C. Sec 1396r(c)(4)].

Is there a Medicaid bed-hold rule for Medicaid recipients?

All nursing homes that participate in the Medicaid Reimbursement Program in New York are required to maintain a bed-hold for a period of 15 days. This means that if a resident is required to enter a hospital, the nursing home must keep his/her bed available for 15 days provided that (a) the nursing home has a vacancy rate of no greater that 5 percent or 15 vacant beds, which ever is less, (b) the Medicaid recipient has been in the nursing home for a minimum of 30 days, and (c) Medicaid has paid the facility a minimum of one day prior to the hospitalization of the resident. An additional five-day bed-hold can be obtained upon request of the hospital physician in charge of the patient's care. Medicaid will pay for the bed during that period of time. If the bed-hold period has expired, the nursing home operator is required to give the returning resident the first available bed. Texas Medicaid on the other hand, does not pay for bed-hold. The elder law professional should check local regulations.

What is the application procedure for obtaining Medicaid assignment benefits?

1. Application must be filed in the local county where the individual resides by the applicant, a relative, or other representative. (A personal interview may be required.)
2. An individual, couple, or family may apply, provided each person meets all requirements.
3. Applicant must provide financial records for the 36 months prior to the date of application:
   - Copies of checks
   - Bank books
   - Check statements
   - Stock transactions
   - All other financial records
4. Applicant must present the following additional documents:
   - Copies of all deeds
   - Rent receipts
   - Leases
   - Affidavits establishing residency
   - Proof of citizenship
   - U.S. passport, Social Security, and Medicare cards
   - Social Security award letter
   - Supplementary health insurance
   - Income tax returns for last three years
   - Birth certificate
   - Marriage certificate, if applicable
   - Death certificate of spouse, if applicable
   - Military discharge papers, if applicable

- Proof of income (German or other war reparation payments are not considered income)
- Insurance policies

If the applicant cannot produce the documents requested by the Medicaid agency, the Medicaid agency is required to assist the applicant in obtaining information and provide assistance in obtaining coverage.

Is it possible to receive Medicaid benefits for the period prior to the filing of the application?

Yes. Medicaid will provide coverage for the 90-day period immediately prior to the application, if all Medicaid requirements are met for that period.

What is the duration of Medicaid certification?

The patient receives Medicaid benefits for 12 months from the original date of Medicaid certification and must be *recertified at least once every 12 months* thereafter to continue receiving benefits.

If a Medicaid application is denied, what recourse does the applicant have?

1. Every applicant has 90 days after application denial to submit additional documentation. This is called a *reconsideration*.
2. An applicant has the right to appeal a denial of coverage. The appellate process is statutory, guaranteeing the appellant's right to an administrative *fair hearing*. The applicant can appeal if he or she feels that the original ineligibility decision is incorrect. In New York, a request for a **fair hearing** must be made within 60 days of the date of denial of coverage. The elder law professional should review local Medicaid regulations for more specific information.
3. In all states, where rights have been denied under federal law, the applicant may sue for relief in federal court.

What is institutional Medicaid?

Institutional Medicaid is payment by the Medicaid Assistance Program to a skilled nursing facility for the care and maintenance of a Medicaid recipient for as long as the patient is in the facility.

What is home care Medicaid?

Home Care Medicaid is a program wherein the Medicaid Assistance Program will pay for the home care of a Medicaid applicant, provided the applicant is medically and financially eligible. When first enacted, the home care program paid for 24 hours a day, 7 days a week. It has become much more restrictive in the last several years. The maximum time most Medicaid agencies will cover now is approximately 8 to 12 hours a day, although in exceptional cases 24-hour coverage may be granted. Medicaid implies that if a patient needs 24-hour care, the patient should be in a skilled nursing facility, and Medicaid will pay for that care. Local regulations vary and should be checked.

Are resource transfer rules different for home care as opposed to institutional care?

As stated above, the resource transfer look-back period for institutional care is 36 months, with penalties for certain transfers. There are no such penalties for home care, except in certain important "waiver" programs in some states. One can transfer assets on Monday and apply on Tuesday. However, if the Medicaid applicant on home care is subsequently required

Reconsideration
The period of time after a denial of Medicaid benefits in which the applicant may submit additional documentation.

Fair Hearing
The appellate process for a declined Medicaid applicant.

Institutional Medicaid
Payment by the Medicaid Assistance Program to a skilled nursing facility.

Home Care Medicaid
Payment by the Medicaid Assistance Program for care in the applicant's home.

to go to a skilled nursing facility and has made transfers in order to become a Medicaid recipient, penalty periods will be calculated and institutional Medicaid could be denied until the penalty periods are overcome.

Can the penalty period be reduced or eliminated by retransferring the assets back to the Medicaid applicant?

Under current Medicaid regulations, retransfers are permissible to reduce or eliminate the Medicaid penalty period. This retransfer technique is used regularly in Medicaid planning to reduce the penalty period.

What are the rules concerning the transfer of tangible personal property of a client who wishes to apply for Medicaid?

Generally, all tangible personal property, regardless of its value, is treated as an exempt resource. Therefore, if an individual owns a Steinway piano valued at $500,000 and transfers it to another person as a gift, Medicaid will treat this as an exempt transaction because it is a transfer of tangible personal property. However, a different result will occur if the piano is sold. In that case the proceeds will be treated as an available resource. If these funds are transferred to another person as a gift, penalty periods will be assessed against the transferor.

Can a New York domicilary who owns a vacation condo in Palm Beach, Florida, obtain Medicaid coverage while still owning the second home?

Prior to 1996, Medicaid eligibility would be granted pending the sale of the second home. This rule has been repealed and eligibility will be denied on the grounds that the applicant has excess nonliquid assets. The condo must be sold, and the proceeds will be considered an available Medicaid resource.

Do transfers for fair market value create penalty periods?

No, where an individual has actually sold something and received its fair market value, it is merely exchange for cash. It is *not* a gift.

Can a penalty be assessed where the asset was transferred exclusively for a purpose other than to qualify for Medicaid?

If it can be established that the transfer was made at the time when the individual had no intent to apply for Medicaid, no penalty period can be assessed. For example, a widow aged 75 lives alone, does her own shopping, goes to church every Sunday, travels, sees her family regularly, and is basically independent, both physically and financially. She decides because of her age to do some estate planning, and she transfers her house and some cash to her son. Two weeks later, she slips and falls down several steps and fractures her hip, is hospitalized, has hip surgery, and is unable to walk. She is now wheelchair-bound and confined to a nursing home. She applies for Medicaid and reveals the transfer. *Medicaid is unable to assess a penalty because at the time she made the transfer, she had no intention of going into a nursing home and she was basically well.* Her lack of intent can be established through medical reports, affidavits from her clergy, financial advisor, bank officer, attorney, and friends. She should qualify for Medicaid regardless of the transfers. The case may have to go to a *fair hearing*, however, because Medicaid may deny it automatically, but coverage is likely to be granted at the fair hearing.

What is a hardship transfer?

A **hardship transfer** occurs when an individual transfers all of his or her assets to another person, leaving the transferor without assets.

No penalty periods can apply where a penalty period would result in undue hardship, [42 U.S.C. Sec. 1396p(c)(2)(D)] i.e.:

Hardship Transfer
When an individual transfers all his or her assets to another person, leaving the transferor without assets.

1. Where the applicant has no way to pay bills after making the transfer.
2. When a transfer is not known or authorized by the Medicaid applicant. In this case, the individual Medicaid applicant assigns his or her rights to recover the transferred asset to the Medicaid Assistance Program.

How does Medicaid treat IRAs and work-related pensions of a Medicaid applicant?

In general, a retirement fund that is owned by an applicant is considered a Medicaid resource if the individual is not entitled to periodic payments but is permitted to withdraw funds from the plan. The amount of the resource equals the sum that the individual can withdraw at any one time. If the entire amount of the fund can be withdrawn at one time, then the entire fund is considered at a countable resource. If only 20 percent can be withdrawn in any one calendar year, then that sum will be considered a countable resource every year that it is available to the Medicaid recipient.

If the fund is now in regular payment status, the law is different. Once the Medicaid recipient has applied for periodic payments or is actually receiving periodic payments, the fund is treated as a countable resource for Medicaid, regardless of the frequency of the payment. **Once the fund is in payment status, the corpus of the fund is no longer available to Medicaid as a countable resource. However, the periodic payments will be counted as income and treated as a countable resource**.

Are IRAs and work-related pension funds of the community spouse treated as an available resource for Medicaid?

Medicaid has held that IRAs and work-related pensions of the community spouse are exempt assets. However, income received from these assets will be treated as part of community spousal income and will be subject to the Community Spouse Resource Allowance (CSRW).

How does Medicaid treat jointly held assets? [42 U.S.C. Sec. 1396p(c)(3)]

According to Medicaid regulations, in the case of an asset held with another in joint tenancy, tenancy in common, or "similar arrangement," the asset is considered to be transferred only when action is taken that will reduce the individual's ownership or control of the asset. For example, a withdrawal of funds by a joint tenant from a bank account is now considered a transfer because it reduces the Medicaid applicant's ownership and control of the account. Generally speaking, there is a presumption that all joint assets are owned by the Medicaid applicant unless the joint tenant who is *not* applying for Medicaid can establish contribution to that account. Medicaid considers these accounts as *convenience accounts*. They actually belong to the Medicaid applicant to the extent they were contributed by the applicant. In every state, the title of the account does not control. The controlling factor rests on contribution to the account.

A spouse of an applicant may refuse to provide support to the Medicaid applicant. Medicaid coverage cannot be denied because of spousal refusal to contribute toward the care of the applicant. Medicaid retains the right to sue the refusing spouse for support. (This is a unique feature in New York State. It is arguably available in every state under federal law, but may require a suit in federal court in states other than New York.)

Can Medicaid recover from the estate of a deceased Medicaid recipient?

There are complex rules involving recovery from the estate of Medicaid recipients, and they vary from state to state. The Medicaid agency will file a claim against the estate and seek recovery from the assets of the decedent up to the amount it expended on the patient's behalf. Medicaid has also been given the statutory right to recovery from the estate of a deceased spouse of a Medicaid recipient who has refused to contribute to the support of the Medicaid recipient spouse.

How does Medicaid treat a spousal right of election?

Most states permit a surviving spouse to file a claim against the estate of a predeceased spouse if the surviving spouse's share of the estate is less than the minimum share prescribed by statute. If the surviving spouse is a Medicaid applicant/recipient and fails to elect against the estate of the spouse, Medicaid considers such a failure as a transfer of assets and subject to a penalty period resulting in a period of ineligibility.

How does Medicaid treat trusts?

Revocable Trust
A trust agreement wherein the settlor reserves the right to revoke the trust at any time.

1. *The revocable trust:* A **revocable trust** is a trust created by the Medicaid applicant during his or her lifetime. It is considered an *inter vivos* trust (amongst the living) and is revocable, which means that the grantor/Medicaid applicant can at any time revoke this trust. Because the applicant has retained the right to revoke the trust, any funds transferred to this trust are considered Medicaid resources and are counted in determining eligibility for Medicaid assistance. There is no transfer penalty when assets are transferred to a revocable trust; however, the assets are considered a Medicaid resource.

Irrevocable Trust
A trust that cannot be revoked after it has been created by the settlor.

2. *Transfer to an inter vivos irrevocable trust:* This is a **irrevocable trust** created by a Medicaid applicant wherein the applicant gives up all right, title, control, and interest in the assets transferred to the trust. The applicant may receive the income from the trust as the income beneficiary. Upon the applicant's death, the principal of trust will go to the residuary beneficiaries. Because the applicant has made the transfer and it is an *irrevocable* transfer, a penalty period will be created. *The look-back rule in this situation is 60 months, not 36 months.* If an individual receives income from an irrevocable trust and is applying for Medicaid, the income from the trust is treated by Medicaid as a resource. The principal, if it meets the 60-month look-back rule and overcomes any penalty periods, cannot be considered a Medicaid resource.

Testamentary Trust
A trust created by the testator within the will. By its nature, this trust does not take effect until the testator dies.

3. *Testamentary trusts:* A **testamentary trust** created in the last will and testament of a Medicaid applicant. These trusts are not funded until death and therefore are not subject to Medicaid restrictions or penalties.

Special Needs Trusts: Exempt Trust Transfers Not Subject to a 60-Month Penalty Period

Special needs trusts allow disabled individuals to remain eligible for mental health, mental retardation, Medicaid or SSI benefits while receiving trust benefits. Funds from the trust can be used for the benefit of the disabled beneficiary, but the funds are not considered available to the disabled person for Medicaid purposes until they are distributed from the trust for the benefit of the beneficiary.

1. *Third-party supplemental needs trust or the common law discretionary trust.* This is a trust established by a third party who funds the trust with his or her own money. The beneficiary can be of any age. The trustee uses the funds for the benefit of the disabled beneficiary. The following factors must be present to establish a valid supplemental needs trust.

   a. the settlor must express an intent that the funds be used to supplement and not supplant public benefits, *i.e.,* available public benefits must be considered before any trust property is distributed, and

   b. the trustee must have absolute discretion to spend or refuse to spend trust assets for the benefit of the beneficiary.

   Note: because the funds are provided by a third party, there is no payback requirement for public benefits received by the Medicaid beneficiary and no penalty period is incurred by the beneficiary. However, a penalty period will be created for the person who funds the trust, unless the trust is irrevocable, is created for the sole benefit of the disabled person and distributions are "actuarially sound" (based on the beneficiary's life expectancy). Also note that any distributions actually made are treated as income to the beneficiary in the month received and subject to the rules against excess income. *See the CD-Rom for a sample Third Party Supplemental Needs Trust used in New York.*

2. *Payback trust* (pursuant to OBRA-93) (also known as a self-settled supplemental needs trust). This trust is funded with the beneficiary's own assets. It is available only to beneficiaries under the age of 65. As with a qualified income trust, any excess principal or accumulated interest is paid back to Medicaid upon the death of the beneficiary. Payback trusts will shelter assets for Medicaid purposes but not SSI purposes. The Social Security Administration treats these trusts as revocable. The following factors are necessary to establish a payback trust:

   a. The trust must be irrevocable and established for the sole benefit of the disabled beneficiary.

   b. The trust must be created by a parent, grandparent, legal guardian of the beneficiary or by a court.

   c. The trustee must have complete discretion to pay or refuse to pay trust resources for the beneficiary's benefit.

3. *Pooled trusts.* Trust assets of *disabled individuals* transferred into a qualifying **pooled trust** may be exempt from being treated as a Medicaid resource. Trust assets are pooled with other similar beneficiaries and administered by a nonprofit organization. The state will receive funds from the trust after the death of the beneficiary, to the extent they are not retained by the trust, up to the amount of medical assistance paid on behalf of the beneficiary. Some states allow transfers to pooled trusts by persons of any age, but other states assess a transfer penalty if the transferor is 65 years of age or older.

4. A **qualified income trust,** also referred to as a "Miller Trust" is created for a resident of an income cap state, such as Florida, Texas and Arizona (see page 247 for the complete list of income cap states). The trust is funded with the income that exceeds the income cap of the state. The trust is not treated as an asset of the Medicaid applicant/beneficiary provided.

   a. The principal of the trust consists of the grantor's excess pension, Social Security benefits, or any other type of income, plus accumulated income payable to the grantor.

   b. In some localities, the trust assets must be used to pay for the beneficiary's personal needs allowance, a spousal income allowance (if any), and the balance used to pay

Supplemental Needs Trust
A trust that is created for the benefit of a disabled person under 65 who receives the income from the trust. Upon the death of the income beneficiary, the principal of the trust is used to pay off any Medicaid liens. The residuary of the trust will go to the family of the deceased income beneficiary.

Pooled Trust
Trust assets of multiple individuals in similar situations that are pooled together and administered by a nonprofit organization.

Qualified Income Trust
A qualified income trust is created for a resident of an income cap state whereby the trust is not treated as an asset of the Medicaid applicant.

for the beneficiary's medical expenses. Any remaining income can be used for the beneficiary or the spouse's benefit.

c. In other localities, the remaining principal and accumulated income will be paid to the local Medicaid program upon the death of the beneficiary up to the sum expended on behalf of the Medicaid recipient in the same way as a payback trust. 42 U.S.C. § 1396p(d)(2)(C).

Check local Medicaid regulations and state law on trusts regarding use of these trusts in Medicaid planning.

When can Medicaid place liens on a Medicaid applicant's assets?

Medicaid Liens and Estate Recovery [42 U.S.C. Sec. 1396p(b)]

A. *Lien authority:* Liens against a Medicaid applicant recipient prior to death are prohibited except in limited circumstances as follows:

1. For benefits incorrectly paid pursuant to a court judgment.

2. On real property of currently institutionalized individuals where the state has determined, after an opportunity for a hearing, that the individual cannot return home. However, if the institutionalized person returns home, Medicaid must remove the lien. Liens cannot be imposed against a homestead of a spouse, disabled child of any age, or dependent child under 21 or certain siblings who legally reside there.

3. The home in which a Medicaid applicant's sibling is residing cannot be the subject of a lien by Medicaid if it can be established that the sibling possesses an equity interest in the applicant's home and was residing in the premises for a minimum of one year immediately prior to the institutionalization of the Medicaid recipient. The sibling who seeks to qualify under this lien exception must verify his or her financial interest by producing the following documentation:

   a. Proof of her or his payment of the mortgage

   b. Proof of payment for home improvements, such as a dormer, finished basement, or any other addition to the living quarters

   c. A valid recorded deed naming the sibling as a grantee or life tenant

   d. Financial proof of an investment in the homestead at the time of purchase or subsequently thereafter

   e. An agreement, preferably in writing, indicating that the sibling has the legal right to use the property without being named on the deed

4. The Medicaid statute neither authorizes nor prohibits liens after the recipient's death

B. *Medicaid estate recovery:* Recovery by Medicaid of benefits paid is prohibited except as specifically set forth in the statute. The state *must* seek recovery of medical assistance paid in the following situations:

1. Individuals against whose property liens are placed, pursuant to a lien authority, from the decedent's estate or upon the sale of the property.

2. Individuals 55 and over who receive Medicaid assistance. Recovery can be made from their estate for nursing home care, home care, community-based services, and related hospital and prescription drugs services. If the recipient is under 55, there can be no Medicaid recovery.

   Example: If Medicaid benefits were paid to a recipient from age 50 to 62, only benefits paid from 55 to 62 can be the subject of a recovery by Medicaid.

3. Individuals who received Medicaid assistance, by having additional resources disregarded in connection with receiving benefits under a long-term care insurance policy. Recovery from their estate for nursing home care and other long-term care services is permitted by statute.

An estate includes all probate assets real and personal that were in the decedent's name alone. Assets that are nonprobatable do not fall into the decedent's probate estate and are not subject to recovery. For example, if a decedent had 1,000 shares of AT&T stock or a home in his own name, that asset is considered a probate asset and is recoverable by Medicaid. If a stock is jointly held with another party, the stock passes to the surviving joint owner by operation of law outside of probate and is not subject to Medicaid recovery. It should be noted that each state has the option of defining an estate to include any property in which the individual had *any* interest at the time of death. This includes joint tenancies, life estates, etc.

Currently, 11 states have elected to extend estate recovery to include all assets, probate and non-probate. They are Maine, Rhode Island, Delaware, Alabama, Illinois, Iowa, Montana, North Dakota, South Dakota, California, and Nevada.

Note: 1. A probate asset is one that is solely in the name of the decedent and must be distributed through the estate.

2. A non-probate asset is one that will pass by operation of law to a surviving joint owner or beneficiary and is not subject to distribution through the decedent's probate estate proceedings; for example; real property which is jointly held with a right of survivorship; assets held in trust for another person; annuities, life insurance, or pension benefits payable to a named beneficiary. If the Medicaid recipient's estate is the named beneficiary, it is treated as a probate asset and subject to Medicaid recovery.

Limitations on Recovery Against the Estate of a Medicaid Beneficiary

1. *Recovery can only be made after the death of the surviving spouse.*
2. Recovery can only be made when there are no surviving dependent children under 21 or disabled children.
3. In the case of recovery of a lien on a homestead, recovery cannot be made while one or more of the following persons is living:
   a. A sibling who resided there for at least one year prior to the beneficiary's admission to the institution.
   b. A son or daughter who resided with the Medicaid beneficiary for two years prior to the institutionalization of the Medicaid recipient who provided care that permitted the individual to remain at home and who resided in the home since the individual's institutionalization.
4. The recovery procedure requires that the Medicaid agency file a claim against the decedent's estate in the probate court. Florida now requires that the personal representative of the estate formally notify the Medicaid agency of any pending estate proceeding in the probate court.
5. Medicaid is subject to two statutes of limitation:
   a. The claim must be filed within six years of the death of the Medicaid beneficiary.
   b. Medicaid's claim can only be perfected for benefits paid within 10 years of the recipients' death. For example, if an individual began receiving Medicaid benefits at age

80 and died at age 97, Medicaid can only recover funds it paid out during the period covered from age 87 to 97.

If the Medicaid authority places a lien against the recipient's estate without giving prior notice and without the opportunity for a medical hearing, the lien must be withdrawn and dissolved.

Effective Dates for Medicaid Liens

Medicaid liens may be placed only for Medicaid payments made on or after October 1, 1993, and do not apply to individuals who died before October 1, 1993.

Hardship Waiver

Special consideration will be given by Medicaid authorities where the assets subject to lien recovery are:

1. The sole income-producing asset of the survivors of the Medicaid recipient.
2. A homestead of modest value.

Medicaid Asset Planning

Spend Down
The process by which an elderly person divests him- or herself of assets in order to qualify for Medicaid programs.

If a Medicaid applicant is required to spend down assets in order to qualify for Medicaid, the following should be considered as methods of **spend down**:

1. Pay off all debts on exempt resources, such as a mortgage on a house, condominium, cooperative apartment, or mobile home. Pay off automobile loans and all personal and legitimate debts, including credit cards.
2. Pay legal fees.
3. Pay nursing home placement fees.
4. Pay off all back taxes on real estate, income tax, or business taxes.
5. Make home repairs, such as a new roof, refurbish a bathroom, put in ramps, or make other necessary repairs.
6. Add on a room to the house in the event that he or she requires home care to remain on the premises.
7. Purchase exempt resources that do not have any limitations as to value, such as a new house, condominium, cooperative apartment, mobile home or trailer, or an automobile.
8. Prepay funeral expenses.

The Medicaid Application

Each state has its own Medicaid application, which the elder law professional should obtain. (See CD-ROM for State Offices on Aging List.)

Criminalization of Medicaid Asset Transfers

In 1996, President Clinton signed into law the Health Insurance Portability and Accountability Act of 1996 (HIPAA), which took effect on January 1, 1997. The act contains provisions that make it a crime punishable by one to five years in prison and a fine of up to $25,000 for an individual to transfer assets in order to qualify for Medicaid benefits, if the transfer results in the "imposition" of a period of ineligibility.

Subsequently, this provision of the bill dealing with criminalization of Medicaid asset transfers was declared unconstitutional and has not been enforced. Elder law professionals can continue to do medical asset planning without the fear of being subject to criminal sanctions. Granny and her attorney will not go to jail! It is important to remember that medical eligibility is subject to change, and the elder law professional needs to keep current on the law.

THE HEALTH INSURANCE PORTABILITY AND ACCOUNTABILITY ACT OF 1996
(Signed law on August 21, 1996; Effective January 1, 1997)

42 USC Sec. 1320a-7b, 01/03/95
Title 42—the Public Health and Welfare
Chapter 7—Social Security
Subchapter XI—General Provisions and Peer Review

PART A—GENERAL PROVISIONS

Sec. 1320a-7b. Criminal penalties for acts involving Medicare or State health care programs

a. *Making or Causing to Be Made False Statements or Representations*

Whoever—(1) knowingly and willfully makes or causes to be made any false statement or representation of a material fact in any application for any benefit or payment under a program, under subchapter xviii of this chapter or a State health care program (as defined in section 1320a-7 (h) of this title),

(2) at any time knowingly and willfully makes or causes to be made any false statement or representation of a material fact for use in determining rights to such benefit or payment,

(3) having knowledge of the occurrence of any event affecting (A) his initial or continued right to any such benefit or payment, or (B) the initial or continued right to any such benefit or payment of any other individual in whose behalf he has applied for or is receiving such benefit or payment, conceals or fails to disclose such event with an intent fraudulently to secure such benefit or payment either in a greater amount or quantity than is due or when no such benefit or payment is authorized,

(4) having made application to receive any such benefit or payment for the use and benefit of another and having received it, knowingly and willfully converts such benefit or payment or any part thereof to a use other than for the use and benefit of such other person,

(5) presents or causes to be presented a claim for a physician's service for which payment may be made under a program under subchapter XVIII of this chapter or a State health care program and knows that the individual who furnished the service was not licensed as a physician, or

(6) knowingly and willfully disposes of assets (including by any transfer in trust) in order for an individual to become eligible for medical assistance under a State plan under title XIX, if disposing of the assets results in the imposition of a period of ineligibility for such assistance under section 1917 (c), shall

i. in the case of such a statement, representation, concealment, failure, or conversion by any person in connection with the furnishing by that person) of items or services for which payment is or may be made under the program, be guilty of a felony and upon conviction thereof fined not more than $25,000 or imprisoned for not more than five years or both, or

ii. in the case of such a statement, representation, concealment, failure, or conversion by any other person, be guilty of a misdemeanor and upon conviction thereof fined not more than $10,000 or imprisoned for not more than one year, or both. In addition, in any case where an individual who is otherwise eligible for assistance under a State plan approved under subchapter XIX of this chapter is convicted of an offense under the preceding provisions of this subsection, the State may at its option (notwithstanding any other provision of that subchapter of such plan) limit, restrict or suspend the eligibility of that individual for such period (not exceeding one year) as it deems appropriate; but the imposition of a limitation, restriction, or suspension with respect to the eligibility of any individual under this section shall not affect the eligibility of any other person for assistance under the plan, regardless of the relationship between that individual and such other person.

THE STATUTORY AMENDMENT
Effective August 5, 1997

BALANCED BUDGET ACT OF 1997

Sec. 4734. PenaltyForFraudulent Eligibility

Section 1128B(a)(47 U.S.C. 1320a-7b(a)), as amended by Section 217 of the Health Insurance Portability and Accountability Act of 1996 (Public Law 104-191; 110 Stat. 2008), is amended:

2. By striking paragraph (6) and inserting the following:
   "(6) for a fee knowingly and willfully counsels or assists an individual to dispose of assets (including by any transfer in trust) in order for the individual to become eligible for medical assistance under a State plan under Title XIX, if disposing of the assets results in the imposition of a period of ineligibility for such assistance under section 1917 c,"; and
3. In clause (ii) of the matter following such paragraph, by striking the following:
   "failure, or conversion by any other person"
   and inserting the following:
   "failure, conversion, or provision of counsel or assistance by any other person."

Current Status of Section 217 Health Insurance Portability and Accountability Act of 1996

The Health Insurance Portability and Accountability Act of 1996, which went into effect on January 1, 1997, was immediately amended by Congress, in its continuing efforts to discourage Americans from becoming eligible for the Medicaid entitlement program. In 1997, Congress passed the Balanced Budget Act of 1997. Section 4734 of the Act replaces Section 217 (known as the "Granny Goes to Jail Law"). The law made it a misdemeanor (crime) for a paid advisor to knowingly and willfully counsel or assist a person to dispose of assets for the purpose of obtaining Medicaid assistance where the disposition of the assets would create the imposition of a period of ineligibility for obtaining Medicaid assistance. Granny would not go to jail, but her lawyer would! This, in effect, put a gag upon attorneys, paralegals, and other professionals who counsel individuals in connection with Medicaid planning that results in a period of ineligibility.

On April 25, 1997, the first recorded decision interpreting Section 217, passed August 21, 1996, effective January 1, 1997, was decided in the United States district court for the district of Oregon in *Peebler & Nay vs. Reno* [965 F. Supp 28 (D. Or. 1997)].

PEEBLER V. RENO

965 F.Supp. 28 (D. Or., 1997)

Haggerty, District Judge:

On February 14, 1997, Plaintiffs filed this action for declaratory relief seeking a judicial declaration that 42 U.S.C. § 1320a-7b(a)(6) is unconstitutional. On April 2, 1997, Defendant filed a motion to dismiss the action for lack of subject matter jurisdiction. For the reasons that follow, Defendant's motion to dismiss is GRANTED.

BACKGROUND

In 1988, Congress passed 42 U.S.C. § 1396p(c) ("§ 1396") which requires a period of ineligibility for Medicaid benefits in response to the applicant's transfer of assets for the purpose of obtaining benefits. The period of ineligibility for Medicaid benefits is directly proportionate to the value of the assets that were transferred. To determine the period of ineligibility, the value of the assets transferred is divided by the statewide average monthly nursing home cost (as determined by the state health agency.)

Margaret Peebler is an 87-year-old widow with no living children or siblings. In November of 1996, while living independently in an apartment, she fell several times. After two stays in the hospital, she went to live in the Centennial Health Care Center in Gresham, Oregon, in December 1996. While Mrs. Peebler is in a wheelchair and is expected to require 24-hour care for the rest of her life, she is not mentally incapacitated.

In January 1997 Mrs. Peebler "gave up" her apartment, and upon discharge from Centennial she will enter an adult foster care or assisted living facility. The cost of care in such a facility is between $1,800 and $3,000 per month. Mrs. Peebler's total assets as of February 1997 were $14,824.22. She has no insurance to cover long-term care and cannot qualify for such insurance. Mrs. Peebler's only income is a monthly $393 Social Security check.

Among other requirements, an individual's assets must be below $2,000 to qualify for Medicaid. When Mrs. Peebler's assets fall to that level, Medicaid will pay for her long-term care. However, all of her monthly Social Security check will be applied towards her long-term care, except for a $30–$75 monthly personal needs allowance.

In an effort to retain the ability to meet her future personal needs, Plaintiff attorney Tim Nay advised Mrs. Peebler to transfer her assets so that she could meet the requirements for Medicaid. On February 12, 1997, Mrs. Peebler transferred $7,785 to her great-nephew. It is intended that the great-nephew use this money to provide for Mrs. Peebler's personal needs for the rest of her life.

Pursuant to § 1396, Mrs. Peebler is ineligible to receive Medicaid benefits for three months. This is due to the application of OAR 461-140-295(2), which sets the average monthly cost of private nursing facility services at $2,595. Put another way, the period of ineligibility [3 months] = the amount transferred [$7,785] / average monthly cost of services as determined by the state [\$2,595]. The period of ineligibility is intended to duplicate the amount of medical care the individual would have been able to afford but for the transfer of assets.

Section 217 of the Health Insurance Portability and Accountability Act of 1996, Pub.L. No. 104-191, 110 Stat. 2008 (codified at 42 U.S.C. § 1320a-7b(a)(6)) was signed into law on August 21, 1996, and had an effective date of January 1, 1997. Section 217 applies to any individual who "[k]nowingly and willfully disposes of assets . . . in order for an individual to become eligible for [Medicaid], if disposing of the assets results in the imposition of ineligibility for such assistance under [42 U.S.C. § 1396p(c)]."

Plaintiffs have been neither prosecuted nor threatened with prosecution under § 217. Nonetheless, they filed this action on February 14, 1997, seeking a declaratory judgment that § 217 is unconstitutionally vague in violation of the Due Process Clause of the Fifth Amendment. Defendant has moved to dismiss the action for lack of subject matter jurisdiction. Specifically, Defendant claims that Plaintiffs lack standing to invoke the jurisdiction of this court.

STANDARD OF REVIEW

The Declaratory Judgment Act (the Act) permits a federal court to "declare the rights and other legal relations" of parties to "a case of actual controversy." 28 U.S.C. § 2201. The "actual controversy" requirement of the Act is the same as the "case or controversy" requirement of Article III of the United States Constitution. *Aetna Life Ins. Co. v. Haworth*, 300 U.S. 227, 239-40, 57 S.Ct. 461, 463-64, 81 L.Ed. 617 (1937). Thus, the Act requires no more stringent showing of justiciability than the Constitution does.

For a case to be constitutionally justiciable, the plaintiff must have standing. In order to have standing to invoke the power of a federal court, a plaintiff must establish, at a constitutional minimum, three propositions. *San Diego County Gun Rights Comm. v. Reno*, 98 F.3d 1121, 1126 (9th Cir.1996) (citing *Lujan v. Defenders of Wildlife*, 504 U.S. 555, 560, 112 S.Ct. 2130, 2136, 119 L.Ed.2d 351 (1992)). First, the plaintiff must demonstrate that he has suffered an "injury in fact" which is "(a) concrete and peculiarized, and (b) actual or imminent, not conjectural or hypothetical." *Lujan*, 504 U.S. at 560, 112 S.Ct. at 2136. Second, the injury must be fairly traceable to the challenged action of the defendant. *Id*. at 560, 112 S.Ct. at 2136. Third, it must be likely, and not merely speculative, that the injury will be redressed by a favorable judicial decision. *Id*. Plaintiff bears the burden of establishing each of these requirements, and failure to demonstrate any one is a fatal defect, mandating dismissal. *Id*.

DISCUSSION

Defendant's motion to dismiss for lack of subject matter jurisdiction under F.R.C.P. 12(b)(1) asserts that enforcement of § 217 against Plaintiffs is neither "actual" nor "imminent" enough to satisfy the standing requirements of Article III of the Constitution and that the Plaintiffs therefore lack standing to challenge the constitutionality of § 217 in federal court. As Defendant points out, "[t]he mere existence of a statute, which may or may not ever be applied to plaintiffs, is not sufficient to create a case or controversy within the meaning of Article III." *Stoianoff v. Montana*, 695 F.2d 1214, 1223 (9th Cir.1983) (citation omitted).

Plaintiffs have not been indicted, arrested, threatened with arrest, or even granted an "advisory opinion" by the Department of Health & Human Services concerning the application of § 217. Further, the government has represented in its motion to dismiss that, if Mrs. Peebler waits until May 13, 1997 to apply for Medicaid benefits, "no period of ineligibility for such benefits will be imposed." *Defendant's Memorandum*, p. 4. If no period of ineligibility is imposed, neither of the Plaintiffs can be prosecuted under § 217. Under these circumstances, enforcement of § 217 against them is not "actual" or "imminent." Consequently, Plaintiffs lack standing to bring this suit in federal court.

CONCLUSION

Based on the foregoing, Defendant's motion to dismiss for lack of subject matter jurisdiction (# 11) is GRANTED and all pending motions are Denied as moot. This action is dismissed with prejudice.
IT IS SO ORDERED.

It is clear from this case that if a transferor of assets waits out the period of ineligibility—does not apply for Medicaid during that ineligibility period—and then subsequently applies for benefits, the transferor would not be subject to any criminal prosecution under Section 217. This is case scenario 2 discussed above.

The above is a clear and precise statement of the government's position. No criminal penalty will be imposed for transferring assets, provided that the transferor does not apply for Medicaid at any time during the penalty period.

Therefore, under no circumstances should an individual apply for Medicaid until after the expiration of the penalty period imposed by said transfer. As long as Section 217 remains on the books, caution is advised when making transfers. Regardless of the interpretation made by the Justice Department in *Peebler vs. Reno*, the government's position can change at any time.

Warning: The elder law professional is advised to be extremely cautious in advising clients in matters concerning asset transfers. An individual who counsels a client in this area of the law could be accused of aiding and abetting a crime and could be prosecuted as a principal under the new law. *(**This law is not being enforced at this time.**)*

THE FAMILY AND MEDICAL LEAVE ACT
[29 U.S.C. SEC. 2601 et seq.]

The **Family and Medical Leave Act** was passed by Congress in 1993. The government recognized that employees very often must take leave of their jobs for short or long periods of time to take care of medical emergencies and family medical problems, such as an elderly parent with Alzheimer's or Parkinson's disease or a family member who has suffered a stroke. When a family member becomes ill, an employee often takes time off to

Family and Medical Leave Act
This act requires employers with 50 or more workers to provide unpaid time off to care for a seriously ill spouse, parent, child, or for the employee's own illness.

care for such a person because the employee does not possess the resources or ability to pay for private care.

The Family and Medical Leave Act protects an employee who takes a leave of absence in order to care for a family member. The act requires employers with 50 or more workers to provide unpaid time off to care for a seriously ill spouse, parent, child, or for the employee's own illness. The eligibility requirements are as follows:

1. The employee must be employed by a firm that employs 50 or more employees within 75 miles of the employee's work site.
2. The length of employment must be a minimum of 12 months, which do not have to be consecutive before the employee will qualify for a leave.
3. During that 12-month period, the employee must have worked 1,250 hours.

The act provides that an eligible employee who meets the above-mentioned qualifications is legally permitted to take a total of 12 work weeks of leave during any 12-month period, when the leave concerns the following:

1. The care of the spouse, child, or parent of an employee, if the family member is suffering from a serious health condition
2. The inability of an employee to perform the job because of a personal serious health condition.

The statute defines "serious health condition" as "an illness, injury, or impairment, physical or mental condition," which involves either:

1. Inpatient care in a hospital, hospice, or residential medical care facility
2. Continuing treatment by a health care provider

Both members of a married couple can simultaneously take time to care for one of their parents under the Family and Medical Leave Act. An employee who is refused leave under this act can commence a civil action in federal or state court.

SCENARIO I

During the initial interview, the legal professional obtains the following information from the client's son, who is present at the interview:

1. *His mother, age 69, suffered a severe stroke 10 days ago and is currently hospitalized.*
2. *Medical condition—patient is comatose, nonresponsive, possibly entering a persistent vegetative state.*
3. *She is a widow, with one adult child.*
4. *She has done absolutely no advance planning. There is no durable power of attorney, no living will, no health care proxy, and no advance directive for the appointment of a guardian.*

5. *She and her son, who is a bachelor, have lived together for the last five years in their one-family house. He has been caring for her for the last several years because she has been in poor health.*

6. *Patient's assets:*

   a. *One-family house, title in the name of the ill mother with a remaining mortgage balance of $25,000. The current fair market value of the house is $250,000.*

   b. *$150,000 in cash and CDs in joint accounts with her son.*

   c. *$25,000 life insurance policy, cash surrender value $15,000. Beneficiary is the son. Policy is owned by the mother.*

   d. *$10,000 in common stocks registered in mother's name alone.*

Problem: The son wants to know if the mother will be eligible for any benefits under the Medicaid Assistance Entitlement Program.

Exercise: Devise a Medicaid eligibility plan based on the facts in the first case scenario.

SCENARIO II

Married couple. Husband, age 75, has been hospitalized for the last two weeks. He has suffered a mild stroke that affected his speech pattern (aphasia) but did not paralyze any parts of his body. The wife states that her husband will be ready for discharge in approximately one week. The wife is concerned about her husband's future health.

She is rightly concerned about financing his catastrophic illness should he suffer a second, more debilitating stroke. The wife, age 70, is in good health; there are two adult children from this, their first and only, marriage.

Their assets are as follows:

1. *A two-family dwelling, with one rental apartment, valued at $250,000, subject to a $15,000 mortgage. Title is registered in the name of both husband and wife as joint tenants by the entirety.*

2. *Joint bank accounts and CDs in the name of both husband and wife in the sum of $150,000.*

3. *Brokerage account in joint name, husband and wife, in the amount of $175,000.*

4. *Veteran's life insurance policy insuring the husband and naming the wife as beneficiary; face value $10,000.*

5. *Series E savings bonds, face value $30,000, purchased from 1970 to 1982 in the husband's name, POD (paid on death) to the wife.*

Problem: Will the ill spouse qualify for home care Medicaid? Will the ill spouse qualify for institutional Medicaid (skilled nursing facility coverage) in the event he must enter a nursing home in the future as a result of his deteriorating medical condition?

Exercise: Devise a Medicaid eligibility plan based on the facts in the second case scenario.

USEFUL TELEPHONE NUMBERS

Medicare: 800-Medicare

Social Security: 800-772-1213

REVIEW QUESTIONS AND EXERCISES

1. Explain the difference between Medicare and Medicaid. Who is entitled to coverage under each program?

2. Explain the difference between Medicare Part A coverage and Medicare Part B coverage. How do you qualify for Medicare Part A and Medicare Part B?

3. What is a Medi-gap insurance policy? Discuss the advantages of obtaining this coverage.

4. What rights does a Medicare beneficiary receive? What are the procedures if a Medicare beneficiary is denied coverage?

5. What is the future of Medicare? How can the Medicare system survive the graying of America?

6. What services are covered by Medicaid? Will Medicaid pay for nursing homes, home care, or hospice care?

7. If a Medicaid recipient enters a nursing home, will Medicaid seize the recipient's assets? Will Medicaid put a lien on the recipient's house? Can Medicaid seek reimbursement from the estate of a recipient after his or her death?

8. What is the Medicaid look-back rule? Discuss Medicaid asset planning. What would make a client eligible for Medicaid? If an elderly client transfers his or her home to a disabled child, will he or she still qualify for Medicaid? Will the elderly client qualify for Medicaid if she transfers her home to a child who has been living with her for two or more years?

9. What is the difference between an income cap state and a non-income cap state?

10. Can a trust be used to shield assets from becoming a Medicaid resource?

11. What is the major holding of *Peebler v. Reno*? How has this case effected Section 217 of the Health Insurance Portability and Accountability Act of 1996?

12. What is the Family and Medical Leave Act? How has this law helped the elderly client and his or her family?

USEFUL WEB SITES

1. www.ssa.gov
2. www.medicare.gov

CHAPTER 11

Patients' Rights in Health Care Decision Making

PREVIEW

What are a patient's rights in determining his or her own health care decision making? What happens when a terminally ill patient wants to stop all lifesaving treatments? What if a patient requires the assistance of a doctor in terminating life support? What if a patient is unconscious and a court appointed guardian decides to terminate lifesaving treatments? What Constitutional protections does the patient have? What is the state's interest in keeping patients alive, regardless of their quality of life? This chapter explores the patient's rights in his or her own health care decision-making process, including the right to refuse lifesaving treatments. A discussion of physician-assisted suicide in America and worldwide is also included.

END OF LIFE ISSUES

The practice of elder law can be very gratifying to the legal professional. In helping clients sort out matters of home, health, and finance, the elder law professional deals with issues at the core of daily human existence. Although often difficult, the practice of elder law can be emotionally rewarding.

Many clients have problems for which there are no happy solutions. These clients need crisis intervention or legal professional help in dealing with issues of declining quality of life due to degenerative and catastrophic illnesses or imminent death. In other words, clients present life-and-death situations on a daily basis. Most elder law professionals, unless they have a background in health care, are not trained to handle these stressful situations. The elder law firm must learn how to be compassionate while remaining objective. The elder law practice often represents clients and their families during the end of life. In fact, the author's practice deals on average with the death of four clients per week. This has an emotional effect upon the entire staff, from lawyer to file clerk. The following situations are typical of those encountered regularly in an elder law practice:

SCENARIO I

A client who is in the early stages of Alzheimer's disease comes in for a consultation. He appears to be very competent and consults the elder law firm about terminating his life with the assistance of a physician or a family member with whom he has not yet discussed this possibility. At this initial visit, our impression is that he is bright, intelligent, and alert, but is aware of his diminishing capacity and knows of the devastating progression of this terrible disease. He has read the medical literature and understands that at the terminal stages of Alzheimer's disease, the patient becomes a "non-person," losing his dignity. He cannot bear the degradation that incontinence will bring. He dreads not knowing who he is and where he is. He knows there is a possibility that he will end up in a hospital or a nursing home and be subject to custodial care without any possibility of recovery.

SCENARIO II

A client who has been represented by the elder law firm for many years advises us that she has just received the results of her CT scan, which revealed the presence of an inoperable brain tumor. Her oncologist informed her that she has between six months and a year to live. The prescribed chemotherapy and radiation treatments will probably not have any permanent effect upon the tumor and will produce terrible side effects. The resulting nausea, loss of appetite, loss of hair, and loss of immune system function are not acceptable to her. She cannot conceive of losing control of her entire body. She wants to know what her rights are.

SCENARIO III

A 50-year-old male who is HIV-positive seeks assistance in estate planning. During the initial meeting, he confides that he has been diagnosed as having an active case of AIDS. He wishes to transfer his assets and needs legal advice concerning assisted suicide, either by a physician, relative, or friend. What are his rights, and how can he protect his friends who might help him to terminate his life and end his agony?

The three case scenarios presented above have a common thread, assisted suicide. They pose the following critical questions:

1. Can a physician assist in a patient's suicide?
2. Can a family member or close friend assist a terminally ill patient without being prosecuted for homicide under the state penal code?

Physician-Assisted Suicide
An act in which a physician helps a competent, terminally ill patient, who has previously authorized the physician, to terminate his or her own life.

Physician-assisted suicide occurs when a physician knowingly assists in causing the patient to die in accordance with the patient's desire. Assisted suicide occurs when someone other than a physician assists in helping a person die, for example, a family member.

According to a decision rendered by the Supreme Court on June 26, 1997 (*Washington v. Glucksberg*; see page 278), physician-assisted suicide still remains a criminal act under the laws of the State of Washington. The Court upheld the state's constitutional right to ban physician-assisted suicide and to pass legislation making it a crime. Therefore, a physician, health care provider, family member, or friend is prohibited from assisting in an individual's suicide. They can be prosecuted for homicide and cannot be protected by the patient who requests assistance in committing suicide. The terminally ill patient has no constitutional "liberty right" to assisted suicide. There is no federal law that prohibits assisted suicides.

HISTORICAL BACKGROUND ISSUES OF THE "PATIENT'S RIGHT TO DIE"

1906 First euthanasia bill is introduced in Ohio, it does not succeed.

1938 National organization is formed to promote euthanasia in the United States; it is known as National Society for the Legalization of Euthanasia.

1941 The New York State legislature receives a bill involving mercy killing; it does not pass.

1968 A Florida legislature accepts a bill legalizing living wills, which is adopted thereafter.

1973 "A Patient Bill of Rights" is endorsed by the American Hospital Association, which recommended that patients, after informed consent, should have the right to refuse treatment when terminally ill.

1976 The Supreme Court of the State of New Jersey hears the *Quinlan* case, and issues an order permitting the disconnection of Karen Ann Quinlan's respirator based on her parents' testimony that such would have been the patient's choice had she been able to make it.

1980 The Hemlock Society is founded. It advocates legal changes permitting physician-assisted suicide, which could become standard medical procedure in the United States.

1988 Physician-assisted suicide is approved by a recognized religious group in the United States—the Unitarian Universalists.

1990 Michigan becomes the physician-assisted suicide hub of the United States. Jack Kevorkian, MD, a retired pathologist, assists in the first reported physician-assisted suicide case.

1990 Congress passes the Patient Self-Determination Act, requiring hospitals that receive federal funds to tell patients that they have a right to demand or refuse treatment. It takes effect the next year.

1990 Historic ground is broken when the United States Supreme Court decides the *Cruzan* case. The court recognizes the right of patients and their next of kin to refuse life-sustaining treatment.

1991 Dr. Timothy Quill, a Rochester, New York, physician, publicly reveals in his book how he assisted a patient in her suicide.

1991 A bill was introduced into the Washington State legislature legalizing physician-assisted suicide, which was voted down. *Final Exit: The Practicalities of Self-Deliverance and Assisted Suicide for Dying* was published by Derek Humphry, president and founder of the Hemlock Society.

1992 The California legislature introduces a bill legalizing physician-assisted suicide, which is defeated.

1993 An organization in Seattle, Washington, known as "Compassion for Dying" is created, which instituted litigation in Seattle and in New York regarding patients' rights in physician-assisted suicide.

1994 Physician-assisted suicide is approved in Oregon, but the enforcement of the statute is stayed pending litigation.

1996 The Ninth U.S. Circuit Court of Appeals and the Second U.S. Circuit Court of Appeals both rule that terminally ill patients have a constitutional liberty interest in their right to physician-assisted suicide.

1997 The U.S. Supreme Court hears arguments on both cases from the Ninth and Second Circuits regarding the patients' liberty interests in their quest for the right to die. On June 26, the Supreme Court upholds a state's constitutional right to prohibit physician-assisted suicide and to pass legislation making it a criminal act. The court decides that terminally ill patients do not have a constitutional liberty right to physician-assisted suicide. We have not heard the last of this issue.

1997 Dr. Kevorkian admits that he has assisted almost 100 people to commit suicide.

1998 Sixteen people die by making use of the Oregon Death With Dignity Act, receiving physician-assisted suicide in its first full year of implementation.

1999 Dr. Kevorkian is sentenced to 10–25 years imprisonment for the second-degree murder of Thomas Youk after showing a video of Youk's death by injection on national television. Kevorkian has admitted being present at 130 assisted deaths since 1990.

2001 U.S. Attorney General John Ashcroft issues a directive stating that assisting suicide is not a legitimate medical purpose and that prescribing, dispensing, or administering federally controlled substances to assist suicide can lead to a suspension or revocation of a physician's license.

2002 Federal District Court for the District of Oregon overrules the Ashcroft directive, stating the directive exceeded the authority delegated to the Attorney General.

2002 Dr. Kevorkian's petition for a writ of certiorari to the Court of Appeals of Michigan is denied.

2003 *Oregon v. Ashcroft* is brought to the Ninth Circuit Court of Appeals (decision pending).

2004 Florida court judge orders Terri Schiavo's feeding tube removed.

2004 Florida Governor Jeb Bush orders Terri Schiavo's feeding tube reinserted.

Legal Context

The debate surrounding the right to die includes a number of challenging legal issues. The cases can be distinguished between those that examine "the right to refuse medical treatment," which is constitutionally protected, and "the right to physician-assisted suicide," which is not federally protected, but may be legal under state law. Some of the legal questions that arise in this chapter include:

1. Does a person have a right to refuse medical treatment?
2. Can medical treatment be denied when there is "clear and convincing evidence" that the patient would refuse such treatment if he or she were competent and able to communicate?
3. Does a person's Constitutional right to privacy include a right to physician-assisted suicide?
4. Does the Due Process Clause guarantee a personal liberty interest in the right to physician-assisted suicide?
5. Does the Equal Protection Clause require that people seeking physician-assisted suicide be treated the same as people refusing medical treatment and be allowed to die without government intervention?
6. Is a physician who assists a suicide subject to prosecution it the United States?
7. Is the dispensing of medication that would painlessly and voluntarily end a terminally ill patient's life in a state where physician-assisted suicide-legal "a legitimate purpose" pursuant to the federal Controlled Substance Act?

The Landmark cases here are *In re: Quinlan* (New Jersey)[1] (see Chapter 3 for full text of this case), and *O'Connor v. Westchester County Hospital*, and *Cruzan v. Director, Missouqi Department of Health* (see Chapter 4 for full text).[2]

O'CONNOR V. WESTCHESTER COUNTY HOSPITAL
531 N.E.2d 607 (N.Y. 1988)

OPINION OF THE COURT

Wachtler, Chief Judge.

Mary O'Connor is an elderly hospital patient who, as a result of several strokes, is mentally incompetent and unable to obtain food or drink without medical assistance. In this dispute between her daughters and the hospital the question is whether the hospital should be permitted to insert a nasogastric tube to provide her with sustenance or whether, instead, such medical intervention should be precluded and she should be allowed to die because, prior to becoming incompetent, she made several statements to the effect that she did not want to be a burden to anyone and would not want to live or be kept alive by artificial means if she were unable to care for herself.

    The hospital has applied for court authorization to insert the nasogastric tube. The patient's daughters object claiming that it is contrary to her "expressed wishes", although they conceded at the hearing that they do not know whether their mother would want to decline this procedure under these circumstances, particularly if it would produce a painful death. The trial court denied the hospital's application, concluding that it was contrary to the patient's wishes. The Appellate Division affirmed, 139 A.D.2d 344, 532 N.Y.S.2d 133. The hospital has appealed by leave of the Appellate Division, which also granted a stay permitting the patient to be fed intravenously while this appeal is pending.

We have concluded that the order of the Appellate Division should be reversed and the hospital's petition granted. On this record there is not clear and convincing proof that the patient had made a firm and settled commitment, while competent, to decline this type of medical assistance under circumstances such as these.

I

The patient is a 77-year-old widow with two children, Helen and Joan, both of whom are practical nurses. After her husband's death in 1967 she lived alone in her apartment in the New York City area where she was employed in hospital administration. In 1983 she retired from her job after 20 years service.

Over the years a number of her close relatives died of cancer. Her husband died of brain cancer. The last two of her nine brothers died of cancer, one in 1975 and the other in 1977. During their final years she regularly visited them in the hospital and cared for them when they were home. In November 1984, after being informed that her stepmother had died of cancer in Florida, Mrs. O'Connor had an attack of congestive heart failure and was hospitalized. She was released from the hospital in December 1984.

In July of the following year she suffered the first of a series of strokes causing brain damage and related disabilities, which rendered her unable to care for herself. She became passive, could only carry on limited conversations, and could not walk, eat, dress or care for her bodily needs without assistance from others. Upon her release from the hospital in August 1985, Mrs. O'Connor resided with her daughter Helen who, together with Joan and another woman, provided her with full-time care.

In December 1987, Mrs. O'Connor had a second major stroke causing additional physical and mental disabilities. She became unresponsive and unable to stand or feed herself. She had to be spoon-fed by others. Her gag reflex was also impaired, as a result of which she experienced difficulty swallowing and thus could eat only pureed foods. In this condition her daughters found that they could no longer care for her at home and, when she left the hospital in February 1988, she was transferred to the Ruth Taylor Institute (the Institute), a long-term geriatric care facility associated with the Westchester County Medical Center (the hospital). In conjunction with this transfer, her daughters submitted a document signed by both of them, to be included in her medical file, stating that their mother had expressed the wish in many conversations that "no artificial life support be started or maintained in order to continue to sustain her life", and that they wanted this request to be honored.

During the initial part of her stay at the Institute the staff found Mrs. O'Connor was cooperative, capable of sitting in a chair and interacting with her surroundings. However, in June her condition deteriorated. She became "stuperous, virtually not responsive" and developed a fever. On June 20, 1988, she was transferred from the Institute to the hospital.

At the hospital it was determined that she was suffering from dehydration, sepsis and probably pneumonia. The hospital staff also found that she had lost her gag reflex, making it impossible for her to swallow food or liquids without medical assistance. She showed marked improvement after receiving fluids, limited nourishment and antibiotics intravenously. Within a few days she became alert, able to follow simple commands and respond verbally to simple questions. However her inability to swallow persisted and her physician, Dr. Sivak, determined that a nasogastric tube should be used to provide more substantial nourishment. When Mrs. O'Connor's daughters objected to this procedure, the matter was brought before the hospital's ethics committee which found that it would be inappropriate to withhold this treatment under the circumstances.

On July 15, the hospital commenced this proceeding by order to show cause seeking court authorization to use the nasogastric tube, claiming that without this relief Mrs. O'Connor would die of thirst and starvation within a few weeks. In an opposing affidavit her daughters stated that this was against their mother's expressed wishes because before becoming incompetent, she had repeatedly stated that she did not want her life prolonged by artificial means if she was unable to care for herself. They noted the number of relatives she had comforted during prolonged final illnesses and urged that the effect of her statements should be evaluated against that background.

At the hearing, two medical experts testified regarding Mrs. O'Connor's condition: Dr. Sivak for the hospital and Dr. Wasserman for the respondents. With respect to the patient's statements concerning life-sustaining measures the respondents themselves both testified and called one additional witness, James Lampasso.

The treating physician, Dr. Sivak, testified that Mrs. O'Connor was suffering from multiinfarct dementia as a result of the strokes. This condition substantially impaired her cognitive ability but she was not in a coma or vegetative state. She was conscious, and capable of responding to simple questions or requests sometimes by squeezing the questioner's hand and sometimes verbally. She was also able to respond to noxious stimuli, such as a needle prick, and in fact was sensitive to "even minimal discomfort", although she was not experiencing pain in her present condition. When asked how she felt she usually responded "fine", "all right" or "ok". The treating physician also testified that her mental awareness had improved at the hospital and that she might become more alert in the future. In fact during the latest examination conducted that morning, in response to the doctor's request she had attempted to sit up and had been able to roll over on her side so that he could examine her lungs. However, Dr. Sivak stated that she is unable to comprehend complex questions, such as those dealing with her medical treatment, and doubted that she would ever regain significant mental capacity because the brain damage was substantial and irreparable.

The doctor stated that Mrs. O'Connor was presently receiving nourishment exclusively through intravenous feeding. However, this procedure was inadequate for long-term use because it does not provide sufficient nutrients and the veins tend to deteriorate. He testified that intravenous feeding is used as a temporary measure which generally must be discontinued within several weeks. He noted that these difficulties could be overcome with a gastric tube connected to the patient's digestive tract through her nose or abdomen. This procedure would provide adequate nutrients and could cause only transient discomfort at the time of insertion. Since the patient's condition is otherwise fairly stable, this procedure would preserve her life for several months, perhaps several years. If the procedure were not employed and the intravenous methods could no longer be used or were otherwise discontinued, she would die of thirst and starvation within 7 to 10 days. The doctor stated that death from starvation and especially thirst, was a painful way to die and that Mrs. O'Connor would, therefore, experience extreme, intense discomfort since she is conscious, alert, capable of feeling pain, and sensitive to even mild discomfort.

The respondents' expert Dr. Wasserman, a neurologist, agreed essentially with Dr. Sivak's evaluation and prognosis. In his opinion, however, Mrs. O'Connor would not experience pain if permitted to die of thirst and starvation. Because of the extensive brain damage she had suffered, the doctor did not "think she would react as you or I would under the circumstances" but would simply become more lethargic, unresponsive and would ultimately die. If she experienced pain, he believed she could be given pain killers to alleviate it. He conceded, however, that he could not be "medically certain" that she would not suffer because he had never had a patient, or heard of one, dying after being deprived of food and water. Thus he candidly admitted: "I guess we don't know".

Interestingly, Dr. Wasserman also admitted that during his examination, which occurred just before the close of the hearing, the patient exhibited further improvement in her condition. He found that she was generally able to respond to simple commands, such as a request to move her arm or foot. He also noted that she was able to state her name, seemed to be aware of where she was, and responded to questions about 50 or 60% of the time, although her speech was slow and halting and her responses were not always appropriate. Most significantly, she was able to converse in short sentences of two or three words which, he noted, she had not been able to do since her admission to the hospital. He also observed that she had a gag reflex. Although he did not know whether Mrs. O'Connor would be able to use it to eat, he recognized the possibility that she might.

Neither of the doctors had known Mrs. O'Connor before she became incompetent and thus knew nothing of her attitudes toward the use of life-sustaining measures. The respondents' first witness on this point was James Lampasso, a former co-worker and longtime friend of Mrs. O'Connor. He was also acquainted with other members of the family and presently worked with the patient's daughter Helen at a local hospital. He testified that his first discussion with Mrs. O'Connor concerning artificial means of prolonging life occurred about 1969. At that time his father, who was dying of cancer, informed him that he would not want to continue life by any artificial method if he had lost his dignity because he could no longer control his normal bodily functions. The witness said that when he told Mrs. O'Connor of this she agreed wholeheartedly and said: "I would never want to be a burden on anyone and I would never want to lose my dignity before I passed away." He noted that she was a "very religious woman" who "felt that nature should take its course and not use further artificial means." They had similar conversations on two or three occasions between 1969 and 1973. During these discussions Mrs. O'Connor variously stated that it is "monstrous" to keep someone alive by using "machinery, things like that" when they are "not going to get better"; that she would never want to be in the same situation as her husband and Mr. Lampasso's father and that people who are "suffering very badly" should be allowed to die.

Mrs. O'Connor's daughter Helen testified that her mother informed her on several occasions that if she became ill and was unable to care for herself she would not want her life to be sustained artificially. The first discussion occurred after her husband was hospitalized with cancer in 1967. At that time Mrs. O'Connor said that she never wanted to be in a similar situation and that she would not want to go on living if she could not "take care of herself and make her own decisions." The last discussion occurred after Mrs. O'Connor's stepmother died of cancer and Mrs. O'Connor was hospitalized for a heart attack: "My mother said that she was very glad to be home, very glad to be out of the hospital and hope[d] she would never have to be back in one again and would never want any sort of intervention any sort of life support systems to maintain or prolong her life." Mrs. O'Connor's other daughter, Joan, essentially adopted her sister's testimony. She described her mother's statements on this subject as less solemn pronouncements: "it was brought up when we were together, at times when in conversations you start something, you know, maybe the news was on and maybe that was the topic that was brought up and that's how it came about."

However, all three of these witnesses also agreed that Mrs. O'Connor had never discussed providing food or water with medical assistance, nor had she ever said that she would adhere to her view and decline medical treatment "by artificial means" if that would produce a painful death. When Helen was asked what choice her mother would make under those circumstances, she admitted that she did not know. Her sister Joan agreed, noting that this had never been discussed, "unfortunately, no".

At the conclusion of the hearing the daughters submitted a counterclaim seeking an order directing the hospital to also discontinue the intravenous feeding.

As noted the trial court denied the hospital's petition and granted the counterclaim concluding that Mrs. O'Connor's "past expressions plainly covered any form of life-prolonging treatment". The Appellate Division affirmed noting that requiring greater specificity would impose an undue burden on those seeking to avoid life-prolonging treatment.

II

It has long been the common-law rule in this State that a person has the right to decline medical treatment, even life-saving treatment, absent an overriding State interest (*Schloendorff v. Society of N.Y. Hosp.*, 211 N.Y. 125, 129-130, 105 N.E. 92). In 1981, we held, in two companion cases, that a hospital or medical facility must respect this right even when a patient becomes incompetent, if while competent, the patient stated that he or she did not want certain procedures to be employed under specified circumstances (*Matter of Storar and Matter of Eichner v. Dillon*, 52 N.Y.2d 363, 438 N.Y.S.2d 266, 420 N.E.2d 64). In *Storar*, involving a retarded adult suffering from terminal cancer, who needed blood transfusions to keep him from bleeding to death, we declined to direct termination of the treatment because it was impossible to determine what his wish would have been were he competent and it would be improper for a court to substitute its judgment for the unascertainable wish of the patient. Commenting on this latter principle in a subsequent case we noted that the right to decline treatment is personal and, under existing law in this State, could not be exercised by a third party when the patient is unable to do so (*People v. Eulo*, 63 N.Y.2d 341, 482 N.Y.S.2d 436, 472 N.E.2d 286).

In contrast to the patient in *Storar*, the patient in *Eichner* had been competent and capable of expressing his will before he was silenced by illness. In those circumstances, we concluded that it would be appropriate for the court to intervene and direct the termination of artificial life supports, in accordance with the patient's wishes, because it was established by "clear and convincing evidence" that the patient would have so directed if he were competent and able to communicate (52 N.Y.2d, at 379, 438 N.Y.S.2d 266, 420 N.E.2d 64, supra; see also, *Matter of Delio v. Westchester County Med. Center*, 129 A.D.2d 1; 516 N.Y.S.2d 677 *Addington v. Texas*, 441 U.S. 418, 424, 99 S.Ct. 1804, 1808, 60 L.Ed.2d 323. We selected the "clear and convincing evidence" standard in Eichner because it "'impress[es] the factfinder with the importance of the decision' * * * and it 'forbids relief whenever the evidence is loose, equivocal or contradictory'" (*Matter of Storar*, supra, 52 N.Y.2d at 379, 438 N.Y.S.2d 266, 420 N.E.2d 64). Nothing less than unequivocal proof will suffice when the decision to terminate life supports is at issue.

In *Eichner*, we had no difficulty finding "clear and convincing" evidence of the patient's wishes. Brother Fox, the patient in *Eichner*, was a member of a religious order who had conscientiously discussed his moral and personal views concerning the use of a respirator on persons in a vegetative state. The conclusion that "he carefully reflected on the subject * * * [was] supported by his religious beliefs and [was] not inconsistent with his life of unselfish religious devotion." (*Id.*, at 379-380, 438 N.Y.S.2d 266, 420 N.E.2d 64.) Further, his

[handwritten in margin: preponderance of the evidence]

expressions were "solemn pronouncements and not casual remarks made at some social gathering, nor c[ould] it be said that he was too young to realize or feel the consequences of his statements" (*id.*, at 380, 438 N.Y.S.2d 266, 420 N.E.2d 64). Indeed, because the facts in Brother Fox's case were so clear, we had no need to elaborate upon the kind of showing necessary to satisfy the "clear and convincing" standard.

The facts in this case present a much closer question and require us to explore in more detail the application of that standard in this context. It would, of course, be unrealistic for us to attempt to establish a rigid set of guidelines to be used in all cases requiring an evaluation of a now-incompetent patient's previously expressed wishes. The number and variety of situations in which the problem of terminating artificial life supports arises preclude any attempt to anticipate all of the possible permutations. However, this case, as well as our prior decisions, suggest some basic principles which may be used in determining whether the proof "clearly and convincingly" evinces an intention by the patient to reject life prolonged artificially by medical means.

III

At the outset, since the inquiry in New York is limited to ascertaining and then effectuating the patient's expressed wishes, our focus must always be on what the patient would say if asked today whether the treatment in issue should be terminated. However, we can never be completely certain of the answer to our question, since the inquiry assumes that the patient is no longer able to express his or her wishes. Most often, therefore, the inquiry turns on interpretation of statements on the subject made by the patient in the past. This exercise presents inherent problems.

For example, there always exists the possibility that, despite his or her clear expressions in the past, the patient has since changed his or her mind. And, as Judge Simons in his dissenting opinion correctly points out, human beings are incapable of perfect foresight. Thus, almost inevitably, the medical circumstances in the mind of the patient at the time the statements were made will not coincide perfectly with those which give rise to the need for the inquiry. In addition, there exists the danger that the statements were made without the reflection and resolve that would be brought to bear on the issue if the patient were presently capable of making the decision.

No person or court should substitute its judgment as to what would be an acceptable quality of life for another (*People v. Eulo*, supra, 63 N.Y.2d at 357, 482 N.Y.S.2d 436, 472 N.E.2d 286). Consequently, we adhere to the view that, the inquiry must always be narrowed to the patient's expressed intent, with every effort made to minimize the opportunity for error.

Every person has a right to life, and no one should be denied essential medical care unless the evidence clearly and convincingly shows that the patient intended to decline the treatment under some particular circumstances (*Matter of Storar*, supra, 52 N.Y.2d at 379, 438 N.Y.S.2d 266, 420 N.E.2d 64). It is appropriate here because if an error occurs it should be made on the side of life.

Viewed in that light, the "clear and convincing" evidence standard requires proof sufficient to persuade the trier of fact that the patient held a firm and settled commitment to the termination of life supports under the circumstances like those presented. As a threshold matter, the trier of fact must be convinced, as far as is humanly possible, that the strength of the individual's beliefs and the durability of the individual's commitment to those beliefs (see, *Matter of Eichner*, supra, at 380, 438 N.Y.S.2d 266, 420 N.E.2d 64) makes a recent change of heart unlikely. The persistence of the individual's statements, the seriousness with which those statements were made and the inferences, if any, that may be drawn from the surrounding circumstances are among the factors which should be considered.

The ideal situation is one in which the patient's wishes were expressed in some form of a writing, perhaps a "living will," while he or she was still competent. The existence of a writing suggests the author's seriousness of purpose and ensures that the court is not being asked to make a life-or-death decision based upon casual remarks. Further, a person who has troubled to set forth his or her wishes in a writing is more likely than one who has not to make sure that any subsequent changes of heart are adequately expressed, either in a new writing or through clear statements to relatives and friends. In contrast, a person whose expressions of intention were limited to oral statements may not as fully appreciate the need to "rescind" those statements after a change of heart.

Of course, a requirement of a written expression in every case would be unrealistic. Further, it would unfairly penalize those who lack the skills to place their feelings in writing. For that reason, we must always remain open to applications such as this, which are based upon the repeated oral expressions of the patient. In this case, however, the application must ultimately fail, because it does not meet the foregoing criteria.

Although Mrs. O'Connor's statements about her desire to decline life-saving treatments were repeated over a number of years, there is nothing, other than speculation, to persuade the fact finder that her expressions were more than immediate reactions to the unsettling experience of seeing or hearing of another's unnecessarily prolonged death. Her comments—that she would never want to lose her dignity before she passed away, that nature should be permitted to take its course, that it is "monstrous" to use life-support machinery—are, in fact, no different than those that many of us might make after witnessing an agonizing death. Similarly, her statements to the effect that she would not want to be a burden to anyone are the type of statements that older people frequently, almost invariably make. If such statements were routinely held to be clear and convincing proof of a general intent to decline all medical treatment once incompetency sets in, few nursing home patients would ever receive life-sustaining medical treatment in the future. The aged and infirm would be placed at grave risk if the law uniformly but unrealistically treated the expression of such sentiments as a calm and deliberate resolve to decline all life-sustaining medical assistance once the speaker is silenced by mental disability. That Mrs. O'Connor made similar statements over a long period of time, does not, by itself, transform them from the type of comments that are often made casually into the type of statements that demonstrate a seriousness of purpose necessary to satisfy the "clear and convincing evidence" standard.

We do not mean to suggest that, to be effective, a patient's expressed desire to decline treatment must specify a precise condition and a particular treatment. We recognize that human beings are not capable of foreseeing either their own medical condition or advances in medical technology. Nevertheless, it is relevant to the fundamental question—the patient's desires—to consider whether the infirmities she was concerned with and the procedures she eschewed are qualitatively different than those now presented. Not that the exact nature of her condition would be dispositive in this analysis—it is but another element to be considered in the context of determining whether her pronouncement made on some previous occasion bears relevance to her present condition.

Thus, it is appropriate for us to consider the circumstances in which Mrs. O'Connor made the statements and to compare them with those which presently prevail.

Her statements with respect to declining artificial means of life support were generally prompted by her experience with persons suffering terminal illnesses, particularly cancer. However, Mrs. O'Connor does not have a terminal illness, except in the sense that she is aged and infirm. Neither is she in a coma nor vegetative state. She is awake and conscious; she can feel pain, responds to simple commands, can carry on limited conversations, and is not experiencing any pain. She is simply an elderly person who as a result of several strokes suffers certain disabilities, including an inability to feed herself or eat in a normal manner. She is in a stable condition and if properly nourished will remain in that condition unless some other medical problem arises. Because of her age and general physical condition, her life expectancy is not great. But that is true of many nursing home patients. The key thing that sets her apart—though there are likely thousands like her—is her inability to eat or obtain nourishment without medical assistance.

It is true, of course, that in her present condition she cannot care for herself or survive without medical assistance and that she has stated that she never wanted to be a burden and would not want to live, or be kept alive "artificially" if she could not care for herself. But no one contends, and it should not be assumed, that she contemplated declining medical assistance when her prognosis was uncertain. Here both medical experts agreed that she will never regain sufficient mental ability to care for herself, but it is not clear from the record that the loss of her gag reflex is permanent and that she will never be able to obtain food and drink without medical assistance.

The record also shows that throughout her life Mrs. O'Connor was an independent woman who found it distasteful to be dependent on others. Unfortunately, she has been unable to care for herself for several years. As a result of her first stroke in July 1985, she has required full-time care, and following her latest stroke in December of 1987, she had to be spoon-fed until her gag reflex completely failed in June of this year. No one contends that the assistance she received up to that point violated her wishes, although there is little question that she would not have survived without this constant attention from others, including some medical professionals. The only change in her condition is the loss of her gag reflex, and the consequent need for medical assistance in eating, which is said to be contrary to her desires.

In sum, on this record it cannot be said that Mrs. O'Connor elected to die under circumstances such as these. Even her daughters, who undoubtedly know her wishes better than anyone, are earnestly trying to carry them out, and whose motives we believe to be of the highest and most loving kind, candidly admit that they do not know what she would do, or what she would want done under these circumstances.

There is no question that Mrs. O'Connor was competent when she made the statements in issue and the only question is whether she intended by those statements to choose death by starvation and thirst in her present circumstances. Thus we are not holding that "an incompetent patient cannot forego the use of artificial life-sustaining machines offering no hope of improvement or cure." (Dissenting opn., at 549, at 904 of 534 N.Y.S.2d, at 625 of 531 N.E.2d.) Indeed such a holding would be inconsistent with our decision in *Matter of Eichner*, 52 N.Y.2d 363, 438 N.Y.S.2d 266, 420 N.E.2d 64, where as noted, the wishes of such a patient were upheld by this court upon clear and convincing evidence that the patient intended to decline the treatment under the circumstances. Our present decision simply demonstrates that the *Eichner* standard is a meaningful one, and that no one should be denied life-sustaining treatment when there is not clear and convincing evidence that this was in fact the patient's choice. In short it is unfair and inaccurate to suggest that mental patients have greater rights of "self-determination" than other patients. In fact, we noted in *Katz* that their wishes to decline a particular treatment for mental illness should not be honored if that would endanger their lives or the lives of others (*Rivers v. Katz*, supra, 67 N.Y.2d at 495, 504 N.Y.S.2d 74, 495 N.E.2d 337).

Accordingly, the order of the Appellate Division should be reversed, the petition granted and counterclaim dismissed, without costs.

Upon reading the three significant cases, the elder law professional will find there is one common thread: the primary issue—the patient's right to have life support systems withdrawn after having entered into a persistent vegetative state. The laws have changed dramatically in favor of patients' rights in the last few years. Most states have enacted legislation permitting the use of living wills and health care proxies to enable individuals who may be suffering from catastrophic illnesses to determine the course of their own treatment.

A health care proxy, a form of advance decision planning, allows a patient to appoint a surrogate who will make decisions for them when they lack capacity and competency.

The living will is an advance directive by a patient to the medical facility, health care provider, and/or physician instructing them whether or *not* to keep the patient alive in the event that there is no hope for recovery. There is no surrogate involved. A patient who is *already* in a vegetative state may now *legally* enlist assistance in dying through the health care proxy or living will that was executed while the patient was competent.

The living will may also state that the patient wishes to be kept alive under any and all circumstances!

It is important to understand the following:

1. A health care proxy cannot authorize a surrogate to decide to actively administer drugs or use some other agent or method to kill the patient.
2. A health care proxy/living will permits withholding/withdrawing of treatment. This is not assisting in suicide.
3. In the absence of an advanced directive, the withholding/withdrawing of treatment may be legally considered as homicide if it is reported to the authorities.

But what are the rights of the individual who is terminally ill but not in a vegetative state? The individual who knows that he or she is going to die, that death will be painful, and that he or she will be a burden to some of the family? The individual who is competent and who agonizes daily about his imminent death? Would it not be merciful, kind, and compassionate to permit him or her to die with dignity and self-respect with the assistance of a physician, a friend, or a family member? Except in Oregon, this is not possible. Likewise, an individual who neglected to execute a health care proxy and a living will while competent must by law be kept alive artificially upon entering a persistent vegetative state. No physician or family member can legally authorize termination of life support systems. If someone *did* assist the patient out of kindness and compassion, as has been happening more and more these days in the United States, such assistance risks being judged as an act of homicide and being vigorously prosecuted. However, as will be seen later in the chapter, two recent cases decided by the Supreme Court of the United States challenge this judgement.

THE LAW AND PHYSICIAN-ASSISTED SUICIDE

In Other Countries

The law on the European continent is different, particularly in Holland, which is one of the most progressive countries in Europe, especially when it comes to physician-assisted suicide. For decades, Holland has permitted physicians to assist terminally ill patients in directly terminating their lives. Literally, the government has "looked the other way." Opponents say that this policy sanctions murder. On April 10, 2002, formal legislation was enacted making it legal for physicians to assist in the suicide of a terminally ill patient without being prose-cuted, provided they follow specific statutory procedures. The guidelines are as follows:

1. The terminally ill patient must undergo a psychiatric evaluation, and there must be a finding of competence.
2. Documentation must be established that the patient has repeatedly requested to termi-nate life voluntarily and consistently over an extended period of time during the illness.
3. The patient's medical records must indicate clearly that the patient is suffering intoler-ably with no hope of relief and no reasonable alternative.
4. The assisted suicide can only be performed by a physician *in consultation with another physician who, as a euthanasia specialist, is specifically so authorized.*
5. Life must be ended in a medically appropriate way.

Belgium, on May 16, 2002, became the second nation in Europe to decriminalize euthana-sia. The Belgian legislation differs from the Dutch law in that it applies to people who are over the age of 18. The law provides different procedures for patients that are declared ter-minally ill and those who have incurable diseases but are expected to live for several years. Any person filing a request to receive euthanasia must be conscious when the demand is made. The patient must then repeat the request. A third medical opinion must be obtained in the case of a patient who is not in the terminal stages of an illness. Finally, the Belgian law requires that every mercy killing be reported with a special commission that determines if the doctors in charge complied with the law.

The author has been deliberate in the use of the term *physician-assisted suicide*. It is defined as an act in which a physician helps a competent, terminally ill patient, who has been previously authorized by the physician, to terminate his or her own life. This is distinguished from the commonly used terms *euthanasia* or *mercy killing*, which do not imply the patient's consent to the termination of life. **Euthanasia** is defined as the act of putting to death pain-lessly a person suffering from an incurable and painful disease or condition. In euthanasia, the decision to terminate life is made by the medical establishment, usually without the patient's consent. This could also lead to the arbitrary termination of life by the state. The basis of the controversy concerning the legalization of physician-assisted suicide is that its indiscriminate use could cause dangerous abuse and may lead us down "the slippery slope of euthanasia." Canada prohibits euthanasia, and in 1993 its highest court denied the right of its citizens to physician-assisted suicide. Australia's Northern Territory became the first place in the world to legalize euthanasia in 1996, but saw the law overturned after nine months.

Euthanasia
The act of putting to death painlessly a person suffering from an incurable and painful disease or condition. The decision to terminate life is made by the medical establishment without the patient's consent.

In the United States

Dr. Jack Kevorkian, the now-famous retired Michigan pathologist, has been in the fore-front of promoting physician-assisted suicide in the United States. As of this writing, he has assisted in nearly 130 suicides in his home state, making Michigan "the assisted-suicide capi-tal" of the country, much to the chagrin of its state legislature and criminal prosecutors. Kevorkian has been tried for murder on several occasions and prior to 1999 was acquitted each time. "Kevorkianism" is now synonymous with assisted suicide and has become a hot media topic and household term. Kevorkian is a national media figure, his picture has appeared on the coveted *Time* magazine cover (May 3, 1993), and his hunger strikes are known worldwide.

However, the tide turned against Dr. Kevorkian in 1999. On April 13 that year, a Michigan judge sentenced him to prison for a period of 10 to 25 years, following his conviction for second-degree murder in the euthanasia death of a man suffering from amyotrophic lateral sclerosis (ALS, Lou Gehrig's disease). Kevorkian injected Thomas Youk with a lethal cocktail of chemicals on September 17, 1998, and videotaped the death. Two months later, Dr. Kevorkian went public with Thomas Youk's death. He arranged to have the videos shown on CBS's *60 Minutes*. That was his downfall. All his subsequent appeals have failed, and he is currently in a Michigan State penitentiary.

PEOPLE V. KEVORKIAN

639 N.W.2d 291 (Mich.App.,2001)

Whitbeck, J.

A jury convicted defendant of second-degree murder and delivering a controlled substance. The trial court sentenced him to concurrent prison terms of ten to twenty-five years for the murder conviction and seven years for the controlled substance conviction. Defendant appeals as of right and we affirm.

I. OVERVIEW

This case is about death; in particular, the death of former racecar driver Thomas Youk in September 1998. Youk was fifty-two years old and had amyotrophic lateral sclerosis (ALS), also known as Lou Gehrig's disease. Defendant twice videotaped himself interacting with Youk. In the first videotape, defendant went to Youk's home to discuss his condition. In the second videotape, defendant administered a lethal drug to Youk. Defendant later was a guest on the television news show *60 Minutes*, during which segments from both videotapes were shown. The jury saw the videotapes and the *60 Minutes* interview at defendant's trial. Nevertheless, defendant attempted to persuade the jury not to convict him because the murder he was charged with committing was, in his view, a "mercy killing."

Euthanasia is at the core of this case. But for defendant's self-described zealotry, Thomas Youk's death would, in all probability, not have been the subject of national attention, much less a murder trial. Defendant, in what is now apparently something of an afterthought, asks us to conclude that euthanasia is legal and, therefore, to reverse his conviction on constitutional grounds. We refuse. Such a holding would be the first step down a very steep and very slippery slope. To paraphrase the United States Supreme Court in *Washington v. Glucksberg*, [521 U.S. 702 (1997)], it would expand the right to privacy to include a right to commit euthanasia and thus place the issue outside the arenas of public debate and legislative action. Such a holding would also involve the judiciary in deciding questions that are simply beyond our capacity. Succinctly put, there is no principled basis for us to legalize euthanasia. ***

II. THE DEATH OF THOMAS YOUK

A. The September 15, 1998, Videotape

On September 15, 1998, at 9:55 p.m., defendant went to Youk's home to discuss Youk's condition. As the videotape of this discussion revealed, defendant stated that he was recording their interaction in "connection with a request from Thomas [Youk] for help in . . . ending his suffering." Youk then described his condition. He recalled that his symptoms of ALS first became obvious to him in 1994 and that he had been confined to a wheelchair since 1997. By September 1998, Youk said, he could not move his left arm or his legs, he had minimal use of his right arm, he had difficulty swallowing and breathing, he was fed through a tube, and he was forced to use a machine to help him breathe. Youk stated that, at the time, he could not do anything for himself, that he had discussed "his wishes" with his mother, brothers, and wife, and that they "understand why. It's my decision."

Defendant then told Youk that he needed to sign a form indicating that he was consenting to a "direct injection instead of using the device, the machine." Defendant asked Youk if he wished to donate his organs, and Youk declined. Defendant then read the consent form, which stated in part:

I, Thomas Youk, the undersigned, entirely voluntarily, without any reservation, external persuasion, pressure, or duress, and after prolonged and thorough deliberation, hereby consent to the following medical procedure of my own choosing, and that you have chosen direct injection, or what they call active euthanasia, to be administered by a competent medical professional, in order to end with certainty my intolerable and hopelessly incurable suffering.

The meeting ended at 10:15 p.m.

B. The September 16, 1998, Videotape

On September 16, 1998, at 9:49 p.m., defendant again videotaped himself and Youk at Youk's home. Youk stated that he "wanted to go through with this" and signed the consent form. Defendant remarked that he would inject Youk in the vein because "it's quicker," and stated, "now I'm going to put on a cardiogram so we know when your heart is stopped, okay." Defendant established a connection between Youk and the electrocardiogram. Defendant injected Youk with Anectine and Seconal before injecting Youk with potassium chloride. During this time, defendant provided a commentary on what was occurring:

> Sleepy Tom? Tom are you asleep? And now we'll inject the Anectine. You asleep Tom? Tom? You asleep? He's asleep. Now the Potassium Chloride. This machine is recording for some reason so I'm pulling it by hand until the heart stops. It's been, it's been about two minutes since I injected the, ah, Seconal, and one minute since I injected the--. Now we're getting agonal complexes and that's about the, the Potassium Chloride will stop the heart, so. Now there's a straight line. A straight line and the cardiogram will be turned off. His heart is stopped.

C. Cause Of Death

The police were dispatched to Youk's house on September 17, 1998, at 1:30 a.m. They found Youk lying on his bed, dead. The police also found a Federal Express receipt with defendant's name at the scene. Officials conducted Youk's autopsy at 10:00 a.m. the same day. The medical examiner listed the manner of death as homicide and the cause of death as intravenous injection of substances. During the autopsy, the medical examiner found two "fresh" needle marks on Youk's left and right wrists that had been covered with makeup. The autopsy protocol stated that the cause of death was "poisoning by intravenous injection of substances."

Oakland County Medical Examiner Ljubisa J. Dragovic, an expert in neuropathology and pathology who later testified for the prosecution at defendant's trial, witnessed the autopsy. Dr. Dragovic found three significant drugs in Youk's bodily fluids. First, Youk had a high level of the barbiturate Seconal, also known as Secobarbital, in his blood. Seconal is a Schedule 2 controlled substance typically used to induce sleep. Dr. Dragovic believed that the amount of Seconal in Youk's blood would have killed him in a few hours. Second, Dr. Dragovic found Anectine, a paralyzing muscle relaxant, present in Youk's body in an amount that could have killed Youk within five to eight minutes by causing brain death. However, Dr. Dragovic determined that it was the third drug, potassium chloride, that defendant injected into Youk that caused his death. As Dr. Dragovic explained, when potassium chloride is injected into the body in a concentrated form at once, rather than in small amounts over time, it stops the heart from beating within a matter of seconds. According to Dr. Dragovic, the toxicology reports did not reveal the presence of potassium chloride in Youk's body because that substance is naturally present in the body after red blood cells die.

Dr. Dragovic also confirmed that Youk had ALS. However, in Dr. Dragovic's opinion, Youk did not die from ALS, ALS was not an underlying cause of Youk's death, and ALS did not contribute to Youk's death in any way. Rather, Dr. Dragovic firmly reiterated that the poisons injected into Youk killed him, constituting a homicide.

D. The 60 Minutes Interview

News correspondent Mike Wallace interviewed defendant for 60 Minutes. In the first clip from the interview shown to the jury, Wallace stated at the outset, "You killed him." Defendant responded: "I did, but it could be Manslaughter not Murder. It's not necessarily Murder. But it doesn't bother me what you call it. I know what it is. This could never be a crime in any society which deems itself enlightened." Defendant indicated that he was making an example of Youk. Wallace then suggested that Youk was initially a little reluctant because Youk "thought he was getting assisted suicide." Defendant replied that "this is better than assisted suicide, I explained that to him. It's better control."

Defendant also explained to Wallace the process leading to Youk's death. According to defendant, the first injection paralyzed Youk's muscles and slowed his ability to take in oxygen. When the oxygen was "cut off" and Youk could not breathe, defendant injected the "potassium chloride to stop the heart." Defendant then told Wallace that "[e]ither they go or I go," apparently meaning that he would be acquitted for killing Youk or, if convicted, he would starve to death in prison. As defendant put it: "I've got to force them to act. They must charge me. Because if they do not, that means they don't think it's a crime. Because they don't need any more evidence do they? Do you have to dust for fingerprints on this[?]"

Wallace suggested that defendant was "engaged in a political, medical, macabre . . . publicity venture," and had a "ghoulish . . . desire to see the deed done." Defendant did not disagree with those assertions, stating: "Well, it could be, I, I can't argue with that. Maybe it is ghoulish. I don't know. It appears that way to you. I can't criticize you for that." In fact, defendant agreed with Wallace, emphasizing that "the main point is . . . that the deed be done." Evidently in response to the argument that legalizing euthanasia could be problematic in practice, defendant commented that "[e]verything can be abused. You learn from abuse, you punish the abuser, and then . . . if you want to control, you say that only certain doctors can do this in certain areas, nobody else. . . . That's the way to control it."

Defendant then returned to one of his main themes, saying:

If you don't have liberty and self-determination, you got nothing. That's what this country's built on and this is the ultimate self-determination to determine when and how you're gonna die when you're suffering.

[Wallace]: And those who say that [defendant], Dr. Death, is a fanatic?

[Defendant]: Zealot. No, not if, sure, you try to take a liberty away and I turn fanatic.... I'm fighting for me, Mike, me. This is a right I want when I, I'm 71, I'll be 71. You don't know what'll happen when you get older. I may end up terribly suffering. I want some colleague to be free to come and help me when I say the time has come. That's why I'm fighting for, me. Now that sounds selfish. And if it helps everybody else, so be it.

III. Euthanasia And The Constitution

P7372 ∧S

Facts And Argument

On appeal, defendant makes two related, but separate, constitutional arguments. First, he argues that the unenumerated rights protected by the Ninth Amendment and its Michigan constitutional counterpart include a patient's right to be free from unbearable pain and suffering. Second, he maintains that the Fourteenth Amendment and its Michigan constitutional counterpart also include this right by proscribing state deprivation of liberty without due process of law either under constitutional privacy concepts or as a "necessary and direct corollary of this position . . . that a person should not be forced to suffer unbearably." Defendant claims that he has standing to raise these due process arguments. Defendant thus contends that he is entitled to have his murder conviction reversed and no further criminal proceedings instituted against him for "aiding in Thomas Youk's assertion of his constitutional right to be free from intolerable pain and suffering."

Constitutional Provisions

The Ninth Amendment of the United States Constitution states that "[t]he enumeration in the Constitution, of certain rights, shall not be construed to deny or disparage others retained by the people." The counterpart provision in the Michigan Constitution states that "[t]he enumeration in this constitution of certain rights shall not be construed to deny or disparage others retained by the people."

The Fourteenth Amendment of the United States Constitution states, in relevant part, that no state shall "deprive any person of life, liberty, or property, without due process of law." The counterpart provision in the Michigan Constitution states, in relevant part, that "[n]o person shall be . . . deprived of life, liberty or property, without due process of law."

The Nature Of Defendant's Arguments

First, defendant does not ask us to hold that he acted properly in furtherance of the right to refuse life-sustaining medical treatment. In *Cruzan v. Director, Missouri Dep't of Health*, [497 U.S. 261, 279 (1990)] the United States Supreme Court "assume[d] that the United States Constitution would grant a competent person a constitutionally protected right to refuse lifesaving hydration and nutrition," likely under a Fourteenth Amendment due process liberty interest analysis. More recently, in *Glucksberg*, the Court strengthened the constitutional basis for the *Cruzan* decision, interpreting *Cruzan* as holding that "the right to refuse unwanted medical treatment was so rooted in our history, tradition, and practice as to require special protection under the Fourteenth Amendment." Here, defendant does not, and could not, rely on Cruzan; factually, this case does not involve removing life support. Further, though not resting their decisions precisely on the Fourteenth Amendment, Michigan courts have arrived at the same conclusion regarding a patient's right to refuse life-sustaining medical care. The limited scope of these cases does not establish a right to be free from unbearable pain and suffering that would make euthanasia legal. There is, of course, a substantial factual distinction between refusing care, even if doing so hastens death, and purposefully ending a life.

Second, defendant does not make any claim that this case concerns medical efforts to relieve pain or discomfort, though these medical efforts may hasten death. Michigan exempts such medical efforts from criminal penalties. Importantly, however, the exemption does not apply to medical efforts designed to cause death. Factually, there is not a scintilla of evidence that defendant administered potassium chloride to Youk to relieve Youk's pain or discomfort. Defendant admits as much in his brief on appeal.

The only medical relief for Thomas Youk's conditions was the relief that he sought from [defendant]. The injection [defendant] gave to Thomas Youk was the only effective medical way to alleviate Thomas Youk's unbearable suffering. No pain medication would suffice, and there was no other beneficial medical alternative that would have aided Thomas Youk.

Third, defendant does not ask us to find that his actions in this matter constituted some form of permissible assisted suicide. In Michigan, assisting in a suicide—that is, providing the physical means by which another person attempts or commits suicide or participating in a physical act by which another person attempts or commits suicide—is illegal. [See M.C.L. § 752.1027]. The Michigan Supreme Court has upheld the statute in question against both a Title Object Clause challenge under the Michigan Constitution and a Due Process Clause challenge under the United States Constitution. In reaching its decision on the due process challenge, a majority of the Court observed:

> Presently, a substantial number of jurisdictions have specific statutes that criminalize assisted suicide and the Model Penal Code also provides for criminal penalties. Further, nearly all states expressly disapprove of suicide and assisted suicide either in statutes dealing with durable powers of attorney in health-care situations, or in "living will" statutes. In addition, all states provide for the involuntary commitment of persons who may harm themselves as the result of mental illness, and a number of states allow the use of nondeadly force to thwart suicide attempts.

Referring to *Cruzan*, the majority observed:

> Indeed, the United States Supreme Court repeatedly and unequivocally has affirmed the sanctity of human life and rejected the notion that there is a right of self-destruction inherent in any common-law doctrine or constitutional phrase.

Several years after the Michigan Supreme Court decision in *Kevorkian I*, the United States Supreme Court in *Glucksberg* upheld a similar Washington statute against a similar Due Process Clause challenge under the United States Constitution. The *Glucksberg* majority held that the prohibition in the Washington statute against " 'caus[ing]' " or " 'aid[ing]' " a suicide did not offend the Fourteenth Amendment of the United States Constitution.

Here, defendant makes no attempt to assert that he was engaged in assisted suicide when he injected Youk with potassium chloride, causing his death. Rather, he asserts that if the Ninth Amendment "is to have any substantive meaning," the right to be free from inexorable pain and suffering must be among the unenumerated rights protected by that amendment and its Michigan counterpart. Further, defendant asserts that the right to be free from unbearable pain and suffering caused by a medical condition is inherently part of the liberty interests secured by the Fourteenth Amendment and its Michigan counterpart. Defendant then contends that he cannot be prosecuted for "aiding in Thomas Youk's assertion of his constitutional right to be free from intolerable pain and suffering." Although defendant's appellate counsel has carefully avoided using the words, as we have already noted, the record indicates that defendant was quite specific when describing his actions; he said he was engaged in "active euthanasia" and the consent form that Youk signed directly refers to such active euthanasia.

In summary, defendant does not, nor could he, ask us to hold that his actions were legally justifiable because he simply helped Youk exercise his right to refuse medical care. Defendant does not, nor could he, ask us to hold that he was lawfully attempting to alleviate Youk's pain and suffering by any means other than causing his death. Defendant does not, nor could he, ask us to hold that his actions constituted a legal form of assisted suicide. In a nutshell, and using his own terminology, defendant asks us to legalize euthanasia.

Reserved Rights

Defendant's argument that the people have reserved the right to euthanasia under the Ninth Amendment and its Michigan counterpart is basically formless. He states that a right to be free from inexorable pain and suffering "must be among" the rights protected by these two constitutional provisions. Further, he argues that states "should recognize such a right and give it force." Defendant does not cite a single case for this extraordinary request. As the Supreme Court said in *Mitcham v. Detroit*, [355 Mich. 182, 94 N.W.2d 388 (1959)]

> It is not enough for an apellant in his brief simply to announce a position or assert an error and then leave it up to this Court to discover and rationalize the basis for his claims, or unravel and elaborate for him his arguments, and then search for authority either to sustain or reject his position. The appellant himself must first adequately prime the pump; only then does the appellant well begin to flow. Failure to brief a question on appeal is tantamount to abandoning it.

We conclude, therefore, that defendant has abandoned this argument on appeal.

Euthanasia As A Due Process Right To Privacy

1. Defendant's Argument

Defendant starts with the proposition that there is a right to privacy that is part of the liberty interest protected by the Fourteenth Amendment and its Michigan counterpart. He then asserts that the "intensely personal and private right of a patient to be free from intolerable and irremediable suffering" is either part of or similar to this privacy right. Citing *Vacco*, he argues that if the administration of aggressive painkilling drugs is acceptable even if this may hasten death, then the "necessary and direct corollary of this position is that a person should not be forced to suffer unbearably."

Defendant then reviews the positions of Justices O'Connor, Breyer, Souter, and Stevens in *Glucksberg* to reach the conclusion that "Justices on the Supreme Court have suggested allowing for interpretation of the Fourteenth Amendment's guarantee of liberty to apply to various privacy rights, including those related to personal and private medical procedures." Finally, defendant argues that he has standing to assert Youk's constitutional right to be free from intolerable pain, claiming that Justice Stevens in *Glucksberg*, "recognized the possibility that an individual who provides assistance to a patient who was suffering interminably could prevail on a Constitutional challenge" and that, if we agree that there is a constitutionally protected right to be free from unbearable suffering, then the charges against him must be dismissed. We do not agree.

2. Encompassing Euthanasia Within The Right To Privacy

It is one thing to assert, as defendant does, that there is a large body of case law suggesting that due process sometimes relies on the right to privacy to protect fundamental liberty interests. It is quite another thing, however, to conclude that the right to privacy encompasses euthanasia. As Justice Jackson once pointedly noted, the enduring nature of precedent gives judicial opinions a force all their own.

The principle then lies about like a loaded weapon. . . . Every repetition imbeds that principle more deeply in our law and thinking and expands it to new purposes. All who observe the work of courts are familiar with what Judge Cardozo described as "the tendency of a principle to expand itself to the limit of its logic."

Defendant urges us to pick up the loaded weapon of the right to privacy cases. He asks us to use this weapon to resolve the situation faced by a person who suffers from literally unbearable pain and who wishes to end that pain by dying. As Justice O'Connor described it: "Death will be different for each of us. For many, the last days will be spent in physical pain and perhaps the despair that accompanies physical deterioration and a loss of control of basic bodily and mental functions."

We decline, however, to pick up this loaded weapon for three basic reasons. First, we can find no meaningful precedent for expanding the right to privacy to include a right to commit euthanasia so that an individual can be free from intolerable and irremediable suffering. To our knowledge, no court of last resort in this country has ever recognized such a right. Even in the assisted suicide cases dealing with an asserted "right to die," courts have steadfastly refused to expand the right to privacy to include the right to commit or receive euthanasia. As Chief Justice Cavanagh and Justices Brickley and Griffin explained while describing the boundaries of the right to privacy in end-of-life cases:

✳ ✳ ✳

Similarly, in *Glucksberg*, a majority of the United States Supreme Court concluded that the asserted "right" to assistance in committing suicide "is not a fundamental liberty interest protected by the Due Process Clause." [*Glucksberg*, supra at 728]. Instead, the Court determined that a state has legitimate and countervailing interests in preserving life, preventing suicide, protecting the integrity and ethics of the medical profession, protecting vulnerable groups from abuse, neglect, and mistakes, and acknowledging the equal value of all people. Most importantly, the *Glucksberg* majority noted that states "may fear that permitting assisted suicide will start it down the path to voluntary and perhaps even involuntary euthanasia." In commenting on the Ninth Circuit Court of Appeals decision in the underlying case, the majority of the Court said:

✳ ✳ ✳

The majority then turned, directly, to the "slippery slope" argument. The majority cited *United States v. 12 200-ft Reels of Super 8MM Film* [413 U.S. 123 (1973)] for the proposition that "'[e]ach step, when taken, appear[s] a reasonable step in relation to that which preceded it, although the aggregate or end result is one that would never have been seriously considered in the first instance.'" The majority referred to Physician-Assisted

Suicide and Euthanasia in the Netherlands [FN49] as suggesting that despite the existence of various reporting procedures, euthanasia in the Netherlands has not been limited to competent, terminally ill adults who are enduring physical suffering, and that regulation of the practice may not have prevented abuses in cases involving vulnerable persons, including severely disabled neonates and elderly persons suffering from dementia. [Glucksberg, supra at 734]

Here, expanding the right to privacy would begin, as the steps in the progression of defendant's argument supporting voluntary euthanasia clearly indicate, the slide down the slippery slope toward euthanasia. No court of final jurisdiction has so expanded the right to privacy. Neither will we conclude that by expanding the right to privacy as defendant suggests, we would, to a great extent, place the matter outside the arenas of public debate and legislative action.

We observe that by expanding the right of privacy to include a right to commit euthanasia in order to end intolerable and irremediable suffering we would inevitably involve the judiciary in deciding questions that are simply beyond its capacity. There is no court that can answer the question of how much pain, or perception of pain by a third party, is necessary before the suffering becomes intolerable and irremediable. The role of the courts is to serve neither as physicians nor as theologians.

3. The "Dutch Cure"

Finally, defendant urges us to recognize that his prosecution "for helping Thomas Youk put an end to his suffering at the request of Mr. Youk" is unconstitutional on its face. He arrives at this position by asserting, first, that Youk had a constitutional right to be free from intolerable pain and, second, that defendant's provision of "Constitutionally guaranteed medical services" allows him to assert Youk's rights.

There is no authority whatsoever for the proposition that a right to be free from intolerable and irremediable suffering, if it exists, somehow migrates to an "individual," such as defendant, who provides assistance to a patient who is suffering interminably.

This is the mercy killing argument—the argument for the "Dutch cure"—taken beyond the position of even its most extreme advocates. Under defendant's theory, if one who is not a doctor became convinced that one's dear friend was suffering from a painful, incurable disease and that the friend wished to die, one could at the request of that friend shoot him between the eyes with a .45 caliber pistol and not be guilty of murder. Indeed, under defendant's theory, the same result might well be obtained if one's friend were severely depressed, or perhaps simply unhappy with his lot in life. This is the slippery slope with a vengeance and we will not take a single step down it, into the abyss.

❋ ❋ ❋

CONCLUSION

We conclude by noting that the jury, no doubt influenced by the gritty realism of the videotapes defendant made as well as his flat statement of culpability in the 60 Minutes interview, convicted defendant of second-degree murder as well as delivery of a controlled substance. Defendant has on the record before us compared himself to Margaret Sanger, Susan B. Anthony, and Dr. Martin Luther King, Jr., all of whom risked imprisonment for their beliefs. How history will view defendant is a matter this Court can neither predict nor decide. Perhaps in the brave new world of defendant's "enlightened" society, acts such as the one he committed in this case will be excused. Still, we find it difficult to hypothesize a rule of law under which this might be so. We deal here, however, with the application of the law as it currently exists to the facts of this case. While defendant has carefully skirted the label of murder in his past actions, he cannot do so now. Justice Levin once stated that "[defendant] is not a murderer." Here, defendant in essence convicted himself of a murder he surely committed. We will not now reverse that conviction on due process grounds. The trial court did not abuse its discretion in refusing to dismiss the charges.

Affirmed.

DONALDSON V. LUNGREN

4 Cal.Rptr.2d 59 (Cal.App. 2 Dist.,1992.), 2 Cal.App.4th 1614

Donaldson v. Lundgren [in an earlier case, a California court found there was no right to assisted suicide]

Gilbert, Associate Justice.

Plaintiff Thomas Donaldson wishes to die in order to live. He suffers from an incurable brain disease. He wishes to commit suicide with the assistance of plaintiff Carlos Mondragon so that his body may be cryogenically preserved. It is Donaldson's hope that sometime in the future, when a cure for his disease is found, his body may be brought back to life.

He and Mondragon appeal a judgment dismissing their action for declaratory and injunctive relief. Despite our sympathy for Donaldson, we must affirm and hold he has no constitutional right to either premortem cryogenic suspension or an assisted suicide. We also decide Mondragon has no constitutional right to aid, advise or encourage Donaldson's suicide.

FACTS

Donaldson and Carlos Mondragon brought an action for declaratory and injunctive relief against the State Attorney General, the Santa Barbara District Attorney, and the Santa Barbara County Coroner. Plaintiffs' first amended complaint seeks a declaration that Donaldson has a constitutional right to premortem cryogenic suspension of his body and the assistance of others in achieving that state. The first amended complaint also seeks an injunction against criminal prosecution of Mondragon and others for participating in the premortem cryogenic suspension and an injunction against the coroner performing an autopsy on Donaldson's body after death. Plaintiffs allege the following:

Plaintiff Thomas Donaldson, a mathematician and computer software scientist, suffers from a malignant brain tumor, diagnosed by physicians as a grade 2 astrocytoma. The astrocytoma, a "space occupying lesion," is inoperable and continues to grow and invade brain tissue. The tumor has caused Donaldson weakness, speech impediments and seizures. Ultimately, continued growth of the tumor will result in Donaldson's persistent vegetative state and death. Physicians have predicted his probable death by August 1993, five years from initial diagnosis.

Donaldson desires to be cryogenically suspended, premortem, with the assistance of Mondragon and others. This procedure would freeze Donaldson's body to be later reanimated when curative treatment exists for his brain cancer. Following cryogenic suspension, Donaldson will suffer irreversible cessation of circulatory and respiratory function and irreversible cessation of all brain function.

He will be dead according to the definition of death set forth in Health and Safety Code section 7180. That section provides: "(a) An individual who has sustained either (1) irreversible cessation of circulatory and respiratory functions, or (2) irreversible cessation of all functions of the entire brain, including the brain stem, is dead. . . ."

Donaldson seeks a judicial declaration that he has a constitutional right to cryogenic suspension premortem with the assistance of others. Alternatively, he asserts he will end his life by a lethal dose of drugs. Mondragon will "advise and encourage" Donaldson through suicide "to minimize the time between his legal death and the onset of the cryonic suspension process."

Recognizing that Mondragon will be committing a homicide, or alternatively, aiding and advising a suicide, Donaldson and Mondragon seek an injunction protecting Mondragon from criminal prosecution. In order not to destroy his chance of reanimation, they also seek a court order to prevent the county coroner from examining Donaldson's remains. Donaldson and Mondragon base their action upon asserted constitutional rights of privacy and free expression.

Defendants on appeal contend: 1) Donaldson has a constitutional right to premortem cryogenic suspension, and 2) Donaldson has a constitutional right to receive and Mondragon has a constitutional right to give advice and encouragement concerning Donaldson's suicide.

DISCUSSION

I

Donaldson wishes to achieve cryogenic suspension of his body, premortem, before his relentlessly advancing brain tumor destroys the quality and purpose of his life, reduces him to a vegetative state, and makes futile his hope for reanimation.

Whatever Donaldson's motivations are for dying, however, he argues his right to privacy and self-determination are paramount to any state interest in maintaining life. He reasons the state has no logical, secular motive to demand his continued existence, given his medical condition and prognosis. Therefore, there should be no balancing of interests where the state has only an abstract interest in preserving life in general as opposed to Donaldson's specific and compelling interest in ending his particular life.

Donaldson rests his contentions upon judicial decisions declaring the right of a competent patient, his guardian, or surrogate to refuse medical treatment or procedures that sustain life. (*Cruzan v. Director, Mo. Health Dept.* (1990) 497 U.S. 261, 110 S.Ct. 2841, 111 L.Ed.2d 224;

A person has a constitutionally protected interest in refusing unwanted medical treatment or procedures. (*Cruzan v. Director, Mo. Health Dept.*, supra, 497 U.S. 261, —, 110 S.Ct. 2841, 2851, 111 L.Ed.2d 224, 241;

This right to medical self-determination also derives from the legal doctrine of informed consent to medical treatment. (*Cruzan v. Director, Mo. Health Dept.*, supra, 497 U.S. 261, —, 110 S.Ct. 2841, 2847, 111 L.Ed.2d 224, 236; *Barber v. Superior Court*, supra, 147 Cal.App.3d

1006, 1015, 195 Cal.Rptr. 484.) A logical corollary of the doctrine is that a patient possesses the right not to consent and to refuse treatment. (*Ibid.*)

Whether asserting rights resting upon the United States or California Constitution or the decisional law of informed consent, a patient may refuse treatment even though withholding of treatment creates a life-threatening situation. (*Bouvia v. Superior Court*, supra, 179 Cal.App.3d 1127, 1137, 225 Cal.Rptr. 297—28-year-old quadriplegic, cerebral palsy victim may assert her constitutional right to refuse nasogastric hydration and nourishment.) Moreover, the right to refuse treatment or life-sustaining measures is not limited to those who are terminally ill. (*Id.*, at p. 1138, 225 Cal.Rptr. 297—patient had life expectancy of 15 to 20 additional years; *Bartling v. Superior Court*, supra, 163 Cal.App.3d 186, 192–193, 209 Cal.Rptr. 220—patient was seriously ill and ventilator-dependent but not "terminal.")

To determine whether Donaldson has suffered a violation of his constitutional rights, we must balance his interests against any relevant state interests. (*Cruzan v. Director, Mo. Health Dept.*, supra, 497 U.S. 261, —, 110 S.Ct. 2841, 2852, 111 L.Ed.2d 224, 242; *People v. Adams*, supra, 216 Cal.App.3d 1431, 1438, 265 Cal.Rptr. 568.) Pertinent state interests include preserving human life, preventing suicide, protecting innocent third parties such as children, and maintaining the ethical integrity of the medical profession. (*Adams*, supra, at p. 1438, 265 Cal.Rptr. 568; Alexander, *Death by Directive* (1988) 28 Santa Clara L.Rev. 67, 78 (hereafter *Death by Directive*).) The state may also decline to assess the quality of a particular human life and assert an unqualified general interest in the preservation of human life to be balanced against the individual's constitutional rights. (*Cruzan*, supra, 497 U.S. at p. —, 110 S.Ct. at p. 2853, 111 L.Ed.2d at p. 244.)

Decisions regarding the right to refuse life-sustaining treatment, including hydration and nourishment, distinguish between artificial life support in the face of inevitable death and self-infliction of deadly harm (suicide). Likewise, decisions hold a physician incurs no criminal liability by terminating life support measures when a patient chooses to abandon such treatment. The rationale of these decisions is that natural death from underlying illness is merely forestalled by life support measures.

Donaldson argues a refusal of further medical treatment is a legal fiction for suicide: "As is often true in times of social transition, case law has created fictions to avoid affronting previously accepted norms. In life support termination, there is a fiction of medical determinism. Patients are seen as passive victims of their illness. They do not choose to die; death overtakes them. Their physicians do nothing to help them die. Death overwhelms them, too."

Donaldson argues that the doctor who disconnects the support system is taking affirmative action that in fact causes the death of the patient. He points out that even if the doctor assists the patient to die by doing nothing, he or she is actively participating in ending the patient's life. "'Not doing anything is doing something. It is a decision to act every bit as much as deciding for any other deed. If I decide not to eat or drink anymore, knowing what the consequence will be, I have committed suicide as surely as if I had used a gas oven.' J. FLETCHER, HUMANHOOD: ESSAYS IN BIOMEDICAL ETHICS 157 (1979)." (Note, *Suicidal Competence and the Patient's Right to Refuse Lifesaving Treatment* (1987) 75 Cal.L.Rev. 707, 740, fn. 213.)

There may be an apparent similarity between the patient and doctor, and Donaldson and Mondragon, but in fact there is a significant difference. The patient, for example, who is being kept alive by a life-support system has taken a detour that usually postpones an immediate encounter with death. In short, the medical treatment has prolonged life and prevented death from overtaking the patient. Stopping the treatment allows the delayed meeting with death to take place.

Donaldson is asking that we sanction something quite different. Here there are no life-prolonging measures to be discontinued. Instead, a third person will simply kill Donaldson and hasten the encounter with death. No statute or judicial opinion countenances Donaldson's decision to consent to be murdered or to commit suicide with the assistance of others. (*Von Holden v. Chapman* (1982) 87 A.D.2d 66, 450 N.Y.S.2d 623, 627—"essential dissimilarity" between right to decline medical treatment and any right to end one's life.)

Donaldson, however, may take his own life. He makes a persuasive argument that his specific interest in ending his life is more compelling than the state's abstract interest in preserving life in general. No state interest is compromised by allowing Donaldson to experience a dignified death rather than an excruciatingly painful life.

Nevertheless, even if we were to characterize Donaldson's taking his own life as the exercise of a fundamental right, it does not follow that he may implement the right in the manner he wishes here. It is one thing to take one's own life, but quite another to allow a third person assisting in that suicide to be immune from investigation by the coroner or law enforcement agencies.

In such a case, the state has a legitimate competing interest in protecting society against abuses. This interest is more significant than merely the abstract interest in preserving life no matter what the quality of that life is. Instead, it is the interest of the state to maintain social order through enforcement of the criminal law and to protect the lives of those who wish to live no matter what their circumstances. This interest overrides any interest Donaldson possesses in ending his life through the assistance of a third person in violation of the state's penal laws. We cannot expand the nature of Donaldson's right of privacy to provide a protective shield for third persons who end his life.

II

Donaldson also argues that at the very least he has a constitutional right to receive advice and encouragement concerning his suicide. Penal Code section 401 provides: "Every person who deliberately aids, or advises, or encourages another to commit suicide, is guilty of a felony." Donaldson asserts this section unconstitutionally interferes with his right to privacy.

Suicide or attempted suicide is not a crime under the criminal statutes of California or any state. (*In re Joseph G.* (1983) 34 Cal.3d 429, 433, 194 Cal.Rptr. 163, 667 P.2d 1176; *Assisting Suicide*, supra, at p. 350, fn. 22—at least one state has a common law crime of attempted suicide.) The absence of a criminal penalty for these acts is explained by the prevailing thought, to which Donaldson and others would disagree, that suicide or attempted suicide is an expression of mental illness that punishment cannot remedy. (*In re Joseph G.*, supra, 34 Cal.3d at pp. 433–434, 194 Cal.Rptr. 163, 667 P.2d 1176.)

A majority of states, however, impose criminal penalties upon one who assists another to commit suicide. One reason for the existence of criminal sanctions for those who aid a suicide is to discourage those who might encourage a suicide to advance personal motives. Another reason is the belief that the sanctity of life is threatened by one who is willing to participate in taking the life of another, even at the victim's request. (*Ibid.*) A third justification is that although the suicide victim may be mentally ill in wishing his demise, the aider is not necessarily mentally ill. (*Ibid.*)

These reasons justify a criminal statute punishing the aiding and encouraging of suicide, although suicide itself is not illegal. The state's interest in such a situation involves more than just a general commitment to the preservation of human life. In *Cruzan*, the state opposed discontinuing nutritional procedures for an unconscious patient with severe brain damage absent clear and convincing evidence this was the patient's wish. *Cruzan* emphasized the state's interest in guarding against potential abuses. Third parties, even family members, do not always act to protect the person whose life will end. *Cruzan* stated, "[w]e do not think a State is required to remain neutral in the face of an informed and voluntary decision by a physically-able adult to starve to death."

The judgement is official * * *

Popular Attitudes

Assisted suicide is a complex, legal, moral, sociological, ethical, and religious matter. It has been long established in our Western culture that life is to be preserved at any cost, not destroyed (except for political causes in war). The Hippocratic Oath, taken by every physician who enters into the practice of medicine, states in essence that the physician will do no harm. Is assisting a patient in committing suicide doing harm? What does the Bible say? "Thou shall not kill." Is assisting a terminally ill spouse or parent to take his or her own life killing?

The American Medical Association does not condone physician-assisted suicide or euthanasia. Its credo is that physicians should become more familiar with pain and the control of pain to relieve suffering and promote the dignity and autonomy of dying patients. This concept of alleviating pain without actually curing it is called **palliative care**.

Palliative Care
The American Medical Association's concept of alleviating pain where no cure is available.

Certain religious groups are against assisted suicide or euthanasia. The religion of a person who commits suicide may forbid burial in consecrated ground. Furthermore, some hospitals that are sponsored by or affiliated with religious charities may not honor living wills.

On the other hand, there are national groups such as The Hemlock Society, founded in California in 1980. An organization with more than 40,000 members, The Hemlock Society actively advocates physician-assisted suicide and euthanasia. Founder Derek Humphry published a book in 1991 entitled *Final Exit: The Practicalities of Self-Deliverance and Assisted Suicide for the Dying*. It was an instant best seller.

At present (July 2003), Oregon is the only state that has a statute permitting doctor-assisted/physician-assisted suicide and only with very narrow guidelines for terminally ill patients. Thirty-nine states have specific statutes prohibiting assisted suicide. Six states prohibit assisted suicide through their interpretation of common law: Alabama, Idaho, Massachusetts, Nevada, Vermont, and West Virginia. Maryland in 1999 became the most recent state to enact legislation outlawing assisted suicide. Only North Carolina, Ohio, Utah, and Wyoming do not have any common law or legislation that prohibits assisted suicide.

On November 6, 2001, U.S. Attorney General Ashcroft took legal action to block Oregon's assisted suicide law. He obtained authorization permitting federal drug agents to punish doctors who prescribed federally controlled drugs to help terminally ill patients to die. However, on April 17, 2002, a federal district judge ruled that the U.S. Department of Justice does not have the legal authority to overturn the Oregon law allowing physician-assisted suicide. In May 2003, the Ninth Circuit Court of Appeals heard oral arguments on the case, and a decision was pending at the time of writing.

A Harris Poll conducted in December 2001 revealed that by an approximately two to one ratio, most adults continue to favor euthanasia and physician-assisted suicide. The poll shows that when people read a brief description of the Oregon law, allowing physician-assisted suicide for patients who have fewer than six months to live, a majority of people interviewed said that they would favor the enactment of such a law in their state. The poll also revealed that most people felt that U.S. Attorney General Ashcroft was acting inappropriately in his actions to overturn the Oregon physician-assisted suicide legislation.

With American graying at a rapid pace, we have not seen the end of this debate. Stay tuned.

The Supreme Court and a Patient's Right to Die

The first case that the Supreme Court encountered concerning the patient's **right to die** was *Cruzan v. Director, Missouri Department of Health*.[3] The case involved a young woman whose car overturned on a slippery road in Missouri, leaving her in an irreversible persistent vegetative state as a result of oxygen deprivation. The patient's parents filed a petition with the state of Missouri requesting permission to withdraw all forms of artificial nutrition and hydration that were being used to sustain her life. The petition contended that the patient had a right to privacy, which included her right to determine how and when she died. The Missouri Supreme Court refused to acknowledge the existence of such right of privacy in either the state or the federal constitution and denied the parents' petition.

The Missouri Supreme Court relied upon the decision rendered in the New York case *O'Connor v. Westchester County Hospital*.[4] The court would only recognize a patient's right to die if it was presented with clear, convincing evidence of the patient's wishes. The doctrine of clear and convincing evidence requires that the patient, while competent state the choice to have life terminated under certain specific circumstances, *e.g.*, persistent vegetative state, brain death, irreversible coma, either:

a. In writing—in a health care proxy, durable medical power of attorney, or living will
b. Orally—as proved by the sworn testimony of a person who heard the statement or declaration issued by the patient who seeks to enforce his or her "right to die."

The Cruzan case was appealed to the Supreme Court of the United States in 1990. The Supreme Court rendered a decision confirming the decision of the lower court by a majority of five votes to four. The Cruzan family had to establish clear and convincing evidence that Nancy Cruzan did indeed wish to terminate her life if she ever entered into a persistent vegetative state. This could only be accomplished by oral testimony of witnesses. She never executed any form of advanced directive.

The Supreme Court upheld the established doctrine of clear and convincing evidence. It also advanced the patient's right to die when Chief Justice Rehnquist wrote that "for the purpose of this case we assume that the United States Constitution would grant a competent person a constitutionally protected right to refuse lifesaving hydration and nutrition." (*Cruzan v. Director, Missouri Department of Health*).[5]

As a direct result of this landmark decision, many states quickly passed legislation legalizing the use of advance directives, including health care proxies, durable medical powers of attorney, and living wills.

Subsequently, the Cruzan case resolved itself. The parents of Nancy Cruzan successfully established in a local probate court clear and convincing evidence that their daughter had stated to family and friends prior to the accident that she did not wish to be kept alive by artificial means if she ever became terminally ill, resulting in a persistent vegetative state. Hydration and nutrition were withdrawn with the court's permission, and she was allowed to die with dignity after a long-fought struggle with the law.

On January 8, 1997, the Supreme Court again took up the gauntlet and deliberated the complex issue of the patient's "right to die" in *Quill v. Vacco* and *Glucksberg v. Washington.* Do adult competent patients who have been diagnosed as terminally ill possess a constitutional right to terminate their lives with the assistance of a physician? Is this any different from the terminally ill patient who refuses life-sustaining medical treatment?

The Supreme Court selected to hear the two cases on appeal because of the public's continuing concern about this issue and the persistence of the controversial Dr. Kevorkian. It considered two cases: one from New York, *Quill v. Vacco*,[6] and the other from Washington, *Compassion in Dying v. State of Washington.*[7] Both federal appellate courts issued dramatic decisions declaring that every citizen is guaranteed the constitutional right to physician-assisted suicide.

The Court had to consider some very complex issues:

1. Which patients, if any, would be eligible for physician-assisted suicide?
2. How could physician-assisted suicide be responsibly monitored?
3. Does physician-assisted suicide violate the Hippocratic Oath? Would physicians cooperate?
4. Does the federal government have the legal right to interfere with a person's individual freedom to take his or her own life?
5. How would legalization of physician-assisted suicide impact upon the terminally ill patient's medical treatment by HMOs and other medical insurers? Would HMOs prematurely deny life-sustaining treatment to increase their profit margin?

Six months later, on June 26, 1997, the Supreme Court rendered a decision on the appeals involving the two cases: *it upheld the state's constitutional right to prohibit physician-assisted suicide and to make it a criminal act.* The decisions in both cases were unanimous, nine to zero.

It is interesting to speculate whether the founding fathers of our country who drafted the Constitution over 200 years ago would have in their wildest dreams considered physician-assisted suicide as a Constitutional right.

VACCO V. QUILL

521 U.S. 793 (1997)

Chief Justice REHNQUIST delivered the opinion of the Court.

In New York, as in most States, it is a crime to aid another to commit or attempt suicide, but patients may refuse even lifesaving medical treatment. The question presented by this case is whether New York's prohibition on assisting suicide therefore violates the Equal Protection Clause of the Fourteenth Amendment. We hold that it does not.

Petitioners are various New York public officials. Respondents Timothy E. Quill, Samuel C. Klagsbrun, and Howard A. Grossman are physicians who practice in New York. They assert that although it would be "consistent with the standards of [their] medical practice[s]" to prescribe lethal medication for "mentally competent, terminally ill patients" who are suffering great pain and desire a doctor's help in taking their own lives, they are deterred from doing so by New York's ban on assisting suicide. App. 25-26.

Respondents, and three gravely ill patients who have since died, sued the State's Attorney General in the United States District Court. They urged that because New York permits a competent person to refuse life-sustaining medical treatment, and because the refusal of such treatment is "essentially the same thing" as physician-assisted suicide, New York's assisted-suicide ban violates the Equal Protection Clause. *Quill v. Koppell*, 870 F.Supp. 78, 84-85 (S.D.N.Y.1994).

The District Court disagreed: "[I]t is hardly unreasonable or irrational for the State to recognize a difference between allowing nature to take its course, even in the most severe situations, and intentionally using an artificial death-producing device." *Id.*, at 84. The court noted New York's "obvious legitimate interests in preserving life, and in protecting vulnerable persons," and concluded that "[u]nder the United States Constitution and the federal system it establishes, the resolution of this issue is left to the normal democratic processes within the State." *Id.*, at 84-85.

The Court of Appeals for the Second Circuit reversed. 80 F.3d 716 (1996). The court determined that, despite the assisted-suicide ban's apparent general applicability, "New York law does not treat equally all competent persons who are in the final stages of fatal illness and wish to hasten their deaths," because "those in the final stages of terminal illness who are on life-support systems are allowed to hasten their deaths by directing the removal of such systems; but those who are similarly situated, except for the previous attachment of life-sustaining equipment, are not allowed to hasten death by self-administering prescribed drugs." *Id.*, at 727, 729. In the court's view, "[t]he ending of life by [the withdrawal of life-support systems] is nothing more nor less than assisted suicide." *Id.*, at 729 (emphasis added). The Court of Appeals then examined whether this supposed unequal treatment was rationally related to any legitimate state interests, and concluded that "to the extent that [New York's statutes] prohibit a physician from prescribing medications to be self-administered by a mentally competent, terminally-ill person in the final stages of his terminal illness, they are not rationally related to any legitimate state interest." *Id.*, at 731. We granted certiorari, 518 U.S. 1055, 117 S.Ct. 36, 135 L.Ed.2d 1127 (1996), and now reverse.

The Equal Protection Clause commands that no State shall "deny to any person within its jurisdiction the equal protection of the laws." This provision creates no substantive rights.

The Equal Protection Clause commands that no State shall "deny to any person within its jurisdiction the equal protection of the laws." This provision creates no substantive rights. *San Antonio Independent School Dist. v. Rodriguez*, 411 U.S. 1, 33 (1973); *id.*, at 59 (Stewart, J., concurring). Instead, it embodies a general rule that States must treat like cases alike but may treat unlike cases accordingly. *Plyler v. Doe*, 457 U.S. 202, 216 (1982) ("'[T]he Constitution does not require things which are different in fact or opinion to be treated in law as though they were the same'") (quoting *Tigner v. Texas*, 310 U.S. 141, 147 (1940)). If a legislative classification or distinction "neither burdens a fundamental right nor targets a suspect class, we will uphold [it] so long as it bears a rational relation to some legitimate end." *Romer v. Evans*, 517 U. S. , (slip op., at 10) (1996).

New York's statutes outlawing assisting suicide affect and address matters of profound significance to all New Yorkers alike. They neither infringe fundamental rights nor involve suspect classifications.

On their faces, neither New York's ban on assisting suicide nor its statutes permitting patients to refuse medical treatment treat anyone differently from anyone else or draw any distinctions between persons. Everyone, regardless of physical condition, is entitled, if competent, to refuse unwanted lifesaving medical treatment; no one is permitted to assist a suicide. Generally speaking, laws that apply evenhandedly to all "unquestionably comply" with the Equal Protection Clause.

The Court of Appeals, however, concluded that some terminally ill people—those who are on life-support systems—are treated differently from those who are not, in that the former may "hasten death" by ending treatment, but the latter may not "hasten death" through physician-assisted suicide. 80 F.3d, at 729. This conclusion depends on the submission that ending or refusing lifesaving medical treatment "is nothing more nor less than assisted suicide." *Ibid.* Unlike the Court of Appeals, we think the distinction between assisting suicide and withdrawing life-sustaining treatment, a distinction widely recognized and endorsed in the medical profession and in our legal traditions, is both important and logical; it is certainly rational. See *Feeney*, supra, at 272, 99 S.Ct., at 2292 ("When the basic classification is rationally based, uneven effects upon particular groups within a class are ordinarily of no constitutional concern").

The distinction comports with fundamental legal principles of causation and intent. First, when a patient refuses life-sustaining medical treatment, he dies from an underlying fatal disease or pathology; but if a patient ingests lethal medication prescribed by a physician, he is killed by that medication.

Furthermore, a physician who withdraws, or honors a patient's refusal to begin, life-sustaining medical treatment purposefully intends, or may so intend, only to respect his patient's wishes and "to cease doing useless and futile or degrading things to the patient when [the patient] no longer stands to benefit from them." Assisted Suicide in the United States, Hearing before the Subcommittee on the Constitution of the House Committee on the Judiciary, 104th Cong., 2d Sess., 368 (1996) (testimony of Dr. Leon R. Kass). The same is true when a doctor provides aggressive palliative care; in some cases, painkilling drugs may hasten a patient's death, but the physician's purpose and intent is, or may be, only to ease his patient's pain. A doctor who assists a suicide, however, "must, necessarily and indubitably, intend primarily that the patient be made dead." *Id.*, at 367. Similarly, a patient who commits suicide with a doctor's aid necessarily has the specific intent to end his or her own life, while a patient who refuses or discontinues treatment might not. See, e.g., *Matter of Conroy*, supra, at 351, 486 A.2d, at 1224 (patients who refuse life-sustaining treatment "may not harbor a specific intent to die" and may instead "fervently wish to live, but to do so free of unwanted medical technology, surgery, or drugs"); *Superintendent of Belchertown State School v. Saikewicz*, 373 Mass. 728, 743, n. 11, 370 N.E.2d 417, 426, n. 11 (1977) ("[I]n refusing treatment the patient may not have the specific intent to die").

The overwhelming majority of state legislatures have drawn a clear line between assisting suicide and withdrawing or permitting the refusal of unwanted lifesaving medical treatment by prohibiting the former and permitting the latter. *Glucksberg*, at 708-711, 713-720, 117 S.Ct., at 2262-2263, 2264-2267. And "nearly all states expressly disapprove of suicide and assisted suicide either in statutes dealing with durable powers of attorney in health-care situations, or in 'living will' statutes." *Kevorkian*, supra, at 478-479, and nn. 53-54, 527 N.W.2d, at 731-732, and nn. 53-54. Thus, even as the States move to protect and promote patients' dignity at the end of life, they remain opposed to physician-assisted suicide.

New York is a case in point. The State enacted its current assisted-suicide statutes in 1965. Since then, New York has acted several times to protect patients' common-law right to refuse treatment. Act of Aug. 7, 1987, ch. 818, § 1, 1987 N.Y. Laws 3140 ("Do Not Resuscitate Orders") (codified as amended at N.Y. Pub. Health Law §§ 2960-2979 (McKinney 1993 and Supp.1997)); Act of July 22, 1990, ch. 752, § 2, 1990 N.Y. Laws

3547 ("Health Care Agents and Proxies") (codified as amended at N.Y. Pub. Health Law §§ 2980–2994 (McKinney 1993 and Supp.1997)). In so doing, however, the State has neither endorsed a general right to "hasten death" nor approved physician-assisted suicide. Quite the opposite: The State has reaffirmed the line between "killing" and "letting die." See N.Y. Pub. Health Law § 2989(3) (McKinney 1993) ("This article is not intended to permit or promote suicide, assisted suicide, or euthanasia"); New York State Task Force on Life and the Law, Life-Sustaining Treatment: Making Decisions and Appointing a Health Care Agent 36-42 (July 1987); Do Not Resuscitate Orders: The Proposed Legislation and Report of the New York State Task Force on Life and the Law 15 (Apr.1986). More recently, the New York State Task Force on Life and the Law studied assisted suicide and euthanasia and, in 1994, unanimously recommended against legalization. When Death is Sought: Assisted Suicide and Euthanasia in the Medical Context vii (1994). In the Task Force's view, "allowing decisions to forgo life-sustaining treatment and allowing assisted suicide or euthanasia have radically different consequences and meanings for public policy." *Id.*, at 146.

This Court has also recognized, at least implicitly, the distinction between letting a patient die and making that patient die. In *Cruzan v. Director, Mo. Dept. of Health*, 497 U.S. 261, 278, 110 S.Ct. 2841, 2851, 111 L.Ed.2d 224 (1990), we concluded that "[t]he principle that a competent person has a constitutionally protected liberty interest in refusing unwanted medical treatment may be inferred from our prior decisions," and we assumed the existence of such a right for purposes of that case, *id.*, at 279, 110 S.Ct., at 2851-2852. But our assumption of a right to refuse treatment was grounded not, as the Court of Appeals supposed, on the proposition that patients have a general and abstract "right to hasten death," 80 F.3d, at 727-728, but on well-established, traditional rights to bodily integrity and freedom from unwanted touching, *Cruzan*, 497 U.S., at 278-279, 110 S.Ct., at 2851-2852; *Id.*, at 287-288, 110 S.Ct., at 2856-2857 (O'CONNOR, J., concurring). In fact, we observed that "the majority of States in this country have laws imposing criminal penalties on one who assists another to commit suicide." *Id.*, at 280, 110 S.Ct., at 2852. *Cruzan* therefore provides no support for the notion that refusing life-sustaining medical treatment is "nothing more nor less than suicide."

For all these reasons, we disagree with respondents' claim that the distinction between refusing lifesaving medical treatment and assisted suicide is "arbitrary" and "irrational." *Brief for Respondents* 44. Granted, in some cases, the line between the two may not be clear, but certainty is not required, even were it possible. Logic and contemporary practice support New York's judgment that the two acts are different, and New York may therefore, consistent with the Constitution, treat them differently. By permitting everyone to refuse unwanted medical treatment while prohibiting anyone from assisting a suicide, New York law follows a longstanding and rational distinction.

New York's reasons for recognizing and acting on this distinction—including prohibiting intentional killing and preserving life; preventing suicide; maintaining physicians' role as their patients' healers; protecting vulnerable people from indifference, prejudice, and psychological and financial pressure to end their lives; and avoiding a possible slide towards euthanasia—are discussed in greater detail in our opinion in *Glucksberg*, ante. These valid and important public interests easily satisfy the constitutional requirement that a legislative classification bear a rational relation to some legitimate end.

The judgment of the Court of Appeals is reversed.

It is so ordered.

unequivocally no

SUMMARY

1. A patient has a Constitutional right to refuse medical treatment under the U.S. Constitution.
2. When a patient cannot communicate, that patient's guardian or health care proxy can express the patient's decision to refuse medical treatment. The guardian or health care proxy cannot substitute his or her own judgment or morals to determine what decision should be made, but merely expresses the wishes of the patient as the guardian believes them to be.
3. The Constitution requires proof by "clear and convincing evidence" that the patient would wish to refuse medical treatment. Protection under state law may be stronger, but cannot offer less protection.
4. A living will, completed before the patient becomes ill, is the most effective way for a patient to make his wishes known. While it is not conclusive, the living will provides the most persuasive evidence of a patient's wishes.
5. There is no federal constitutional right to suicide, and there is no federal protection for physicians who participate in a patient's suicide.
 6. Oregon is the only state that expressly permits physician-assisted suicide, protecting both patient and physician from prosecution by state authorities. A physician, however, may still be subject to federal prosecution pursuant to the federal Controlled Substance Act.

REFERENCES

Derek Humphry. *Final Exit: The Practicalities of Self-Deliverance and Assisted Suicide for the Dying*. The Hemlock Society, 1991.

Derek Humphry and Ann Wickett. *The Right to Die—A Historical and Legal Perspective of Euthanasia*. The Hemlock Society, 1986.

David Lester and Margot Tallmen, Eds. *Now I Lay Me Down*. Suicide in the Elderly. Philadelphia: The Charleston Press, 1994.

Sherwin B. Nuland. *How We Die*. Vintage Books, 1995.

Timothy E. Quill. *Death and Dignity—Making Choices and Taking Charge*. W.W. Worton & Co., 1993.

(The author is one of the plaintiffs in the case the Supreme Court heard on January 10, 1997.)

Timothy E. Quill. *A Midwife Through the Dying Process*. Johns Hopkins University Press, 1996.

ORGANIZATIONS

New York State Task Force on Life and the Law.
Health Education Services
P. O. Box 7126
Albany, NY 12224

When Death is Sought: *Assisted suicide and euthanasia in the medical context* (1994).
When Others Must Choose. Deciding for patients without capacity (1994).
The Proposed Legislation and Report of the New York State Task Force on Life and the Law, April 1986, 2nd ed. August 1988.

End-of-Life Choices
P. O. Box 101810
Denver, Colorado 80246
800-247-7421
www.endoflifechoices.org

REVIEW QUESTIONS AND EXERCISES

1. Discuss the changes in patient's right to die over the last 100 years.
2. Discuss the holding in *O'Connor v. Westchester County Hospital*, and compare it to *Quinlan*.
3. Explain how surrogate health care decision making has changed in the light of *Quinlan*, *Cruzan*, and *O'Connor*. How would the execution of a health care proxy have helped to avoid the problems faced in these three cases?
4. *Quinlan, Cruzan*, and *O'Connor* deal with patients in a vegetative state. What effect do these decisions have on terminally ill patients?
5. Discuss physician-assisted suicide in Holland and Belgium.
6. What is the distinction between physician-assisted suicide and euthanasia? Explain how physician-assisted suicide may lead us down the "slippery slope" of euthanasia.
7. What is the major holding of *People v. Kevorkian*? How did Dr. Kevorkian's actions cross the line from physician-assisted suicide to murder? Why did the court refuse to extend the right to privacy to include the right to euthanasia?
8. What is the major holding of *Donaldson v. Lungren*? How does the Supreme Court describe the difference between a patient's right to refuse medical treatment and a patient's right to assisted-suicide? What is the state's interest in not allowing a patient to die?
9. Discuss physician-assisted suicide and euthanasia in the United States. Should these practices be allowed?
10. Discuss palliative care. What role should palliative care take in health care practice?
11. Discuss the holdings in *Quill v. Vacco* and *Washington v. Glucksberg*. How are these decisions similar? How are these two decisions different? What effect do these decisions have on the area of physician-assisted suicide?
12. To what effect did *Quill v. Vacco* and *Washington v. Glucksberg* answer the following questions:
     a. Which patients, if any, would be eligible for physician-assisted suicide?
     b. How could physician-assisted suicide be responsibly monitored?
     c. Does physician-assisted suicide violate the Hippocratic Oath?
     d. Does the federal government have the legal right to interfere with a person's individual freedom to take his or her own life?
     e. How could legalization of physician-assisted suicide impact upon the terminally ill patient's medical treatment by HMOs and other medical insurers?

NOTES

1. *In re: Quinlan* (New Jersey), 647 N.J. (1976), cert. denied 429 U.S. 922 (1976).
2. *Cruzan v. Director, Missouri Department of Health*, 497 U.S. 261 (1991).
3. *Cruzan v. Director, Missouri Department of Health*, 497 U.S. 261 (1991).
4. *O'Connor v. Westchester County Hospital*, 72 N.Y.2d 517 (1988).
5. *Cruzan v. Director, Missouri Department of Health*, 497 U.S. 261 (1991).
6. *Quill v. Vacco*, 97 F.3d 708 (2nd Cir., 1996).
7. *Compassion in Dying v. State of Washington*, 79 F.3d 790 (1996).

CHAPTER 12

Managed Care and Long-Term Care Insurance

PREVIEW

Issues relating to the health care system in America are changing. This chapter covers the health care delivery system, especially managed care in which a corporate health management organization, the HMO, organizes and controls the nature and amount of medial care available to a patient-subscriber. This chapter explores the ins-and-outs of HMOs, including a discussion of their creation, operation, abuses, and effect on Medicaid. This chapter focuses on how the health care delivery system affects the elderly. People are living longer, and the likelihood of developing catastrophic illnesses increases greatly with aging. Financing these illnesses is a major concern of the elder law practice. Traditional medical insurance, HMO medical coverage, and traditional Medicare are not currently designed to pay for long-term catastrophic illness. This chapter, therefore, details the need for long-term care insurance.

INTRODUCTION

Managed care has hit the United States and is the talk of the country. It spans the generations, from infants to the elderly. It affects the rich and the poor, even Medicaid recipients. Contracts are being negotiated now between the **Centers for Medicine, Medicaid Services (CMS)** formerly known as the Health Care Finance Administration (HCFA) and private HMOs to provide medical services for Medicare beneficiaries. State Medicaid agencies are also negotiating with HMOs to provide medical services for their recipients. It is imperative that the legal professional understand how this system of health care operates, because our elderly clients, accustomed to traditional systems of health care, have become quite anxious about HMOs and their continuing access to medical benefits. The future indicates that there will be extensive litigation in this area because the HMOs have not provided all the services they are required to deliver according to the terms of their contracts.

    Managed care is the term currently used to describe a delivery system of health care in which a corporate organization, the HMO, organizes and controls the nature and amount of medical care that is made available to a patient-subscriber. As our country struggles to provide universal health care, the concept of managed care is frequently suggested as a viable alternative to the traditional private pay system.

    Unlike an insurance company, an HMO does more than simply pay for care. It contracts to *provide* care by assuming responsibility for arranging quality care for patients through the physicians and facilities with which it contracts to provide such care. It sets fees for doctors and determines the amount of the patients' co-payments.

Managed Care
The delivery system of health care in which a health maintenance organization (HMO) organizes and controls the nature and amount of medical care that is made available to a patient-subscriber.

THE HMO

The federal government became increasingly aware that unregulated health care was not working. Both government and business agreed that the cost of health care had to be brought under control because costs were rising much faster than the rate of inflation. Consequently, in 1970 Congress passed the Federal HMO Act to provide financial and regulatory support for the development of HMOs.

Three major factors led to governmental support and legislation in favor of creating HMOs:

1. The need to control skyrocketing medical costs.
2. The need to reduce existing barriers to outpatient care.
3. The need to control and regulate under- and overutilization of medical services.

HMO Operation

An HMO operates according to contract law in two basic areas:

1. It contracts with patient-subscribers, individually or as part of a specific group, who enroll in a particular program of health benefits. They, in return, pay a specified premium to the HMO.
2. It contracts with individual or groups of physicians to provide services as specified in the HMO's health benefits contract.

Gatekeeper
A physician who practices within a health maintenance organization, whose job is to control the number of referrals that the primary care physician gives to a specialist.

Medical personnel are divided into two categories:

1. Primary care physicians such as the family practitioner, general practitioner, internist, and the pediatrician.
2. Specialists such as radiologists, orthopedists, etc.

Managed Care Plan
Often called health maintenance organizations (HMOs), these plans are a combination of insurance company and a health care delivery system (doctor/hospital). These plans cover health care costs in return for a premium paid by the insured. The plan restricts the health care providers, physicians, etc., the subscriber can use for care and treatment. There may be a small co-payment, *e.g.,* $5–15 per visit.

The primary care physicians are designated as **gatekeepers**. Their function is to ration health care utilization as necessary, containing costs on the one hand and maintaining high standards of ethical quality medical care on the other. They coordinate diagnostic testing and referrals to specialists as they deem necessary.

Regardless of the specific situation, the gatekeeper must always keep in mind the HMO's contractual obligations to provide:

1. Consistent preventive medical care (which will save the HMO money in the long run)
2. Appropriate use of diagnostic tests
3. Appropriate use of medications
4. A system with high subscriber satisfaction
5. Sufficient access for patient-subscribers

The above procedure is commonly referred to as case management.

SCENARIO

At the onset of illness, the patient first consults with a designated gatekeeper who determines if a primary care physician can deliver the required medical care or if the services of a specialist or specific diagnostic testing measure are required. The patient is then treated and discharged or referred to the appropriate specialist or medical facility. The patient-subscriber is not charged or is charged a minimal fee for primary care services by an HMO-designated physician, pursuant to the terms of the contract.

Ideally, the HMO has a moral obligation, which it shares with its contracted physicians, to provide:

1. Competent medical personnel
2. State-of-the-art treatment facilities
3. Patient advocacy on behalf of its subscribers
4. A program of preventive health care

In this regard, the gatekeeper's decision should not be motivated by any financial gain or loss to the employer, the HMO. In fact, current legislation requires the HMO to provide outcome analysis data clearly demonstrating that its parsimonious use of specialists, labs, x-ray facilities, etc. does not adversely affect the length or severity of a patient's illness. A cause for concern would arise if an HMO physician avoided performing a test on an HMO patient-subscriber that the physician would have deemed medically necessary for a fee-for-service patient. The HMO saves money by regulating and possibly *not* performing unnecessary or excessive diagnostic testing. The cost saving is often passed on to the patient-subscriber in the form of lower premiums.

By contrast, in a **fee-for-service program**, the patient-subscriber is often subjected to superfluous diagnostic testing, producing too many medical possibilities, high expense for the patient, and potential conflicts of interest for the physician who profits from the tests. The resulting situation may be dangerous.

The HMO's paramount concern should be providing the appropriate medical care for a patient, advocating personal and longstanding relationships between the patient and the primary health care provider. The HMOs are moral agents with attendant ethical duties analogous to those of a physician. Institutional pressures to provide dividends for investors or to reduce costs should not be the driving force. Clearly, fiscal considerations should not be allowed to interfere with ethical medical decisions.

In sum, the HMO seeks to create a cost-conscious environment, and the doctor, keeping this in mind, is expected to obstruct the patient to a certain degree. The physician becomes a double agent, representing the patient and the HMO, which wants dividends for its investors and salaries for its highly paid executives. Therein lies the conflict of interest. Therefore, HMOs must be carefully monitored by a specially designated governmental agency to assure the public of ethical and quality medical care.

Capitation

Capitation is a term used to describe the fundamental structure of the HMO. It is, ironically, also the root of the conflict of interest. Capitation is a monthly sum paid in advance by an HMO to a health care provider as remuneration for providing contractually covered services

Capitation
The fee a health maintenance organization pays a physician-provider who is a member of the organization for services rendered to each patient. The physician receives a specific fee per patient per year, regardless of the number of times or the amount of treatment that is provided to the patient.

to a subscriber of the plan. The provider receives a flat monthly fee per patient. This fee remains constant regardless of the frequency of the patient's visits or intensity of the patient's treatment. Therefore, because the provider receives the patient capitation fee, regardless of whether or not the provider sees the patient, it is in the provider's best financial interest to see the patient minimally, limiting visits as well as treatment and diagnostic testing.

The capitation system also affects medical specialists. Under a managed care system, specialists have become casualties due to their high charges. The loss of the expertise of the specialist in treating patients is one of the consequences of changing to a system that promotes profit and low cost over maximization of knowledge applied to patients' needs.

Gag Clauses

Gag Clause
Clause found in a contract between a health maintenance organization and a physician-provider that prohibits the physician from giving certain information to the patient regarding treatment options.

Another aspect of the HMO structure that can create conflicts of interest is the **gag clause.** A gag clause, contained in many HMO provider contracts with physicians, hinders the provider-physician from giving patients full medical information about costly treatment options not covered by the HMO. The HMO may offer appropriate and adequate medical options, but because it is cost-conscious, it instructs its provider physicians *not* to disclose all the options available, including experimental procedures that the private physician might advise the patient to explore. Some gag clauses restrict the physician from telling the HMO patients about policies that link the compensation of doctors to their successes in holding down health care costs. Some HMO plans are so tightly managed that the physician must first receive authorization from the HMO before discussing proposed treatments with a patient. A typical gag clause in an HMO contract might read:

> *The physician shall make no communication that undermines or could undermine the confidence of enrollees, their employers, or the public.*

California has been in the forefront of utilizing health maintenance organizations. Its managed care companies have set the pace in efforts to manage a physician's communication with patient subscribers. One California HMO provider's contract states that a *"provider will not knowingly or directly advise any member to disenroll."* This is designed to prevent a physician provider from advising a patient-subscriber to obtain medical treatment not covered or deemed unnecessary by the HMO from a fee-for-services physician or to disenroll and join another plan that would cover these services. Failure to adhere to this clause on the part of the physician can result in termination of a physician-provider for reasons other than quality of care. In fact, during the 1996 elections, California voters rejected legislation that would have outlawed the use of gag clauses in that state. On the other hand, also in 1996, sixteen states *did* vote in favor of banning the use of gag clauses.

Gag clauses have come under intense examination. An article in the *New York Times* (December 7, 1996) "U.S. Bans Limits on HMO. Advice in Medicare Plan, Says Gags Violate the Law," comprehensively discussed the status of gag clauses. The Department of Health and Human Services issued a policy directive effective January 1, 1997, stating that:

> *Medicare HMO patients were entitled to all benefits available in the standard Medicare program which pays doctors a separate fee for each service. One of those benefits was advice from doctors on medically necessary treatment options. It concluded that any contract that limits a doctor's ability to advise and counsel a Medicare beneficiary was a violation of the federal Medicare law. Federal health officials said that they intended to issue a similar policy for HMOs serving Medicaid patients.*

In January 1996, the American Medical Association called upon all managed care plans to expunge gag clauses from their contracts. The following is an excerpt from the AMA report:

> *[A]fter reviewing over two hundred HMO contracts and consulting with doctors, they concluded that Americans could be short-changed because the contracts prohibited doctors from telling patients of superior treatment available from specialists outside of the HMO or of other costly alternatives. It was also noted that, in numerous instances, physicians were disciplined or threatened with termination for discussing said treatment options."* (New York Times, December 7, 1996). *Many states (including New York) now restrict HMOs from including provisions in their contracts with providers prohibiting them from discussing any treatment or procedure with any enrollee of an HMO.*

Fraud

As with some fee-for-service physicians, some HMOs have been guilty of fraudulent practices, including upcoding billing for higher reimbursements from Medicare and Medicaid and billing for services not medically necessary and not performed. Studies have established that health care fraud is costing the government approximately $100 billion annually. The federal government must continue to monitor the health care delivery system to prevent fraud and protect the American taxpayer, who ultimately pays the bill.

Antitrust Issues

There is very little antitrust litigation involving HMOs. Until now, small competing companies have been available to serve the needs of the general market. However, as large insurance companies begin to enter the field, creating giant health maintenance organizations, the patient-consumer will be at an increasing risk and at the mercy of these large conglomerates. It appears that this trend of mergers and acquisitions will continue at a rapid pace. Government intervention in the form of antitrust legislation will be necessary. The Antitrust Division of the Justice Department will be employed to investigate violations.

There has never been a time in American history when the medical delivery system has been in such a state of flux and uncertainty as today. The HMO has presented itself as an alternative to traditional dispensation of medical services. In spite of all its problems, managed care already has made substantial contributions to American health care. Already, it has been clearly demonstrated that HMOs have made primary medical care more available to more Americans than ever before. Their preventive treatment plans, including prenatal care and counseling, mammography, and immunizations, will result in better future health for their subscribers. HMOs are clearly the most economical way to deliver the best quality health care to the greatest number of people. If monitored properly, HMOs should be able to live up to their own high expectations.

The pendulum, however, has begun to swing against managed care companies. In a 5–4 ruling, handed down on June 20, 2002, by the Supreme Court of the United States (*Rush Prudential HMO v. Moran*, 535 U.S. 355 (2002)), the states' authority to protect the rights of patients involved in disputes with managed care companies over denial of recommended treatments was upheld. The ruling guarantees outside review of an HMO's refusal to pay for a procedure that a patient's physician has authorized. This ruling only applies to individuals who receive medical coverage from employer-sponsored benefits plans that contract with an outside medical provider. There is current legislation in Congress to provide this protection to all members of any managed care plan.

Managed Care and Medicaid

At the end of 2001 according to government statistics, 22 million Medicaid beneficiaries, or 58 percent of all enrollees, were in managed care programs. The U. S. Department of Health and Human Services issued new regulations giving Medicaid beneficiaries enrolled in managed care plans the same types of protection that participants in private plans would receive under the patient right's legislation now under consideration in Congress.

Under these new regulations that took effect on August 13, 2002, beneficiaries have the following rights:

- *Emergency Room Care.* Health plans must pay for a Medicaid beneficiary's emergency room care whenever and wherever the need arises.
- *Access to Second Opinion.* All beneficiaries are allowed to get a second opinion from a qualified health professional.
- *Direct Access for Women's Health Services.* Women are allowed to directly access a woman's health specialist in the network for the same routine and preventive health care services as is available in Medicaid fee-for-service.
- *Patient-Provider Communication.* Managed care plans are prohibited from establishing restrictions, such as gag rules, that interfere with patient-provider communications.
- *Network Adequacy.* Managed care plans are required to ensure that they have the capacity to serve the expected enrollment in their service area.
- *Marketing Activities.* States are required to approve marketing materials used by the managed care plans to enroll Medicaid beneficiaries. Plans are prohibited from using door-to-door, telephone, and other forms of cold-call marketing.
- *Grievance Systems.* All managed care plans must have a system in place to accommodate enrollee grievances and appeals. Grievances must be resolved within state-established time frames that may not be longer than 90 days and must be resolved by managed care organizations within 45 days. However, expedited time frames exist for resolving appeals when life or health is in jeopardy.

Managed care plans serving Medicaid beneficiaries also must provide consumers with comprehensive, easy-to-understand information about the program in which they are enrolled.

The HMO and Long-Term Care

Long-Term Care
The medical and support services needed to attain an optimum level of physical, social, and psychological functioning by persons who are frail and dependent due to chronic physical and mental impairments.

The American College of Physicians has described **long-term care** as:

> *the medical and support services needed to attain an optimum level of physical, social, and psychological functioning by persons who are frail and dependent due to chronic physical and mental impairments.*

The future of American health seems to indicate that the HMOs will eventually be dealing with long-term care treatment. The basic purpose of an HMO is to control spiraling medical costs. Americans spend more than half of their lifetime medical expenditures in the last six months of their life, but they die anyway. These expenditures are normally covered under the traditional fee-for-services medical insurance plan, regardless of the physician's ability to cure the patient. This country does not permit euthanasia, and the medical community will spend enormous sums of money to keep the elderly or terminally ill patient alive. If they do not, they would be subject to prosecution for assisted suicide, manslaughter, or murder. It is quite possible that the HMO in its cost-cutting procedures could decide to limit the amount of care it provides for terminally ill patients because it can claim it is wasting precious assets that could be used for the treatment of patients that will recover. It may view these expenditures as not cost-effective. Some fear that if this scenario does occur, it could start this nation on the slippery slope to euthanasia.

LONG-TERM CARE INSURANCE

In the 21st century, **long-term care insurance** (a/k/a nursing home insurance) will play a significant role in life planning for people over the age of 50. As previously noted, people are living longer, and the likelihood of their developing illnesses in their later years that cannot be treated at home has increased. Financing these illnesses is a major concern of the elder law practice. Traditional medical insurance, new HMO medical coverages, and traditional Medicare are not currently designed to finance long-term catastrophic illness. Unless expanded coverages are made available in the future, providing indemnification against such illnesses, senior citizens have only the following alternatives:

1. *Private Pay:* The individual directly pays the facility. Under certain circumstances, costs may be tax-deductible,
2. *Medicare:* Partial coverage of the first 100 days for rehabilitation only.
3. *Medicaid:* One must be impoverished to access this entitlement benefit.
4. *Long-Term Care Insurance:* Specifically designed to provide financial coverage for long-term catastrophic illness. As of January 1, 1997, premiums are also tax-deductible, with certain restrictions.

Changes in governmental policy have led to increased interest in long-term care insurance as a method of financing catastrophic illness. Just prior to the end of the Reagan administration, Congress enacted legislation expanding Medicare benefits to include coverage in a long-term care facility for approximately 150 days per year. For the first time in the history of our country, the government provided coverage for long-term catastrophic illness. When President Bush the first took office, however, this unique benefits program was repealed. Congress responded to constituents who deemed it too costly. Currently there is no federal program to provide such benefits except the Medicare benefits package, which is designed only to cover short-term rehabilitation and is severely restricted as follows:

1. Patient must be hospitalized for 72 hours immediately prior to admission to a skilled nursing facility or at least be admitted to a nursing home within 30 days of hospital discharge.
2. Coverage is only for rehabilitation and not custodial care.
3. Patient must require physical therapy or skilled nursing care.

Long-Term Care Insurance
An insurance policy designed to protect an individual against catastrophic illness. It covers nursing care, home care, and, depending on the policy, assisted-living facilities and hospice care. The cost of the premium is deductible from federal income tax, depending upon the age of the insured and the amount of the premium. Some states also allow the deduction.

4. Period of coverage: maximum 100 days.
   a. Medicare pays 20 days in full.
   b. Medicare pays for all skilled nursing home care from the 21st to 100th day, except $109.50 (2004) per day. This deductible is paid by the patient and increases annually. This 100-day coverage is also restricted. If the patient no longer requires skilled care or rehabilitation, if the patient refuses such treatment, or if the patient ceases to benefit from such care and treatment, this coverage can be terminated before the completion of the 100-day period.

The only other program available to aging clients to pay for long term-care is the Medicaid Entitlement Program, a federal program administered by state and local agencies. As was discussed in detail in Chapter 10, one must be impoverished to be entitled to this benefit.

Without proper advance planning, long-term catastrophic illness can be devastating, both physically and financially. The benefits of long-term care insurance coverage must be discussed with the client because nursing home costs are staggering: $80,000 to $120,000 per year in the Greater New York area, less in other parts of the country. Twenty-four-hour home care can cost as much as $7,500 per week if a registered nurse is required. The cost of an assisted-living facility with home care services can exceed $60,000 per year. Some policies provide coverage for assisted-living facilities. If transfers of assets are to be made by the patient or the agent designated in a durable power of attorney in order to qualify for Medicaid, they must be done well ahead of time.

Under the current Medicaid laws, any transfers made within 36 months prior to the date of application are questionable and may make the transferor ineligible for Medicaid benefits at that time. However, if long-term care insurance was already in place upon entry into a nursing home or another long-term care facility, the client would be able to preserve assets. The transfer could be made at any time prior to entry into the nursing home or even upon entry, as long as the policy remains in effect for at least the current Medicaid look-back period of 36 months and the patient does not apply for Medicaid for 36 months in accordance with the transfer law that took effect January 1, 1997. (Kennedy-Kassenbaum Health Insurance Bill).

THE KENNEDY-KASSENBAUM HEALTH INSURANCE BILL

On August 21, 1996, President Clinton signed into law the Kennedy-Kassenbaum Health Insurance Portability and Accountability Act of 1996, which officially went into effect January 1, 1997. It is part of the government's continuing effort to limit the expansion of entitlement programs such as Medicaid. Worried that aging baby boomers and their parents will cause too great a strain on the federal budget, the law is designed to encourage the middle class to purchase long-term care insurance. It provides an incentive for individuals and employers to purchase long-term care insurance by amending the Internal Revenue Code to permit tax deductions for premiums paid for such insurance for chronically ill individuals. These deductions can also apply to policies that have been issued prior to January 1, 1997. They are grandparented in. The government is determined to get out of providing long-term care benefits for its citizens and is encouraging the private insurance industry to take on this role. The new law provides the following:

A. Employers will be granted tax deductions for the funds paid out for long-term care employee benefit packages, similar to their current deductions for medical benefits.
B. Individuals who purchase long-term care insurance will also be allowed to deduct such insurance premiums as a medical expense, provided they file itemized tax returns to qualify for the deduction. The long-term care insurance premiums (and other medical expenses) must exceed 7.5 percent of the individual's adjusted gross income.

C. Limitations as to the amount of premiums that are eligible for tax deduction. In 2003, the limitation is based upon the age of the person filing the tax return:

Age	2004 Limitation
under age 41	$260
age 41 to 50	$490
age 51 to 60	$980
age 61 to 70	$2,600
above age 71 or older	$3,250

For example, an individual age 65, paying a $2,500 annual premium, can only take the tax deduction of $2,000 due to the above limitations. The $2,000 is then subject to the 7.5 percent deductibility floor. The dollar limits are indexed to inflation.

D. The law provides that benefits received from long-term care insurance will be tax free, subject to certain statutory limitations. The exclusion from income is limited to $175/day on per diem contracts. This limit is indexed to inflation.

E. The provisions apply only to Federal income tax. State law determines deductibility for long-term care insurance for state tax purposes.

Long-Term Care Insurance Defined

Long-term care insurance is an insurance contract between a licensed private insurance carrier and an insured designed to pay for the following services:

1. Skilled nursing home
2. Assisted-living facility
3. Home care
4. Hospice care

A long-term care insurance policy can work as part of Medicaid planning:

1. The individual purchases a long-term care policy.
2. Simultaneously executing a durable power of attorney, the insured individual appoints an agent and at least one or two substitute agents who are designated to handle the affairs of the insured in the event the insured is unable to act for any reason.
3. At this point, the insured pays the annual premium until such time as the insured suffers a catastrophic illness and is required to enter a nursing home or other covered facility. When the policy is accessed, the insurance carrier waives the premium.
4. Upon the insured's accessing the benefits of the policy:
   a. The agent designated in the durable power of attorney should transfer all of the assets of the principal to the designated individuals. (In *January 1, 1997, a federal statute went into effect that criminalizes certain asset transfers by an individual who seeks to obtain Medicaid coverage.* This statute, the Health Insurance Portability and Accountability Act of 1996, is discussed in detail in Chapter 10. This law is not being enforced at this time because it has been determined to be unconstitutional.)
   b. The insurance carrier will begin to pay benefits under the policy for 36 months. At the end of 36 months, the principal will be eligible for Medicaid under the current 36-month look-back rules. Medicaid will ask the applicant to the entitlement

program, "Did you transfer any of your assets within the past 36 months?" The answer will be "No," because the application will be made at least 36 months and one day after the transfer.

5. There are certain long-term care insurance policies issued under the Robert Wood Johnson Plan (AKA The Partnership Plan) that allow the insured to retain possession of all assets and, at the end of the 36-month look-back period, apply for Medicaid benefits. Under this plan, Medicaid can only use as a resource the income from the assets not transferred. The assets themselves are not treated as a Medicaid resource. They belong solely to the insured. Certain drawbacks to this type of policy are:

   a. The premium is usually twice that of the standard policy.

   b. In most situations, once the insured enters a facility, he or she will usually remain there until death and will no longer need the assets. Retaining assets in this way could lead to costly guardianship proceedings upon becoming incapacitated. Dying in possession of these assets could necessitate probate proceedings, which would result in an additional expense to the decedent's estate, as well as possibly creating an estate tax burden on the heirs.

   c. The policy is only available in four states: California, Connecticut, Indiana, and New York. The Omnibus Reconciliation Act, effective August 10, 1993, prohibited the expansion of this type of policy into other states.

Long-term care insurance is a desirable method of asset preservation because the insured who purchases a policy no longer has to worry about transferring assets and an impoverished lifestyle before entering the nursing home or accessing the policy in another way. Long-term care insurance allows the individual to retain assets and to maintain dignity, self-respect, and independence. The elderly are very reluctant to transfer their assets. Long-term care insurance permits them to avoid this.

Baby Boomers and Long Term Care Insurance

In 2030 baby boomers will be between the ages of 65 and 84. By 2050, all baby boomers will be at least age 85. They will have an increasing need for long-term care services. Baby boomers should incorporate long-term care insurance into their retirement and life course estate planning.

The Basic Long-Term Care Insurance Policy

The basic long-term care policy usually begins to pay benefits when the insured requires assistance with at least *two activities of daily living (ADLs)*. These ADLs include bathing, toileting, walking, feeding, dressing, and moving from bed to chair. Some policies start immediately upon meeting the above criteria. However, under some policies the insured can elect to take a 20- or 100-day deductible, thereby delaying the payment benefits by the insurance carrier, resulting in a reduction of the cost of the premium.

1. *Policy Rating:* Insist that the company issuing the policy has a Best's rating of A or A+. (Best's is an insurance company-rating guide.) One must go with a reputable company that has the greatest probability of remaining in business until the policy is accessed.

2. *Levels of Care:* The policy must benefit all of the following levels of care: skilled, intermediate, custodial, and hospice.

3. *Hospital Stay:* The policy should require no prior hospital stay. The insured patient should be able to go directly from home to a nursing facility without prior hospital admission.

4. *Coverage for Certain Illnesses:* Coverage must be provided for Parkinson's disease, cognitive impairments, *e.g.,* Alzheimer's disease, senile dementia, organic brain syndrome, etc.

5. *Covered Facility:* The definition of a covered facility must be clearly explained within the policy. The facility must be a licensed, skilled nursing home, not a hospital, drug rehabilitation center, or sanitarium. The client should be aware of the fact that not all policies cover assisted-living facilities and home care.

6. *Preexisting Conditions:* Review the policy to determine what the restrictions are concerning preexisting conditions. Some of the better policies contain no exclusions or limitations for preexisting conditions. Make sure the policy does not have a "post-claims underwriting clause." This prevents denial of coverage at the time a claim is made because of a preexisting condition.

7. *Waiver of Premium:* Make sure the premium is waived when the policy benefits are accessed. Determine when the waiver period commences and when it ceases.

8. *Guarantee of Renewability:* The policy should contain a clause representing to the insured that the insurance company will guarantee the insured's right to renew the coverage for life if desired. This means that as long as the insured pays the premiums, the company cannot cancel the policy. The policy should contain a liberal reinstatement clause to protect the insured if the premium is late. A provision for third party notification should be included in the policy. This would avoid the policy lapsing for nonpayment.

9. *Daily Benefit Amount:* This sum should be sufficient to pay the current private-pay rate for a facility where the client intends to seek care, taking into account the client's other sources of income, other anticipated expenses, and reasonable assumptions about inflation of long-term care costs.

10. *Payment of Long-Term Care Insurance Benefits in Addition to Other Coverages:* Benefits should be paid by the policy even though there may be other policies in force. For example, the patient may be receiving Medicare benefits or other insurance benefits through employment.

11. *Level Premium:* The premiums should not be affected by advances in age or deterioration of health. The rate should be fixed on the date of application and should not increase during the term of the policy.

12. *Age Limits:* Most policies commence coverage at age 40 and can be purchased only up to an age designated by the company, typically age 80 or 84. Most companies provide full coverage to age 80. Policies issued after age 80 contain lower benefit coverage. The lower the age at which the individual purchases the policy, the lower the premium, which is then fixed at that rate, unless state law and the policy allow premium adjustments for all in the same category.

13. *Coverage to Be Reviewed after Policy Issued:* The legal professional and the client should immediately scrutinize the policy from cover to cover. Most policies contain a short-term cancellation clause allowing the proposed insured to cancel and obtain a full refund for any reason within the first 30 days or so of issuance. Contact the agent to discuss the coverages and compare them to other policies to make sure that the best coverage is provided for a competitive premium rate.

14. *Inflation Guard:* Very significant! Most policies offer at a moderate additional premium an automatic increase in benefits, *e.g.,* five percent of the original daily benefit each year the policy is in effect. Benefits are designed to increase with this option upon the anniversary date of the policy. Strongly urge the client to opt for this coverage, at the highest compounded rate available, as a hedge against the upward spiraling costs of health care.

15. *Term of the Policy:* This is defined as the period for which coverage extends upon the activation of the policy. In other words, an individual purchases a policy, pays the annual premium until such time as the insured becomes ill, and receives the benefits. The policy has no fixed expiration date, but once the benefits are accessed, the *term* begins.

    It is generally recommended that the term of the policy should extend, at a bare minimum, for a period of 36 months, which is the current Medicaid penalty look-back period. Under certain circumstances, if assets have been transferred to an irrevocable trust, it is highly recommended that the term of coverage obtained be for a minimum of six years (this allows for an increase of the penalty period to 72 months), because in 1993 Congress extended the Medicaid penalty look-back period to 60 months to penalize transfers to irrevocable trusts. Long-term care experts predict that the current penalty period will continue to increase. In view of this, clients should consider purchasing lifetime coverage, which in effect obviates the need to plan for transfer of one's assets to meet Medicaid requirements of impoverishment. With lifetime coverage, an insured need never apply for the Medicaid entitlement program, and assets will be protected. The client should be advised to shop around to locate the best deal (the lowest premium for the most coverage). Insurance companies in this field have become very competitive.

    When advising a client in the purchase of long-term care coverage, the attorney must take into account the sources of income, anticipated expenses, and a reasonable assumption as to the inflating costs of long-term care in the future.

16. *Deductible Period:* The general rule is that the longer the deductible period, the lower the premium. The typical policy contains options regarding the deductible period such as 20, 60, 100, and 365 days. The 100-day deductible coverage is preferred because:

    a. It brings the cost of coverage down substantially;

    b. Medicare may pay for up to 100 days for rehabilitation, thus covering the 100-day deductible period. (As of 2004, for the first 20 days Medicare pays in full, and during an additional 80 days, Medicare pays everything except $109.50 per day.)

17. *Convalescent Benefits At Home:* Some policies provide for continuing coverage after the patient returns home from a stay at a nursing facility. The benefits payable under this provision of the policy are usually lower than the daily benefits payable while the patient is confined to a nursing home.

18. *Assisted-Living Facilities:* Some policies provide coverage in assisted-living facilities.

19. *Hospice Care:* Some policies provide coverage for hospice care.

Long-Term Care Home Health Care Policies

This type of coverage can be included as an optional rider within a long-term care insurance policy for an additional premium. Some insurance carriers will also issue a separate policy if an individual does not wish to purchase nursing home coverage.

1. *Qualification for Benefits*
   a. The patient requires assistance with at least two activities of daily living.
   b. Cognitive impairment: Alzheimer's disease, senile dementia, irreversible dementia, organic brain syndrome, etc.
   c. Injury or sickness not necessarily long-term, such as a hip injury or automobile accident at any age.

2. *Benefits:* The policy will usually pay for assistance from a professional home health care agency, registered nurse, licensed practical nurse, speech therapist, occupational therapist, home health aide, or personal care attendant. Most policies require that the patient need continual assistance in at least two of the ADLs or continual supervision, *e.g.,* for Alzheimer's or some form of senility. The clause of the contract must be studied carefully to determine the full extent of coverage. Most frequently, a physician's certificate is also required to access the coverage.

3. *Prior Hospital Stay:* You should advise your client to obtain a policy that does not require a prior hospital stay.

4. *Daily Benefits:* They should be at least 50 percent of the daily nursing home benefits.

5. *Deductible Period:* Review this carefully. There may be several options to consider. Remember, the shorter the period, the higher the premium.

6. *Term of Policy:* Most policies run from one to five years. Obviously, the longer the coverage, the higher the premium. Recommended coverage is for a minimum of four years and should be for at least four days per week.

7. *Inflation Guard:* This rider is usually available at a moderate increase in premium. It is used as a hedge against inflation.

8. *Treatment Plans:* Some companies, as an integral part of their coverage, provide the patient with treatment plans and monitor the case. They often provide the patient with a case manager who visits on a regular basis.

9. *Respite Care:* Most often a home-bound individual is cared for by a family member or a friend. This can be physically exhausting and emotionally distressing. Respite care provides temporary relief for the primary caregiver. This can be in the form of providing for the hiring of home health care aides or for the patient to go to a facility for a short stay while the primary caregiver gets some *respite.*

10. *Drug Abuse Treatment or Alcoholism:* Most policies do not afford coverage for these illnesses.

Group Benefit Policies

Many employers provide long-term care coverage for employees, as well as their parents, as part of their employee group benefits package. In order to qualify for coverage, the parents must meet certain medical requirements. The coverage is provided so that employees will only take minimal time off from work to care for their ill parents. They are entitled to do so pursuant to the Family and Medical Leave Act. It should be ascertained whether the client has such a benefit provided by the employer. Most often these group policies provide minimal coverage, and the client may wish to buy supplemental coverage from a private carrier.

REFERENCE

LONG-TERM CARE INSURANCE

American Council of Life Insurance
1001 Pennsylvania Ave. N.W.
Suite 500 South
Washington, D.C. 20004–2599

REVIEW QUESTIONS AND EXERCISES

1. Discuss some of the interactions you have had with HMOs in your lifetime. What are the benefits and deficiencies of the HMO process? How might the interaction with an HMO differ as you age?

2. What is a gatekeeper? What are the gatekeeper's responsibilities? How does the gatekeeper balance the two competing interests of a patient's needs versus the HMO's need to keep costs under control? Discuss ways to regulate these competing interests.

3. Discuss the gag rule's effect and any potential conflict of interest that it raises.

4. What effect does fraud in the HMO delivery system have on the total cost of coverage? What strategies would you employ to overcome fraud in the HMO system?

5. What is long-term care insurance? How has long-term care insurance changed in the last 20 years?

6. Discuss the essential elements of coverage in a long-term care policy.

7. How does long-term care insurance affect the Medicaid planning process?

8. How does long-term care insurance work? When purchasing long-term care coverage, what should the recipient look for? What should the elder law professional advise her or his client?

Chapter 13
Viatical Settlements and Accelerated Life Insurance Benefits

PREVIEW

Medical technology has had a significant effect on the lifespan of people. As technology continues to advance, people are living longer and longer, even people with terminal illnesses. However, these medical advances come at a significant price. How can terminally or chronically ill patients finance escalating costs of health care? Two ways are through viatical settlements and accelerated life insurance benefits. This chapter explains in detail what each of these strategies are and the benefits of each.

INTRODUCTION

In order to raise money for medical and funeral expenses, terminally ill people have been known to borrow money from friends and family and, in return, irrevocably name them as beneficiaries on life insurance policies to repay the debts they insured. Then, upon death, the loan was paid in full from the proceeds of the life insurance policy.

In direct response to the AIDS epidemic in America and the resulting financial havoc for AIDS patients, private viatical settlement companies were created. Viatical companies buy at a discount the life insurance policies of terminally ill patients, thereby creating a cash fund that can be used by policyholders during the last months of life. Ninety percent of the policies that have been viaticated to date involved AIDS patients. However, as the population continues to age, a vast market will exist for viatical settlements among the elderly stricken with other terminal or chronic illness. The costs of medical care and nursing home care are skyrocketing. (In the New York area, the cost of nursing home care can exceed $100,000 per year, though the national average is somewhat less.) Viatical settlements can help pay for some of these costs.

The legal professional should be familiar with viatical settlements, as part of financial planning for the elderly.

VIATICAL SETTLEMENTS

The term *viatical* is derived from the Latin word *via*, meaning road or way. A *viaticum* is a supply of money or other necessities for a journey or prayer, which is for someone about to die. Thus, in this discussion, the word viatical relates to those on the road to death.

A **viatical settlement** is the sale of an in-force life insurance policy to a viatical settlement company by the policyholder, also referred to as the insured or the *viator*. The payment to the policyholder is usually in the form of a lump sum representing a certain percentage (40 percent to 80 percent) of the face value of the policy.

Viatical Settlement
Involves the assignment, transfer, or sale of an insurance policy to a viatical settlement company for consideration. The viator is the one who sells the policy. The viatical settlement company is the one that pays the viator for the policy based upon life expectancy.

VIATICAL SETTLEMENTS

HOW THEY OPERATE

A terminally ill patient wishing to **cash in** on a life insurance policy seeks out a viatical settlement company to buy the life insurance policy in return for a lump sum payout. In order to be eligible to participate in a viatical settlement, the viator and the policy must meet certain criteria:

1. The policyholder must be terminally ill with a two-year maximum life expectancy. There may be special circumstances, however, wherein the provider may purchase the policy knowing that the viator may continue to live for a maximum of seven years. This, of course, will reduce the amount of the final payout.
2. The policy must be in full force and effect for at least two years, the usual incontestability period.
3. The face value of the policy must be sufficient to make a viatical settlement profitable for both the viator and the provider.
4. The policy must be assignable—most policies such as whole universal life, term, employee group life and even federal group life are assignable.
5. The policy must be issued by a highly rated insurance company able to pay the death benefit at the appropriate time.
6. The viator must produce releases from the primary and contingent beneficiaries.
7. The viator must permit the release of all medical records to the provider.
8. The viator must complete a viatical underwriting application.

The viator, having met all of the above criteria to the satisfaction of the viatical company, will receive an offer in a short time. If the offer is accepted by the viator, the agreed lump sum payment will be transferred to an independent escrow agent by the viatical company to protect the viator. The viator will simultaneously execute an assignment of the policy to the provider who in turn will present said assignment to the insurance company. The insurance company will then issue an endorsement changing ownership and beneficiary to the viatical company. As soon as the escrow agent is notified that the transfer is complete, the funds will be released to the viator.

At this point the viatical company owns the policy and must continue to pay all future premiums to the life insurance company unless the company has issued a waiver of the premium due to the disability of the insured. Upon the death of the insured, the provider will receive the full proceeds of the death benefit provided for in the policy. However, the provider may resell the policy to an investor to make a quicker profit.

The Offer of Settlement

Due to the increasing use of viatical settlements, the Federal Trade Commission has issued a pamphlet entitled *Viatical Settlements: A Guide for People with Terminal Illness*. It advises terminally ill consumers considering viatical settlements to do the following:

- Contact two or three providers to get offers on your policy. The market is very competitive, so it is wise to shop around.
- Check with state insurance department to see if the provider or brokers must be licensed. If so, check their status. Check also with local Better Business Bureau for any complaints.
- Resist high-pressure tactics. The offer does not have to be accepted. Some states have a 15-day rescission period before the viatical settlement transaction is complete.
- Verify that the investor or the viatical company has money on hand for payout.

- Request that the company set up an escrow account with a reputable financial institution at the beginning of the transaction, so the funds are available to fund the offer.
- Insist on a timely payment. No more than a few months should elapse from the contract to the closing.
- Ask the company about possible tax consequences and the effects of viatical settlements on public assistance benefits, *e.g.*, Medicare, Medicaid.
- Check with the insurance company on the availability of accelerated death benefits.
- Ask about privacy during the transaction.
- Contact a lawyer to check on the possible probate and estate tax considerations.

Elder law legal professionals must keep these considerations in mind when advising clients.

Regulation of Viatical Settlement Companies

Viatical settlement companies are subject to regulation by the insurance departments of each state. About 50 percent of the states have enacted laws to protect consumers against unethical viatical providers. The federal government does not currently regulate the viatical industry. Florida, due to its aging population and its increasing number of AIDS victims, has taken an active role in regulating viatical companies. Check local state insurance departments to see if viatical settlement firms are subject to state regulations.

Tax Implications

The elder law professional should also have a basic understanding of the tax consequences of viatical settlements. Under Internal Revenue Code Section 101(a), amounts received "by reason of death" of the insured are not taxable as income. In Private Letter Ruling 944 3020 (July 22, 1994), however, the IRS concluded that viatical settlements were not payments received "by reason of death" and, therefore, would be subject to income taxation even though the insured was terminally ill. The IRS contended that the assignment to a viatical settlement company is really a sale of property and was a gain to be treated as a capital gain under IRS Section 1001(b) and is taxable. Until 1997, then, the IRS treated all accelerated death benefits as ordinary income and taxed them pursuant to IRS section 72(e).

As of 1997, however, viatical settlements are tax exempt pursuant to HIPAA. Congress passed the Health Insurance Portability and Accountability Act in 1996 (H.R. 3103, Public Law No. 104-191). This law, designed to protect terminally and chronically ill life insurance policyholders, exempts proceeds from viatical settlements and accelerated death benefits from federal income tax. However, with regard to state income tax, the only states to date that treat these proceeds as nontaxable are New York and California. More than likely, other states will follow their lead. (This legislation does not change the **federal estate and gift tax law**. If the insured owned the policy on date of death, the proceeds are includable in his or her gross estate and subject to estate taxation. The transfer of a policy as a gift still has the three-year add-back rule [IRS Section 2035], and the beneficiary does not have to pay income tax on the proceeds.)

The Internal Revenue Code has been amended to add Section 101(g). It excludes from gross taxable income any amounts paid by reason of terminal illness of an insured as a direct result of the sale or assignment of a life insurance policy to a qualified viatical settlement company. The law defines a **qualified viatical settlement company** as a person (or business) that regularly purchases or takes assignments of life insurance contracts on the lives of terminally ill individuals; it is either licensed by the state in which the insured lives (or conducts business) or meets requirements set forth in the **Viatical Settlements Model Act** adopted by the **National Association of Insurance Commissions**.

This law defines **terminal illness** as life expectancy of 24 months or fewer from the date of certification of terminal illness. There is no limit to the amount that can be received tax free by certified terminally ill insured.

Chronically ill insureds are also covered under this sweeping legislation. The proceeds received by a chronically ill insured will also receive tax-free treatment under IRS Section 101(g), with certain restrictions. A chronically ill individual is defined as someone who has been medically certified within the previous 12 months as being unable to perform without assistance at least two activities of daily living (*e.g.,* bathing, eating, toileting, walking, moving from bed to chair, and dressing) for at least 90 days. This will include insureds with Parkinson's disease, Alzheimer's disease, symptomatic AIDS, etc. There is a cap on the total proceeds of a viatical settlement that can receive tax free treatment, either $175 per day (per diem contract) or $63,875 annually (lump sum contract). The legislation provides that the aforesaid amounts will be indexed for inflation. It appears that any excess payment will be subject to income taxation.

This law, effective January 1, 1997, benefits many elderly clients and increases the potential for viatical settlements and accelerated death benefit claims. Terminally ill clients are now able to gain access to tax-free assets not available before the new legislation. These funds can now be used to pay off mortgages, high medical and nursing home bills, and even permit a family to relocate prior to the death of the insured.

This legislation making viatical settlements tax free also helps the viatical industry. Ironically, the development of new drugs, while prolonging the life expectancy of AIDS patients, caused a substantial reduction in profit to the viatical companies. The tax-free status of viatical settlements will allow the industry to market its product to patients with other terminal diseases such as cancer and heart disease as well as chronic illnesses such as Parkinson's and Alzheimer's.

THE ACCELERATED DEATH BENEFIT OPTION

Sometimes it is not necessary to seek out a viatical company because an existing insurance policy may include an accelerated death benefit option. In electing the **Accelerated Death Benefit (ADB)** option, the policyholder approaches the insurance company that originally sold the policy with a requesting to *cash in* on a portion of the death benefits while the policyholder is still alive.

Conditions

1. The ADB option may be a standard benefit or may be purchased as an additional rider.
2. The maximum life expectancy must be one year or less.
3. The average payout is 25 percent to 50 percent of the face value of the policy.
4. The portion of the death benefit that remains in effect is paid to the named beneficiaries upon the death of the insured.

Terminal Illness
Life expectancy of 24 months or fewer.

Chronic Illness
Illness where someone is unable to perform without assistance at least two activities of daily living for at least 90 days.

Accelerated Death Benefit (ADB)
A benefit found in a life insurance policy permitting a terminally ill person to cash in a life insurance policy during lifetime. The amount of the benefit will depend upon the insured's length of illness.

Many life insurance policies contain "waiver of premium clauses" that are activated upon the disability of the insured. It is incumbent upon the elder law office to inform the client of potential rights in connection with this coverage.

Options for Special Situations

Some insurance companies, in response to catastrophic illness needs, are offering nursing home confinement benefits as a provision within their life insurance policies. This permits a terminally ill policyholder who has fewer than six months to live to exercise the accelerated death benefit if the policyholder is permanently confined to, or expects to be confined to, a nursing home.

Federal employees who have purchased federal employee group life insurance may also exercise their ADB option to receive a full or partial lump sum payment, provided that the policyholder is terminally ill and has a documented a life expectancy of nine months or fewer. The payout can be up to 94 percent of the face value of the policy.

The Loan Option

Another option available to a terminally ill policyholder is borrowing the cash surrender value of the policy. The insured immediately receives a lump sum, though the policy still remains in effect. Upon death, the loan plus any accrued but unpaid interest is deducted from the gross death benefit proceeds, and the net proceeds are then paid to the beneficiaries.

REFERENCES

Lyn Asinop. "Tax Change Could Make Life Easier for Chronically Ill." *Wall Street Journal*, August 15, 1996, Section C, p. 1.

Gary J. Casper. "Viatical Settlements: New Tax Free Treatment for 'Cashing Out' Life Insurance Provides Tax and Estate Planning Opportunities," 1997. Washington Counsel, PC.

Michael Cavendish. "Policing Terminal Illness Investing." Florida Bar Journal, Feb. 2000, pp. 10–21.

Gary Chodes, Marilyn Saunders. "Viatical Settlements and the Elderly: An Emerging Market."

David W. Dunlap. "Recalculating Death Benefit Math & AIDS Progress Alters Industry." *New York Times*, July 30, 1996, Section D, p. 1.

Federal Trade Commission. "Viatical Settlements: A Guide for People with Terminal Illness," 1996.

Carolyn T. Gear Forbes. "Cashing in Your Chips." *New York Times,* June 17, 1996, Section D, p. 208.

National Association of Insurance Commissions. Compendium of State Laws Regarding Viatical Settlements.

Jack Taylor. Income Tax Treatments of Accelerated Death Benefits and Viatical Settlement Payments. (IRS Report for Congress) September 14, 1995.

FOR MORE INFORMATION

Affording Care
4293 52nd Street, Unit 4-G
New York, NY 10022–6431

American Council of Life Insurers
1001 Pennsylvania Avenue, N.W.
Washington, D.C. 20004–2599
www.acli.com

Federal Trade Commission, Public Reference
6th & Pennsylvania Avenue, N.W.
Washington, D.C. 20580
http: www.ftc.gov
877 FTC HELP

National Association of Insurance Commissioners
444 North Capitol Street, N.W.
Washington, D.C. 20001
www.naic.org

National Association of People with AIDS
1413 K Street, N.W.
Washington, D.C. 20005
www.napwa.org

National Viatical Association
1200 G Street, N.W., Suite 760
Washington, D.C. 20005

North American Securities Administrators Association
10 G Street, N.E., Suite 710
Washington, D.C. 20002

Viatical Association of America
1200 19th Street, N.W., Suite 300
Washington, D.C. 20036

Your State Attorney General
Office of Consumer Protection
Your State Capital

Your State Insurance Commissioner
Department of Insurance
Your State Capital

REVIEW QUESTIONS AND EXERCISES

1. What is a viatical settlement? How does the viatical settlement operate? What are its benefits and drawbacks?

2. What should the terminally ill person look for when negotiating a viatical settlement? What should the elder law professional advise a client about a viatical settlement?

3. What are the tax implications associated with a viatical settlement? What effect does the Health Insurance Portability and Accountability Act of 1996 have on viatical settlements?

4. What is an accelerated death benefit (ADB)? How does this differ from a viatical settlement? What are the benefits of utilizing an ADB?

5. Discuss the regulation on viatical settlements. Should there be more or less restrictions placed on viatical settlement companies? What are some of the issues that legislatures might need to address?

6. Discuss your opinion of viatical settlements. Is this an effective way for terminally ill patients to cover expenses? Is there an alternative way?

CHAPTER 14
Living Facilities for the Elderly

PREVIEW

The media portrays the "old-aged home" in a very poor light. The retirement home has been viewed as drab, dull, and filled with sick old men and women. However, this view of senior living facilities is not accurate. With older Americans becoming more vital in their later years, new living facilities are being created to address this new lifestyle. This chapter focuses on living facilities for the elderly, discusses in depth independent living facilities, assisted-living facilities, and skilled nursing homes, and explains what the elder law professional should advise clients when choosing where to live out their remaining "golden years."

INTRODUCTION

There is a new, upbeat elderly generation. They are returning to school at 50, starting careers at 60, jogging into their 70s, and playing tennis into their 80s. Florida has 285,000 drivers over the age of 85, and the number is rapidly growing. Seniors are divorcing in their 70s and 80s and remarrying. These vital seniors are scattered throughout the country—the traditional family as we know it has changed in many sectors of American society. Parents have relocated to warmer climates, and children have moved away to enjoy other parts of the country, to marry, or to find employment. Many children can no longer care for their elderly parents, who in the past lived down the street or in neighboring communities. Many parents want to be independent of their children.

Alternative lifestyles have developed to meet the needs of the graying population of the 21st century, serving them in varying degrees:

1. **Independent Living Facilities:** Similar to resort communities, providing maid services, dining rooms, recreational activities, and transportation for the healthy elderly.
2. **Assisted-Living Facilities:** Providing the above services and more, they are attuned to the medical and social needs of their residents who require limited supervision and try to function at their optimum level.
3. **Skilled Nursing Homes:** Providing the highest degree of care for residents who are admitted only when they are seriously ill and in need of skilled nursing care and rehabilitation.

Helping the elderly choose the appropriate lifestyle is a primary role of the elder law attorney and the legal professional staff, who should be familiar with various types of living arrangements and with specific facilities in their area. Because financial considerations play a key factor in the selection of living facilities, the elder law firm staff, familiar with the facilities' specific financial requirements, will be of great assistance in this area. Their expertise in health issues, financial planning, and contract law ensures that the clients will be protected as they make appropriate choices. See the CD-ROM for Checklist for Clients and Their Families When Altering

Independent Living Facility
A residence for the elderly who are healthy. This type of facility is similar to a resort community, often providing maid services, dining rooms, recreational activities, and transportation.

Assisted-Living Facility
A living facility for the elderly who require some assistance, but are not in need of skilled nursing care.

Skilled Nursing Facility (SNF)
Facility providing skilled nursing care, a subacute care facility for patients who do not require hospitalization but who cannot be cared for at home.

Their Living Arrangements. It is advisable for legal professionals to visit all the different types of living facilities in their area so that they can provide firsthand knowledge to their clients.

INDEPENDENT LIVING FACILITIES

Don't be surprised if one day an elderly client informs you that he and his wife have decided to move to an independent living facility in another state. It is happening all over the country. They may own a one-family house, a condo, or a co-op that they find unsuitable because aging often leads to isolation. They find it more difficult to drive, to shop, to clean, to prepare meals daily, to see their friends, or to go to the movies and the theater. They do not wish to become dependent upon their family and friends. They seek desperately to maintain their dignity, self-respect, and independence during these precious years. There are many issues with which elderly Americans and their families will have to cope when this moving process begins. Sometimes the emotional ramifications of relocation create problems that are hard to face and require even more delicate planning than the financial issues.

The housing industry in America has risen to meet the needs of older Americans. Independent living facilities have begun to proliferate throughout our nation, especially in retirement areas such as Florida, California, Texas, and Arizona. They can also be found in many states in the Midwest and Northeast. They allow senior citizens to maintain as independent a lifestyle as they wish in a somewhat protected environment that provides multiple services. In many parts of the country, unused public schools and even parish schools are being transformed into housing for the elderly. Funding for these conversions is made available by the federal Department of Housing and Urban Development. Section 202 of the Federal Housing Act is designed to provide low-cost rental housing for the elderly. To date, more than 300,000 units have been built nationwide.

The prospective resident is usually required to sign two instruments upon entry into the facility: a residency agreement and a lease.

Residency Agreement

Residency Agreement
A legal document prepared by the facility that states in detail the services provided to the resident by the facility.

A **residency agreement** is a legal document prepared by the facility that states in detail the services provided to the resident by the facility. It should be examined carefully to determine whether the services provided are suitable to the needs of the prospective resident. The facility may *not* provide additional health care services if the resident's condition deteriorates and may, in fact, ask the resident to leave. This agreement must be signed by the resident, acknowledging and consenting to the terms therein. The services may include the following:

1. Furnished and unfurnished apartments. Many people bring their own furniture as if they were simply moving to another residence. Others may prefer to rent a furnished apartment. In certain situations, however, where the elderly may have mixed emotions about this new way of life, it is recommended that they bring some of their own furniture or other personal property to ease the transition. For individuals who may have difficulty walking, it is recommended that they request a unit easily accessible to the public areas and to the dining room.
2. Weekly maid service.
3. Dining room service (two to three meals per day). Most facilities provide dietary services by a staff dietitian when requested.
4. Courtesy shuttle to take residents to local shops, movies, museums, banks, doctors, etc.

5. Recreational facilities, including swimming pools, golf courses, shuffleboard, tennis courts, libraries.
6. Organized activities, including lectures, aerobics classes, arts and crafts, outings to theaters, concerts, museums, etc.
7. Emergency response systems in public rooms and every apartment room.
8. Parking facilities for those residents with cars.
9. Full- or part-time registered nurse and/or social worker.
10. Available medical services.

Lease Agreement

Parties

The lessor is the facility, and the lessee is the resident. The lease agreement must state clearly who are the lessees, what is their legal relationship, and who will ultimately be liable to the lessor in the event of a breach of a lease.

- If a husband and wife are the lessees, are they jointly or severally liable?
- If an unmarried couple executes the lease, are they jointly or severally liable?
- If a single individual signs the lease and subsequently marries, must the new spouse sign the lease?
- If multiple occupants are the lessees, are all the current occupants required to sign the lease?

Terms of the Lease

- Is it a month-to-month tenancy? In this type of lease, the lessor or the lessee can terminate the lease on written notice of 30, 60, or 90 days, or whatever is agreed to by both parties.
- Is it a term for a year or more? This lease will automatically expire at the end of the term, unless it is renewed pursuant to the terms of the lease.
- Is it a **life care lease**? Some agreements permit residents to live in the facility for their entire life, no matter what their health condition may be. In exchange for this arrangement, the residents are required to pay an inordinate amount of money up front.
    A life care lease is not recommended where there is a risk that the facility may go out of business, leaving the resident no alternative but to leave. Another scenario is the early death of the resident, who has paid a substantial amount of money in advance and did not live long enough to make ample use of the facility. Refunds to the estate of the resident are not common.

Life Care Lease
A lease allowing the resident to live in the facility for his or her entire life, no matter what his or her health condition may be.

Rent

1. How much is the rent?
2. When is the rent due?
3. Is there a late fee?
4. Is a security deposit required?

5. Is interest paid on security deposit?
6. What are the conditions under which the security deposit will be released to the lessee?
7. Are there any hidden charges?
8. Does the lease require a guarantee by a third party?
9. Is there a provision in the lease prohibiting the assignment of the lease to a third party? (subletting)

Admission Procedures

Medical Model Role
A standard profile into which the resident of the living facility must fit. This condition precedent must be met in order to reside in the facility.

The lease will contain a provision describing the **medical model role** for the residents of the facility. The medical model role is a standard profile into which the resident must fit and is referred to as a **condition precedent** in order to reside in the facility. Most leases contain provisions that the owner of the facility reserves the sole and exclusive right to determine what the criteria shall be concerning the resident's medical suitability. This is standard in every independent living facility lease. The resident must, upon the request of the lessor, submit to a medical examination by a licensed physician, who then files a medical report with the lessor. The lessor, after reviewing the medical report, then determines with absolute discretion the suitability of the resident for occupancy in the facility. The prospective lessee may be excluded for the following reasons:

• The applicant may have early stages of Alzheimer's disease. At a later time the applicant may cause damage to the premises, such as causing floods or fires by forgetting to turn off water taps or appliances. Or the applicant may be a wanderer and may suffer injury or death as a result.

• The applicant may have difficulty ambulating in the not-too-distant future, and wheelchairs are not allowed in the facility's public area. This is not an old-age home, but rather an independent living facility for the well elderly.

• The applicant's medical records may indicate a recent history of behavioral disorders, *e.g.,* acting irrationally on occasion. The landlord is not looking for unnecessary problems or disruption to the other residents.

The individuals who are denied admission to the independent living facility may be more suitable for an assisted-living facility.

Termination of the Lease

1. *Medical.* The independent living facility lease provides provisions under which the lease may be terminated by either party for medical reasons. If the facility determines that the resident is no longer medically suitable, it may terminate the lease by giving the resident written notice and provide ample time to vacate the premises. The resident may also terminate the lease if it can be proved that the resident is medically unsuitable to reside in the facility.

2. *General.* Most leases contain a clause that permits the lessor to terminate the lease arbitrarily with reasonable notice for any reason whatsoever. This arbitrary termination provision in effect gives the facility complete control as to the type of resident it finds most suitable.

   A problem that often confronts the independent living facility occurs when a resident wishes to remain even though not medically suitable as stipulated in the criteria established by the facility. Court decisions tend to favor the facility when they commence an eviction proceeding on these grounds.

3. *Death.* Another problem often arises when one spouse dies. This does not automatically terminate the lease because the spouse occupying the apartment may still be medically suitable to remain as a resident and may be a lessee, having signed the lease.

Do your care for life Care?

LIFE-CARE COMMUNITIES

Life-care communities are springing up all over the United States. Some are privately funded. Others are not-for-profit, funded and operated by charitable foundations and religious groups. In this type of living arrangement, the residents transfer all or a substantial portion of their assets to the life-care community. A resident signs a *life-lease* agreement, permitting the resident to reside there for the rest of his or her life, provided the resident continues to pay the monthly maintenance.

Some life-care agreements provide for the refund of some portion of the initial down payment upon the death of the resident or upon his or her leaving the facility for any other reason. The majority of agreements do not have this provision.

Many life-care communities provide a campus-like setting that includes an independent living facility, an assisted-living facility, and a skilled nursing home. In such a community, the resident can move from one level of care to the next as dictated by his or her health. There is no need for the resident to renegotiate the lease agreement with the life-care community as the resident moves from one facility to another.

The problem with life-care communities is that they could fail, go into bankruptcy, or go out of business, leaving residents homeless and penniless. Another situation that can arise is that the facility may have no available space when the resident is required to go to the next level of care. In that case, the resident will be placed off-campus at another facility. This could create undue hardship for a married couple. Not all states permit life-care communities for this very reason. The states that do permit them have enacted legislation affecting these communities. However, such legislation usually focuses on full disclosure rather than setting up a system providing complete protection for purchasers. Such legislation facilitates, but does not supplant, careful investigation by a potential resident.

> **Life-Care Communities**
> Residential facilities where a resident usually turns over all assets to the facility and it agrees to take care of him or her during the person's entire lifetime regardless of medical or physical conditions. These facilities are composed of independent living facilities, assisted-living facilities, and skilled nursing facilities. The individual starts out at one level and continues until reaching the level of highest care or death.

COLLEGE CAMPUS COMMUNITIES

Colleges and universities are trying to lure their older alumni back to the campus by providing housing facilities for them along with medical care provided by their own medical schools and hospitals. They invite their alumni to partake in the college's intellectual programs and to use their recreational facilities. The colleges and universities have developed financing packages that benefit the college and promote tax savings for the individual.

> **College Campus Communities**
> Living facilities for the elderly established by colleges and universities for their older alumni.

ASSISTED-LIVING FACILITIES

The long-term care industry is undergoing dramatic changes. Assisted-living housing is being constructed in every state and is a booming area. It is the fastest growing type of housing for elders and is increasing at the rate of approximately 20 percent per year. Older Americans who do not wish to live alone are selling their homes, vacating their apartments, and moving into the safety and security of assisted living. These residents can no longer manage their activities of daily living by themselves, but are not ill enough to require the skilled intensive care provided by a nursing home. This type of living arrangement is a hybrid, a cross between an independent living facility and a skilled nursing home. There are over one million residents now residing in assisted-living facilities. In 2001, the industry received more than $20 billion in revenue.

Residential Agreement

The assisted-living facility uses primarily a residential agreement that is similar to a lease, but is not a true lease. The terms of the residential agreement are similar to those of an independent living facility, the main differences pertain to admission and discharge procedures. Many residential agreements are vague, incomplete, and misleading. The prospective residents are not given ample time to study the document. Elder law attorneys should advise their clients not to sign any agreements before they seek the advice of competent counsel.

Admission

Admission to the assisted-living facility is based solely upon the medical condition of the prospective resident. These facilities are not designed to house people with catastrophic illness, contagious diseases, or substance abuse problems. They will automatically exclude potential residents who exhibit destructive behaviors that will endanger other residents of the facility. Prior to admission, a medical report must be submitted, along with a list of the prescribed medication that the potential resident is taking. The facility may also require a medical examination by an in-house physician or nurse prior to admission.

Discharge

The facility may establish its own procedures for discharging a resident. It has broad latitude in this area. Sometimes the family of a resident will protest a discharge and file litigation against the facility, but recent cases indicate that the facility will prevail because of its overriding interest to protect the other residents. The usual conditions for discharge are:

- The resident's condition has deteriorated, requiring a higher level of care that can only be provided by a skilled nursing home.
- The patient is disruptive and is in danger of harming himself/herself or other residents.
- The patient becomes nonambulatory and bedridden.

Services Provided by the Assisted-Living Facility

Services provided are similar to those of the independent living facility: Residents live in private or semi-private rooms, and meals are provided. Assistance in dressing, bathing, taking medications, and other activities of daily living is also provided to the residents. The assisted-living facility staff supplies these services and supervises the dispensing of medication.

Appropriate cultural and recreational programs, as well as transportation into the community, are provided.

Living Accommodations

One- to two-bedroom furnished or unfurnished units are usually offered.

Cost

The average cost is $2,000 per month. In the New York area, the average is $3,000 to $5,500, depending upon the amenities provided. Residents pay privately unless they are covered under a long-term care insurance policy. So far 39 states have received permission from the federal government to transfer some of their Medicaid funds from nursing homes to assisted-living facilities. The only states that have not been approved are Alabama, California, Kentucky, Mississippi, Ohio, Oklahoma, Pennsylvania, Tennessee, Utah, West Virginia, and Wyoming. Oregon was the first state to use Medicaid funding to pay for long-term care residents in assisted-living facilities as an alternative to skilled nursing facilities. States that use Medicaid funds for assisted living save because the cost of housing in an assisted-living facility is significantly less than in a skilled nursing facility.

The facility may provide certain ancillary services during the day, such as health care aides to assist residents in dressing, going to the dining room, and other activities of daily living. The facility may also provide an in-house bank where funds can be deposited up to a usual amount of $500, which can be withdrawn for incidentals such as going to the barber or to the movies, ordering outside meals, newspapers, etc.

Regulation

Currently there is no federal or state regulation of the assisted-living industry. Several states have investigated the possibility of passing regulatory legislation. The elder law professional should refer to a local state legislator for more information.

NURSING HOMES

In March 2001, the Centers For Disease Control and Prevention released a report entitled *The Changing Profile of Nursing Home Residents: 1985–1997*. The report examined America's nursing home residents and how they have changed over the period 1985–97. The report came to the following conclusions:

1. In 1997, more than one-half of elderly nursing home residents were 85 years of age or older, compared with only 45 percent in 1985.
2. Female nursing home residents outnumber male residents 3 to 1.
3. About 58 percent of nursing home residents in 1997 were admitted directly from a hospital or different nursing home, and about 33 percent came from private homes. The vast majority of admissions were widowed.

4. Circulatory diseases and cognitive and mental disorders were the most common admission diagnoses in both 1985 and 1997. Cognitive impairment, incontinence, and functional decline were strong contributing factors to nursing home admissions.

5. Admissions to nursing homes between 1985 and 1997 indicated a dramatic increase in the level of disability of the residents. More residents needed help with the activities of daily living (ADLs) such as bathing, dressing, eating, transferring from bed to a chair, toileting, and walking.

6. The demand for nursing home and health care services will increase as baby boomers age. In 2030, approximately 70 million Americans will be 65 years of age and older, and approximately 8.5 million will be 85 years of age and older.

7. The report concludes that informal, unpaid caregivers such as spouses, children, other relatives, and friends will provide for the majority of daily care for older Americans. Programs must be developed to alleviate *caregiver burnout*.

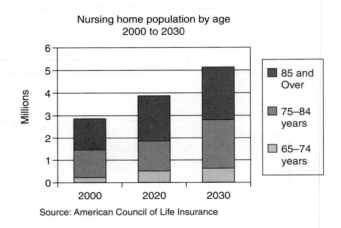

Nursing home population by age
2000 to 2030

Source: American Council of Life Insurance

SKILLED NURSING FACILITY (SNF)

The skilled nursing facility of today is not an *old age home* in the traditional meaning. Rather, it is a subacute care hospital for seriously and chronically ill patients who require the services of skilled health care professionals on a 24-hour-per-day basis. It also provides custodial care for patients suffering from Alzheimer's, Parkinson's, or senile dementia, who cannot easily remain at home or in another type of facility. The skilled nursing facility may be very large, accommodating hundreds of patients, or quite small, serving fewer than 100 patients. It may accept patients with a variety of medical problems, or it may be specifically oriented to patients with illnesses such as Alzheimer's or patients who are ventilator-dependent. There are basically two kinds of nursing facilities—rehabilitation and extended care:

Rehabilitation Facility
A skilled nursing facility that provides short-term, intensive rehabilitation services to patients who have recently suffered a stroke or other injuries.

1. *Rehabilitation Facility:* The mission of the **rehabilitation facility** is to provide intensive rehabilitation services, including, but not limited to, physical, occupational, and speech therapy. The typical patient has been released from a hospital after suffering a stroke or injuries, most commonly resulting from a fall. The object is to restore the vital functions and daily activity skills of the patient to such an extent that the patient can return home. The average length of stay is 100 days, and the coverage is provided by Medicare. If after 100 days the patient still requires rehabilitation services, the patient will then be transferred to an extended care facility.

2. *Extended Care Facility:* The **extended care facility** provides nursing care services until the patient recovers sufficiently to return to the community or dies.

Selecting a Nursing Home

Patients enter a skilled nursing facility when they are no longer able to function in their homes without skilled nursing care or when they are discharged from a hospital as a result of a severe illness. The majority of patients, once they enter the extended care facility, never return to their homes.

Declining Standards of Care

When considering placing a loved one into skilled nursing facility, a person must be cognizant of the findings issued in a report by the U.S. Department of Health and Human Services (2002).

1. Most of America's 17,000 nursing homes have inadequate staffing to care for their residents properly. The annual staff turnover in nursing homes has been estimated to be as high as 100 percent.
2. The nation's 1.6 million nursing home residents are being exposed to a significant increase in serious health problems, *i.e.,* bedsores, blood-borne infections, malnutrition, dehydration, and pneumonia.
3. There is minimal federal oversight of the nursing home industry.

Cost

There are a number of options for paying for a nursing home that could cost from $75 to $350 a day:

- Private pay
- Under certain conditions, Medicare will pay for the first 100 days. Medicare will pay 100 percent for the first 20 days of rehabilitation and requires a copayment of $109.50 (in 2004) per day from days 21–100.
- Medicaid—if the patient is impoverished
- Long-term care insurance
- V.A. benefits—if available at all, usually for a limited time, but in a few situations unlimited.
- Health insurance sometimes supplements Medicare benefits and occasionally pays for a few months to a year of nursing home services.

Location

Location is a prime consideration in the selection of a skilled nursing facility. The facility should be situated close to the homes of family members so that they can make regular visits without inconvenience and can monitor the care of the patient. The more the family becomes involved, the less likelihood there will be for patient *neglect and abuse.*

Other Factors to Consider

- Presence of the odor of urine. *This is an overt warning that the patients may not be well cared for and that this facility should not be considered.*
- Ambiance. Is the environment cheerful or institutional? Are the premises well lit, well ventilated and does it appear to be clean? *Hint: Step into the men's or ladies' room for a further look.*
- Reception by a staff member upon entering the facility.
- Behavior of residents. Are residents sitting in their wheelchairs staring into space, or do they seem to be involved in some activity? Families should be aware of the fact that nursing homes have been accused of warehousing the residents for whom they are supposed to be caring.
- Dining room. Is it pleasant? Are the patients feeding themselves? Are there patients who have difficulty feeding themselves? Are those who cannot express what they would like to eat, *e.g.,* stroke patients, being assisted and attended to? Does the weekly menu seem healthy and appealing? *Hint: Eat a meal there. See for yourself.*
- Presence of strength training programs; occupational, physical, and speech therapy.
- Visiting hours. Are they convenient? Can children visit elderly relatives?
- Telephone calls. Are they permitted?
- Suitable recreational activities and programs.
- Frequency of bathing. Does this meet the family's standard?
- Hiring of personal health care aides acceptable if the patient requires additional care or if the family so desires.
- Medication Policies. Do the patients appear to be overmedicated? It is not uncommon for nursing facilities to overmedicate patients to keep them under control.
- Use of physical restraints. This may be another warning sign that the facility is not appropriate.
- Facility's policy concerning the use of psychotropic drugs, *e.g.,* Haldol®, Prozac®. What is the facility's policy concerning chemical restraints?
- Availability of private and semiprivate rooms. Are there two or four people in a room? Are there private bathrooms or adjoining bathrooms?
- Security. Can a resident wander out?
- Adequate equipment—emergency help buttons, handrails in shower stalls, and other protective measures for the elderly.
- Are services sufficient for the client for the foreseeable future.

Ombudsman Program
A federal program administered by each state's office on aging that accepts complaints involving nursing home neglect and abuse. An ombudsman investigates these claims and reports on them to the proper authorities.

If the superficial examination of the facility, taking the above factors into consideration, is positive, then the following should be done by the client:

- Review the annual state inspection report of the facility, which by law in some states must be displayed in a visible place or be available upon inquiry. Also review all complaint investigation reports for the last year and determine what, if any, regulatory actions may have taken place.
- Contact the local ombudsman. Inquire if there have been any complaints against the facility and the nature of these complaints.
- Check with the Better Business Bureau and the state Medicaid agency for the same purpose.

- Contact the facility's residents or families' committee. (This is a committee or council made up of the residents' family members.) They are a good firsthand source of information about the facility and how the residents there are treated.
- Check out the facility with a social worker, physician, or family member of a current resident.
- Determine who owns the facility and whether the facility has changed hands recently. What is the reputation of the owner? Who is really in charge?
- Inquire into the experience and reputations of the administrator and director of nursing. Meet with them, if possible, after gathering information and preparing questions. Make inquiries as to their hiring policies. Check if it is the policy to do background checks on prospective employees. Recent studies have revealed that the nursing home industry employs many persons with criminal records and does not do pre-employment screening.

The Nursing Home Contract

A nursing home contract is a legally enforceable contract that is usually executed by a family member or by the resident, if the resident has the ability to do so. Because this contract is such an important document, an elder law attorney should review it along with the entire admission package. That attorney may give advice regarding making certain amendments to the standard preprinted contract provided by the nursing home. It is important to carefully scrutinize all terms of the contract prior to execution.

Signing of the Contract

If someone other than the resident executes the contract, make absolutely certain that person will in no way be held personally liable for the charges incurred by the resident. It should be clearly spelled out in the contract that only the resident and the resident's assets will be held liable, even if another person, called *the sponsor,* has signed the nursing home contract. (Prior to the signing of the nursing home admission's contract, the resident or sponsor will have been required to complete a financial questionnaire.) Remember that nursing homes are usually for-profit organizations, in business for themselves and not for the resident. Therefore, the client should not reveal any more financial information than is absolutely necessary. What the facility is actually seeking in many cases is a guarantee of the ability to pay privately for at least six months to a year.

The Daily Rate Payable Monthly

The agreement should state what the daily rate is, and the facility's policy regarding change of daily rate, *e.g.,* notice, percentage of increase, frequency of rate change. Inquire when the last rate change went into effect.

Security Deposit

1. Amount
2. Refundable
3. Interest paid on the security deposit

Most nursing homes require two months' security and one month's room and board to be paid upon admission. Any payments demanded in excess of this amount should be questioned. Most states prohibit additional financial demands by long-term care facilities.

Refund Policy

What is the refund policy? If the contract is terminated by death before the end of the month, are charges prorated and a refund issued to the patient's estate? If the patient desires to leave the facility permanently for any reason before the end of the month, how much notice is required? Is the patient entitled to a refund?

Bed-Hold Policy

Bed-Hold Agreement
An agreement between a patient and a skilled nursing facility that preserves the patient's right to return to the same nursing home after a temporary hospitalization.

If a private pay, nursing home patient requires hospitalization and has to leave the facility temporarily, the patient continues to be responsible for the daily nursing home charges during the period of hospitalization, provided the patient or family has signed a **bed-hold** agreement. In this situation, the nursing home facility will hold the bed until the patient returns. If no bed-hold agreement has been signed, the nursing home may not charge for the period the patient remains out of the facility. However, if the patient is ready to return and there are no beds available, placement must be made at another facility. The bed-hold agreement preserves the patient's right to return to the same nursing home.

If the patient is on Medicaid, the Medicaid local agency in some states will pick up the patient's nursing home charges for a period usually not exceeding 15 days. An additional five-day bed-hold can be obtained upon request of the hospital physician in charge of the patient's care.

If the Medicaid patient remains hospitalized for longer than 15 days or if a state's Medicaid program does not pay for bed-hold, the patient's family should be advised that if they want to be sure the patient can return to the same facility, they must pay privately for the bed-hold during the patient's stay in the hospital after the Medicaid bed-hold payment ceases. If the family chooses not to do this, they should be aware that the nursing home is not required to hold the bed for longer than a specified period (20 days in New York and other lengths of time in other states). There is a risk that a bed will not be available when the patient is ready to be discharged from the hospital. In the event this occurs, the patient will be discharged to another nursing home. However, when a bed becomes available at the original nursing home, the patient is entitled to such bed. This should be made clear in the bed-hold clause of the contract.

Change in Source of Funding

If a patient on private pay has exhausted all funds and is picked up by Medicaid, will the patient have to leave the facility? If the patient is allowed to remain in the facility under the circumstances, will the services remain the same?

Federal law requires that a patient cannot be discharged from a facility simply because of a change in financial status from private pay to public assistance. However, if the patient is in a private room, the patient is required to transfer to the next available semi-private room. All other services should remain the same. However, some states allow nursing homes to designate only limited numbers of Medicaid beds, which permits the facility to discharge patients who run out of money if a Medicaid bed is unavailable. Although common in some states, this practice probably violates federal law. This policy should be clearly stated in the nursing home contract.

Discharge Policy

The facility has the right to discharge patients under the following circumstances:

1. Failure to pay the monthly charges.
2. Disruptive or abusive behavior, endangering themselves or other residents.
3. Medical reasons, *e.g.,* patient becomes too ill to be treated in the facility or no longer needs skilled care.

Policy Regarding Living Wills and Do-Not-Resuscitate Orders

If a patient has expressed how he or she wishes to be treated under certain circumstances involving terminal illness, it is important to know beforehand if the nursing home facility will enforce a living will or a do-not-resuscitate order.

Patient-Resident's Bill of Rights

Obtain a copy of the **Patient-Resident's Bill of Rights**. Each nursing home must provide a statement of the patient's rights while in the facility. See the CD-ROM for the statutory form of a Patient's Bill of Rights commonly used in nursing homes.

REFERENCES

SKILLED NURSING HOMES
Sahyoun N. R., Pratt L. A., Lentzer H., Dey, A., and Robinson, K. N. *The Changing Profile of Nursing Home Residents: 1985–1997. Aging Trends*, No. 4. Hyattsville, Md.: National Center for Health Statistics, a subdivision of the Center of Disease Control, 2001.

ASSISTED-LIVING FACILITIES
Assisted-Living Federation of America
10300 Eaton Place, Suite 400
Fairfax, VA 22030
http://www.alfa.org

American Association of Homes and Services for the Aging
901 E Street, N.W.
Washington, D.C. 20004
http://www.aahsa.org/public/consumer.htm

REVIEW QUESTIONS AND EXERCISES

1. What is an independent living facility? What are its advantages and disadvantages?
2. When a client is considering moving to an independent living facility, what advice should the elder law professional give to the elderly client?
3. What is a life-care community? What are its advantages and disadvantages?
4. What is an assisted-living facility? What are its advantages and disadvantages?
5. How have nursing homes changed since 1985? How will nursing homes continue to change in the coming years?
6. What is a skilled nursing facility? What are its advantages and disadvantages?
7. What is the difference between a rehabilitation facility and an extended care facility?
8. When a client needs to enter a skilled nursing facility, what advice should the elder law professional give to the elderly client?
9. Of what should a client be aware when placing a family member or friend in a skilled nursing facility?

An independent living facility is a resident for the elderly who are healthy.

CHAPTER 15

Elder Abuse

PREVIEW

Unfortunately, elder abuse is on the rise in America. This increase is directly related to the growing number of elders in our society. The incidence of elder abuse will become more prevalent in the coming decades. Millions of men and women over 65 have been subject to one form or another of elder abuse. Among the elderly population, the incidence of abuse occurs at all economic levels and in all age groups. This chapter explores the different forms of elder abuse and their indicators. The forms of abuse discussed include physical abuse, psychological abuse, passive and active neglect, self-neglect, emotional, abandonment, caregiver abuse, marital abuse, sexual abuse, and financial abuse.

INTENTIONAL OR UNINTENTIONAL ELDER ABUSE

The elderly, often frail and unable to defend themselves, are easy targets—on the streets, in their own homes, in nursing homes, and in hospitals. On the streets, it is very easy for thieves to snatch their handbags, wallets, and jewelry and then run away—or to follow them into their homes, taking their valuables and sometimes their lives. In their own homes, in nursing homes, or in hospitals their personal possessions may be stolen by health care aides. Equally distressing is the verbal and physical abuse that these aides often inflict upon the elderly if they demand too much, complain, soil themselves, or are simply uncooperative.

The harm immediate family members inflict upon their elderly parents may be the most devastating. It could be subtle, as in **undue influence,** or it can take the form of physical violence. It can be intentional, unintentional, or the result of neglect. Technically, abuse and neglect are distinct. Children could slowly steal their parents' assets under the guise of a power of attorney or try to confine a parent to a facility against the parent's wishes when he or she does not really belong there. Sometimes a neighbor will befriend an elderly person, hoping to gain his or her confidence and be named as an agent in his or her power of attorney, enabling the neighbor to misappropriate the person's assets during his or her lifetime, or to be named a principal beneficiary of the estate upon his or her death. The abuse takes many forms, but the results are the same: The elderly suffer, and in the end, society also suffers because it has failed to protect its more vulnerable members.

Spousal abuse and partner abuse is also prevalent among elderly men and women. Elderly wives are often severely abused by their spouses. Elderly husbands are quite often the subjects of abuse by their spouses. This could occur as a form of retaliation for prior mistreatment by a spouse, as self-defense, or for many other reasons, such as frustration over loss of abilities and feelings of helplessness. The results are the same. The risk factor of abuse and neglect increases significantly in close living arrangements between the victim and the

Undue Influence
The improper use of power or trust in a way that deprives a person of free will and substitutes another's objectives.

abuser. This type of abuse is also classified as domestic violence and is subject to prosecution under those state laws.

Forms of Elder Abuse
- Physical abuse
- Neglect—passive and active
- Self-neglect
- Psychological—emotional abuse
- Abandonment
- Caregiver abuse
- Marital abuse
- Sexual abuse
- Financial abuse

In June 2002, congressional hearings were held to investigate elder abuse. It concluded that the public is not fully aware of this problem or the societal need to correct it. It is critical to our national interest that more attention is focused on this growing epidemic. Elder abuse frequently takes place in the 17,000 nursing homes in the United States. Currently, there are approximately 1.6 million persons residing in these facilities, and hundreds of thousands of occupants in assisted-living facilities. These individuals, due to their frail health, are often the targets of abusers, with most incidents going unreported. Detection, reporting, and prevention are the key issues. A federal investigation of the nursing home industry must be started to prevent further abuses.

Federal legislation and funding of local adult protection service agencies is also necessary to begin to deal with this enormous problem. Currently, the Elder Justice Act is being considered by Congress. All 50 states have enacted some form of elder abuse legislation. Considerable variation exists from one state to another as to the reporting requirements and criminal sanctions to be imposed on violators. The federal government must establish an agency to coordinate local, state, and federal efforts on this front. Federal criminal legislation must be enacted to punish those who mistreat the elderly.

Until now, the federal government has done little. It first ventured into the field of elder abuse in 1987. That was the year that Congress passed amendments to the Older Americans Act. The act provided statutory definitions of elder abuse and exploitation of the elderly population. These are only guidelines for identifying the problem; the federal government was not yet concerned with enforcement and prosecution.

In order to more effectively serve the elderly clients and their families, it is important for the elder law professional to understand the nature of this growing problem. We must be aware and sensitive to the needs of our clients in this critical time in their lives. The following discussion will focus on the types of elder abuse, how to detect its existence, how it affects the client, and what the obligations of the legal professional are in reporting incidents of elder abuse.

Causes

Elder abuse can occur in a domestic or an institutional setting. If it takes place within the family, it is considered a form of domestic violence. There are many causes for the maltreatment of defenseless elderly. Elder abuse is a complex combination of social, psychological, and economic factors fusing the psychopathology of the abuser with the deteriorating physical and mental status of the abused.

1. Many abusers have serious psychiatric disorders and have often been hospitalized for schizophrenia and other forms of psychoses. They are often abusers of drugs and alcohol.

2. Stress caused by financial problems is a common factor. Many abusers are financially dependent upon their victims for money and housing. There is a greater risk of violence in situations where the abuser lives with the victim, *e.g.,* adult children living with the elder parent.

3. Dysfunctional families have an increased risk of elder abuse.

4. Caregivers' stress is a significant causal factor. The extreme frustration that can result from caring for an elderly spouse or parent is often expressed in acts of violence, neglect, or abandonment. The majority of reported elder abuse cases indicate that the perpetrators are family members who reside with the victim and are in a caregiving role.

5. Elderly persons suffering from dementia, disruptive behavioral patterns, or impaired cognitive ability are at an increased risk of abuse.

6. Transgenerational violence is a factor. Studies indicate that a cycle of domestic violence exists. Violent behavior and anger are learned responses, often expressed in responding to difficult and stressful life situations. This behavioral pattern can be passed on from one generation to the next.

Physical Abuse

Physical abuse is the intentional infliction of pain or injury upon an elderly person by one who is directly responsible for the care and custody of the victim. Physical abuse can also be inflicted by a person who is in a position of trust in relation to the care of an individual. Common types of abuse are random acts of violence, direct beatings, hitting (with or without an object), pushing, shoving, shaking, slapping, kicking, pinching, burning, unreasonable physical restraint, inappropriate use of drugs, force feeding, and prolonged deprivation of food and water.

Physical Abuse (of the Elderly)
The intentional infliction of pain or injury upon an elderly person by one who is directly responsible for the care and custody of the victim.

SCENARIO

A family member strikes an elderly relative out of frustration when the relative fails to carry out certain ordinary functions, e.g., *spilling food, becoming incontinent, or forgetting to do certain things. The law treats this act of violence as an assault.*

Indicators of Physical Elder Abuse

- Wounds, cuts, abrasions, discoloration of the skin, black and blue marks, bruises, welts, rope burns, punctures, sprains, fractures, dislocation of joints, or paralysis
- Physical restraint or confinement, *e.g.,* rope burns; missing hearing aids, eyeglasses, dentures, or prostheses
- Unexplained or unexpected deterioration of health, *e.g.,* injuries for which there appears to be no rational explanation
- Malnutrition or dehydration without apparent illness-related causes
- Weight loss
- Inappropriate use of medication, *e.g.,* overdose of drugs resulting in emergency room treatment

- Burn marks that could have been caused by cigarettes, lye, acids, or friction from the elder being tied or chained to a chair, bed, or post
- Hair loss due to pulling
- Unexplained venereal disease and unusual urinary or genital infections
- Evidence of poor skin condition such as untreated bedsores
- Soiled clothing or bed linen

Psychological-Emotional Abuse

Emotional Abuse (of the Elderly)
The willful infliction of mental pain and suffering upon an elderly person by an individual in a position of trust.

Emotional abuse is the willful infliction of mental pain and suffering upon an elderly person by an individual in a position of trust, *e.g.,* threats, implanting fear, isolation, humiliation, or intimidation. This could also occur in the form of giving harsh orders to an elderly family member or by not including the elderly in certain decision-making processes involving their own well-being. **Infantilism** is a common form of psychological abuse of the elderly. The victim is treated like a child and is forced to accept a dependent role in the relationship, thereby essentially giving up control of his or her own life.

Infantilism
A common form of psychological abuse whereby the victim is treated like a child and forced to accept a dependent role in the relationship.

Indicators of Psychological Elder Abuse

Stress

- Agitation
- Ambivalence
- Anger
- Denial
- Depression
- Disorientation and marked confusion
- Excessive fears
- Helplessness
- Hesitation to converse openly
- Insomnia
- Marked change in appetite
- Low self-esteem
- Sleep deprivation
- Unexplained paranoia
- Unusual weight gain or loss
- Withdrawal

Neglect

duty
Care actual damage

Neglect (of the Elderly)
The lack of care provided by a person responsible for the care or custody of an elderly person.

Neglect is a lack of care by a person responsible for the care or custody of an elderly person, whether willful or not. Failure to assist in personal hygiene or failure to provide proper clothing, medical care, mental health, and dental treatment constitutes neglect. Lack of protection from ordinary health and safety perils is also evidence of neglect.

Self-Neglect or Self-Abuse

Not all elder abuse is by others. Self-neglect is the most common form of maltreatment among the elderly population. This form of abuse is evidenced by the neglect an elderly person inflicts upon his or her own health, personal hygiene, safety, and financial affairs. The misuse of prescription drugs, alcohol, or other substances is also considered self-neglect.

Indicators of Self-Neglect or Abuse

- Lack of ability or consistent failure to properly manage finances, *e.g.,* failure to deposit checks, pay bills, or answer correspondence
- Dissipation of assets, giving funds or other assets away to family, friends, and strangers
- Attempted suicide
- Wandering about the neighborhood appearing confused and improperly clothed
- Refusing necessary medical and dental treatment
- Substance abuse and overdose of medications
- Inability to manage the activities of daily living, *e.g.,* eating, shopping, preparation of meals, housework, and personal hygiene
- Hoarding food
- Lack of proper toilet facilities
- Inoperable heating, air-conditioning, and electrical systems
- Residence infested with animals
- Living in isolation, not permitting anyone to enter his or her residence.
- Changes in the ability to communicate, *e.g.,* inappropriate responses, refusal to respond, disorientation as to time and place, confusion, short-term memory loss, and incoherence
- Urine or fecal odor, rashes, boils, sores, malnutrition, and dehydration

Caregiver Abuse-Neglect

Caregiver abuse-neglect is abuse or neglect that occurs when a caregiver abuses or neglects to give reasonable and proper care to the elderly person in his or her charge. The neglect can take place at home, in a hospital, in a nursing home, in an assisted-living facility, or anywhere the elderly reside. If the aide accompanies an elderly client to an appointment at the elder law office and insists upon being present during the consultation, the legal professional should be aware of the possibility of caregiver abuse. Home visits are often a required part of the practice of elder law. It is important to be cognizant of living conditions of the elderly client. Is there any evidence of caregiver abuse?

Caregiver Abuse-Neglect
Abuse or neglect that occurs when a caregiver abuses or neglects to give reasonable and proper care to the elderly person in his or her charge.

Its Indicators

In addition to the physical and psychological abuse indicators discussed above, other indicators include:

- Inadequate clothing
- Malnutrition

- Dehydration
- Untreated rashes and bed sores
- Unexplained black and blue marks
- Lice and fleas present on the body
- The elderly person is prevented from seeing an elder care attorney or speaking for himself or herself during a consultation without the caregiver being present
- Improper expression of affection by the caregiver
- Inappropriate sexual relationship with the caregiver
- Isolation from family and friends
- Not being able to answer the telephone without the caregiver being present
- Inappropriate behavior by the caregiver towards the elderly victim, *e.g.,* aggressiveness, threats, harassments, insults, etc.
- Caregiver, family, and the elderly victim provide conflicting accounts of an incident in which the elderly person was injured
- Prevention or obstruction of the observance of religious holidays, dietary restrictions, and meetings with clergy

MACK V. SOUNG

95 Cal.Rptr.2d 830 (Cal.App. 3 Dist., 2000)

Callahan, J.

This case presents the question of whether plaintiffs, the surviving children of Girtha Mack, can state a cause of action against her former physician for either violation of the Elder Abuse and Dependent Adult Civil Protection Act ("the Elder Abuse Act" or "the Act," Welf. & Inst.Code, § 15600 *et seq.*), or for intentional infliction of emotional distress. The trial court sustained demurrers to both causes of action without leave to amend.

ELDER ABUSE (THIRD AMENDED COMPLAINT)

Plaintiffs are the children of decedent Girtha Mack, who passed away on October 13, 1996. Defendant Soung is a licensed medical practitioner who attended to Girtha during her final days, during which she resided at Covenant Care Nursing and Rehabilitation Center (Covenant). Both Dr. Soung and Covenant were health care providers within the meaning of the Elder Abuse Act.

Despite assurances by Covenant to plaintiffs that steps were being taken to prevent their mother from getting bedsores, in August 1996 (all further calendar references are to that year) Girtha was left in a bedpan for 13 consecutive hours, with the result that she developed an untreatable stage III bedsore. Covenant and Dr. Soung concealed the existence of the bedsore until September 4, and Covenant's employees refused to permit plaintiffs to inspect the injury until an ombudsman intervened on their behalf on September 10.

Knowing that Girtha's mental faculties were deteriorating, Dr. Soung entered into a consultative relationship with plaintiffs regarding her care and treatment. Dr. Soung not only concealed Girtha's injury but he also consistently opposed Girtha's hospitalization in

September and October, representing that Covenant's care was "appropriate." When her condition worsened in October, Dr. Soung abruptly abandoned Girtha as her physician without further notice and refused to respond to repeated requests by Covenant's staff to permit Girtha's hospitalization, thereby endangering her health. His actions were "reckless." Girtha died on October 13, a few days after Dr. Soung gave written notice of his withdrawal as her physician.

INTENTIONAL INFLICTION (FIFTH AMENDED COMPLAINT)

The fifth amended complaint expanded on the allegations set forth above. It noted that Dr. Soung had a high volume geriatric practice with many patients from long-term care facilities. On September 8, despite having received a message that Girtha has sustained a stage III bedpan injury, Dr. Soung conducted a monthly exam and wrote that she had "not much change in condition" without mentioning the bedsore. Dr. Soung was aware Girtha had a preference for medical intervention unless she was permanently comatose. On September 18, over the objection of Dr. Soung but consistent with Girtha's wishes, Girtha was admitted to the hospital for treatment of her injury; she was readmitted to Covenant on September 23, by which time Dr. Soung noted she was unable to understand her condition.

As Girtha's communicativeness waned, Dr. Soung spoke increasingly to plaintiffs about her care, thereby entering into a consultative relationship with them. On September 3 and 10, the doctor was called to testify at an administrative hearing to revoke the license of a nursing care home, based on the same issues that had arisen between Covenant and Girtha. He also learned the Department of Health Services was investigating the treatment that led to Girtha's bedpan injury. Consequently, Dr. Soung became openly hostile to plaintiffs, whom he viewed as "troublemakers."

On October 8, Dr. Soung mailed a notice of withdrawal of care to Girtha's former address. Though he knew plaintiffs were capable of making surrogate decisions for her care, he failed to contact them. On October 9, he advised plaintiff Sylvester Mack that he would withdraw in 30 days unless plaintiffs found another physician earlier. At that time he had examined Girtha and found that she had a large swelling on the side of her face. On October 11, plaintiffs were advised by nurses at Covenant that Girtha was dying, but that Dr. Soung refused to permit her hospitalization. Since Dr. Soung's authority was essential to transfer Girtha to the hospital, plaintiffs were forced to remove Girtha's wristband and tell the emergency room staff that she had no primary physician, in order to secure Girtha's admission to the hospital. Dr. Soung's "wilful and abrupt abandonment" of Girtha with "no warning" was "despicable and malicious, and with conscious disregard for the rights and feelings of [Girtha] and her family." As a result of Dr. Soung's actions, plaintiffs were "shocked and humiliated," causing them to suffer "serious distress."

I

THE ELDER ABUSE CAUSE OF ACTION

Plaintiffs contend the trial court abused its discretion in sustaining Dr. Soung's demurrer to the elder abuse cause of action without leave to amend. As amended in 1991, the Elder Abuse Act was designed to protect elderly and dependent persons from abuse, neglect, or abandonment. (§ 15600; see *ARA Living Centers-Pacific, Inc. v. Superior Court* (1993) 18

Cal.App.4th 1556, 1559, 23 Cal.Rptr.2d 224.) In addition to adopting measures designed to encourage reporting of abuse and neglect (§ 15630 et seq.), the Act authorizes the court to award attorney fees to the prevailing plaintiffs and allows survivors to recover pain and suffering damages in cases of intentional and reckless abuse where the elder has died. (§ 15657; see *Delaney v. Baker* (1999) 20 Cal.4th 23, 33, 82 Cal.Rptr.2d 610, 971 P.2d 986.)

In order to be entitled to these heightened remedies, section 15657 provides that the plaintiff must establish "recklessness, oppression, fraud, or malice in the commission of this abuse" by "clear and convincing evidence." "'Recklessness' refers to a subjective state of culpability greater than simple negligence, which has been described as a 'deliberate disregard' of the 'high degree of probability' that an injury will occur [citations] [.] Recklessness, unlike negligence, involves more than 'inadvertence, incompetence, unskillfulness, or a failure to take precautions' but rather rises to the level of a 'conscious choice of a course of action . . . with knowledge of the serious danger to others involved in it.' [Citation.]" (*Delaney*, supra, 20 Cal.4th at pp. 31–32, 82 Cal.Rptr.2d 610, 971 P.2d 986.)

A liberal construction of the pleading discloses the following salient facts: (1) Girtha developed a serious untreatable bedsore injury in August 1996 while she was housed at Covenant and Dr. Soung was her attending physician; (2) Covenant, with assistance from Dr. Soung, covered up and concealed the existence of the bedsore until intervention by a county ombudsman finally compelled Covenant to reveal the injury to plaintiffs; (3) over Dr. Soung's objection, Girtha was hospitalized for three days for treatment of the injury and then returned to Covenant; (4) Dr. Soung subsequently became aware of Girtha's inability to communicate and turned to plaintiffs for consultation regarding her care and treatment; (5) as Girtha's conditioned worsened, plaintiffs expressed the desire that she be transferred to a hospital, which was consistent with her wishes; Dr. Soung responded by criticizing the power of attorney by which Girtha gave plaintiffs decisionmaking authority over her treatment and opposed hospitalization; and (6) when Girtha's condition reached the critical stage, Dr. Soung gave notice of withdrawal as her physician, refused to respond to requests by Covenant's staff to hospitalize her, and abruptly abandoned her care. In pursuing this course of conduct, Dr. Soung acted recklessly.

Section 15610.07 states that "abuse of an elder" includes "neglect." "Neglect" is defined in section 15610.57, as "either of the following: (1) The negligent failure of any person having the care or custody of an elder or a dependent adult to exercise that degree of care that a reasonable person in a like position would exercise. . . . (b) Neglect includes, but is not limited to, all of the following: . . . (2) Failure to provide medical care for physical and mental health needs. . . . " (Italics added.) As stated in Hongsathavij v. Queen of Angels etc. Medical Center (1998) 62 Cal.App.4th 1123, 73 Cal.Rptr.2d 695, "[a] physician cannot just walk away from a patient after accepting the patient for treatment. A physician cannot withdraw treatment from a patient without due notice and an ample opportunity afforded to secure the presence of another medical attendant." (*Id.* at p. 1138, 73 Cal.Rptr.2d 695, citing *Payton v. Weaver* (1982) 131 Cal.App.3d 38, 45, 182 Cal.Rptr. 225.)

A doctor who conceals the existence of a serious bedsore on a nursing home patient under his care, opposes her hospitalization where circumstances indicate it is medically necessary, and then abandons the patient in her dying hour of need commits neglect within the meaning of the Act. Further, if it can be proved by clear and convincing evidence that such acts were committed with recklessness, oppression, fraud, or malice, the heightened remedies of section 15657 will apply.

The Act was expressly designed to protect elders and other dependent adults who "may be subjected to abuse, neglect, or abandonment . . . ." (§ 15600, subd. (a).) Within the Act, two groups of persons who ordinarily assume responsibility for the "care and custody" of the elderly are identified and defined: health practitioners and care custodians. A "health practitioner" is defined in section 15610.37 as a "physician and surgeon, psychiatrist, psychologist, dentist, . . . " etc., who "treats an elder . . . for any condition." (Italics added.) "Care custodians," on the other hand, are administrators and employees of public and private institutions that provide "care or services for elders or dependent adults," including nursing homes, clinics, home health agencies, and similar facilities which house the elderly. (§ 15610.17.) The Legislature thus recognized that both classes of professionals—health practitioners as well as care custodians—should be charged with responsibility for the health, safety and welfare of elderly and dependent adults. This recognition is made explicit in the "reporting" section of the Act which states that "[a]ny person who has assumed full or intermittent responsibility for care or custody of an elder or dependent adult, whether or not that person receives compensation, including . . . any elder or dependent adult care custodian, health practitioner, . . . is a mandated reporter." (§ 15630, subd. (a), italics added.)

Unlike, for example, section 15610.07, subdivision (b), which imposes liability only upon "care custodians," the statute defining "neglect" is not restricted to care custodians. Instead it applies generally to anyone having "care or custody" of an elder, and specifically mentions the "[f]ailure to provide medical care for physical and mental health needs." (§ 15610.57, subd. (b)(2).) Similarly, the heightened remedies section is not limited to care custodians but targets any "defendant" who commits abuse or neglect and does so with "recklessness, oppression, fraud, or malice." (§ 15657.)

In *Delaney*, supra, 20 Cal.4th 23, 82 Cal.Rptr.2d 610, 971 P.2d 986, the defendant, a nursing care home, was found liable for reckless neglect in failing to care for an elderly decedent who contracted a horrible bedsore. (*Id.* At pp. 27–28, 82 Cal.Rptr.2d 610, 971 P.2d 986.) The defendant claimed that since it was a licensed health care provider, it could be liable only for professional negligence, and was exempt from liability under section 15657. The defendant predicated this claim on section 15657.2, which states that actions based on a health care professional's negligent act or omission shall remain governed by those laws applicable to professional negligence. (*Delaney*, supra, at p. 27, 82 Cal.Rptr.2d 610, 971 P.2d 986.)

The Delaney court rejected this argument, noting that the distinction between "reckless neglect" within the meaning of section 15657 and "professional negligence" as described in section 15657.2 was one of degree, and did not turn on the defendant's status as a health care professional or custodian. "Section 15657.2 can . . . be read as making clear that the acts proscribed by section 15657 do not include acts of simple professional negligence, but refer to forms of abuse or neglect performed with some state of culpability greater than mere negligence." (20 Cal.4th at p. 32, 82 Cal.Rptr.2d 610, 971 P.2d 986.) The court held that health care professionals are not exempt from the heightened remedies triggered by section 15657 when they are guilty of "reckless neglect." (20 Cal.4th at pp. 31–32, 82 Cal.Rptr.2d 610, 971 P.2d 986.)

Delaney establishes that health care providers are not exempt from liability for reckless neglect simply because the cause of action arises from the rendition of health care services. Rather, health practitioners who assume care or custody of the elderly are subject to liability if their misconduct rises to the level of neglect, abuse, or abandonment.

Dr. Soung's interpretation would impose liability on residential institutions housing the elderly for willful deprivation of medical care, but exempt physicians from engaging in the same conduct. The statutory language does not so provide. Moreover, there is no evidence the Legislature intended to leave such a loophole in the Act. As Delaney teaches, liability

never read Ginsty—
put the state
to its taste
like a lawyer

under the Act should not turn upon the licensing status of the defendant. (20 Cal.4th at p. 35, 82 Cal.Rptr.2d 610, 971 P.2d 986.) We conclude that Dr. Soung's status as a physician does not immunize him from liability for elder abuse.

✱ ✱ ✱

DISPOSITION

The judgment is affirmed as to the court's ruling regarding the intentional infliction of emotional distress cause of action and reversed as to the court's ruling on the elder abuse cause of action. The cause is remanded to the trial court with directions to vacate its order sustaining the demurrer to the elder abuse cause of action of the third amended complaint and enter a new order overruling the demurrer as to that cause of action only. Plaintiffs shall recover their costs on appeal. (Cal. Rules of Court, rule 26(a).)

SCOTLAND, P. J., and NICHOLSON, J., concur.

Abandonment

Abandonment
The willful and intentional desertion or forsaking of an elderly person by any individual who is responsible for the care and custody of that elder, under circumstances in which a reasonable person would normally continue to provide care and custody.

Abandonment of the elderly generally is the willful and intentional desertion or forsaking of an elderly person by any individual who is responsible for the care and custody of that elder, under circumstances in which a reasonable person would normally continue to provide care and custody. A common form of this abuse is *granny dumping*. In this form, the elder is taken to an emergency room and left there without any identification or money. Other forms include desertion of an elder at a shopping mall, bus depot, train station, airport, or other public location. In a recent case, a daughter took her father from a nursing home, stole his Social Security funds, and abandoned him in a racetrack. Abandonment is a particularly heartless abuse of the elderly.

Sexual Abuse

Sexual Abuse (of the Elderly)
The non-consensual sexual contact of any kind with an elderly person. Additionally, sexual contact with any person who lacks the mental capacity to consent to the act.

Non-consensual sexual contact of any kind with an elderly person is considered **sexual abuse.** Additionally, sexual contact with any person who lacks the mental capacity to consent to the act is also sexual abuse. Unwanted touching, fondling, any type of sexual assault or battery, such as rape, sodomy, coerced nudity, and sexually explicit photography, are all considered sexual abuse. Incidences of sexual abuse often occur under circumstances where the victim is in a dependent or helpless state. Many cases have been reported in nursing homes and hospitals.

Signs and Symptons

- Trauma to the breasts or genital areas
- Unexplained vaginal or anal bleeding
- Unexplained genital infections or venereal disease
- A report by an elderly victim of sexual assault or rape

Financial Abuse

Financial abuse is financial exploitation of the elderly and it is evidenced by the theft, misuse, or unauthorized use of an elder person's money, property, or resources by an individual or institution who is placed in a position of trust. Financial abuse of the elderly is very common and often occurs at home. The financial exploiter is usually a close family member, a relative, a friend, or a care provider who has won the confidence and trust of the elderly individual. This so-called trusted individual may have persuaded the victim to sign a durable power of attorney enabling the family member to gain control of the elderly person's income and assets, slowly and sometimes very quickly, appropriating them for personal gain. The family member may even have wiggled his or her way into the will to be named as a beneficiary and/or executor. This may have been done under the guise of devotion and friendship, or it may have been accomplished through threats of abandonment or even by physical abuse. Frequently, other family members seek advice from the elder law attorney when they suspect financial exploitation and abuse. The elder law attorney should investigate this immediately and, if good cause is found, encourage the concerned family member to take legal action to stop this abuse by:

- Arranging for the revocation of the durable power of attorney and other documents in which authority has been delegated to the so-called trusted individual.
- Commencing civil legal action based on fraud or conversion to recover the misappropriated funds.
- In certain cases, filing a criminal complaint with the local district attorney's office unit that investigates claims against the elderly.
- Filing a claim with the local adult protective service agency. This agency is directed to receive reports of elder abuse, investigate them, and report to the appropriate authorities for further legal action.

Financial Abuse.
The financial exploitation of the elderly, encompassing theft, misuse, or unauthorized use of an elder person's money, property, or resources by an individual who is placed in a position of trust.

Indicators of Financial Abuse

- Activity occurring in a bank account that is unusual and does not fit the normal financial profile of the elderly person, *e.g.,* large unexplained withdrawals by check or cash, checks to unfamiliar persons, certificate of deposits closed before maturity, accounts being transferred to other financial institutions without a rational explanation, unexplained bank charges being placed against the accounts, or the sale, liquidation, or transfer of stock or assets for no apparent reason.
- Signatures on checks, stock powers, deeds, etc., that appear different from the normal signature of the older person. This is especially suspect when the elderly person no longer has the ability to sign his or her name.
- Cashing of an elder's check without specific authorization.
- Forging an older person's signature.
- Signing of a power of attorney, or making a new will or codicil when the individual lacks the legal capacity to execute such documents.
- Improper use of a guardianship or conservatorship.
- Bills, rent, or mortgage payments that remain unpaid for a period of time when they were usually paid by the individual who had the responsibility for managing the financial affairs of the dependent elder.
- Mysterious disappearance of valuables, *e.g.,* jewelry, silverware, artwork, or collectibles.

- Circumstances leading to the isolation of the elder, making him or her totally dependent and under the control of the caregiver.
- Use of the elder's residence or possessions for illegal activity, *e.g.,* a son, while living with his mother, sells controlled substances from the house.

Telemarketing Fraud

Another recognized form of financial abuse of the elderly is telemarketing fraud. The elderly are particularly vulnerable to this fraud, which has become widespread in the United States. Certain telemarketing firms specifically target the elderly. They are selling something, demanding a contribution to some bogus charity, or trying to induce the elderly to subscribe to some magazine, open an investment account, or enter a contest or some type of sweepstake. The Federal Bureau of Investigation, as well as the state and local authorities, have begun vigorous prosecution of these cases.

A Do Not Call List now exists and many states have no-solicitation programs. The elder client should be advised to register for these programs. To avoid unwanted phone calls from many national marketers, clients should be advised to:

1. Register with the federal "Do Not Call List." This can be done online at http://www. DoNotCall.Gov.
2. Telephone 888-382-1222
3. TTY 866-290-4236

This will not prevent calls from charities, political candidates, and companies with whom you have done business in the last 18 months. However, requests can be made that they do not call again, and the caller must honor this or be subject to penalties. Individual states have enacted stronger laws. Some states provide automatic registration on the federal list once a person registers on the state list.

IDENTITY THEFT

Identity theft affects all segments of the population and is yet another form of financial abuse of the elderly. The elderly are prime targets of identity theft, and frequently consult elder law attorneys when they become a victim of this relatively new crime. The focus on identity theft began in the early 1990s. Federal investigations also revealed that identity theft played a significant role in the terrorist attack that occurred on September 11, 2001.

Identity Theft
A crime whereby someone illegally obtains personal identifying information such as the victim's name, address, credit card number, and driver's license number or Social Security number without the knowledge of the owner and then using it to commit fraud or theft.

Identity theft involves illegally obtaining personal identifying information such as the victim's name, address, credit card number, and driver's license number or Social Security number without the knowledge of the owner and then using it to commit fraud or theft. The information obtained is used to open new charge accounts, and then purchase merchandise or borrow money. The primary object of identity theft is to secure personal identification about an individual and then completely take over his/her identity. The perpetrator may buy cars, airline tickets, houses, take mortgages on properties, and even submit false resumes in the victim's name to obtain employment. In the past several years, hundreds of thousands of unsuspecting Americans have been the victim of this relatively new crime.

Federal legislation making identity theft a federal crime was enacted for the first time in 1998. Currently, 47 states have enacted identity theft criminal statues. In 1992, only 35,000 cases were reported to credit agencies. Today, estimates indicate that between $2 and $3 billion dollars are stolen annually as a direct result of identity theft.

On the federal level, the Federal Trade Commission (FTC) is coordinating all government agencies and organizations in providing information to the public about identity theft. A network has also been organized to register complaints from the victims. A toll-free hotline has been installed to receive information about identity theft and provide advice to victims. (877-IDTHEFT; 877-438-4338). More than 400 reports a week were filed in 2000. The FTC anticipates that the volume of reports will increase to 200,000 per year. The Social Security Administration (SSA) is also involved in preventing this crime. The Inspector General's Office of the SSA reports that it received information about 39,000 incidents of misuse of Social Security numbers in 2002.

How Identity Theft Occurs

Skilled identity thieves abound, looking for an opportunity to steal your good name. No matter how careful you are, they seem to have the upper hand. They employ a variety of methods involving low and high technology. If a thief is determined to obtain some piece of your personal information, you really cannot prevent it. Today, in order to participate in the fast paced commercial markets in our society, it is necessary to provide personal information to a whole host of organizations and individuals. As this information flows through commercial transactions, skilled thieves can access it.

The following is a list of the common methods employed by thieves to illegally obtain information about people and then actually take over their lives:

1. Stealing wallets and purses containing personal identification, including Social Security card, driver's license, and credit and bank cards.
2. Stealing mail, including bank and credit cards statements, pre-approved credit card offers; telephone calling cards, and income tax information.
3. Completing and filing a change of address with the post office in order to divert mail to another location
4. Engaging in a practice called *dumpster diving,* which involves rummaging through personal trash or the trash of a business looking for personal data
5. Fraudulently obtaining a person's credit report by posing as a employer, landlord, or someone else who may have a legitimate need or legal right to the information.
6. Obtaining business or personnel records at the victim's place of employment.
7. Illegally penetrating the victim's residence and finding information located therein.
8. Obtaining personal information provided on the Internet.
9. Purchasing personal information from inside sources, *e.g.,* employees may sell information that appears on a credit application or even provide the felon with credit card numbers and driver's license information.

Once the initial step in the crime has been completed, the perpetrator has obtained all the information necessary to advance to the next stage of the crime. This is how the crime is completed:

1. A call is placed to the credit card issuer, and the thief assumes the new identity, requesting a change of mailing address on the credit card account. The imposter then

begins to use the card. It will take some time before the legitimate owner of the account realizes what has happened because the mail has been diverted to a new address.

2. With the personal information at hand, the thief proceeds to open a new credit card account, providing the name, date of birth, and Social Security number of the victim. The card is then used for expensive purchases, and then the thief does not pay the monthly statement. The delinquent account is then reported on the victim's credit history. Eventually, the victim learns what has happened.

3. The criminals establish phone and/or wireless service in the name of the victim.

4. Bank accounts are opened in the name of the victim, and bad checks are written on the new account.

5. New cars are purchased by taking out auto loans employing the victim's identity.

6. Counterfeit checks or debit cards are used to deplete the victim's account.

7. Finally, the identity thief may even file a bankruptcy proceeding under the victim's name to avoid paying debts secured under the victim's name.

Minimizing the Risk

Identity theft cannot be completely eliminated. However, a careful person can minimize the risk of being victimized by cautiously managing the flow of personal information. It is imperative to know to whom you are revealing information. Verify the legitimacy of the person or institution requesting information. The Federal Trade Commission states that by being aware of the increased possibility of identity theft and acting in a cautious and prudent manner, a person can help guard against being a victim. The following procedures are designed to help:

1. Before revealing any personally identifying information, it is imperative to find out how it will be used and whether it will be shared with other commercial establishments. Inquire about the use of the information you are providing. Is it possible to keep it confidential?

2. Pay close attention to your billing cycles. If bills don't arrive on time, follow up with the creditors to find out what has occurred. If a credit statement is missing, it could possibly indicate that identity theft has taken place and your credit card account has been taken over. The address could have been changed, and the card used fraudulently without out your knowledge.

3. Guard your mail from theft. Deposit all your mail at a local post office or at post office collection boxes. Very important mail should always be taken to the post office. Remove all mail from your mailbox promptly. If you are planning to be away, arrange for the post office to hold your mail until you return.

4. Passwords must be placed on credit cards and on bank and phone accounts. It is wise to avoid using easily available information like a person's mother's maiden name, birth date, last four digits of your Social Security number, or your phone number or a series of consecutive numbers.

5. Reduce the amount of personal information and credit cards you carry on a daily basis to the absolute minimum.

6. **Do not give out personal information on the phone, through the mail, or over the Internet unless you have initiated the contact or know with whom you are dealing.**

Identity thieves often pose as representatives of banks, Internet services providers, or even government agencies in order to get you to reveal your Social Security number, mother's maiden name, financial account numbers, and other identifying information.

7. **Shred or tear** all personal information such as charge receipts, copies of credit applications, insurance forms, physician statements, cancelled checks, bank statements, or expiring charge cards that may be useful to an identity thief. Make sure to destroy any credit card offers sent by mail. The thief can pick through your trash and find these items. If left intact, they can be used to apply for credit in the victim's name.

8. The elderly should be especially cautious about where they leave any personal information in their home. Personal items should be kept in a safe place not easily accessible to caregivers, maintenance workers, or delivery people.

9. **Provide your Social Security number only when absolutely necessary. Use other forms of identification wherever possible.**

10. **Do not carry your Social Security card; leave it in a safe place.**

11. **Order a copy of your credit report annually, and verify the accuracy of its contents. If you find errors, contact the credit-reporting agency immediately and proceed to clear up any discrepancies.**

There are the three major credit reporting agencies recognized by the Federal Trade Commission. See Identity Theft on the CD-ROM.

What To Do If Your Client Is a Victim of Identity Theft

1. Contact the fraud departments of each of the three major credit bureaus. Request a *Fraud Alert* be placed in your client's file. Require all creditors to call before they open any new accounts.

2. Order new credit reports, and examine them carefully to detect any fraudulent activity. Report any fraud immediately to the credit bureau.

3. Contact the creditor for any accounts that have been tampered with or opened fraudulently. Follow up with correspondence to these creditors by certified mail, return receipt requested. Close all accounts that have been tampered with.

4. File a report with local police in the community where the identity theft took place. Retain a copy of the report for your file.

5. Report stolen mail to U.S. Postal Inspection Service.

6. Open all new accounts with password-only access.

7. If securities or investment accounts have been compromised, report this immediately to your broker and to the Securities Exchange Commission.

8. Cancel all phone service immediately if an identity theft has occurred, and establish new service with new **PIN** (Personal Identification Numbers).

9. If someone has used your Social Security number to obtain a job or to work, report this crime to the SSA's fraud hotline at 800-269-0272.

10. If a person's name or Social Security number is being used by an identity thief to obtain a valid driver's license or a nondriver's ID card, immediately contact the local department of motor vehicles.

11. If a victim believes that a thief has filed a bankruptcy proceeding using stolen identity, he or she must immediately contact the local bankruptcy court, the regional U.S. Attorney's Office, and the FBI in the city where the bankruptcy was filed.

See the CD-ROM for an Identify Theft Affidavit.

New Technology

Biometric technology is currently being used to deter identity theft. Biometrics register and store biological information about an individual for the purpose of verifying their identity. Examples of biometric identification include fingerprint biometrics that are used worldwide by police agencies, DNA identification, retinal and iris scans, hand geometry, facial feature recognition, ear shape, body odor, brain fingerprinting, signature dynamics, and voice verification. The most accurate of all biometrics is iris identification. This is currently being employed by banks at their ATM operations. It is used at airports and hospitals to verify premises access. Since September 11, 2001, airlines have used iris identification to verify the identity of employees and prevent terrorism. Computer software has been designed to take a digital snapshot of an employee's iris and store it in a hard drive. When the employee seeks to enter a secured area, his iris is matched to the one on file. This new technology of iris biometrics appears to be almost 100 percent accurate. Many countries are testing this form to increase passport and customs' control. The U.S. government is also studying the use of *smart cards,* ID cards where a person's iris code and other biometric information can be stored and used for future identification. This may be a way to control and possibly prevent future terrorist acts.

The Law

Identity Theft and Assumption Deterrence Act of 1998

The Identity Theft and Assumption Deterrence Act was enacted by Congress in October 1998 and can be found in 18 U.S.C Sec. 1028. It is the federal law directed at punishing identity theft. Violations of the act are investigated by federal enforcement agencies, including the U.S. Secret Service, the FBI, the U.S. Postal Inspection Service, and the SSA's Office of the Inspector General. The U.S. Department of Justice prosecutes federal identity theft cases.

The *Identity Theft and Assumption Act* makes it a federal crime when someone:

> knowingly transfers or uses, without lawful authority, a means of identification of another person with the intent to commit, or to aid or abet, any unlawful activity that constitutes a violation of federal law, or that constitutes a felony under any applicable state or local law.

The Act defines the following as a *means of identification*: a name, Social Security number, credit card number, cellular telephone electronic serial number, or any other piece of information that may be used alone or in conjunction with other information to identify a specific individual.

In most instances, a conviction for identity theft carries a maximum penalty of 15 years imprisonment, a fine, and forfeiture of any personal property used or intended to be used to commit the crime.

Schemes to commit identity theft or fraud also may involve violations of other statues, such as credit card fraud, computer fraud, mail fraud, wire fraud, financial institution fraud, or Social Security fraud. Each of these federal offenses is a felony and carries substantial penalties—in some cases as high as 30 years in prison, fines, and criminal forfeiture.

State Laws

Many states have also passed laws related to identity theft; others may be considering such legislation. Where specific identity theft laws do not exist, the practices may be prohibited under other laws. Contact your state attorney general's office or local consumer protection agency to find out about your state laws related to identity theft, or visit http://www.consumer.gov/idtheft.

State identity theft laws in effect as of 2002 are listed in the CD-ROM section on identity theft.

LEGISLATION AGAINST ELDER ABUSE

In response to the dramatic increase in elder abuse, many states have enacted legislation designed to protect the elderly. For example:

1. Revised power of attorney statutes to make it more difficult for these documents to be used for financial abuse.
2. Agencies, such as adult protective services, have been created to receive reports of elder abuse, investigate them, and report their findings to law enforcement authorities who will act upon them.
3. Public health laws of the individual states have been amended to require health care providers, doctors, hospitals, and social workers to report any suspected incidents of elder abuse to the proper authorities for prosecution.
4. Criminal statutes have been enacted specifically to protect the elderly. Florida, for example, passed legislation in 1989 creating a third-degree felony for "the knowing and willful financial exploitation of an aged person by improper or illegal use of the management of his or her funds, assets, property, power of attorney, or guardianship." The elder law firm should check its local law to see what, if any, legislation protects the elderly.
5. The federal government ombudsman program, administered by each state's agency on aging, has been created to investigate claims of abuse in nursing homes.
6. Federal standards exist on patient's rights in nursing homes. This "Resident's Bill of Rights" (see the CD-ROM) must be given to each resident upon his or her entry into a nursing home. The following are the rights to which the patient is entitled:
   • To be treated with dignity and respect.
   • Safety and security of personal possessions.
   • Ability to raise issues concerning complaints and general care.
   • Receive general information concerning treatment and care.
   • Participate in planning all aspects of the patient's care.
   • Make choices and independent personal decisions.
   • Enjoy privacy, care, and confidentiality in medical, personal, and financial affairs.
   • Protection against unwarranted transfer.

THE ROLE OF THE ELDER LAW TEAM

1. To report elder abuse to the proper authorities if the elder law team suspects that the client is the subject of such abuse.
2. Not to participate in any transactions where it appears that the elderly are being coerced into doing something against their own free will, such as transferring assets under undue influence.
3. To recommend to the families of the elderly that they should consider guardianships or conservatorships to protect the rights of their elderly relatives.

See the CD-ROM for information on where to report elder abuse.

Bibliography

"Detecting Financial Abuse of the Elderly." *The Elder Law Report*, XIII, 5, December 2001.

"Financial Abuse of the Elderly: Risk Factors, Screening Techniques, and Remedies." *Bifocal, Newsletter of the American Bar Association Commission of Legal Problems of the Elderly*, 23, 4, Summer 2002.

Federal Trade Commission. *ID Theft: When Bad Things Happen to Your Good Name.*

Merck Manual of Geriatrics, 2nd Ed.

REFERENCES

American Bar Association Commission on Domestic Violence
http://www.abanet.org/domviol/home.html
Advice for domestic violence victims, plus a guideline to doing safety planning, contains statistics, teaching resources, legal research, and analysis.

Biometrics—Iris Identification
http://iridiantech.com

Federal Trade Commission
600 Pennsylvania Ave., N.W.
Washington, D.C. 20580
http://www.consumer.gov/idtheft
An excellent source of information concerning identity theft.

National Aging Information Center
http://ww.aoa.dhhs.gov/naic
This service of the U.S. Administration on Aging offers searchable databases on aging and elder abuse.

National Center for Victims of Crime (NCVC)
http://www.ncvc.org
Resources for all types of victims of crime, includes domestic violence and every state.

U.S. Administration on Aging
http://www.aoa.gov
Resources on all aging topics, including elder abuse.

REVIEW QUESTIONS AND EXERCISES

1. What is elder abuse, and what are its causes? What should the elder law professional do to protect against the abuse of clients?

2. What is physical abuse, and what are its indicators? How can it be prevented?

3. What is psychological/emotional abuse, and what are its indicators? How can it be prevented?

4. What is neglect? What is self-neglect? What is caregiver abuse-neglect? What are the indicators of neglect, self-neglect, and caregiver abuse-neglect? How can they be prevented?

5. What constitutes sexual abuse, and what are its signs and symptoms? How can it be prevented?

6. What is financial abuse, and what are its indicators? How can undue influence result in financial abuse? How can it be prevented?

7. Discuss identity theft. Can it be prevented? What should a client do to protect himself or herself from identity theft?

8. What can the elder law professional do to assist a client who has been the victim of identity theft?

9. What is the role of the elder law professional in preventing elder abuse?

CHAPTER 16
Resources for the Elder Care Law Team

The elder law office is often called upon to function as a senior community resource center and, as such, must be equipped to handle a variety of needs. Clients, community leaders, professionals in allied fields, and the general public go there seeking financial planning advice, assistance in placing a loved one into a skilled nursing facility, direction in solving out-of-state issues for elderly relatives, or referrals to other professionals ranging from gerontologists for medical assistance to real estate brokers and tax specialists for disposing the contents of a senior citizen's residence.

As a client's individual needs become apparent, the elder law office will be able to direct the client to the appropriate resource. The office should have readily available, up-to-date resource material in the following areas:

- Air ambulance services (see Yellow Pages®).
- Banks and mortgage brokers that handle reverse mortgages.
- Day care programs, including those that provide transportation to and from the site, medical care, meals, and custodial care for patients during the day.
- Directories of hospitals, rehabilitation facilities, nursing homes, including VA facilities.
- Directories of medical professionals, social workers, and occupational, physical and speech therapists. (Especially helpful are health care professionals who make home visits.)
- Elder care attorneys in other localities.
- Home health care agencies, employment agencies specializing in home health care aides for the elderly, and visiting nurses services.
- Hospice programs.
- Housing facilities: congregate care, independent living facilities, life care communities, and assisted-living facilities.
- Directories of insurance specialists who can advise clients about long-term care insurance and medi-gap insurance.
- Directories of national organizations that are involved with the elderly.
- Programs designed for the homebound elderly, *i.e.,* Meals on Wheels.
- Programs that assist the elderly in making home repairs at minimal cost.
- Programs that assist the elderly in paying utility bills and reducing their real estate taxes and rent.
- Religious organizations providing services to the elderly.
- Information concerning special services for the elderly provided by local utility companies, *i.e.,* third-party billing notification, augmentative hearing devices, etc.
- Directories of support groups for various illnesses, such as cancer, diabetes, Parkinson's, and Alzheimer's disease.

- Directories of transportation alternatives for the elderly.
- Federal, state, and local agencies directly related to issues of aging:
    Adult protective service agencies.
    Better Business Bureau.
    District attorney's office (division dealing with crimes against senior citizens).
    Long-term care ombudsman program.
    State insurance departments.
    Social Security offices.
    Veteran's Administration offices.
- Directories of local service organizations that have programs to assist the elderly: Kiwanis, Rotary, Lions, United Way.

The Internet has become an invaluable tool to the elder law professional. Every elder law office should have access to the Internet to provide the most up-to-date resources for clients.

The Resource Directory for Older People on the CD-ROM provides a comprehensive compendium of resources for the elderly compiled by the National Institute on Aging and the Administration on Aging.

CONCLUSION

The preceding chapters have described various areas to be explored by the elderly and their families as they proceed in their journey toward the end of life. The informed and sensitive legal professional can guide them through that often turbulent road, making their paths easier to tread.

The work is challenging, rewarding, and certainly a noble endeavor. The author has certainly found it to be so.

GLOSSARY

Abandonment (of the Elderly)   The willful and intentional desertion or forsaking of an elderly person by any individual who has the care and custody of that elder, under circumstances in which a reasonable person would normally continue to provide care and custody.

Accelerated Death Benefit (ADB)   A benefit found in a life insurance policy permitting a terminally ill person to cash in a life insurance policy during lifetime. The amount of the benefit will depend upon the insured's length of illness.

Adjusted Gross Estate   The gross estate less estate administration expenses.

Administration Proceeding   A court proceeding to distribute the assets of a person who dies intestate (*i.e.,* without a will).

Advance Directives   Legal instruments executed by an individual identifying who may handle his or her legal and medical affairs, and in some cases, providing specific instructions.

Agent/Attorney-in-fact   The beneficiary of the power of attorney transferred by the principal, who is authorized to act on behalf of the principal.

Alternate Gift Over   A stipulation in a will bequeathing property to a secondary beneficiary or beneficiaries, in the event that the primary recipient does not survive testator.

Anatomical Gifting   The donation of human organs and tissues for transplantation or research and development.

Ancillary Jurisdiction   The power of a court to decide matters incidental to its primary jurisdiction, e.g., a will is probated in New York and, because the decedent has real estate in New Jersey, ancillary jurisdiction is required in New Jersey to distribute the real property in the ancillary state in accordance with that state's laws.

Annual Gift Tax Exemption   The federal gift tax law that provides every individual with an annual $11,000 exemption per donee from gift tax. A married couple has a $22,000 exclusion, per donee.

Assisted-Living Facility   A living facility for the elderly who no longer can live independently and require some assistance but are not in need of skilled nursing care.

Bed-hold Agreement   An agreement between a patient and a skilled nursing facility that preserves the patient's right to return to the same nursing home after a temporary hospitalization.

Beneficiary   An individual who benefits from the act of another.

Bequest   The testamentary disposition of personal property.

Bonding   A guarantee by a surety company that protects the assets of the estate from gross negligence, malfeasance, and theft by the fiduciary.

Capacity   An individual's ability to understand the nature, effects, and consequences of his or her acts.

Capital Gains   The taxable profits made on the sale of stocks, bonds, property, and other capital investments or assets.

Capital Gains Exclusion on Residence   The Internal Revenue Code as of May 6, 1997, provides that every individual is entitled to $250,000 (married couples filling jointly, $500,000) capital gains tax exclusion in connection with the sale of a personal principal residence, provided that the residence was the principal residence and that the taxpayer lived there for two of the last five years.

Capital Gains Tax   A tax levied upon any gains derived from the taxable sale of a capital asset. For example, if one purchases stock for $10 and sells it for $30, there is a gain of $20. That gain is a capital gain subject to tax.

Capitation   The fee a health maintenance organization pays a physician-provider who is a member of the organization for services rendered to each patient. The physician receives a specific fee per patient per year, regardless of the number of times or the amount of treatment that is provided to the patient.

Caregiver Abuse-Neglect (of the Elderly)   When a caregiver neglects to give reasonable and proper care to the elderly person who is in his or her charge.

Catastrophic Insurance Coverage   A form of long-term care insurance may also include coverage for catastrophic medical expenses.

Charitable Trust   A trust agreement for the benefit of a charity. In general, it is created for charitable, educational, religious, or scientific purposes.

Chronic Illness   Illness where someone is unable to perform without assistance at least two activities of daily living for at least 90 days.

Codicil   A separate legal testamentary instrument used to explain, modify, add to, subtract from, qualify, alter, restrain, or revoke provisions in an existing last will and testament, acknowledged in the same manner as a will.

Cohabitation   The act of living with a partner without being legally married. Cohabiting couples are not entitled, under state laws, to the same benefits as married couples by the state.

College Campus Communities   Living facilities for the elderly established by colleges and universities for their older alumni.

Common Law Marriage   A marriage that takes legal effect, without license or ceremony, when a couple lives together as husband and wife, intend to be married, and hold themselves out to others as a married couple.

Competency   The state or condition of having the ability to handle one's personal affairs, not suffering from any mental disability or incapacity.

Competency Proceeding   Legal proceedings conducted in court to determine an individual's mental capacity.

Constructive Trust   When a person has title to property and/or takes possession of it under circumstances in which he or she is holding it for another even though there is no formal trust document or agreement. The court may determine that the holder of the title holds it as constructive trustee for the benefit of the intended owner. This may occur through fraud, breach of faith, ignorance, or inheritance.

Coordination of Benefits (COB)   Provision in group policies that usually limits the total benefits payable under two or more group policies so that benefits do not exceed the actual amount of covered expenses incurred. COB is particularly important when a husband and wife each have obtained family coverage under separate group policies. Group policy benefits are usually not reduced by benefits payable under an individual health insurance policy. However, some individual policies may reduce the amount of benefits payable if benefits are payable under another individual insurance policy a person owns, or may establish primary and secondary priorities of payment.

Co-payment   The share of a covered hospital or medical expense, usually a percentage or fixed dollar amount, which the insured patient is required to pay after meeting the deductible. Doctor visit co-payments and drug co-payments are usually assessed without reference to a deductible and do not count toward the policy deductible.

Cost of Living Adjustments (COLA)   Annual increases in Social Security benefits to offset the effects of inflation on fixed incomes.

Custodial Care   Room and board in a nursing home where assistance with activities of daily living are provided. Most care in a nursing home is custodial care and is not covered by Medicare. Medicaid provides the majority of nursing home reimbursement for custodial care.

Deductible   The initial amount of covered expenses an insured will have to pay privately before benefits are paid under the terms of the policy. The insurer is self-insured up to the deductible amount.

Deed   A legal instrument executed by a grantor transferring right, title, and interest in real estate to a grantee. The document must be notarized and is usually recorded in the county clerk's office. There are several different types of deeds, such as a bargain and sale deed, a quitclaim deed, a trust deed, a warranty deed, etc. An unrecorded deed is valid upon delivery to the grantee, but it can be superceded by a later deed that is recorded first.

Devise   The testamentary disposition of real property.

Diagnostic Related Grouping (DRG)   Medicare regulations that assign specific lengths of hospital stays to particular illnesses.

Dipping in Power A provision in a will that does not suspend or prevent absolute vesting of the bequest in the named minor beneficiary. The will would then empower the executor or a trustee in his or her sole and nonreviewable discretion to retain the bequest in a separate fund to be used for the benefit of the beneficiary and withdraw assets for that purpose.

Direct Deposit Allows for the Social Security or Supplemental Security Income to be deposited into a specified bank account electronically. This procedure eliminates the possibility of theft or loss of the check and guarantees a quick and safe deposit.

Disclaimer The renunciation of a gift or claim to which an individual is entitled, such as an individual disclaiming the right to inherit from an estate. The party actually refuses to accept any or all of an inheritance that has been devised or bequeathed to him or her. Medicaid treats a disclaimer as a transfer of assets subject to the 36-month look-back rule.

Domicile A place where an individual has a fixed permanent home to which he or she always has the intention of returning when absent. An individual may have only one domicile, but may have several residences. Domicile is significant because it controls the jurisdiction of taxing authorities, voting rights, etc.

Do Not Resuscitate (DNR) Order A legal document stating that in the event the patient goes into cardiac or respiratory arrest, the patient requests not be resuscitated or maintained on life support equipment.

Durable Power of Attorney A legal instrument executed by a competent adult authorizing another individual agent to act in a fiduciary capacity on his or her behalf. It is designed to survive the incapacity of the principal in the event that the principal becomes incompetent. It automatically terminates on the principal's death. It can be general or limited in its powers.

Elder Law The area of law concentrating on the legal problems of aging.

Emotional Abuse (of the Elderly) The willful infliction of mental pain and suffering upon an elderly person by an individual in a position of trust.

Escheat The reversion of property to the state when there are no heirs to inherit the property.

Estate Tax A tax levied by the federal government or a state on the assets of a decedent as they are transferred to the heirs of the decedent. Sometimes called *Transferred Inheritance Tax*.

Euthanasia The act of putting to death painlessly a person suffering from an incurable and painful disease or condition for reasons of mercy. The decision to terminate life is made by the medical establishment or the state without the input or consent of the patient. However, if a patient has a living will or health care durable power of attorney, then the agent or spouse named in the advance directive makes the decision and it is still considered euthanasia.

Exclusions Conditions or circumstances under which insurance coverage will not be provided or may be limited.

Executor A person(s) or corporate entity (bank or trust company) named in a will to carry out the orderly administration of the testator's estate.

Extended Care Facility A skilled nursing facility that provides nursing care services to the patient until the patient recovers sufficiently to return to the community or dies.

Fair Hearing The appellate process for a declined Medicaid applicant.

Family and Medical Leave Act This act requires employers with 50 or more workers to provide unpaid time off to care for a seriously ill spouse, parent, child, or for the employee's own illness.

Federal Estate Tax Credit The IRS allows an exclusion of the first $1.5 million of a decedent's estate in 2004 (combined with any gift tax exclusion claimed during the decedent's lifetime) from estate tax. If utilized effectively, a married couple can protect up to $3 million through a credit shelter trust. The exclusion limit is increasing until 2009. In 2010 the limit decreases to $1 million.

Federal Gift Tax Credit The IRS allows an exclusion for the first $1 million given away during a person's life. Any amounts given thereafter and not subject to another exclusion (such as charitable donations or the $11,000 annual exclusion) are subject to gift tax.

Federal Insurance Contributions Act (FICA) The vehicle by which the mandatory contributions are made into the Social Security system.

Federal Patient Self-Determination Act of 1990 An act that requires every medical facility or nursing home that accepts Medicare to provide and inform each new patient of his or her right to execute a health care proxy and living will.

Fiduciary A person or entity who has the power and obligation to act for another under

Immediate Review　A review by the medical Peer Review Organization (PRO) of a Notice of Noncoverage. The Medicare beneficiary is not responsible for paying the costs of any hospital stay until after the immediate review.

Issue　Issue are all people descended from a common ancestor. A decedent's issue includes his or her children, grandchildren, and great-grandchildren.

Income Beneficiary　The individual who receives income earned on assets held in a trust.

Independent Living Facility　A residence for the elderly who are healthy. This type of facility is similar to a resort community, often providing maid services, dining rooms, recreational activities, and transportation.

Individual Retirement Account (IRA)　An account that allows a person the opportunity to save for the future on a tax-sheltered basis.

Infantilism　A common form of psychological abuse whereby the victim is treated like a child and forced to accept a dependent role in the relationship.

Institutional Medicaid　Payment by the Medicaid Assistance Program to a skilled nursing facility.

Interrorem Clause　A clause in a will that states that if a named beneficiary contests the will, the beneficiary forfeits any gift the testator provided for that beneficiary in the will. However, if the beneficiary wins the will contest, this clause usually becomes void.

***Inter Vivos* Trust**　A trust created during the lifetime of the settlor, literally, a trust *among the living,* in contrast to a testamentary trust.

Intestate　The condition of being without a will, *i.e.,* Mary is an intestate or Mary's estate is intestate.

Irrevocable Trust　A trust that cannot be revoked.

Judgment　A decision or opinion given by a court of law that's enforceable. There are many different types of judgments, such as a money judgment, which authorizes a payment of money from one person to another.

Jurisdiction　The authority of a particular court to hear a certain type of case, *i.e.,* it has jurisdiction over the case by virtue of the subject matter of the case or authority granted by statute.

Last Will and Testament　A legal instrument by which an individual makes a disposition of probate property, real and personal, which is to take effect after his or her death. A will is completely revocable during the testator's

lifetime, provided the testator is competent to make the revocation.

Legacy　Gift or bequest by will of personal property.

Lien　Generally speaking, a claim or charge on property for the payment of a debt. Liens can be placed against real and personal property.

Life-Care Communities　Residential facility where a resident usually turns over all assets to the facility that agrees to provide care during the resident's remaining lifetime, regardless of medical or physical conditions. These facilities are composed of independent living facilities, assisted-living facilities, and skilled nursing facilities. The individual starts out at one level and continues until reaching the highest level of care or dies.

Life Care Lease　A lease allowing the resident to live in a life care facility for his or her remaining life, regardless of health condition.

Life Estate in Residence　An interest in real property that allows the life tenant the right to possess and use the property for life. For example, a life estate in a home permits the life tenant to live in the residence for life. The interest of the life tenant ceases upon his or her death, at which time, in most cases, the remainderman owns the property in fee simple absolute.

Life Insurance Trust　An *inter vivos,* irrevocable trust most often employed to create tax-free life insurance proceeds that may be used to pay inheritance tax. The trustee owns the life insurance policy, the beneficiary of the policy is the trust. Proceeds from life insurance policies owned by the trust are free from estate and income tax.

Life Tenant　An individual who has a life interest in real estate, *i.e.,* a residence for a lifetime. A life tenancy ceases on the death of the life tenant.

Lifetime Estate Tax Exemption　The federal estate and gift tax law that provides an individual with a lifetime exemption of $1,500,000 (2004). A married couple has a $3,000,000 exemption (2004). This exemption increases until 2009, after which it returns to $1 million in 2010.

Limited Guardianship　Guardianship whereby the court limits the powers of the guardian to those powers that are absolutely necessary for caring and for conducting the affairs of the incapacitated person. The guardianship may also be limited in time.

Limited Power of Attorney　An individual known as the agent or attorney-in-fact authorized by another, called the principal, to act his or her place for some particular purpose or to perform a particular act or to transact some particular business. This authority is usually conferred by a written instrument, called a power of attorney. The attorney-in-fact is not necessarily an attorney; it is usually a private individual or a corporate entity.

Living Trust *Inter vivos* trust created by the settlor and operating during the lifetime of the settlor, usually for the benefit of the settlor and family members, which becomes irrevocable on the death of the settlor. It is often used to avoid the probate process.

Living Will An advance directive instrument wherein an individual states that in the event the signer goes into a persistent vegetative state or has a terminal illness, he or she does not wish to be kept alive artificially.

Long-Term Care The medical and support services needed to attain an optimum level of physical, social, and psychological functioning by persons who are frail and dependent due to chronic physical and mental impairments.

Long-Term Care Insurance An insurance policy designed to protect an individual against catastrophic illness. Each policy is different but cover most nursing care, home care, and, depending on the policy, assisted-living facilities and hospice care. The cost of the premium is deductible from federal income tax as a medical expense, depending upon the age of the insured and the amount of the premium. Some states also allow a deduction for state income tax purposes.

Lucid Interval A period of time when a person who is known to be confused due to illness has a clear perception and understanding of the nature of his or her acts.

Managed Care The delivery system of health care in which a health maintenance organization (HMO) or preferred provider organization (PPO) controls the nature and amount of medical care that is made available to a patient-subscriber.

Managed Care Plan Often called health maintenance organizations (HMOs), these plans are a combination of insurance company and a health care delivery system (doctor/hospital). These plans cover health care costs in return for a premium paid by the insured. The plan restricts the health care providers, physicians, etc., the subscriber can use for care and treatment. There may be a small co-payment, *e.g.,* $5–15 per visit.

Medicaid A federal program officially known as the Medicaid Assistance Program, administered by the states to provide medical assistance, nursing home care, home care, etc., for poor, indigent people. It is a needs-based program, not based on age.

Medicaid Assistance Program (See **Medicaid.**)

Medicaid Look-Back Rule In order to obtain Medicaid assistance, the applicant must provide an asset trail (detailing financial information) for a period immediately before the date of the application. (The look-back period is currently 36 months).

Medicaid Penalty Period The period during which a person is ineligible for Medicaid benefits due to nonexempt transfer of assets. The Medicaid penalty period is determined by the amount transferred divided by the average cost of a skilled nursing home in the community where the applicant lives. For example, if a transfer is made of $100,000 and the average cost of a skilled nursing care is $5,000, the penalty period will be 20 months.

Medicaid Resource Limits The maximum amount of countable resources that an individual can have in order to be eligible to qualify for the Medical Assistance Program.

Medically Necessary Description for medical treatment covered by insurance policies due to medical necessity. For example, plastic surgery for cosmetic purposes and experimental therapy as defined in the policy by the insurance carrier is usually not considered a medically necessary treatment.

Medical Model Role A standard profile into which a prospective resident of a living facility must fit in order to reside and continue to reside in the facility.

Medicare A federal program based on age designed to provide hospital and medical insurance for people over 65 years of age, established under the Social Security Act.

Medicare Approved Charges The amount Medicare recognizes as the reasonable charge for certain care or services, which is often below what the provider typically charges for the care or service.

Medicare Part A Hospital insurance that helps to pay for care in a hospital, skilled nursing facility, home health care, and hospice care.

Medicare Part B Medical insurance which helps to pay for doctor's bills, outpatient hospital care, and other medical services not covered by Part A.

Medicare Participating Doctor or Supplier   A doctor or medical supplier who agrees to accept assignment on all Medicare claims as payment in full.

Medi-gap Insurance Policy   Medicare supplement insurance policy sold by private insurance companies to fill gaps in Medicare coverage. They must be issued in accordance with strict federal and state regulations, and are designed to cover the 20 percent deductible existing under the Medicare program.

Miller Trust   A qualified income trust created for a resident of an income cap state whereby the trust is not treated as an asset of the Medicaid applicant.

Mortgage   Legal instrument that creates a lien against real estate for the purposes of providing security for the performance of a payment of a debt. Must be in writing, notarized, and usually recorded.

Neglect (of the Elderly)   The lack of adequate care provided by a person responsible for the care or custody of an elderly person.

Notice of Noncoverage   A written explanation for why a Medicare beneficiary is denied medical services. A patient must have this in order to exercise the right to request a review by the PRO.

Nuncupative Will   An oral will declared or dictated by a testator who is terminally ill or a soldier on a battlefield about to die. This type of will is valid only in certain states and under certain circumstances.

Ombudsman Program   A federal program administered by each state's office on aging that accepts complaints involving nursing home neglect and abuse. An ombudsman investigates these claims and reports them to the proper authorities.

Order to Show Cause   Order of the court directing individuals to appear before the court in connection with a particular matter, such as a guardianship. It usually is used in a proceeding where time is of the essence.

Palliative Care   Care that alleviates pain where no cure is available.

Payback Trust   A trust created for the benefit of a disabled person under 65 who receives the income from the trust. Upon the death of the income beneficiary, the principal of the trust is used to pay off any Medicaid liens. The residuary of the trust will go to the family of the deceased income beneficiary.

Peer Review Organization (PRO)   Physician-sponsored organizations that review services provided to individual beneficiaries to determine whether or not the care given meets community and professionally recognized standards of quality.

Per Stirpes   Heirship provision in a will whereby the lineal decendents of a deceased beneficiary inherit in his or her place.

Pet Trust   A trust usually created in a pet owner's will for the future care and benefit of a beloved pet.

Physical Abuse (of the Elderly)   The intentional infliction of pain or injury upon an elderly person by a person who is directly responsible for the care and custody of the victim.

Physician-Assisted Suicide   An act in which a physician helps a competent, terminally ill patient to terminate his or her own life. Legal only in Oregon, Holland, and Belgium.

Pleadings   The documents used in lawsuits and court proceedings that state the formal allegations of the parties, including their claims and defenses.

Pooled Trust   Trust assets of multiple individuals in similar situations that are pooled together and administered by a nonprofit organization.

Postnuptial Agreement   Legal agreement executed by a couple after marriage concerning their property rights in the event of separation, divorce, and death. These agreements are widely used in second marriages to protect parties and their heirs.

Pour-Over Will   A provision in the last will and testament of an individual, wherein the testator leaves the residuary of his or her estate to a trustee of a living trust for the purposes of distribution by the trustee according to the terms of the living trust.

Powers Clause   A clause in a will that grants to the fiduciary the powers necessary to carry out his or her duties.

Power of Attorney   A legal instrument executed by a competent adult authorizing another individual to act in a fiduciary capacity on his or her behalf according to its terms. It can be general or limited.

Preferred Provider Organization   An arrangement between a group of doctors or providers and an entity such as an employer or other group. This arrangement makes it possible for price discounts on services in exchange for a higher volume of patients.

Pre-existing Condition   An illness or condition that manifested itself or existed and was treated or diagnosed before the policy was issued. Many medical insurance policies will not pay benefits for pre-existing conditions, or will only cover treatment of them after the policy has been in force for a specified period of time, usually two years.

Prenuptial Agreement Legal agreement executed by two individuals who are contemplating marriage that sets forth their respective rights into their own and each other's properties in the event of separation, divorce, or death. A prenuptial agreement is executed before the marriage, but only has legal effect if the marriage is solemnized.

Present Interest A present interest in real and personal property gives the interest holder the right to own that property until their interest expires. They can own it outright, in the form of a life estate, or upon the occurrence of a condition.

Primary Insurance Amount (PIA) The benefit amount received from Social Security.

Principal The person from whom the power of attorney originates.

Principal-Agent Rule Rules governing the relationship between a principal and the agent to act for the principal's benefit subject to his or her direction and control. The principal is the master, and the agent is the servant. The acts of the agent are recognized and treated as the acts of the principal until revocation of the agent's powers by the principal expressly or by the death of the principal. The durable power of attorney and health care proxy operate pursuant to the principal-agent rule.

Probate A procedure that takes place in the probate or surrogate's court by which the last will and testament is offered to the court for authentication. The result of the probate proceeding will be the validation of the will, and letters testamentary will be issued to the executor establishing the authority of the executor to act on behalf of the estate. The probate court retains jurisdiction over the administration of an estate until the administration is completed and closed by the court. The probate court could also declare the will to be null and void due to improper execution, undue influence, or lack of testamentary capacity and/or remove or refuse to recognize the executor.

Quarters The credits a working individual earns in order to qualify for Social Security benefits. The Social Security Administration will not pay out benefits unless the required number of quarters are in the account (40 quarters, or 10 years, if the individual was born after 1929).

Reconsideration The period of time after a denial of Medicaid benefits in which the applicant may submit additional documentation.

Rehabilitation Facility A skilled nursing facility that provides short-term, intensive rehabilitation services to patients who have just suffered a stroke or similar problem or are recuperating from surgery and/or other injuries.

Remainderman A person who inherits property, real or personal, after the present interest holder's interest expires.

Residence Place where an individual may live. One may have several residences in different localities.

Residency Agreement A legal document prepared by the facility that states in detail the services provided to the resident by the facility.

Residuary Article The provision in a will or trust disposing of the remainder of a testator's estate after the payment of debts and expenses and the distribution of specific bequests, legacies, and devises.

Residuary Beneficiary The individual who receives the remaining corpus of a trust at the time it terminates, or one who receives the residuary of an estate.

Residuary Estate That which remains after debts and expenses of administration, legacies, bequests, and devise have been paid. The residuary estate is paid out to the residuary beneficiaries.

Reverse Mortgage A mortgage used for people over 65 who are living at home and who wish to access the equity in their homes so that they can use these funds to pay their bills and remain at home. Repayment of the mortgage is due upon the death of the owner or sale of the residence.

Revocable Trust A trust agreement wherein the settlor reserves the right to revoke the trust at any time.

Revocation The power to recall authority or to void some document such as a power of attorney health care proxy or certain revocable trusts. Some revocations occur by operation of law, such as a power of attorney that is automatically revoked upon the death of the principal.

Right of Election A surviving spouse's statutory right to choose either the gifts given by the deceased spouse in the will or a forced share of the estate as defined in the probate statute.

Roth IRA/IRA-Plus Account   An individual retirement account that allows withdrawals without tax penalties.

Rule Against Perpetuities   A common-law rule stating that in order for a future interest to be good, it must vest after its creation, (*e.g.,* at the death of a testator) within a living being plus 21 years plus the period of gestation of any beneficiary conceived but not yet born.

Self-Proving Affidavit   An affidavit executed by the witnesses to a will, swearing to the proper execution of the will. This document eliminates the need for the witnesses to appear at the probate court to testify as to the validity of the will. They may, however, be required to testify in a will contest.

Settlor of Trust   The individual who creates the trust and signs the trust agreement.

Sexual Abuse (of the Elderly)   The non-consensual sexual contact of any kind with an elderly person. Additionally, sexual contact with an elderly person that lacks the mental capacity to consent to the act.

Situs   The location of an event for the purposes of legal jurisdiction.

Skilled Nursing Facility (SNF)   Facility providing skilled nursing care, a subcute care facility for patients who do not require hospitalization but cannot be cared for at home.

Spend Down   The process by which an elderly person divests himself or herself of assets in order to qualify for Medicaid programs.

Springing Durable Power of Attorney   A legal instrument executed by a competent adult authorizing another individual agent to act in a fiduciary capacity on his or her behalf that takes effect upon the happening of a condition precedent, usually incompetence or incapacity of the principal. Medical proof of incapacity will have to be obtained before this durable power of attorney can *spring* into effect.

Sundown Syndrome   The concept that many elderly clients tend to be more alert during the day than in the late afternoon or evening.

Supplemental Needs Trust   A category of trusts established for a person receiving means tested public benefits such as Disability or Medicaid. Assets from the trust can be used for the disabled person to the extent it does not interfere with their benefits by paying for food, shelter, clothing or medical care. Types of supplemental needs trusts include payback trusts, pooled trusts and third-party trusts.

Supplemental Security Income (SSI)   Benefits payable to people who are 65 or older, blind, or disabled and who have minimal income.

Taxable Estate   The total assets of a decedent, minus all allowable deductions, that can be subject to estate taxation.

Tenants by the Entirety   Joint tenancy of real property only between spouses. The interest of either spouse cannot be sold or transferred individually. They must be transferred or sold simultaneously. Upon death, the surviving spouse retains complete possession of the entire property. Joint tenants with right of survivorship other than those that are husband and wife can sell or transfer without the other's consent. However upon death, the survivor retains complete control.

Terminal Illness   Life expectancy of six months or fewer.

Testamentary Capacity   In order for an individual to execute a will properly, the individual must have testamentary capacity, which means an understanding of the following:
1. The general nature and extent of his or her property.
2. His or her relationship to the people named in the will and who his or her natural heirs are.
3. That he or she is signing a will and understands generally to whom the will gives his or her property.

Testamentary Trust   A trust created by the testator within the will. By its nature, this trust does not come into being until the testator dies.

Trust   A written, contractual agreement between one person called the *settlor* and another person called the *trustee*, wherein a trustee is the legal title holder of the property received from the settlor for the benefit of another known as the *beneficiary*. There are many types of trusts, a living trust or charitable trust, etc. The beneficiary has the equitable right to the trust property as defined in the trust instrument.

Trustee   Fiduciary who holds the property in trust. While the property is in the trust, the trustee owns the property, at best, for the benefit of the beneficiaries.

Trust Res   Property transferred by the settlor of the trust to the trustee. Refers to the subject matter of a trust.

***Ultra Vires* Acts**   Acts by an agent beyond the scope of the powers granted to the agent. An *ultra vires* act by an agent may not be binding upon the principal.

Undue Influence   The improper use of power or trust in a way that deprives a person of free will and substitutes another's objectives.

Venue   The proper or most convenient location for the trial of a case.

Viatical Settlement   Agreement that involves the assignment, transfer, or sale of an insurance policy to a viatical settlement company for consideration. The viator is the one who sells the policy. The viatical settlement company is the one that pays the viator for the policy based upon life expectancy of the insured.

Will Construction Clause   A clause in a will that states that the probate courts should apply the laws of the testator's domicile rather then the laws of the state where the testator died.

MEDICAL GLOSSARY

Common Diseases of Aging & Medical Terminology

Alzheimer's Disease   A progressive neuropsychiatric disease caused by metabolic change in the brain cells and neuron degeneration. The disease affects the brain and is characterized by the loss of cognitive functions, as well as behavioral disturbances. It is the fourth leading cause of death of people 65 years or older and appears to occur twice as frequently in females as males.

Amyotrophic Lateral Sclerosis (ALS)   A degenerative disease affecting the central and peripheral motor neurons. It is of unknown cause. Speech difficulty may be among its earliest signs. It causes flaccidity and paralysis. The disease is almost always fatal. The term of the disease is usually three years, and then death occurs.

Aphasia (Expressive)   An acquired impairment of language process (inability to express oneself properly through speech, loss of verbal comprehension) caused by damage to areas of the brain that are primarily responsible for the language function, usually the result of a stroke.

Aphasia (Receptive)   Patient recognizes words or instructions but is unable to comprehend their meaning.

Bradykinesia   A slowness of all voluntary movement and speech.

Capitation   The fee a health maintenance organization pays a physician-provider who is a member of the organization for services rendered to each patient. The physician receives a specific fee per patient per year, regardless of the number of times or the amount of treatment that is provided to the patient.

Catastrophic Illness   A severe illness requiting prolonged hospitalizaton or recovery.

Cerebro Vascular Accident (CVA)   Damage to the brain as a result of a pathological condition of the blood vessels, especially the arteries. The blood supply to the brain is suddenly interrupted. CVAs, or strokes, are the third most common cause of death in the United States, after heart attacks and cancer.

Cognitive Impairment   A decrease in intellectual functioning.

Coma   The medical state of a deep stupor, being completely unaware of one's surroundings, and unable to hear or respond.

Comatose   The patient's inability to respond to any external stimuli.

Custodial Care   Basic activities of daily living care (ADL) provided on a 24-hour basis, usually in a nursing home, *i.e.,* feeding, bathing, dressing, or toileting an Alzheimer's patient.

Dementia   Refers to a large number of brain diseases in which there is slow, progressive deterioration of cognitive ability and personality traits, and severe behavior changes. Results in memory loss, disorientation as to time and place, intellectual decline, and, finally, impaired judgment.

Diabetes   A disease in which the pancreas does not produce or properly use insulin, a hormone that is needed to convert sugar, starches, and other food into energy needed for life.

DNR   Do not resuscitate order. A patient or family member signs this order indicating that in the event the patient goes into cardiac or respiratory arrest, the patient is not to be resuscitated. Used in cases where the patient is terminally ill.

Dysphasia   Patient's inability to swallow, usually resulting from a stroke.

Embolism   A clot that originates in another part of the circulatory system and then travels through the system to block an artery supplying a vital organ, causing serious damage.

Euthanasia   The act of putting to death painlessly a person suffering from an incurable and painful disease or condition. The decision to terminate life is made by the medical establishment or the state without the input or consent of the patient.

Gag Clause   Clause found in a contract between a health maintenance organization and a physician-provider that prohibits the physician from giving certain information to the patient regarding treatment options.

Gatekeeper   A physician who practices within a health maintenance organization, whose job is to control the number of referrals that the primary care physician gives to a specialist.

Geriatrics   The care of the aging population,

HIPAA   The Health Insurance Portability and Accountability Act of 1996. Federal legislative health care reform bill that has resulted dramatic changes in the health care industry.

Hospice Care   A freestanding health care facility caring for terminally ill individuals. Hospice care is also provided at home for terminally ill individuals and is covered under Medicare for up to six months. It provides medical care and support services such as counseling to terminally ill patients and their families.

Incontinence   The inability to control bodily elimination functions.

Organic Brain Syndrome   Form of dementia caused by brain damage.

Osteoarthritis (OA or Arthritis)   The breakdown of bone cartilage in the joints, which causes bones to rub against each other, causing pain and loss of movement.

Osteoporosis   Loss of bone density, making the bones brittle. When the elderly suffer from this disease, they often fracture their bones either from a fall or even turning over in bed.

Palliative Care   Medical procedure of relieving the pain of a terminally ill patient.

Parkinson's Disease   A degenerative process that occurs in the basal ganglia. A chronic nervous system disease, it generally appears in midlife or later and progresses slowly in severity. It results in rigid posture and an expressionless face. There is a slow, regular tremor of the hands. The gait is slow and shuffling, and turning is done in one piece. Muscles are rigid and weak, and movements tend to be limited in range and force.

Persistent Vegetative State   A coma-like condition in which the autonomic nervous system continues to function (*i.e.,* heart, lungs, digestion, and elimination), but the voluntary nervous system (muscles) is nonfunctional.

Physician-Assisted Suicide   The act of a physician assisting the suicide of a terminally ill patient with the consent of that patient. To date, physician-assisted suicide is legal in the U.S. only in the state of Oregon.

Pneumonia   A major infection or inflammation of the lungs where the air sacs in the lungs fill with pus and other liquid causing oxygen to have trouble reaching the blood.

PRI & Screen   Patient review instrument form used to evaluate a patient who is a candidate for entry into a nursing home. It enables a skilled nursing facility to determine what level of care the patient requires.

Respite Care   The admission of a patient from home to a SNF for a short period of time. This will provide the primary caregiver with a brief rest period, vacation, etc., before again resuming the role of primary caretaker.

Resting Tremor   A tremor of a limb that increases when the limb is at rest.

Restraints   Chemical or mechanical devices that restrict a patient's movement. Permission from the patient or family members is required.

Skilled Nursing Facility (SNF)   Facility providing skilled nursing care, a subacute care facility for patients who do not require hospitalization but cannot be cared for at home.

Stroke   A sudden loss of brain function caused by a blockage or rupture of a blood vessel to the brain.

Transient Ischemic Attack (TIA)   Happening suddenly, it is a precursor to a major stroke. TIAs usually result from a reduction of the blood supply caused by a buildup of plaque. The symptoms that the patient experiences are a sudden transient blurring or loss of vision, weakness (motor) or numbness (sensory) of one side, difficulty with speech, vertigo, or diplopia (double vision).

INDEX

" motion to dismiss "

circumstances which require total trust, good faith, and honesty.

Fiduciary Bond   A guarantee by a surety company that protects the assets of the estate from gross negligence, malfeasance, and theft by the fiduciary. There are many types of other bonding guarantees.

Financial Abuse (of the Elderly)   The financial exploitation of the elderly, encompassing theft, misuse, or unauthorized use of an elder person's money, property, or resources by an individual who is placed in a position of trust.

Gag Clause   Clause found in a contract between a health maintenance organization and a physician-provider that prohibits the physician from giving certain information to the patient regarding treatment options.

Gatekeeper   A doctor, usually a primary care physician, who has the responsibility to refer his or her patients to specialists within the same health maintenance or preferred provider organization. In some cases, the gatekeeper is a physician who monitors and controls (limits) the referral power of the primary care physician within the organization.

General Power of Attorney (Non-Durable)   A legal instrument executed by a competent adult authorizing another individual agent to act in a fiduciary capacity on his or her behalf. The power automatically ceases upon the incapacity of the principal. (See Limited Power of Attorney.)

Generation-Skipping Transfer Tax (GST)   An additional federal tax imposed upon assets transferred by a donor to a donee at least two generations removed, *e.g.,* a grandparent to a grandchild.

Gift Tax   A federal and state tax, if applicable, imposed upon assets transferred by a donor to a donee during the donor's lifetime.

Grace Period   A special period of time, usually 10 to 60 days, after a premium on an insurance policy is due, during which time the policyholder may make payment of the premium without the policy protection lapsing.

Grantor of a Trust   One who funds a trust.

Gross Estate   Any type of property, real and personal, of any kind or nature, that was owned by a decedent at death and which passes to a beneficiary, regardless of how it passes, whether by will, beneficiary designation, or some other means.

Guardian/Conservator   An individual who has been invested with power by a court of law having jurisdiction and charged with the duty of taking care of a person and managing that person's property and/or rights. The person who is the subject of a guardianship is incapable of handling his or her own affairs.

Hardship Transfer   The transfer of all assets to another, leaving the transferor without assets. Transfers could occur without the consent of the owner of the asset, *i.e.,* a transfer via a power of attorney or a withdrawal from a joint bank account by a joint tenant without the consent or approval of the other tenant, a fraudulent taking.

Health Care Proxy   An advance directive legal instrument wherein an individual appoints another to make medical and health care decisions for him or her in the event the individual is unable to do so. It operates on the principles of agency law.

HIPAA   The Health Insurance Portability and Accountability Act of 1996. Federal legislative health care reform bill that has resulted dramatic changes in the health care industry.

HMO   Healthcare Maintenance Organization (HMO). (See Managed Care Plan.)

Holographic Will   A will written by the testator wholly in his or her handwriting, regardless of whether or not it is witnessed. Each state has specific laws as to whether it recognizes such a will.

Home Care Medicaid   Payment by the Medicaid Assistance Program for care in the applicant's home.

Homestead   The family residence and surrounding land that the Medicaid applicant owns and where he or she resides. Under local laws, homesteads usually receive a reduction in property taxes.

Hospice Care   Care provided by a health care facility for terminally ill individuals. Hospice care is also provided at home for terminally ill individuals and in both cases is covered under Medicare for up to six months. It provides palliative care and support services such as counseling to terminally ill patients and their families.

Identity Theft   A crime whereby someone illegally obtains personal identifying information about another such as name, address, credit card, driver's license or Social Security numbers or actual documents without the knowledge of the owner, and then uses it to commit fraud or theft against the owner.